THE ROYAL NAVY IN
POLAR EXPLORATION

from Frobisher to Ross

THE ROYAL NAVY IN
POLAR EXPLORATION
from Frobisher to Ross

E.C. COLEMAN

TEMPUS

First published 2006

Tempus Publishing Limited
The Mill, Brimscombe Port,
Stroud, Gloucestershire, GL5 2QG
www.tempus-publishing.com

British Library Cataloguing in Publication Data.
A catalogue record for this book is available from the British Library.

ISBN 0 7524 3660 0

Typesetting and origination by Tempus Publishing Limited
Printed in Great Britain

CONTENTS

INTRODUCTION

In addition to its light, human beings need the sun for warmth. It is not surprising, therefore, that having reached a stage of development that allowed them to expand their horizons through travel, the earth's people should have looked first to the warmer places of their planet. Their success, however, was, in time, to force them away from equatorial and temperate zones and to come face-to-face with those parts of the globe where ice and snow reign in seeming perpetuity and the sun itself disappears for half the year.

The key that unlocked this enforced expansion was turned in 1492 by the westward voyage of Christopher Columbus in his search for a new route to the treasures of Cathay and the Indies. Instead of gaining an Oriental shore, Columbus stumbled across a huge land barrier which was to prove so vast that it stretched from a stormy cape far to the south to the ice-gripped and mist-shrouded north.

Unaware of the extent of the northern reach of this land mass, and restricted by Papal authority and the Spanish-Portuguese Treaty of Tordesillas from trespassing on the shores of the southern Atlantic, the English decided to seek access to the east via a presumed route to the north-west.

Sponsored by the merchants of Bristol and with the king's approval, John Cabot – like Columbus a Genoese seaman – set sail in the *Mathew* in May 1497 and reached the coast of North America (probably Newfoundland) a month later. Despite the pine-clad shores and, due to a belief that the earth's circumference was roughly 7,000 miles less than it actually was, Cabot was convinced that he had reached the fabled lands described by Marco Polo. A year after the start of his first voyage, Cabot sailed once again in search of a north-west route to the Orient. His five ships reached Ireland before one was damaged by bad weather and was forced to return. The remainder sailed on to vanish into history – the search for a north-west passage had not been long in claiming the first of its many victims.

Cabot's son, Sebastian, followed his father's wake ten years later and managed to reach the coast of North America before his crew mutinied and forced his return.

The French then entered the lists, sending the Florentine seaman, Giovanni da Verrazano to seek a northern passage. Sailing in January and opting for a warmer route, Verrazano made landfall in the region of South Carolina and sailed northwards

Martin Frobisher

as far as Nova Scotia before returning to France with a tale that he had found a mile-wide isthmus (in fact the Carolina Outer Banks) beyond which lay a great ocean which would lead towards Cathay. Four years later, Verrazano was to end up as a cannibal meal on a West Indian island.

As a result of Verrazano's voyage, and the reports of fishermen that a channel north of Newfoundland trended to the west, the French sent Jaques Cartier with two ships to continue the search in April 1534. Eighteen weeks later he was back at St Malo having probed a couple of likely inlets and finding nothing apart from two young Indians who were persuaded to accompany him on the return voyage. A year later he set out again, this time to probe almost 1,000 miles up the St Lawrence (and to return the Indians). Leaving his departure too late, he found himself trapped by the winter ice. By the time of the spring thaw and his setting sail for France, he had lost twenty-five of his men chiefly through scurvy. He had, nevertheless, established a French colonial foothold in North America.

In the meantime, England, shaking itself free of European religious and treaty ties as a result of Henry VIII's divorce, had begun to establish itself as an independent maritime nation whose dependence upon the sea for trade and defence was to lead to the burdens of empire. In 1553, the newly-formed Company of Merchant Adventurers decided that the North East offered a better trading option than the shores of North America and sent out three ships in that direction under the command of Sir Hugh Willoughby. Before long the ships had separated, and beyond North Cape, Willoughby found his little fleet reduced to two ships. Pressing on, he discovered Novaya Zemlya before being caught by the Arctic winter. Before long the entire ships' companies had frozen to death.

The third ship, under the command of the expedition's senior pilot, Richard Chancellor, had reached the White Sea and made contact with the natives who informed him that he was on Russian territory. Using borrowed sledges, Chancellor made his way over 1,000 miles to Moscow and arrived just as the Tsar was breaking off his treaty with the merchants of the German Hanseatic League. Promptly offering a new trade association with his masters in the Company of Adventurers, Chancellor secured for England a vast new market for her wool in return for furs, tallow and hemp.

Twenty years after Chancellor's return, a newly formed Cathay Co., with the backing of Queen Elizabeth, sent three small ships to continue the search for the north-west passage. The commander of the expedition was the bluff no-nonsense Yorkshire-born seaman Martin Frobisher. He had spent most of his life at sea and had started by taking part in expeditions to West Africa. Only a third of the men on his first voyage had survived and on a subsequent expedition Frobisher had been captured by the natives and handed over to the Portuguese who imprisoned him before eventually shipping him back to England. He was later to end up in an English gaol for one of a number of sea-borne incidents that verged closely upon piracy.

Frobisher's ships, the *Michael*, the *Gabriel*, and an un-named pinnace, found themselves in stormy seas off the Shetland Isles. After a week of pounding gales, the pinnace had vanished with all hands and, in early June, with the coast of Greenland in sight, the crew of the *Michael* turned about and headed home where they spread rumours that Frobisher had been lost at sea. The expedition's leader had, however, continued westwards in the *Gabriel* until he came across a small island he named Queen Elizabeth's Foreland (later Resolution Island). Steering northwards, he found more land with a coastline that was broken by a wide inlet which, after having sailed up for 150 miles, he named 'Frobisher's Straits' in the belief that it would, eventually, prove to be the sea-route to the west. The passage had, however, not been without incident. During visits ashore it had been noticed that there were numerous signs that natives were active in the area. Before long Frobisher had made contact with what were later to be known as Eskimos. Initial contacts based upon the trading of trinkets proved to be successful, but an attempt by five of Frobisher's men to do some private dealing turned to disaster when the natives kidnapped them along with their boat. Frobisher retaliated by grabbing a native whose curiosity about the sound of a hand-bell had overcome his caution. Lifting the man off the water complete with his seal-skin kayak he attempted to bargain for the return of his men, but to no avail.

After a final visit ashore to pick up what souvenirs they could from the beach, Frobisher decided to take advantage of favourable winds and set sail for home where he arrived in early October. As his captured native rapidly sickened and died, Frobisher was fêted for his 'discovery' of a north-west passage. But that news was to pale into insignificance when a black rock, picked up from the beach by one of his seamen, was examined and believed to contain gold. Instantly, all noble thoughts of exploration were abandoned as another expedition was mounted – this time with a third ship being sponsored by the queen herself. Sailing in May 1577, Frobisher found his way back to his 'Straits' and soon had 200 tons of the black rock on-board, albeit at the cost of several Eskimos' lives falling to the primitive firearms of the Englishmen.

On his return, Frobisher found the gold-lust still raging and plans were made for yet another voyage. In addition to simply stocking up with the black rocks, he was

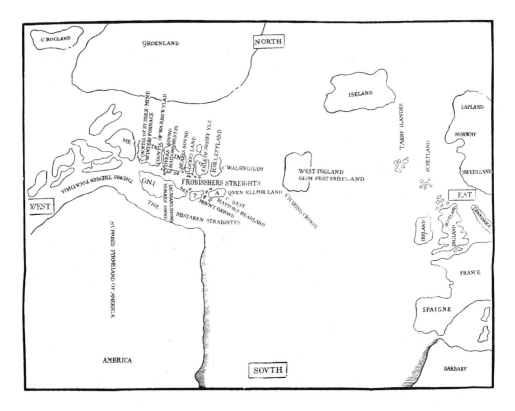

Contemporary map based on Frobisher's discoveries.

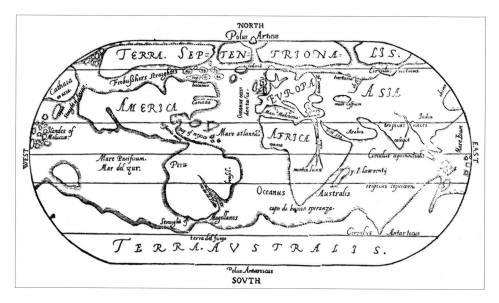

Above: *World map showing Frobisher's Strait leading to the Pacific Ocean.*

also to take out the nucleus of a mining colony. It was not long before that part of the enterprise received a crippling blow when the ship carrying the 100 would-be colonists and all their stores sank after colliding with an iceberg. No lives were lost in the incident and Frobisher pressed on with his cramped vessels into what he took to be his 'Straits', only to find himself in unknown waters that promised yet another westerly breach in the continent's coastline. Gold, however, had now become the sole aim of his voyage, and so he turned about, passed out of the wide entrance (after naming it 'Mistaken Straits') and turned northwards to his intended destination. In the late summer of 1578, his men toiled in uncomfortable conditions to get as much of the black stone as they could before the approaching winter would force them to leave the area. Their efforts, heavily underlined by muttered discontent, netted them over 1,300 tons of ore before the ships left for home. On arrival in late October, they found none of the rejoicing they might have expected from their effort. In their absence the rocks had been studied more closely and had proved to contain nothing more valuable than iron pyrites – fool's gold.

Frobisher's punishment was to be given blockading duties off the coast of Ireland before he was allowed to join Sir Francis Drake in a voyage to the West Indies. Three years later he took part in the Armada campaign where he earned a knighthood. He died in 1594 after being wounded in action against the Spaniards. His 'Straits' later proved to be a bay, and his hard-earned black rocks were used to make roads in Kent.

As Frobisher headed towards the warmth of the West Indies, two ships, the *Sunshine* and the *Moonshine,* under the command of John Davis and sponsored, in the main, by wealthy businessmen, set off to once again look into the possibility of a passage to China over the top of North America. The Devon-born commander took his ships 400 miles up the west coast of Greenland where he charmed the local Eskimos by getting his men to dance to the tune of the ship's musicians. After a peaceful trading session, Davis headed westwards across the expanse of water that was to be named 'Davis Straits' in his honour. Striking the coast at a point he named 'Exeter Sound', he turned south and reached a westward-trending inlet. Sailing 180 miles up the promising waterway, Davis was delighted to see whales spouting even further to the west. To him, such a sight could only mean that there had to be an outlet to the west making 'Cumberland Sound' the passage he had been seeking. With a shift of the wind making further progress difficult, Davis elected to return home with his news. On his arrival, his enthusiasm for his newfound route soon attracted sponsors for another expedition.

With his fleet doubled by the addition of the *Mermaid* and the *North Star,* Davis set off in 1586 to return to northern waters. Sending the *Sunshine* and *North Star* up the east coast of Greenland to search in that direction for a westerly passage, Davis took the *Moonshine* and *Mermaid* up the west coast where, once again, he made contact with the natives. In the beginning, the two races met in amicable trading and wrestling matches (with the Eskimos beating the Englishmen), but the natives soon began to display an aptitude for the theft of metal and wooden objects. When he found that one of his anchors had been stolen, Davis decided that the time had

Henry Hudson.

come to move on. An attempt to reach further north failed due to ice blocking the route and, with a number of his men falling ill, Davis transferred the sick to the *Mermaid* and ordered her home.

With the departure of the *Mermaid*, Davis may have hoped his ill luck might have gone with them – but it was not to be. He missed the entrance to Cumberland Sound and did not find Frobisher's or Mistaken Straits. Two of his men were killed by the natives and others wounded before he decided that the time had come to return home. There, he was to learn that the *North Star* had been lost, and there had been no achievements of note by the other branch of his expedition.

Despite this setback, Davis was still able to find backers for an expedition to sail in 1587. The *Sunshine, Elizabeth,* and the tiny pinnace *Ellen* had not reached far into the Atlantic when the crews of the *Sunshine* – by now starting to leak – and the *Elizabeth,* decided that fishing provided a better option than exploration and sailed off to leave Davis with only the pinnace to enter his strait. Undeterred, he pressed on to reach beyond 72 degrees north where he was stopped by contrary winds. A large headland on the Greenland coast was named 'Sanderson's Hope' after his main backer before he headed south-west to avoid a large field of pack ice. Coasting down the shores to the west, Davies entered Cumberland Sound only to confirm that there was no western exit. After passing Frobisher Bay, he almost fell foul of the great rush of water and ice that poured from Frobisher's Mistaken Straits before making his way home to inform his backers that 'The passage is most probable, the execution is easy'.

Davies was later to sail in an attempt to reach the Pacific via Magellan's Strait. He had hoped to take a look at a north-west passage by approaching it from the west. He did not get through the straits, but having been separated from other ships in the fleet, he discovered the Falkland Isles. Davies was to meet his death at the hands of Japanese pirates twelve years later whilst off the coast of Malaya.

In an attempt to further extend the discoveries of Davies, the East India Co. sent George Waymouth with the *Discovery* and the *Godspeed* to spend a year in the search for the north-west passage. He claimed to have reached beyond 61 degrees north before being forced to return by a mutinous crew. Waymouth returned to obscurity, but his ship, the *Discovery*, was soon to play a part in one of the north's best-known tragedies.

Henry Hudson, with eleven men on board the *Hopeful*, left Gravesend in May 1607 'to discover the pole' on behalf of the Muscovy Co. Making his way up the east coast of Greenland, Hudson found his way barred by ice and turned eastwards to sail along the rim of the barrier in the hope of finding a way through. His progress brought him as far east as Spitsbergen before he gave up and returned to the Thames in mid-September with enough tales of abundant whales to set off a new branch of the whaling industry. Seven months later, again under the sponsorship of the

Muscovy Co., and in the wake of Willoughby and the Dutchman, Barents, Hudson sailed to search for a north-east route to the Orient. After four months he was forced to return having failed to find a way through the ice blocking his path.

With a loss of further interest in the possibility of a north-east passage by the Muscovy Co., Hudson found new employment with the Dutch East India Co. He was ordered back to the Barents Sea to continue the search on the *Half Moon* with the *Good Hope* as escort. This time, his mainly Dutch crew refused to go beyond Novaya Zemlya and, having parted company with the *Good Hope,* Hudson decided to head for warmer waters on the coast of North America. After checking the Chesapeake and Delaware bays in the hope of a western passage, he entered what later became known as the Hudson River. A voyage of 150 miles up the waterway (at the cost of five of his men to Indian attack) led to disappointment when he found he could go no further. Hudson decided to return home. His discoveries led to Dutch involvement on the coast of North America, and their later purchase of Manhattan Island from the natives. The English, however, were less impressed with his work on behalf of the Dutch and the king (James I) forbade his continued employment by what was seen as the opposition.

A small group of leading businessmen, supported by Henry, Prince of Wales, commissioned Hudson to try once again to find a north-west passage. Obtaining the use of Waymouth's old ship, the *Discovery*, he sailed from London in April 1610, and reached the turbulent mouth of Frobisher's Mistaken Straits the following June.

Passing through the narrow entrance, Hudson first kept to the northern shore before ice forced him to swing south into a wide bay. Finding his route barred by land to the south-east he returned to the north to find a group of islands he named 'Isles of God's Mercie'. Once again, Hudson sailed southwards into the bay reaching the bottom on 16 July. This time he kept to the coast as it led first to the north-west and then westwards until a gap between an island and the mainland appeared to offer a southward route. Naming the tip of the island 'Cape Digges' and the opposing mainland 'Cape Wolstenholme' after two of his sponsors, Hudson began his voyage south along the western coast of Labrador. The third of his sponsors, Sir Thomas Smyth, had a cape named in his honour before Hudson found himself passing through a 'labyrinth' of islands. But it was not to be problems in navigation that gave Hudson his chief difficulties – it was the unrest amongst his ship's company.

The *Discovery*'s first mate, Robert Juet, had sailed with Hudson on two previous voyages. It did not take long before he was in serious conflict with Henry Greene; a dissolute young man whom Hudson insisting on taking along for little better reason than he liked him. Before long, Juet had turned against Hudson. Their conflict came to a head just as Hudson found the coast beginning to trend westwards, then to the north. His patience, by now sorely tested by both his situation and his disgruntled first mate, Hudson replaced Juet with the inexperienced but promising, Robert

Bylot. He followed this action by replacing the boatswain, and Juet found himself gathering a core of support in opposition to Hudson.

Whatever the situation might have been amongst his crew, Hudson found he had no choice but to spend the winter in a shallow, sheltered bay at the point where the coastline turned to the west. It was a desolate spot that provided little in the way of supplies. Before long, the ship's gunner had died, possibly from scurvy. Hudson then fell out with one of his most loyal men, the ship's carpenter, and then went on to enrage even his favourite, Greene, over a petty squabble concerning the allocation of the dead gunner's coat. Bylot's time as first mate did not survive the winter as he was replaced by the ship's carpenter and Hudson commandeered all the ship's navigation instruments.

By the beginning of June 1611, the ice had begun to thaw and the scurvy-ridden men began to prepare the ship to break free from her dismal winter's captivity. Hudson issued out the remaining bread and cheese but followed this with searches amongst the crew's personal belongings in the belief that some of them had been hiding their own caches of food. The final straw came when the boatswain, Wilson, formed the opinion that Hudson was giving extra rations to his favourites. When Greene heard this, he and Wilson went to Abacuck Prickett – an educated servant of one of the sponsors, Sir Dudley Digges – and told him that they intended to take over the ship. They needed Prickett on their side because of his contacts through whom he could later put their case. He could also write down the events leading up to the insurrection, and an account of what was to follow. Prickett could easily see that his choice was, in reality, limited to supporting the mutineers or facing death. He chose to give his support.

On the morning of 21 June, north-west of their recently vacated winter harbour, Hudson and his young son, John, were grabbed and hustled into one of the ship's boats. They were followed by three of the crew who had shown loyalty to their captain, and a further four men suffering from scurvy. The boat was cast off and was soon to be lost to sight amongst the ice floes. No trace of Hudson or his companions was ever to be found.

Under the leadership of Greene, the *Discovery* sailed northwards until she reached Cape Digges. The crew spotted a group of Eskimos on the island and Greene, Wilson, Prickett and three others rowed ashore in an attempt to trade for some meat. Without warning, the natives turned and attacked the Englishmen. One of the seamen died instantly as the others fled towards the beach. Prickett, standing by the boat, received several stab wounds before being able to use his knife to fend off his attacker. One of the seamen, on reaching the boat, used an axe to fell another of the attackers as the wounded Greene, Wilson, and the final seaman, clambered aboard and pushed themselves off the beach. A shower of arrows from the Eskimos caused yet more wounds.

Conflict between Eskimos and English Tudor seamen.

By the end of the day, only two of the shore expedition remained alive. Greene and Wilson were both dead. Only nine men remained to get the ship home. Bylot took command and, after getting in a stock of seabirds from the coast near Cape Wolstenholme, headed eastwards through Hudson's Strait to face a journey of over 2,000 miles across the north Atlantic. As the battered ship with its starving crew closed with the shores of England, Robert Juet died. On their arrival in September, it was not too difficult to explain to a number of formal inquiries and tribunals that Greene, Wilson, and Juet had been the instigators of the mutiny. None of the survivors were ever to be found guilty of being involved in the death of Henry Hudson and the other men cast adrift on that bleak June day.

Despite the losses and suffering of the expedition, it had, at least, come home with evidence of real exploratory achievement. Hudson had charted the eastern edge of a great body of water and seemed to have reached its southern limit. This meant that the question of what lay to the west remained open. Once again the fortunes of the merchant adventurers were made ready to sponsor another expedition. This time, however, there was to be the addition of royal patronage. The young Henry, Prince of Wales, offered his support with the services of an experienced captain from the royal fleet along with one of his vessels, the *Resolution*.

Captain Thomas Button had served his country with distinction for about twenty-three years. He had seen action in the West Indies and off the coast of Ireland where his efforts had earned him a pension of *6s 8d* per day. His expedition sailing orders from the Prince of Wales demanded that daily prayers be observed and that any threats by his men against the good order of the expedition receive prompt punishment. Upon passing through Hudson's Strait he was to observe the direction

Captain Thomas Button.

of any flood and follow it to its source in the hope that it would prove to be a passage to the west.

In addition to the *Resolution* he was also to have Waymouth's and Hudson's old ship the *Discovery*, now under the command of Captain Ingram. Two further names were added to the ships companies – Robert Bylot and Abacus Prickett were to go as pilots. Although there was at least a reasonable chance that Hudson and some of the men cast adrift the year before could still be alive, there was no plan to attempt a rescue.

The expedition sailed in early May 1612. After naming a large island at the northern entrance of Hudson's Strait after his ship, Button – although delayed by ice – reached Digges Island with little difficulty. A party who were landed at Cape Wolstenholme to collect seabirds came under attack by a large number of natives who were only repulsed when one of their number was killed by a musket. A subsequent attempt to get fresh water was ambushed and five of the party killed. The situation may have been caused by the commandeering of four kayaks by the landing parties in order to supplement the ship's boats. Despite the deaths, Button returned two of the skin canoes in a hopeful gesture of reconciliation.

Sailing westwards, the expedition then came across an island (Coats Island) with a prominent cape on its southern coast which Button named 'Cary's Swans Nest'. From there he set out on a course just south of west and raced over clear waters in a fever of expectation, his hopes only to be dashed as he came up against a coast that trended both north and south. He named the spot 'Hopes Checked' and, after getting caught in a northerly storm, headed southwards. On 15 August he came across a six-mile wide river estuary that promised shelter for the approaching winter. Button named the site 'Port Nelson' after his sailing master who had died shortly after their arrival.

With his ships secured and surrounded by a wall of earth and pine logs, Button turned his attention to keeping up the morale of his ships' companies. He decided that idle minds were his greatest risk and came up with a series of proposals for the following spring which he insisted were to be discussed at great depth by all his men. The elements surrounding them, however, were unimpressed and, before they found release from their icy prison, several men had succumbed to the conditions.

The ice finally gave way in June 1613, and Button threaded his way northwards through the drifting ice floes. Following the line of the coast, he pushed on until he reached a point just short of 65 degrees. He had land in sight both to the east and west – land that appeared to be closing in on him. It seemed as if he had found himself in a narrow bay. With July almost ended, and without being prepared to spend another winter in those waters, Button turned his ships around and headed home. After passing to the south of a large land mass (Southampton Island), he returned to Cary's Swans Nest before coming across another island he named after his kinsman, Sir Robert Mansel. He then shaped his course northwards prior to going west about Nottingham and Salisbury Islands. To the west of the former island, Button noticed a flood from the north-west. It was this information that kept alive the prospect of a north-west passage through Hudson's Strait.

On his return, Captain Button continued to serve on the royal ships and was eventually appointed to the position of admiral off the coast of Ireland. He was to fall foul of political in-fighting between the Admiralty and the Navy Board and died in 1634 in the midst of squabbles over his pay shortly before a distant relation, Oliver Cromwell, had achieved the required eminence to come to his aid.

Whilst Button had been away, his merchant adventurer backers had organised themselves into the grandly named 'Company of Merchants of London, Discovers of the Northwest Passage'. They sent out two ships, the *Patience* and the *Heart's Ease* to have a look at the west coast of Greenland. Little came of the affair apart from its commander, James Hall, being killed by the natives. One of the ship's pilots, however, was to make his name well known in the near future. William Baffin had produced the only real benefit of the expedition by being the first navigator known to have used the sun, moon and stars in an attempt to find his longitude.

With Button's information at their disposal, the newly-formed company gave the command of the *Discovery* to a near relative of Button who had been with him on his voyage. Unfortunately, Captain William Gibbons lacked the good fortune of Button and spent several months in an inlet on the east coast of Labrador before returning to England. His ship's company showed their contempt by referring to the site of their miserable confinement as 'Gibbon's Hole'.

Despite this setback, the Merchant Co. refitted the *Discovery* and appointed Robert Bylot as her commander with William Baffin as his pilot. The ship sailed from Blackwall on 17 March 1615 and reached the entrance to Hudson's Bay two months later. Slowed down by the ice and contrary winds, Bylot made his way along the northern edge of the strait until they reached a group of islands in a large bay (North Bay). On the islands they met a number of natives whom they considered to be 'rude and uncivil' before pressing on to Salisbury Island. For some time their way was blocked by giant ice floes grinding against each other and the ship 'But God, which is still stronger than rocks, ice, eddy, or streame, preserved us and our shippe from any harme at all.' Continuing on in a north-westerly direction in pursuit of the flood reported by Button, they found the land trending to the north and, before long, they had entered clearer waters. Soon, however, more ice blocked their way. At this, they swung first east, then back on to their north-westerly course which took them up the north-east coast of Southampton Island until they reached a headland Bylot named 'Cape Comfort' in the belief that, once they had rounded the cape, they would find the source of the flood. But it was not to be. The tide died away, the wind fell to little more than a breeze, and they were frequently 'pestered' by ice. After spending over two weeks testing the tide, and with the end of July approaching, Bylot returned to Digges Island with the intention of having one last attempt to find a way to the west. The matter was taken out of his hands by a series of storms, fog, and contrary winds and he headed out of the bay to reach Resolution Island on 3 August. Five weeks later they were back in Plymouth without the loss of a single man.

The seamanship of Bylot and the navigational skills of Baffin had proved to be a good combination and so, upon Baffin's suggestion, the Merchant Co. sent them with the *Discovery* (now on her sixth attempt to find a north-west passage) to follow the path first forged by Davis almost thirty years earlier. Bylot's orders included the instruction that he could 'touch the north part of Japan…to bring home one of the men of the country.'

Greenland was sighted on 14 May 1616 followed by a clear passage up the west coast as far as Davis's 'Sanderson's Hope'. There they were held up by ice, giving them the opportunity to visit a group of islands where they found a number of native women hiding from them. Bylot treated them well and persuaded them to return to their huts before naming the place 'Women's Islands'.

Attempts to sail to the west failed, so the expedition continued north until they reached beyond 76 degrees where they came across a dominant headland backed by mountains. This was named 'Cape Dudley Digges' after one of their most prominent backers. To the north, a bay was named 'Wolstenholme Sound' followed by another named 'Whale Sound'. Just beyond 78 degrees, Bylot reached his most northerly point at the entrance to another large sound. Prevented from entering by the weather, he named the sound after Sir Thomas Smyth (later to be corrupted to 'Smith Sound'). He also stared with astonishment as his compass needle pointed 56 degrees west of true north 'a thing almost incredible and matchless in all the world'. A favourable wind took the *Discovery* south-west to the foggy entrance to another sound which Bylot named after Alderman Jones. The coastline then began to trend to the south before it opened out into a forty-mile wide entrance to a sound that appeared to Bylot and Baffin to offer no passage to the west. They named the sound after another director of the Merchant Co., Sir James Lancaster.

Their voyage down the east coast provided little of interest as the ice constantly fended them off the shore. At last they reached the point already covered by Davies and decided to return home. On their arrival, Baffin wrote to Sir John Wolstenholme 'There is no passage, nor hope of a passage, in the north of Davis Strait, we having coasted all or nearly all the circumference thereof, and find it to be no other than a great bay.' 'Baffin's Bay' it seemed, had little to offer other than to those who hunted the whale.

Of Robert Bylot, history has little more to record, but William Baffin, eager to have an attempt at a north-west passage from the north Pacific, worked for the East India Co. in an effort to reach that part of the world. On 23 January 1622, he

Far left above: *Sir Thomas Smyth, one of Bylot's sponsors for whom Smith Sound was named.*

Far left below: *Title page of Foxe's account of his voyage.*

Left: *Captain Thomas James.*

found himself surveying the walls of a castle on an island in the Persian Gulf whilst the castle was under attack by English forces. As he was working out the angles 'he received a shot from the castle into his belly, wherewith he gave three leaps, and died immediately.' Six years later his widow 'of advanced years and deaf' was awarded £500 compensation and promptly remarried.

It was now time for the English to draw breath. Baffin's reports had dampened the enthusiasm of the merchants and there appeared no others to provide the impetus or sponsorship to send out expeditions. In 1619, the challenge was taken up by the Danes who sent out two ships under the command of Jens Munk. After wintering in Hudson's Bay, only three men – one of who was Munk – managed to return to Denmark.

The possibility offered by a north-west passage, however, still nagged at the merchants of England, and by 1631, they found themselves in a position to sponsor not just one, but two expeditions. Sir Thomas Roe and Sir John Wolstenholme of the London Merchants obtained the services of the experienced sea captain, Luke Foxe, and the use of the *Charles* pinnace. Not to be outdone, the merchants of Bristol provided for a pinnace of their own, the *Henrietta Maria,* under the command of Captain Thomas James. Both vessels had a crew of twenty-two, both captains had virtually the same instructions – to sail north from Digges Island or, failing that, to search the western shore and further the work done by Button. Both captains had letters for the Emperor of Japan.

James sailed from Bristol on 3 May, followed two days later by Foxe setting out from Deptford. Both ships experienced difficulty with the ice in Hudson's Strait, yet reached the western exit within a day of each other. Further problems with the ice prevented their passage to the north and both steered south-west. Foxe passed Cary's Swans Nest on 17 July, a day after James – but neither of the ships had caught sight of the other during any stage of the journey so far. At this point, their courses diverged with Foxe heading north-west and James turning south-west.

The *Charles* reached the Sound that had last been entered by Button before he had turned for home. Foxe stopped at a small island off the north-west coast and named it 'Sir Thomas Roe's Welcome' – a name that later became applied to the entire waterway. He then turned southwards, naming Brooke Cobham (Marble) Island and – after a scientifically-minded friend – a group of small islands as 'Briggs Mathematicks'. On 9 August, he reached Port Nelson where he rested his crew and carried out repairs to his ship, discovering as he did so a cross and an inscribed board raised by Button nineteen years earlier. Ten days later he set off southwards once again. On 29 August, Foxe sighted sails ahead of him and, on the following day, he came up alongside the *Henrietta Marie* and joined Captain James for dinner.

James had not had a particularly successful voyage. After leaving Cary's Swans Nest he had headed almost south before returning northwards and finally turning to the west. He had made landfall at about 59 degrees and followed the coast south in the wake of Foxe. At Nelson Shoal he ran aground, but managed to free himself in order to pass Port Nelson on 15 August – the harbour at that time sheltering Foxe. Five days later, an accident with the capstan removed the leg of Richard Edwards (the *Henrietta Maria*'s gunner) and injured a number of other seamen.

Foxe proved to be a less than grateful dinner guest, noting on the return to his own ship, that he found James to be 'no seaman' but a 'practitioner in the mathematicks'. As if to prove his superior ability, Foxe forged ahead until, on 2 September, he reached a cape from which the land veered sharply to the south. Naming the prominence 'Cape Wolstenholme's Ultimum Vale', Foxe now decided that he had gone far enough to the south and turned his bows to the north.

Two weeks later he found himself north of Salisbury Island and within sight of a mountainous foreland he named 'King Charles Cape'. With the ice clear ahead of him, Foxe pressed on northwards keeping in sight of the rugged land to the east. Just beyond the Arctic Circle, the coast turned abruptly eastwards. For a few hours he maintained his northwards course but, with no further land in sight ahead of him, with signs of scurvy beginning to show in his crew, and with the approach of winter, Foxe turned about and headed for home. He arrived to a somewhat muted welcome.

Not only had he failed to find a passage to the west, but had returned home whilst the Bristol merchant's ship had apparently chosen to winter in Hudson's Bay, thus snatching the advantage. Both the merchants of Bristol and of London would have to wait another year to see the outcome.

As Foxe's topsails had disappeared over the horizon on 2 September, James arrived at Wolstenholme's Ultimum Vale. Unaware that it had already been named, he bestowed upon the cape the name of his ship and of his sovereign's queen, 'Henrietta Maria' (its royal connection thus securing permanence over Foxe's sponsor). Unlike Foxe, James had decided to spend the winter as far to the south in the bay as possible and continued to follow the coast in that direction whilst taking a look at a number of small islands. On several occasions he ran aground, once having to throw overboard much of the coal he had brought with him to provide fuel for his winter stoves. After a month of rather aimless cruising, he decided to winter on Charlton Island – almost within hailing distance of where Hudson had been abandoned.

Unfortunately, the site proved less than had been hoped for. With the completion of three huts built on the shore (during which time John Barton, the gunner's mate, drowned), it was found that the ship could not be secured for the winter. In an attempt to deal with the problem, James took the extraordinary measure of sinking the *Henrietta Maria* just as high winds drove her against the shore. His confidence in his action might be judged from the fact that he kept his crew occupied through the dismal winter in building a replacement vessel. The task was complicated by the loss of the ship's carpenter and another man through scurvy. This had brought the total deaths of the expedition to four (the gunner had died as a result of his lost leg the previous November).

In April 1632, as the first signs of a thaw began to appear, James and his crew began the task of breaking up and removing the ice that filled the hold and lower deck of their ship. After weeks of backbreaking work, and whilst the ice around the vessel remained solid, the ship was emptied and repaired. On 22 July, they managed to set sail and head north through a mass of ice floes. Upon achieving Cape Henrietta Maria, James had intended to continue directly north, but the ice forced him to return to the coastal passage he and Foxe had forged the year before. It was not until he had reached just north of Button's Hopes Checked that he was able to veer eastwards across the bay. By 24 August, he had arrived off the northern coast of Nottingham Island and, despite problems with the ice, chose to investigate towards the north-west, following a course parallel to, but to the north of, Bylot and Baffin. To his disappointment, on reaching latitude in the region of 66 degrees, he found himself in great danger of being trapped by the ice. James consulted the senior members of his crew and decided that the time had come to go home. They arrived in Bristol on 22 October with, to Foxe's relief and the disappointment of the Bristol merchants, no evidence of a passage to the north-west via Hudson's Strait.

Thus ended the first wave of assaults against the seemingly impregnable frozen fortress of the north. The last of the Elizabethan adventurers had gone, and the merchants found that the wealth of India provided a better investment for their money. If the flag of Britain were to be flown again in polar seas it would have to be done for the sake of the nation's honour, by someone with courage, skill – and access to considerable funds.

CHAPTER ONE

BY ROYAL COMMAND

The English Navy received the distinction of 'Royal' in 1673 on King Charles II's assumption of the title 'Lord High Admiral'. The unique position of the service in being the sole 'standing' (i.e. permanent) force could only be affected in the future by the funds allocated to it by Parliament or by government-approved international treaties. The Royal Navy was also unique in that it was the country's chief prerogative force, its loyalty remaining to the sovereign rather than Parliament (the Army was not allowed to be a standing force and depended for its existence upon an annual 'Mutiny Act'). It followed, therefore, that if the monarch could be interested in a proposed plan that needed royal ships or men, the proposal stood an excellent chance of gaining royal, and thus Admiralty, approval. It was Edmund Halley's knowledge and use of this fact that led to the Royal Navy's first involvement with polar exploration.

Halley had shown very early promise in the astronomical field. Whilst still at school he had built his own scientific instruments, researched the variation of the compass, and studied the night skies to such a depth that a prominent globe maker remarked that 'if a star were displaced in the globe he would presently find it out'. At seventeen he entered Queen's College, Oxford, along with his own 24ft telescope and was soon presenting scientific papers to the Royal Society. After three years at the university, Halley abandoned his degree and petitioned the king, Charles II, for transport to St Helena where he proposed to plot the fixed stars of the southern hemisphere. The king lent his support and a ship of the East India Co. gave him a southbound passage in November 1676. Unfortunately, the weather over the island did little to help Halley in his astronomical observations, but he did manage to determine the position of 341 stars and observe a transit of Mercury across the sun.

After almost two years away, Halley returned to present the king with a model of the southern sky complete with a new constellation named by him 'Robur Carolinum' in the king's honour. His success led to his being elected a fellow of the Royal Society at the age of twenty-two. In 1680, whilst touring France, he made observations of the great comet which, subsequently, took his name. Four years later, the bottom fell out of his world when his father died and most of the family fortune went into settling debts. He found assistance with his problems through his friendship with Isaac Newton who allowed him to publish the newly completed 'Principia'.

As early as 1683, Halley had been of the opinion that the great problem of global positioning by means of the longitude could be solved by studying and mapping the variation between the true and magnetic poles. Latitude could be found with relative ease by measuring the angle of the sun or fixed stars but, with no means of finding the longitude, a ship had to sail north or south until the latitude of the destination was reached and then a 'westing' or 'easting' took them along the line of latitude to their intended landfall.

With the sponsorship of a Mr Middleton, Halley submitted to the Royal Society a 'Proposal of Mr Middleton and Mr Halley to compasse the Globe for Improvement of Navigation'. He intended to sail around the world from east to west recording the magnetic variation as he went. Once this had been completed, and the known movement of the magnetic poles compensated for, it might be possible to produce a means of position-finding using the longitude. Such knowledge would, however, be dangerous. If it were to fall into the hands of an enemy or a commercial competitor, the loss of advantage would have been serious to an island nation with imperial ambition. With this in mind, Halley probably realised that his best course lay in obtaining Royal approval for his ideas. Accordingly, he submitted his ideas to the Lords of the Treasury who reported to Queen Mary II that they supported the cost of the proposed voyage (about £600). The queen indicated her approval to the Admiralty who, in turn, ordered the Navy Board to build a ship at Deptford especially for the voyage. The vessel was to be a 'Pink', a three-masted, flat-bottomed ship of Dutch design, and would be named *Paramour*. She was launched in April 1694, just a year after she had been ordered but it was to be another two years before she was ready to sail. On 4 June 1696, the Admiralty granted Halley a commission as 'Master and Commander' of the *Paramour* and the Navy Board gave warrants to the boatswain, gunner and carpenter. Halley's qualifications to have been so commissioned cannot have extended much further than his royal contacts. It meant that he had leap-frogged all the lieutenants who had been required to do sea-time as midshipmen before passing their Admiralty Board examinations for their rank. The situation was, however, not to be tested. By August 1696, Halley had accepted a job as deputy-controller at the Chester Mint and the *Paramour* was left at her moorings.

By early 1698, Halley had completed his work at the mint and, despite offers of work from Newton, expressed an eagerness to get back to his magnetic variation project. A delay of a month, however, was occasioned when the Czar of Russia, Peter the Great – visiting England to gain experience of shipbuilding – asked to be allowed to practise his sailing in her. At last, in July, Halley heard from the Admiralty that the ship was available for his voyage. The following month, the Navy Board was instructed to sheath the vessel with extra planking for 'a voyage to the East Indies or South Seas' and Halley was re-commissioned as her master and commander. This form of commission (i.e. equivalent, but senior, to a lieutenant, and as the only commissioned officer on-board) placed him in the same situation that William Bligh was to find himself in almost a century later. Bligh, however, was a highly experienced seaman and navigator whereas Halley could boast little, if any, skills in seamanship and no experience in commanding sailors. In almost certain recognition of this fact – and in a revealing letter – Halley wrote to the secretary of the Admiralty 'Your Honour knows that my dislike of my Warrant Officers made me Petition their Lordships that my Mate might have the Commission of Lieutenant, thereby the better to keep them in obedience'. Under normal circumstances, his mate (actually 'master's mate') would have been rated as a petty officer and been borne to assist

Edmund Halley

Halley – in his rank as master – with the ship's navigation. This would still have left the highest skills in seamanship in the hands of the boatswain – a warrant officer, one of those whom Halley had expressed a dislike of. In accordance with his wishes, the Admiralty appointed Lieutenant Edward Harrison to the *Paramour*.

Whether coincidence or accident chose Harrison, it is not known, but he had already had dealings with Halley. Four years earlier he had put forward a proposal to the Royal Society for the finding of longitude by means of magnetic variation and the use of eclipses. Not only were these ideas very similar to the thoughts Halley had long held, but the scientist had actually read Harrison's paper to the society, probably in support of his own theories. When nothing had come of this exposure of his ideas, Harrison had them published in 1696. He had spent about eight years in the Royal Navy when he was appointed to Halley's ship.

The *Paramour* left Deptford on 20 October 1698 with its commander, one Lieutenant, three warrant officers, one midshipman, seven able seamen, two warrant officer's mates, one captain's clerk, and four servants. Halley's sailing instructions ordered him to 'make the best of your way to the southward of the equator, and there to observe on the east coast of South America, and the west coast of Africa, the variations of the compass, with all the accuracy you can, as all the true situations both in longitude and latitude of the ports where you arrive'. It continued '…if the seasons of the year permit, you are to stand so far into the south, till you discover the coast of Terra Incognita, supposed to lie between Magellan's Straits and the Cape of Good Hope, which coast you are carefully to lay down in its true position'.

So, in addition to mapping the magnetic variation along the length of the Atlantic, Halley had also been given the task of finding the great continent which, for centuries, it was believed existed to the south – if only to act as a balance to the northern continents.

The start of the expedition was less than auspicious. Halley soon found that, with the addition of extra sheathing, the nails used had caused the inner hull planks to split, thus giving rise to a number of leaks. To make the matter worse the sand used for ballast blocked the pumps as they tried to rid the bilges of excess water. By the time he had reached Portland, it became clear to Halley that he would have to turn back to get his vessel repaired and the ballast changed to shingle. As the work was being carried out at Portsmouth, Halley was dismayed to find that his ship's company, having heard tales of pirates at work off the coast of West Africa, were reluctant about entering those waters alone. Halley countered this alarm by sending Harrison over to Admiral Benbow, about to sail for the West Indies, with a request for permission to join the admiral's fleet. This was granted and the *Paramour* sailed in company on 29 November.

After an uneventful voyage to Madeira, Halley parted company with his escort and continued on south towards the Cape Verde Islands where he suffered the indignity of being fired on by two English merchantmen who took his unusual vessel to be a pirate. Having taken on water, the *Paramour* headed towards the coast of Brazil but found herself trapped in the windless Doldrums. A month had passed when Halley decided to call in at the island of Fernando de Noronha in the hope of finding water to replenish their fast disappearing supplies. As they approached their immediate destination, he ordered the boatswain – who was the officer on watch – to continue on course for the island. He then retired for the night. Waking early the next morning, he took to the upper deck where he was outraged to find the boatswain deliberately sailing past the island. His annoyance was, no doubt, considerably increased when, after taking the vessel to the island, he found the place to be barren. There was no water to be had and the boatswain was proved to be correct in his disobedience.

After spending some time off the coast of the Brazilian Paraiba region, where he carried out observations of an eclipse of the moon, Halley decided to head northwards to Barbados rather than winter further south. The voyage proved difficult and it became clear that the ship's company were less than happy with their commander. Things came to a head when Harrison, in front of the ship's company, told Halley that he 'was not only incapable to take charge of the Pink, but even of a longboat' (somewhat surprising behaviour from someone who had written in the dedication of his book '...it is the Duty of Servants to be Faithful, Humble and Submissive to their Masters'). Halley had him confined to his cabin and took over his watch-keeping and navigational duties.

Whilst at Barbados, Halley used the eclipses of Jupiter's moons to determine the longitude, and recorded the magnetic variation before deciding to return home in the face of discontent amongst his ship's company.

The *Paramour* arrived at Plymouth on 23 June and Halley immediately sent a letter to the secretary of the Admiralty informing him that he had '…buried no man during the whole voyage …the ship being in very good condition.' Having established his leadership and reliability he then went on to blame the early return on

> ...the unreasonable carriage of my Mate and Lieutenant, who, because perhaps I do not have the whole Sea Directory so perfect as he, has for a long time made it his business to represent me, to the whole Ship's company, as a person wholly unqualified for the command their Lordships have given me, and declaring that he was sent on board here because their Lordships knew my insufficiency.

Halley continued '...by his example my Warrant Officers have not used me much better;...'. The secretary replied that Lieutenant Harrison would be tried by court martial – in the meantime, Halley should take the *Paramour* to Deptford where she would be paid off and laid up.

The court martial met on-board HMS *Swiftsure* on 3 July 1699, under the presidency of Admiral Sir Clowdsly Shovell. Three further admirals and seven captains looked into Halley's complaint against Harrison '...and other officers of the said Pink for misbehaviour and Disrespect towards him the Commander.' Harrison did little to help himself by declaring that Halley had deliberately misrepresented his book to the Admiralty some years earlier thus revealing (according to Halley) 'his spite and malice to me'. The court, however, was not impressed by such clashes of personality and allowed common sense to be their guide. Halley, they decided, had 'produced nothing to prove that the said officers have at any time disobeyed or denied his command though there may have been some grumbling among them as is generally in small vessels...' All the defendants were given severe reprimands and acquitted.

Harrison, despite his acquittal, came to the opinion that his future probably lay in the Merchant Service and never again served with the Royal Navy. Halley, furious that the court had '...very tenderly styled the abuses I suffered...', was compensated by being commissioned by the Admiralty as captain in command of the *Paramour* for a second voyage. Instead of a lieutenant, a master's mate was to be carried, with extra seamen to assist the newly appointed – and one-armed – boatswain. As an addition to his previous orders Halley, at his own request, was instructed to penetrate as far south as 55 degrees.

The ship sailed on 16 September 1699, in company with the well-armed Royal African Co. vessel *Falconbird*, as a protection against pirates. The ships separated off Madeira just as a storm approached. Before long, waves were breaking over the ship and washing down the length of the upper deck. As one of the waves broke over the vessel, Manley White, a young boy acting as the captain's servant, lost his grip and was swept overboard, never to be seen again. So affected by the loss was Halley that, for the remainder of his life, he could never speak of the incident 'without tears'.

The Equator was crossed on 16 November and stores, including rum, were taken on board in late December whilst at Rio de Janeiro. Three days before the turn of the century, the *Paramour* weighed anchor and continued southwards carrying out a series of recordings and observations. Soon the temperature began to fall and, once the 'roaring forties' had been reached, penguins and whales were frequently encountered.

On 1 February 1700, Halley reached beyond 52 degrees – his furthest south. In the late afternoon, as a gale forced them through the rough seas, the men of the *Paramour* came across a staggering sight. They found they 'were fair by three islands...being all flat on the top, and covered with snow, milk white, with perpendicular cliffs all around them....The great height of them made us conclude them land, but there was no appearance of any tree or green thing on them....'Fog and wind prevented them from attempting to land on the islands until the following day. As they approached one of the islands, already given the name 'Beachy Head', a gap in the fog revealed that they were looking at 'nothing else but one body of ice of incredible height'. That was all Halley needed to know. With ice of that dimension loose in his area, the sensible thing to do was to get out of it. Weaving his way northwards through the fog he found more and more masses of ice, surrounded by smaller pieces, threatening his vessel. Halley noted in his log 'This danger made my men reflect on the hazards we run, in being alone without a consort, and of the inevitable loss of us all, in case we staved our ship which might so easily happen among these mountains of ice in the fogs, which are so thick and frequent....' For the next three days, in weather 'very cloudy uncomfortable', they made their way through ice as 'hard and white as alabaster' before they hauled clear at last into a 'serene night'. The Royal Navy had had its first taste of the massive ice floes of the far south – and had found the experience to be deeply alarming.

Swept northwards past the Cape of Good Hope, Halley headed for St Helena where he replenished stores damaged by seawater. He then made sail for the West Indies after touching on the coast of Brazil. On completing a call on the Governor of Barbados, Halley returned to his ship to find that he had contracted a tropical disease which resulted in the peeling of his skin. The mate took over command as the surgeon looked after the captain on their departure for Bermuda. The *Paramour* was cleaned and careened at the island's naval dockyard, and her paint work was freshened as Halley recovered from his illness. The mate then requested permission to leave the ship to take up another post and was replaced by Mr Tucker, an experienced master.

Halley had intended to land in New England, but the weather deteriorated to such an extent that he was forced to continue northwards, persisting throughout in making his magnetic observations. Off the coast of Newfoundland, he came across a fleet of French fishing boats whose timely warning prevented him from running aground on the foggy coast. The next group of vessels he came across were English fishermen who greeted their countryman with a flash of cannon in the belief that he was a pirate. The outraged Halley sent a boat over to collect the skipper of the fishing vessel and was only placated by the man's plea that the fishermen had been recently pestered by pirates, and a strange vessel such as His Majesty's Ship *Paramour*, had caused them alarm.

The coast of Newfoundland was visited for supplies of water before Halley turned his bows and sailed southwards until he reached the Scilly Isles 'parallel', at which he made an easting home, thus demonstrating a lack of faith in any work he had done in finding the longitude. He touched at Plymouth before making his way up the channel to arrive at Deptford on 7 September.

By February the following year Halley was able to demonstrate to the Royal Society his 'isogonic' chart of the Atlantic based upon the almost 150 computations of magnetic variation connected by 'Halleyan lines'. Although he had not discovered the means of finding the longitude, he had begun a scientific survey that was to continue for the next 200 years. He had also taught himself to be a competent seaman and navigator to such an extent that, in 1701, the king commissioned him to take command of the *Paramour* once again for a survey of the tides and coasts of the English Channel. On completion of this task, Halley returned to the scientific and academic world. By 1713 he had been appointed secretary to the Royal Society and, eleven years later, Astronomer-Royal.

In 1729, Queen Caroline visited the Royal Observatory at Greenwich to find that Halley's salary amounted to no more than £100 per year with no allowance for an assistant. When she learned that, thirty years earlier, he had held a commission as a captain in the Royal Navy, the queen arranged for him to receive the current salary of a post-captain to make his position more comfortable. Ten years later, his health failing, Halley was forced to give up his post as Astronomer-Royal. On 14 January 1742, at eighty-six years old, he refused the medicines prescribed by his doctor and drank a glass of wine instead. He died shortly afterwards.

Halley was buried near Greenwich as the clockmaker, John Harrison, was working on his second chronometer for use in the finding of longitude. Harrison had been prompted by the government's promise of a prize of £20,000 for such an instrument. The award, in turn, had been inspired by the wreck on the Scilly Isles of the fleet commanded by Sir Clowdsly Shovell – the court martial president who had taken a lenient view of Halley's disciplinary difficulties.

Following Halley's survey of the English Channel, the *Paramour*, due, almost certainly, to her flat bottom and solid construction, was fitted with a heavy mortar to become a 'Bomb' and saw service with Admiral Rooke against the Spanish. She remained in the Mediterranean for a further three years before being sold in 1706.

The Irishman, Arthur Dobbs, born in 1689, was unquestionably a man of achievement. Son of a high sheriff, he became the High Sheriff of Antrim in 1720 and was elected a member of the Irish Parliament seven years later. Before long the Prime Minister had appointed him to be the Engineer-in-Chief and Surveyor-General in Ireland. Having completed essays on the Aurora Borealis, Irish trade, and the failure to make full use of the American colonies, he then turned his mind to the problem of the supposed north-west passage.

On a visit to London in 1734, Dobbs met the First Lord of the Admiralty, Admiral Sir Charles Wager, and gained his support. Wager put him in contact with the Hudson's Bay Co. This company had been in existence since 1670 and had been given the sole English trading rights over the huge area drained by the rivers flowing into Hudson's Bay. Its original charter had required the company to seek 'a new passage into the South Sea', but little had been done in the face of the overwhelming benefits that the expansion of trade had brought about through the trading forts it had established on the western shores of the bay. They had, reluctantly, authorised an expedition under the leadership of James Knight in 1719. Taking the ships *Albany* and *Discovery*, Knight had reached Hudson's Bay in company with another vessel but then disappeared. The Hudson's Bay Co. showed no eagerness to go in search of their vanished companions and it was another forty-eight years before their remains were found on Marble Island off the bay's north-west shore.

Through his new contacts, Dobbs was introduced to Captain Christopher Middleton, one of the company's most experienced officers. Middleton had not only spent a considerable time on the waters of Hudson's Bay, but had also taken a great interest in magnetic variation and the finding of longitude by means of the quadrant – an instrument introduced in 1731 to measure the height of heavenly bodies. The only problem was that Middleton appeared to have no interest in the discovery of a north-west passage.

For the next six years Dobbs tried to persuade Middleton to take up the challenge, but to no avail. The Admiralty also showed little interest as a war with Spain and a looming conflict with France diverted their attention. Dobbs pressed on with his idea until at last, word of his proposals reached George II. The king, considering Dobbs requirements to be a 'trifle', urged the Admiralty to help. Soon Dobbs was to learn that the Admiralty had agreed that two ships, the sloop HMS *Furnace* and the pink, HMS *Discovery* would be made available for 'a voyage towards Hudson's Strait, in order to attempt the discovery of a passage that way into the western American Ocean'. With this news, Middleton became more interested in the proposed expedition and, when Dobbs prevailed upon the Admiralty to grant him a commission as master and commander – at seven shillings and six pence per day, he undertook to command the expedition. The Admiralty also appointed Lieutenant John Rankin as second-in-command, and the Navy Board issued warrants to William Moor, to be master of the *Discovery*, and to Robert Wilson, as master of the *Furnace*.

Middleton then found himself faced with the problem experienced by almost every captain of a Royal Naval ship at that time. A ship's company had to be found whilst there was a war on with Spain. All the best men had volunteered, bounties had attracted the less worthy, and the press gangs had swept through the coastal towns to top up the men-of-war. With sixty-three men needed for a voyage that was most unlikely to bring glory or prize money, and could promise little more than the chance of an icy tomb, Middleton would have been hard-pushed to achieve the numbers required. But, with the probable occasional bribing of Press masters, he was able to report to the Admiralty that his ship's companies were complete although he considered them to be a 'set of rogues' who 'deserved hanging before they entered with me'.

The two ships set sail on 8 June 1741 towards Leith where they were joined by HMS *Dolphin* who escorted them to the Orkney Islands against the fear of enemy ships known to be operating in that area. Once safely beyond the threat, the escort was dropped and Middleton headed out into the north Atlantic. His orders from the Admiralty were to make his way to Sir Thomas Roe's Welcome from where, after taking note of the tides, coastlines, sea depth, and magnetic variation, he was to enter the waterway last seen by Button in 1613. If, after going around Whalebone (Whale) Point, he was to discover a strait or open sea, he was to continue on until he reached the western side of the American continent. There he was to leave a record of his voyage on the coast of California and attempt to make contact with Captain Anson who would be waiting for Spanish treasure ships off the coast of southern California. If he was to be threatened by any Japanese ships he was to retreat and make his way back home via Hudson's Strait, an armed expedition would be sent to follow his path the succeeding year. He was to 'cultivate a friendship' with any of the native peoples he came across, treating them with 'all possible civility and respect'. If he found any 'civilised nations' he was to present them with 'seeds of fruit trees, plants, grain and pulse' and to 'make them sensible of their use and manner of culture'. Should, however, problems arise he was 'to proceed as, upon advice with your officers, you shall judge may be most advantageous to the service on which you are employed'.

The two ships arrived at the entrance to Hudson's Strait on 25 July and, finding it clear of ice, made an easy passage through, arriving off Cary's Swans Nest on the 31st. The following day, Middleton called a meeting of his officers. With the season so advanced would it 'be proper to proceed upon a discovery of a passage from Hudson's Bay to the South Sea directly, or to repair with His Majesty's sloop *Furnace*, and *Discovery* pink, to Churchill River?' The decision was unanimous. Better to accept the hospitality of the Hudson's Bay Post at Churchill, than to risk the rigours of a winter frozen in at some remote corner of the bay. Unfortunately, the people of Churchill were not of the same opinion.

Faced with an unwelcome drain on their meagre resources from an expedition that might lead to a challenge to their monopoly, the settlers were less than forthcoming in their welcome. Middleton was forced to take over an abandoned fort that had fallen into a state of complete disrepair. The building was barely restored by his men when the winter arrived leaving them little time for hunting and getting in firewood. The increasing cold shocked even the most experienced of them and many of the men turned to the ample supplies of brandy in an attempt to keep warm. Soon, frostbite was causing the amputation of fingers and toes and scurvy began to make its presence felt. Sores broke out on the sufferers' bodies, their gums began to blacken, and they collapsed into morose dejection. By the following spring, ten men had died and others survived only as cripples.

Middleton had spent much of the winter turning over in his mind some problems with the design of his ship. Before they had left England he had requested that the

Furnace's quarterdeck be made flush with the main deck, and a new hatchway be cut in order that the forward part of the ship could be reached without risk from the capstan bars which blocked any forward passage when the capstan was in use. In the event, however, there had been no time to carry out these modifications and it was, no doubt, with some annoyance, that Middleton had the 'sad experience' of 'being jammed between the end of a capstan bar and the companion'. He called a meeting of his officers near the end of March to gain agreement for his alterations which, by now, included replacing the ship's tiller with a wheel, and placing hinged deadlights to his cabin windows.

With the work completed, and the river clear of ice, Middleton grabbed the 'first spurt of wind' on 1 July 1742, to get clear of the unwelcoming community. He took with him a small number of Indians to act as translators should he meet any tribes to the north. Three days of easy sailing brought them to Marble Island (still known by the name 'Brooke Cobham' bestowed upon it by Foxe, and the home of the whitening bones of Knight and his men). On the 5th, the ships were in sight of Whale Point and Middleton carried out tests on the tide to see if he could pick up any flood to indicate a northern outlet into the bay. He was encouraged by a modest flow from the north-east and pressed on into the southern entrance to Sir Thomas Roe's Welcome only to find himself surrounded by ice. Ordering both ships to be anchored to a large ice floe in an attempt to avoid being blown ashore by a strong wind, Middleton found to his alarm that the wind was also forcing the ice towards the land. For three days they were unable to do anything about their situation until, with less than two miles between them and the shore, the wind fell and the westward drift slowed down. The calm also meant that the ice-floes began to separate, allowing the ships to attach ice-anchors to the floes and, by hauling on the capstan, to 'warp' their way between the obstructions and away from the menace of the shore.

It still seemed, nevertheless, that they were in great danger of being trapped by the ice or forced upon the shore. Middleton called a council of his officers to discuss the matter. To the north of them they could see what appeared to be a cape guarding a strait or inlet that suggested a westward break in the coast. This might have been what they had been sent out to discover, but it was as a refuge from the threatening ice that the officers agreed to make their way over to the gap in the western shore.

As they rounded the cape, Middleton named it 'Dobbs' – 'after my worthy friend'. Anchoring off the entrance to the inlet, Middleton soon found it to be a poor choice of position as the tide threw a succession of ice floes against him. At first he tried to protect his ships by getting his men to fend the ice off with ice-poles but, before long, the anchor of the *Furnace* was wrenched off the bottom (minus one of its arms), and Middleton was forced to steer the ship around the oncoming ice.

The next day, Middleton sent Lieutenant Rankin in the ship's boat through the entrance to the inlet (named by Middleton as 'River Wager' after the First Lord) to see if he could find a suitable anchorage out of the main ice flow. Rankin soon located a small bay on the northern shore protected from the ice by a group of islands. The *Furnace* and *Discovery* had not been long secured at their new anchorage when a group of 'Uskimay savages' paid the ships a visit. Middleton gave the Eskimos some small gifts and sent them away, naming his anchorage 'Savage Sound' in their honour.

For the next few days, all the officers were employed on testing the tides of the inlet. It was found that, although they appeared to be at the mouth of a river with its flow from the west, there was also a strong flood that entered from the east. This action caused the ice to be forced first in one direction and then in another. Such a situation, Middleton felt, would hazard his ships and, until the position improved, it would be better to remain secure in Savage Sound. There was a possibility, however, that Rankin might have missed a better anchorage closer to the inlet entrance. Consequently, Middleton sent the lieutenant and Wilson, his master, in the ship's boat to take a closer look along the northern side of the inlet. Rankin found nothing, but noted that there seemed to be a number of coves on the southern side. He set out to have a look at these likely harbours, but found it impossible to make his way through the ice blocking the centre of the river. Turning back towards the ships, he had just reached the islands guarding Savage Sound when a sudden tidal rush forced his boat back into the river. As soon as the boat met the main stream with its strong ice-bearing tide, it became surrounded by streams of jostling ice floes that constantly threatened to crush them. For several hours it looked as if there was to be an inevitable tragedy as the rowers fought for control of their craft in the midst of the swirling ice. Suddenly a large floe bore down upon them. Although it could have easily crushed the boat it was, instead, to prove their salvation. The threatening ice had a large indentation at its base into which the boat's crew forced their craft. Thus protected from the grinding and collision of other floes, the boat and its protective ice drifted clear out of the inlet and into Sir Thomas Roe's Welcome. In the calmer waters of the Welcome, the men recovered their strength until the arrival of the flood tide from the east. Setting a course to the northern side of the inlet, they were borne in on the flood and, by keeping close to the land, managed to make their way back to the ships after an ordeal that had lasted for more than thirty-six hours.

Rankin and Wilson were rewarded for their endeavours by being sent out again on the following day to take a boat upriver. This time they kept to the northern shore as far as Deer Sound, so-named when Rankin dropped off two of the Indian translators to hunt deer for the ship's sick. The expedition continued up the river for another forty-five miles taking soundings and going ashore to view the terrain. Climbing to the top of a hill, Rankin noted that the river narrowed to the west of them but, to the north, he could see 'a large collection of water' containing several islands and surrounded by mountains. His overall impression was that they had not discovered a way through to the western ocean, but that the tides that came downriver occurred as a result of another opening to the east through which the water flowed. On his return to Deer Sound to pick up the Indians, Rankin noted a number of large, black, whales which, he felt, supported his view of another, eastern, entrance to the river.

After three weeks anchored in Savage Sound, Middleton noted that the ice had begun to clear. He immediately gave orders that the ships be prepared to sail and weighed anchor on 3 August. On leaving the River Wager, Middleton continued to follow the coastline in a generally northerly direction 'much pestered by ice'. Two days later he came upon a large headland, to which he gave the name 'Cape Hope' in the belief that, once it had been rounded, he would find himself on the north coast of America. At first, Cape Hope suggested that it might have been well named. The clear water continued for about eighteen miles until Middleton saw, looming over the horizon, the unmistakable appearance of land that curved northwards across his front. Turning eastwards he was dismayed to find the land continuing to follow his direction. There was no doubting that he was in a bay. There was, however, still cause for hope. By testing the sea for any tidal action, he came to the conclusion that there was no large river or strait out of the bay, but he knew that, further to the south, he had picked up a strong tide flowing towards the North East. Naming the area of his disappointment 'Repulse Bay', Middleton steered south-east until, on 7 August, he picked up the flood he had been looking for.

It soon became clear that he was not going to be able to follow the tide to its source. A solid sheet of ice blocked the entire eastern sea. To try and get a full picture of what lay along the path of the ice, Middleton went ashore at a point he named 'Cape Frigid' and walked inland for about fifteen miles before climbing a high hill. From its summit he could see both ends of a strait about thirty miles in length. He had no doubt that beyond the eastern end of the strait lay Bylot's Cape Comfort but, with the waters 'froze fast from side to side', there was no possibility of taking his ships through. After naming the barrier 'Frozen Strait' Middleton returned to his ships and organised a council of his officers. They agreed that, not only were they unprepared for a second winter in the north, they had also failed to find a suitable bay or estuary for wintering, and they had a large number of their ship's company ill with scurvy. After just one more search of the coast west of the entrance to Sir Thomas Roe's Welcome, they would head for home.

The ships reached Marble Island on 11 August and dropped off their Indian helpers suitably rewarded with gifts of a boat, guns, ammunition, and axes. One of the Indians 'being used to the English customs' as a result of his time spent with the Hudson's Bay Co., requested to be allowed to accompany the ship to England. Because Middleton had found him to be 'a willing handy man', his wish was granted. Before setting sail for home, an island-cluttered inlet to the west of Marble

Island was given the name 'Rankin Inlet' by Middleton in appreciation of the work done by his lieutenant.

On arrival at the Orkney Islands, Middleton had so many of his men ill with scurvy that he was forced to put them ashore and press local men into working his vessels back to London where he arrived on 2 October 1742.

Despite his clear disappointment, Arthur Dobbs seemed, at first, prepared to accept Middleton's account of his voyage, but his suspicions that the captain was holding something back, flared into antagonism when he received an anonymous letter (possibly from William Moor, the Master of the *Discovery*) that the River Wager was actually a strait leading to the west. Not only was there the evidence of a strong tidal flow down the waterway, but whales had been seen to the west of the ships. There was also the incontrovertible fact that Middleton had spent much of his life in the pay of the Hudson's Bay Co. Could he have discovered a route to the west, but was now denying such knowledge until it could be turned to the advantage of his old employers? There was also the question of the fact that the expedition had used Royal Navy vessels under the command of a commissioned officer. Consequently, the Admiralty became embroiled in the debate and sent for Middleton to explain the charges Dobbs had brought against him. Middleton denied that he was withholding any information of a route to the west. Although their lordships accepted Middleton's word, they were to prove slow to heap praise or reward upon him for his work.

After a pamphlet war between Dobbs and Middleton had died down, Middleton was appointed as master and commander of the sloop HMS *Shark* in which he saw action against the Scottish rebels and their French allies. With the end of the war, he was put ashore on half-pay of four shillings a day, never again to receive an appointment from the Admiralty. He died in February 1770.

The *Furnace* was converted to a bomb before being sold in 1763. Her consort, the *Discovery*, was converted to a storeship and sold in 1750.

With the failure of the Middleton expedition to reveal a passage to the west from Hudson's Bay, Dobbs had suffered no diminution of enthusiasm for the search for a north-west passage – and he was still convinced that the answer lay in the great bay. Through his contacts in the Admiralty, he managed to persuade their lordships to offer a prize of £20,000 for the first British voyage to succeed in discovering the passage. Not surprisingly, the first to organise an attempt to win the prize was none other than Arthur Dobbs.

Obtaining financial support from the nobility, members of Parliament, and merchants, Dobbs obtained two ships, the *Dobb's Galley* and the (encouragingly named) *California*. The commander of the expedition was to be William Moor, Middleton's master on the *Discovery*.

Setting out from Yarmouth at the end of May 1746, the two ships reached Sir Thomas Roe's Welcome Sound on 11 August. Driven south by bad weather, they decided to winter up the Hayes River about three miles from Fort York, the Hudson's Bay Co. post at Port Nelson. They soon quarrelled with their neighbours, resulting in the being unable to obtain any fresh meat from the local Indians. They did, however, manage to get two kegs of brandy, the consumption of which, in conjunction with a lack of fresh meat, led to a severe outbreak of scurvy.

In June 1747, the ships managed to get clear of the river and sailed north to search the coast for the elusive route to the west. But the winter seemed to have done little for the cooperation between the two ships, and much time was spent setting out on individual forays to such an extent that the same ground was covered and named several times over. Eventually it was agreed that Middleton had been right all along and, with the approach of winter, it was decided to 'bear away for England without further delay'.

Dobbs blamed the failure of the voyage on the 'timidity' of Moor and turned his back on the subject of the north-west passage to become an expert in bee keeping. In 1752, he was appointed Governor of North Carolina where his constant squabbling with the colonists did little to encourage support for the Crown in the approaching war of independence. Dobbs was not to know this, having died in his post on 28 March 1765.

A year before Dobbs' death, the Royal Navy had embarked upon its first ever specifically polar exploration. Not, as might be expected from the disappointments of the past two centuries, a hesitant probe either to the north or south, but a bold attack at both – with a single expedition. Not only was Commodore John Byron expected to find 'Terra Australis' and return via the north-west passage, but he was also expected to secure British territory in the south Atlantic and examine the western coast of America last seen by Francis Drake. His orders instructed him to travel as far south as 53 degrees, and as far north as 54 degrees. If anybody (including his ship's companies) was to ask him, however, he was to tell them that he was going to India.

The reason for following in the wake of Halley was straightforward exploration and the hope of a great discovery, but his intended call at the Falkland Islands was for a very different reason. The islands, first discovered by John Davies, claimed for the British by John Hawkins, and then forgotten about, had been settled by a group of French colonists who claimed the territory for the French crown. In the meantime, the Spanish were feeling their way up the west coast of America and had already reached the southern end of California. They would need to be forestalled in their search for new lands. Further to the north, with the penetration by the Dane, Vitus Bering, of the strait which took his name, there was the fear that the Russians might begin an eastern expansion that could close off the western exit of any north-west passage.

The man given the awesome responsibility of leading this expedition, John Byron, had begun his career in the Royal Navy in a most singular manner. He had been a fifteen-year-old midshipman on the storeship HMS *Wager* as part of Anson's 1740 circumnavigation in search of Spanish treasure. The *Wager* had been wrecked on the west coast of South America and, as the seamen and soldiers struggled ashore, they broke up into quarrelling factions, each with their own idea of how to escape their dire situation. Byron stuck by his captain and undertook a desperate journey across the width of the continent to Montevideo. During their epic march across mountains and through rain forests they were helped by the local Indians before being captured by the occupying Spaniards. One result of the disaster was Anson's introduction of an Act of Parliament for the maintenance of naval discipline amongst ships' companies of Royal Navy vessels that were wrecked, lost, or taken by the enemy. It also led to the Royal Navy acquiring its own soldiers – marines – who were also to be subject to naval discipline. As for Byron, as he had risen in his career, he had become known as 'Foul Weather Jack' through his almost supernatural tendency to attract the worst weather any climate had available.

In addition to its exploratory and political aspects, Byron's expedition was also in the vanguard of naval innovation. His ship, HMS *Dolphin*, had been amongst the very first to have her hull sheathed with copper as a protection against the teredo worm and other marine borers. A machine invented by Lieutenant Phillip Orsbridge, which was intended to purify water by pumping air through it, was to be given its initial trials. A concentrated meat extract known as 'portable soup' was to be tried and, finally, cork jackets, as an aid to keeping men in the water afloat, were to undergo their first tests.

The *Dolphin* and her consort, HMS *Tamar*, left Plymouth on 3 July 1764. True to their commodore's reputation, after leaving the Cape Verde Islands, the ships found themselves without wind and drifting beneath a burning sun from which no relief could be found. It took them six weeks to reach Rio de Janerio where Byron found himself with an unexpected problem of diplomacy. Shortly after his arrival, an East Indiaman had limped in with many of its crew suffering from scurvy. Chief amongst her passengers was no less than Lord Clive, the former clerk who had snatched India for the British crown. He was, of course, delighted to hear that Byron's ships were on their way to the sub-continent and urgently requested that he and his staff be given passage. Much to his embarrassment, yet still insisting that he was on his way to India, Byron found he had to turn down the great man's request without adequate reason and without revealing his true destination.

With the loss of a few seamen through desertion to the attractions of the city, the two ships left Rio in late October and set a southerly course. Before long they found themselves amidst a succession of gales and storms. Byron – no stranger to bad weather – was moved to write 'It is certainly the most disagreeable sailing in the world, forever blowing and that with such violence than nothing can withstand it, and the sea runs so high that it works and tears a ship to pieces.' The waters, he

Byron arrives at Patagonia to be greeted by giants.

noted, were 'all in heaps'. On 13 November, the ship's lookouts shouted a warning and pointed towards something that sent a surge of fear through both vessels. In conditions that were already extremely rough, the lookouts had seen a line of pounding foam that stretched all along the horizon. Tall plumes of spray were thrown into the air above which circled a mass of screaming seabirds – the whole confusion speeding down upon the *Dolphin* and the *Tamar*. It was a squall, the like of which had not been seen by anyone on-board. Byron shouted out orders to haul up the sails, or at least let them fly, but he was too late. The shock of the wind hit the vessel with enormous power on the beam and forced her hard over. Sails were split, ropes torn asunder and the first lieutenant lay among the injured. The *Tamar*, gaining some slight shelter from being in the lee of the *Dolphin*, suffered less, but still had her mainsail shredded. Byron's ship had almost been lost in the squall. He wrote that he had never 'seen anything more dreadful'. Choosing to run for cover in Port Desire, Byron's spirits were tested even further when the *Dolphin* ran aground.

Two weeks were spent in the port carrying out repairs before they left for the entrance to the Straits of Magellan. On their arrival Byron went ashore to meet the local Patagonians. Legend had stated that these natives were a race of giants and Byron had promised the First Lord of the Admiralty that he would seek out these 'giants' and find out the truth. The men he found were, indeed, tall, but not remarkably so. Byron gave them beads and ribbons during an amicable meeting before returning to his ship. Through an extraordinary sequence of exaggerations, by the time the reports had returned to England, the Patagonians were confirmed as

Captain the Honourable John 'Foul Weather Jack' Byron.

having feet 18in long and being over 8ft tall. Among the foremost of the pens which helped promote this legend was that of Midshipman Charles Clerke whose paper for the Royal Society reported that they saw 'hardly a men less than eight feet; most of them considerably more.' The reading and publication of the paper by the Royal Society did little to give an accurate picture of the Patagonians, but was to assure Clerke's future place alongside the greatest of the Royal Navy's navigators.

Turning eastwards, Byron set off to find the Falkland Islands. Within five days he had landed in a sheltered bay he named after the First Lord, Lord Egmont. Taking the Union Flag ashore and raising the banner in confirmation of his sovereign's right to the territory, Byron then put his ship's surgeon to work building and planting a garden for the benefit of the colonists that were bound to follow. He noted that the island was abundant with plant-life that could help combat scurvy (although he actually believed that the coconut was the true answer to the condition), and suggested that iron might be found beneath its surface.

Returning to the coast of Patagonia where he had arranged to meet the supply ship *Florida,* Byron found the vessel to be in a serious state of disrepair due to the constant bad weather. As a result, he took her and his two ships back into the entrance to the Straits of Magellan in order to transfer her stores in calmer water.

With repairs having been carried out on all the vessels, Byron should then have headed south in search of unknown lands, but he had had enough of the weather off the south-east tip of the continent and decided to pass through the straits to reach the calmer waters of the Pacific. But 'Foul Weather Jack' found he had to fight for every mile along the narrow, dangerous waterway and did not emerge to the west for two months. Here also, he found that the gales had followed him as he struggled northwards in the direction of California and the, hoped-for, north-west passage beyond. As well as the weather, Byron found he had to contend with an increasing number of his ship's company going down with scurvy. He was able to recoup some of their strength with a visit to the island of Mas Afuera but, on leaving, and picking up the first traces of the south-easterly winds known to reach across the Pacific, he abandoned his instructions and decided to go westwards in search of the Solomon Islands with their legendary wealth of precious metals – and to keep up a supply of coconuts to keep scurvy at bay.

He found nothing beyond a few unimportant islands and returned home via Batavia and the Cape of Good Hope, arriving at Plymouth in May 1776. Despite his failures, both in the south and in the north, the Admiralty was pleased with his re-planting of the flag on the Falkland Islands. The Royal Society, however, was less pleased with his 'dearth of scientific results'.

The Spanish had watched Byron's work on the Falkland Islands with some alarm and decided to counter this thrust into, what they considered as, their territory, by claiming sovereignty over the islands and re-naming them the 'Malvinas'. The French, realising that their colony was about to be taken over by the British, readily agreed to the Spanish move and withdrew. The remaining international tangle was still to be causing problems more than two hundred years later.

Byron was promoted to rear admiral and appointed as Governor of Newfoundland. Following the outbreak of rebellion among the American colonists, he was promoted to vice admiral and given a fleet to operate against the colony's French allies. Almost from the day the fleet sailed from Spithead in June 1778, they were battered by a succession of gales that eventually scattered the ships. Reforming at Halifax, Nova Scotia, he set off again in pursuit of the enemy only to lose two ships which rolled over and sank in the continuing great storms.

Having helped to chase the French out of St Lucia, he made his way to Grenada where he found his fifteen ships facing twenty-seven of the enemy. Following a scrappy, indecisive, fight, Byron withdrew against French lack of determination to bring the matter to a proper conclusion – an end which, almost certainly, would have resulted in the utter defeat of Byron.

He returned to England after the battle and never put to sea again, dying eight years later. His son became known as 'Mad Jack Byron' and his grandson added to the family reputation by becoming 'Mad, bad, and dangerous to know'. He was the poet, Lord Byron, who used his grandfather's story in his poems *Childe Harold* and *Don Juan*.

CHAPTER TWO

TO THE EDGE OF THE ICE

James Cook was born in October 1728, the second son of a Yorkshire agricultural worker. After a rudimentary education he joined his father to work on the land before arrangements were made to apprentice him to a haberdasher who had premises at Staiths, a fishing village on the north Yorkshire coast. Luckily for all concerned, Cook demonstrated an interest in the sea before his apprenticeship was confirmed. Faced with a clear lack of interest in the retail trade from the young man, his employer took him to the nearby port of Whitby where he became apprenticed to John Walker, a Quaker ship owner. Walker's ships were used mainly in the coal trade, transferring their cargoes down the east coast of England from the northern ports to London. It was an ideal training ground for an apprentice with ability, as the vessels − flat-bottomed for the shallow waters of the North Sea − had to operate in a region known for its dangerous coasts, winds and tides.

Cook also served in ships that were used as troop transports and on the Baltic trade before John Walker considered him to have achieved the standard required to be a mate on one of his vessels. So well did Cook carry out his duties that it was soon felt that he had all the seamanship and leadership skills required to become the master of his own ship and Walker offered him the command of the collier *Friendship*. With ten years of hard schooling behind him, the farm worker's son, at the age of twenty-six, could face a secure future with the deck of his own ship beneath his feet. Instead, he entered the Royal Navy as an able seaman.

Cook was in the Thames when he learned that war had broken out with the French. The immediate concern of his ship's captain would have been the protection of his men against the press gangs that roamed up and down the wharves and jetties looking for men 'used to the sea'. Under normal circumstances, Cook would have been able to avoid the attentions of the press by relying on his position as mate to keep him out of their hands. But this was, almost certainly, a 'hot press' where such niceties were ignored in the national interest. Whether this threat of capture was the cause, or whether it was the simple direct patriotism that Cook was clearly capable of, is not known, but the mate of a Whitby coaster presented himself at the Wapping 'Rendezvous' to volunteer for the Royal Navy.

Cook would have had little difficulty in negotiating with the first lieutenant of the *Eagle* for his 'rate' as able seaman, an acceptable position for someone with obvious experience at sea but no previous time on-board one of His Majesty's ships. With time to demonstrate his ability, the newly rated able seaman could look forward to being re-rated as a petty officer if a vacancy occurred. Cook had worked diligently for six months when his proficiency was brought to the attention of the *Eagle's* new captain, Hugh Palliser.

Cook's star began to rise under Palliser. It soon became obvious to the captain that Cook was no ordinary seaman and he had him transferred to the quarterdeck by rating him master's mate to serve under Mr Thomas Bissett, the *Eagle's* master. For the next two years Cook improved his skills as Palliser ranged the *Eagle* from the coast of Spain to the North Sea in search of French ships. In June 1757, Cook successfully took his examinations for master and, two years later, received his first warrant as master when he was appointed to HMS *Solebay* to spend the next three month on the look-out for smugglers. At the end of this time he was re-appointed to HMS *Pembroke*, a new ship of sixty-four guns about to leave for North American waters.

On *Pembroke's* arrival she was promptly pressed into service at the bombardment of Louisburg. For five weeks, cannon balls and mortar shells rained down on the city before the French surrendered. Cook went ashore to see for himself the effect of the siege and, in doing so, made the acquaintance of Samuel Holland, a British Army surveyor who helped him to extend his knowledge of land surveying.

With the melting of the ice in the St Lawrence River the following spring, the time had come to mount an attack against the French forces holding Quebec. But, if the ships carrying General Wolfe's soldiers were to reach their destination in safety, the St Lawrence had to be accurately charted. Cook was chosen to take soundings of the channel, a task that had to be carried out over several nights, right under the noses of the French. Just as he was about to complete the work he was discovered by the enemy who sent a band of Indians in canoes after him. A desperately close encounter ensued in which the Indians boarded his boat at the stern whilst Cook, clutching his charts, leapt out at the bow. The task, however, had been done and Cook was able to present a superbly detailed chart of the river to Admiral Saunders. Through Cook's work, Wolfe's attack on the city by scaling the Heights of Abraham led to the defeat of the French, and to the addition of Canada to the growing British Empire. In Cook's home village the news of the victory was greeted by the expenditure of one shilling on the ringing of the church bells throughout the entire day. Subsequently, a further sixpence had to be spent in the repair of bell-ropes.

Shortly after the fall of Quebec, Cook was appointed to HMS *Northumberland*, the flagship of Admiral Lord Colville. The ship returned home in 1762 where he married Elizabeth Batts at Barking, in Essex. After little more than a few weeks of marriage he was offered the job of marine surveyor under the command of Captain Graves, the Governor of Newfoundland. Accepting the appointment, Cook soon found himself in the middle of a potentially dangerous diplomatic incident. The islands of St Pierre and Miquelon were to be handed over to the French, but the British were keen to obtain accurate charts of the islands before the French took over. To his annoyance Graves found that a delayed passage had meant that the French governor, his family, and a number of settlers, had already arrived and were about to land. To forestall their lawful taking over of the islands, Graves invited them on board his ship and plied them with lavish hospitality whilst Cook was sent to carry out a covert survey. It was to take more than a month of entertainment – wearying to both sides – before Cook's work was completed and the French could be released, unaware of what had been going on behind their backs.

Cook returned to England in HMS *Tweed* to spend a few months with his wife and newly born son. In the meantime, Palliser was appointed to take over the governorship of Newfoundland and requested that Cook join him as marine surveyor to carry out a survey of the island. The work took him five years to complete, returning home during the cold, ice-bound winters. His survey of Newfoundland proved to be of the greatest accuracy and made a lasting impression on all whom were required to refer to it. In August 1766, Cook revealed the skills he had attained in astronomy by carrying out an observation of a solar eclipse which he used to determine the longitude of an observatory he had built at Cape Race. The paper he produced as a result was considered good enough to be placed in the Royal Society's Philosophical Transactions.

Whilst at Newfoundland, Cook made the acquaintance of Joseph Banks, a young, wealthy traveller who asked him to take home an Indian canoe to add to his collection. Cook agreed, but whilst bringing the schooner *Grenville* across the Atlantic he ran into a succession of storms which threatened to capsize the tiny vessel. There was no option but to jettison everything that was not necessary and so Banks' canoe found itself floating in a far larger area of water than it was ever intended to travel.

On 15 February 1768, the Royal Society addressed a 'memorial' to King George III. Their document brought to his Majesty's attention the forthcoming transit of the sun by the planet Venus. The event would take place on 3 June the following year and, if accurately measured from a number of different sites on the globe, would lead to the distance between the Earth and Venus, and the distance between the Earth and the Sun, being calculated. The king ordered the commissioners of the Admiralty to make a vessel available for the Royal Society's purpose and gave £4,000 of his own money towards the project.

It was thought that an East India Co. captain, Alexander Dalrymple, would command the expedition, but the secretary to the Admiralty – perhaps with memories of the complications caused by the appointment of Christopher Middleton three decades earlier – suggested that Mr Cook, master in the Royal Navy, and recently marine surveyor of Newfoundland, would be better qualified. Sir Hugh Palliser gave his support to the proposal and, accordingly, Cook was appointed with the rank of lieutenant, Royal Navy, to commence from the date of his taking command.

There still remained the problem of the vessel to be used. In company with Palliser, Cook turned down a number of small naval ships before searching along the cluttered Thames waterfront. Among the ships available for sale was a Whitby-built collier named the *Earl of Pembroke* – exactly the type of vessel that Cook had learned his trade in. The Admiralty purchased the ship and changed its name to His Majesty's Bark *Endeavour*. She was re-masted and rigged, extra wooden sheathing was added and she had her hull covered in large, flat-headed, nails – tried as an alternative to copper. Lieutenant Cook took command on 25 May 1768.

As the *Endeavour* was being prepared for her voyage, HMS *Dolphin* returned home from her circumnavigation of the world. Her captain, Samuel Wallis, had been asked to find a site suitable to make the observation of the Venus transit, the key element being cloudless skies. Wallis had discovered the island he first named 'George's Island' but later changed to the native name of 'Otaheite' (Tahiti). This, he felt, would make an excellent site for the observation.

Fortunately, the voyage was to be undertaken during one of the lulls in the wars between Britain and France and there would have been little difficulty for the Impress Service's 'Rendezvous' at Tower Hill and elsewhere in London to provide men for the ship's company. They were to be accompanied by the twenty-five-year-old botanist, Joseph Banks. Forgetting the loss of his canoe during Cook's homeward voyage from Newfoundland, Banks was keen to become involved and had the approval of the Royal Society to join the expedition. He had undertaken to pay all his own personal expenses and those of eight other men who were to join him on-board. Further, he brought with him a mass of scientific instruments and books.

The *Endeavour* left Deptford on 30 July 1768, reached Plymouth two weeks later, and with good winds, left England on 26 August. Her route was to be the standard one to reach Cape Horn with calls at Madeira, the Cape Verde Islands and Rio De Janeiro. At Madeira, the officers and scientists had been entertained at the local convent where the nuns, on finding that they were mixing with learned men, asked them when it would next thunder, and if there was an underground spring within the walls of the convent. Much to their disappointment, the guests failed to provide the answers. Fresh meat had been taken on-board at the island but Cook insisted that the – by now decaying – meat brought out from England had to be eaten first. This led to the first floggings of the voyage. The captain then tried a different tack when dealing with the refusal of his men to eat pickled cabbage – a supposed method of avoiding scurvy. Cook let it be known that only the officers were to eat the 'sour

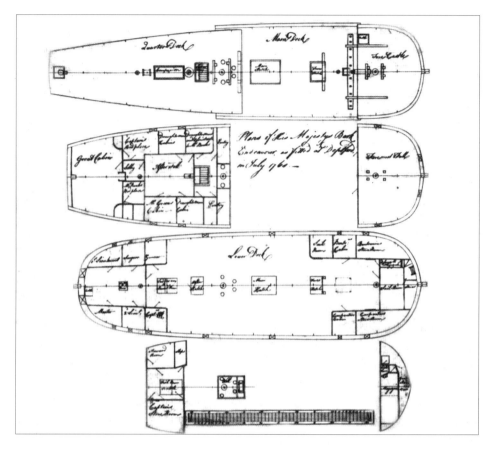

Sheer plan of HMS Endeavour.

krout'. This led instantly to grumblings from the lower deck and the determination that the officers should not be granted special privileges with food that had been put on board for the consumption of everyone. Cook was happy to oblige, with the result that scurvy was kept at bay for the entire voyage.

The hospitality of the Portuguese viceroy at Rio left much to be desired. Unable to accept that the *Endeavour* was actually a ship of the Royal Navy, and treating tales of planets passing before the sun with severe scepticism, the viceroy held up the ship's departure. Cook retaliated by using the time to quietly survey the harbour and its fortifications. At last, permission to sail was granted, and Cook set off only to come under cannon fire from the Santa Cruz fort at the entrance to the harbour. His patience by now sorely tested, Cook demanded to know why he was being so treated. The viceroy, it turned out, had omitted to inform the commander of the fort of his grant of permission.

After a rough voyage down the coast, Cook visited the coast of Tierra del Fuego to take on water. Banks, his Swedish naturalist; Daniel Solander, the ship's surgeon; Dr Monkhouse and the astronomical observer, Charles Green, along with their servants, went ashore to climb a mountain with the intention of carrying out research into the local flora. Exhausted by their climb, they were suddenly subjected to a massive drop in temperature with the approach of night. By the following morning Solander had collapsed into unconsciousness and two black servants had died. All the survivors were restored on their arrival at the ship.

Penguins were seen and warm clothing issued before Cook approached the entrance to Cape Horn. He had agreed with the Admiralty before leaving that the route around the cape would be quicker than passing through Magellan's Strait. There was, of course, always the risk of encountering the storms which had made the cape notorious, but Cook's known ability to find longitude by using the angles of the moon and stars combined with the lunar predictions contained in the Nautical Almanac should keep them clear of dangerous coasts. The outcome, however, was a reassuring anti-climax. The passage around the feared cape was, at times, so quiet that Banks could even take a boat from the ship to obtain bird specimens for his collection.

Two months after his bowsprit had entered the Pacific, Cook ordered the anchor to be dropped in Port Royal Bay, Tahiti. Within days friendly relations had been established with the natives and an observatory site set up ashore.

It did not take long to find out that the Tahitians had an almost uncontrollable urge to steal anything they could get away with. Cook even had a pair of stockings stolen from under his head whilst he was sleeping. Metal objects were considered most desirable and it was soon learned by the ship's company that the native women would be extremely grateful for even the most useless piece of iron. Cook was forced to include in his instructions an order forbidding the trading of iron except for provisions (one iron nail could be traded for twenty coconuts). However, the continuing disappearance of the flat-headed nails coating the ship's hull was only halted when the ship's butcher was flogged in front of the natives. The worst incident of all occurred when, just as the day of the transit was approaching, one of the natives stole the quadrant – the most vital instrument for recording the event. It took all the charm and prestige that Banks had achieved with the natives to get the, by now, broken up and damaged quadrant back in time for the observation.

Following a sleepless night at the 'Venus Point' tented camp (brought on by anxiety about the weather), Cook and the scientist saw the dawn of 3 June lighten beneath clear skies. Reserve camps had been set up on a nearby island and further along the coast from Venus Point just in case they were able to get a better view should bad weather interrupt the main observation. Banks had joined the American-born Lieutenant Gore and the surgeon, Monkhouse, on the island whilst Lieutenants

Hickes and Pickersgill, Midshipman Saunders and Master's Mate Charles Clerke (who, as a midshipman had 'seen' eight-foot tall Patagonians on Byron's voyage) manned the third site.

At Venus Point Cook, Solander and Green aimed their telescopes skywards and recorded that the planet made its first contact with the sun just after twenty-five past nine in the morning. A little over six hours later the last fraction of Venus left the disc of the sun and the expedition knew that it had been a success. A success marred, unfortunately, by some of the *Endeavour*'s ship's company, taking advantage of the officers' absence ashore, broke into the storeroom and stole a large number of nails. A flogging, followed by others for the theft of native weapons and strings of plaited hair, was carried out. Then two of his seamen deserted causing Cook to take native leaders captive until the men were handed over. Clearly the time had come to leave the pleasures of Tahiti.

The Admiralty, in its wisdom, felt that they had further use for a ship such as the *Endeavour* with its skilful captain and its scientist passengers. To this end they had given Cook a package of secret orders which he was to open on the completion of the observation of the transit. When he opened them, Cook found that their lordships intended that he should tackle, what seemed to be, the greatest remaining question of geography. His orders read

> You are to proceed southwards in order to make discovery of ...(Terra Incognita Australis)... until you arrive in the latitude of 40 degrees, unless you sooner fall in with it. But, not having discovered it or any evident signs of it in that run, you are to proceed in search of it to the westward between the latitude before mentioned and the latitude of 35 degrees until you discover it, or fall in with the eastern side of the land discovered by Tasman and now called New Zealand.

The *Endeavour* left Tahiti on 13 July after three months anchored off its shores. Cook carried out a survey of the neighbouring islands (naming the entire group the 'Society Islands' because of their lying close to each other) before beginning his voyage to the south.

Several undiscovered islands were encountered and recorded as they headed towards the expected new continent, but Cook pressed on southwards until bad weather forced him to return northwards. He now decided that, rather than risk his ship, he would begin his voyage to the west. On 6 October, one of the ship's boys, Nicholas Young, shouted from the masthead that he could see land ahead. At 'Young Nick's Head' the *Endeavour* made her first contact with New Zealand amidst great excitement that this could be the great continent for which they were searching.

Two days later Cook, Banks and Solander, went ashore in the attempt to make contact with the natives. Having found a village, they discovered that a number of natives had come behind them and had attacked the ship's boys left to guard their boat. Muskets were fired over the heads of the attackers but they pressed home their assault until the coxswain shot one of them dead. At this, the native retreated. A further attempt to meet the natives the following day led to more firing and deaths so Cook decided to leave the place that he named 'Poverty Bay' from its lack of anything of use to his ship. It was a sad start to a most remarkable voyage of discovery around the two main islands of New Zealand. Other, more satisfying contacts were made with the cannibalistic natives before Cook felt he had achieved enough before continuing westwards towards Van Diemen's Land (Tasmania).

The first sight of land was made by the *Endeavour*'s first lieutenant, Zachary Hickes, but Cook decided that the first person to land on 'Hickes Point' would be his wife's cousin, the young Isaac Smith who stepped ashore 29 April 1770. For the next five weeks the *Endeavour* sailed north along a continuing coast. Landings were made so that Banks could obtain plants and kangaroos and the flag of Great Britain could be unfurled to mark the taking of possession of the new territory. Everything was new and strange, but nothing was so impressive as the size of the land that filled their western horizon. Clearly, they were in the midst of a great and significant discovery.

They were also in the midst of a very great danger. Cook had noted frequent shoaling and soundings were constantly taken to check the depth of the sea beneath them. But, as the ship floated on a high tide on the night of 10 June, there came a jarring shock as she stuck fast on a ridge of coral. The Great Barrier Reef fought to claim a victim as the surge lifted and dropped the stricken vessel time and again onto the jagged pinnacles below. With the light of lanterns, large baulks of timber could be seen floating around the ship – the sheathing at the bows had been ripped off. Below decks, amidst the appalling noise of the ship grinding against the ledge, water could be seen pouring in, its force being checked only by a large chunk of coral that had become wedged in the hole torn in the ship's bows.

Two actions had to be taken immediately. Men were sent down to man the chain pumps in an effort to reduce the level of water inside the vessel whilst Cook and the other officers superintended the lightening of the ship by pitching overboard six cannons and anything else that could safely be jettisoned.

With the dawn came the realization that they were about twenty miles off shore. If the land could be gained there was every chance that repairs could be carried out and the ship saved. The next high tide was due at eleven o'clock in the morning, but it failed to lift them clear. With a sense that time was running out, Cook prepared for the following high tide by sending his ship's boats to try and pull the ship clear. Anchors were also dropped ahead in an attempt to haul the vessel forward using the capstan and windlass. At Cook's command, every hand heaved on the oars and capstan bars. The huge effort worked and the straining ropes pulled the *Endeavour* off the ridge.

Although floating free, the ship was not yet out of danger. The hoisting of sails gave her way, but this increased the volume of water being forced in at the bows, all but defeating the pumps. At this, Midshipman Jonathan Munkhouse approached the captain with an idea based on an incident he had been involved with whilst crossing the Atlantic. Munkhouse suggested that a sail, secured by ropes at its corners, be lowered over the bows. The water pressure would force the canvas into the hole and dramatically reduce the flow into the ship. Cook ordered this to be put into effect with the result that the ship safely reached a small estuary where the damage could be looked at in detail.

It was to be a month before the repairs were completed and the voyage northwards continued. The escape from the Great Barrier was not without further incident and it was only the sheer skill of Cook's seamanship that brought them through the maze of coral ridges and out into the open sea. In late August Cook was able to confirm the existence of the Torres Strait and five weeks later arrived at Batavia where the *Endeavour* was given a thorough refit. Unfortunately, after keeping his men clear of scurvy since he had left England, the captain was now mortified to find that his men were succumbing to a variety of tropical diseases. When the time came to sail, there were only twelve men left capable of working the ship and extra hands had to be taken on. By the time he reached the Cape of Good Hope thirty men had died of dysentery and malaria including Charles Green, the Royal Society's astronomical observer, and the enterprising midshipman, Jonathan Munkhouse.

As the *Endeavour* left the Cape and headed towards St Helena, the first lieutenant, Zachary Hickes, died. Cook appointed Master's Mate Charles Clerke as acting lieutenant to complete the complement of officers.

The voyage from the island, mainly in company with East India Co. ships, brought Cook and his ship safely into home waters. At midday on 10 July 1771, Nicholas Young, the ship's boy who had been the first to see the coast of New Zealand, called out from the tops that he had sighted land. The coast he had sighted was Land's End.

There was no doubting the success of the voyage. The transit of Venus had been accurately recorded, New Zealand had been secured for all time on navigator's charts, the 'New Holland' of Dutch exploration had become Cook's 'New South Wales' and the Royal Society were agog with the specimens brought back by Banks. In recognition of his achievements, Cook was given a commission as master and commander six weeks after his return. There was more than mere recognition and reward in this promotion. Both the Admiralty and Cook were eager that the work that he had started should be continued at the earliest opportunity. The French had begun to take an interest in the strategically important Society Islands. The islands' central position made them a vital base for further exploration and commercial expansion in the Pacific, and Britain's claims in the region had to be secured. Cook, in particular, was keen to search the southern Pacific for the elusive Terra Australis

Captain James Cook

Incognita. Before long the Navy Board had been instructed by the Admiralty to obtain two ships for a second voyage of discovery.

As the *Endeavour* was considered to be no longer fit for such an arduous service (she was sold four years after her return and ended her life as a wreck off Rhode Island), two ships, each less than two years old, were purchased from Captain Hammond of Hull. In accordance with Cook's wishes, the *Marquis of Granby* and the *Marquis of Rockingham* were both based on a similar design to his previous Whitby collier. The Admiralty decided that the *Marquis of Granby* should be re-named *Drake* and the *Marquis of Rockingham, Rayleigh,* but someone pointed out to their lordships that, as Britain was now at peace with Spain, such names might not be well received by the Spanish. What the personal views of the lords of the Admiralty were at the time is not known, but the ship's names were quickly changed to, respectively, *Resolution* and *Adventure*.

Cook was given command of the *Resolution* and the Devon-born Lieutenant Tobias Furneaux, who had already circumnavigated the world in the *Dolphin*, was commissioned as master and commander of the *Adventure*. Lieutenant Clerke (his promotion confirmed on his arrival back in England) joined Cook on the *Resolution*

Captain Tobias Furneaux

but the appointment as first lieutenant went to Robert Palliser Cooper who was not merely senior to Clerke, but also had a middle name which gives a clue to his important connections (Captain Hugh Palliser was now Comptroller of the Navy).

It seemed obvious to all concerned that Joseph Banks should head the scientific effort. With the work he had done for the Royal Society, and through his friendship with the First Lord of the Admiralty, Banks was given the job and immediately began to amass a large number of servants to accompany him on the voyage. In addition, he collected a prodigious amount of scientific instruments and personal luggage. But, owing to her design, the *Resolution* could not accommodate Banks' extra requirements, so he demanded that he take over Cook's quarters and an extra deck be built complete with a superimposed cabin for the captain. Cook was less than keen on the idea, but as Banks had the support of the Navy Board, he felt that he had to go along with it. When the work had been completed, Cook felt that the ship would now prove to be 'crank', and Clerke told Banks that he would go to sea in a 'grog tub' but thought the *Resolution* was the most dangerous ship he had ever seen. Both were proved to be right when the ship carried out trials from Deptford. Even a modest amount of canvas threatened to turn her over and the Thames pilot refused to remain her in beyond the Nore. On the ship's return all the new work was removed and the vessel restored to stability. Banks – outraged at this challenge to his authority – withdrew himself and his staff and set off on an expedition to Iceland.

In the place of Banks, the Royal Society sent the German naturalist Johann Reinhold Forster and his son, Johann Georg. The Board of Longitude sent William Wales and William Bayley to carry out astronomical observations. They, along with Cook, had an extremely important additional task. The early attempts by the clockmaker John Harrison to produce a working marine chronometer had, by now, been refined to an instrument similar in appearance to a large pocket watch. Harrison had used a tiny bar of dissimilar metals, which bent as it expanded with an increase in temperature. The bending bar affected the chronometer's hairspring which, in turn, speeded up the balance wheel. But, as the balance wheel itself also expanded with the increased temperature, the expansion caused it to slow down, thus compensating for the effect of the bi-metal bar. Early trials had proved encouraging, and longitude could be determined with greater ease and accuracy than by the measuring of lunar angles. The time had come, therefore, to give the instruments the severest test of all – an expedition that was intended to take in the cold of the southern high latitudes and the heat of the central Pacific islands. Three chronometers were manufactured by Arnold, a fourth by Kendall. The chronometer's keys, and the responsibility for keeping the watches wound, were to be held by each of the ships' captains, first lieutenants, and astronomers. If accurate, Greenwich time could be maintained, all that would be needed would be a 'fix' of the sun at noon to determine the meridian.

Resolution's muster book contained two names that would not be going on the voyage. Cook had recorded the names of his sons James and Nathaniel as being members of his ship's company. By this method, should the boys later wish to enter the Royal Navy, they would appear to have already completed their 'sea-time' requirement for immediate rating as midshipmen – a commonly accepted practice at the time.

Almost exactly a year after he had arrived in England from his first voyage of discovery the forty-three-year-old Cook sailed from Plymouth in the *Resolution* accompanied by the *Adventure*. After calling at Madeira and the Cape Verde Islands the ships anchored in Table Bay on 30 October 1772. Cook gave his ships' companies three weeks to prepare themselves for their southern voyage before leaving for the uncharted waters that lay before them.

The two ships left the Cape on 22 November, and headed directly southwards with the intention of not stopping until they met ice or land. In case of separation, Cook instructed Furneaux that they should rendezvous at Queen Charlotte Sound, New Zealand. Within a week the temperature had dropped enough for Cook to authorise the issue of jackets and trousers made of 'fearnought' – a dense, heavy woollen material. The increasing cold had also had an effect on the pigs, sheep, and geese that he had brought along for fresh supplies. When they began to die through exposure he had them all killed and their meat issued or preserved.

A week of gales drove the vessels to the east as the thermometer continued to fall. Cook decided to issue an extra glass of brandy to his men to enable them 'to bear the cold without flinching'. At the same time he began to ration his fresh water in case he did not find land along his course.

On 10 December ice was encountered for the first time. The sea was strewn with 'floating rocks'; small at first but soon rising to heights of over 50ft with waves crashing against them. Banks of fog hid some of these flat-topped ice islands and all of Cook's skill had to be used to avoid finding himself on the weather side of them with the grave risk of being dashed against them by the wind. Four days later the ships were stopped dead in their tracks. Ahead of them the sea lay frozen in a jumbled, sullen, grey sheet of ice that extended to the east, west, and southern horizons. Huge blocks of ice, miles in circumference, were locked in the pack. Some, far in the distance and softened by haze, gave many on-board the idea that they were looking at distant land, but the drifting of the fog confirmed their icy natures.

To his great satisfaction Cook found that the ice provided him with a constant supply of fresh water thus relieving him of one of his greatest concerns. Now, with that problem out of the way and with ample victuals on-board, he could concentrate on trying to penetrate further south. At first that task looked as if it was going to be easier to say than to do. The ice had linked up behind him and appeared to have trapped his ships – a situation that could easily lead to their getting stuck fast in its grip. Determined hauling on the icicle-draped rigging and sheer seamanship saved the situation and Cook broke though to the open water once again.

There was a strong belief at the time that such ice, especially ice supplying them with fresh water, had to come from rivers. Therefore, if fresh-water ice meant rivers, rivers had to mean land. Cook decided to coast eastwards along the edge of the ice field until he could find a route to the south.

The ships companies were, by now, beginning to complain of the cold. To help, Cook allowed them to extend their sleeves with cuffs of baize and had caps made of baize-lined canvas. It was, after all, the season of goodwill and Christmas day was spent under bare masts in case a squall should catch them unawares as the men drank themselves into a drunken stupor (much to the elder German biologist's disapproval).

As the final days of 1772 slipped by, Cook found he had to constantly dodge around a sea full of floating ice. Just prior to the new year, ice was seen thickly congregated to the north of his position and Cook found that he was forced to head southwards driven by a rising gale. Although still under threat from the giant ice islands, he was able to continue to the south beneath a clearing sky that, eventually, revealed the moon – only their second sighting since leaving the Cape of Good Hope.

Resolution *sailing passed a giant iceberg.*

Cook using ice to water his ships.

On Sunday 17 January 1772, at 39 degrees, 35 minutes east, HM Ships *Resolution* and *Adventure* crossed the Antarctic Circle – the first ships, carrying the first men, to do so. They were not to go much further. Ahead of them the ice barred their way to the south. Cook climbed to the masthead to see if land could be sighted or if there was an alternative route, but none could be seen. He had no choice but to order his ships about and retreat in the face of the barrier. As he gave the order, the sixteen-year-old George Vancouver, rated as an able seaman but living in the midshipman's mess, climbed out along the jib-boom to claim the prize of being the most southerly man in the world.

For the next three weeks the two ships searched for land to the south, chasing every cloud formation in the hope that it would prove to be the shore they were looking for. In early February, thick fog descended and the ships lost touch with each other. Cannons were fired and other signals were made, but no answer came from the *Adventure*, When the fog cleared, Cook found himself alone among the mass of ice.

On the 17th, the officer of the watch called the captain on to deck. With the approach of the Antarctic winter, the days were losing to the lengthening nights and Cook was treated to an Aurora display that swept across the darkening skies. It was the first time that such a sight had been seen at high southern latitudes. It also warned Cook that the end of the summer was in sight and, although no sighting had been made of the *Adventure*, the time had come to leave the splintered ice fields of the Antarctic. After a hectic race amongst the ice floes of the Roaring Forties, Cook, at last, ordered a course to be steered north-east towards New Zealand. To the relief of all on-board, on 26 March, the *Resolution* dropped anchor in the shelter of a safe harbour found by Lieutenant Richard Pickersgill on the dramatic fiord-like shores of Dusky Bay. They had been at sea for 122 days without sight of land and had travelled over 10,000 miles.

In an almost holiday atmosphere the officers, seamen and scientists roamed over the green-clad hills. The *Resolution* was so close to the shore that a tree trunk was manoeuvred into position to act as a gangplank between the ship and the bank. Hunting parties brought back fresh fruit and meat and the astronomers set up a camp ashore to carry out their observations. They were able to compare their determination of the longitude with the chronometers which were found to be impressively accurate – especially the Kendall model. Some natives were seen. At first they were hostile, but were soon placated by Cook presenting one of the chiefs with a red baize cloak. Another chief collected enough hatchets and nails to make him the richest man in New Zealand.

Whilst at Dusky Bay, a number of seals were caught. Cook felt that the meat of the animal should be tried in case it proved to be an important resource for future expeditions (he may have gained some experience of the use of northern seals during his time in Newfoundland). Not only was the flesh found to be edible (Lieutenant Clerke thought it to be 'little inferior to beefsteak') but the skins could be used to make extremely strong cord and its fat provided oil for the ship's lamps.

At the end of April, Cook took the *Resolution* up the west coast of the island to reach Queen Charlotte Sound in the hope that he would find Furneaux and the *Adventure* safe at the agreed rendezvous. On 17 March, the sky clouded over and six water spouts appeared around the ship. Keen to test a theory that cannon fire would disperse such a phenomenon Cook had one of the weapons loaded. As one of the spirals swirled past his stern, Cook, along with his men, watched in awe. So intent were they in their amazement at the sight that Cook forgot to fire the cannon.

On the following day the *Resolution* rounded the southern point of Queen Charlotte Sound to find the *Adventure* safe inside at Ship Cove. Upon his separation from Cook, Furneaux had made his way to Van Diemen's Land and had come to the opinion that it was connected to the mainland of New South Wales. Cook had been eager to have a look for himself but, now that the question seemed to have been resolved, he decided that another voyage into the yawning emptiness of the south Pacific should be undertaken.

Before he left Queen Charlotte Sound in early June, Cook noted with distaste the effect the mixing of his men with the natives had brought about. He wrote

> We debauch their morals, already too prone to vice, and we introduce among them wants and perhaps diseases which they never before knew and which serve only to destroy that happy tranquility they and their forefathers had enjoyed. If anyone denies the truth of this assertion, let him tell me what the natives of the whole extent of America have gained by the commerce they have had with Europeans.

The next six weeks were spent in the rough conditions of a Pacific winter with nothing learned but the fact that scurvy had broken out among the ship's company of the *Adventure*. Cook had been scrupulous in his efforts to combat the disease and had insisted that his officers and men ate the celery and scurvy grass he obtained whenever possible. When they were not in sight of land he provided them with malt, salted and pickled cabbage, mustard, and carrot marmalade. To drink, he supplied a southern version of the spruce beer he had known in Canada. Furneaux, on the other hand, had not been so insistent in the use of these supposed anti-scorbutics, and, as a result, had already lost his ship's cook to the disease. At least twenty more of his men were suffering from it. No doubt to the approval of both ship's companies, Cook ordered the ships to head for the warmer climes of Tahiti.

Their stay was not to be a long one. Old friendships were renewed and the local King was entertained to a night of bagpipes and seamen's hornpipe dancing. There was the usual spate of thefts by the natives but, by now, Cook had come to the belief that the imposition of European standards on people of a totally different background was futile. He still punished offenders when they were caught but more for the example of his own people than for anything else.

With his men refreshed and his ships well provided with livestock, meat, fresh fruit and water, Cook departed a month after their arrival. A new group of islands was discovered which was named after the First Lord, the Earl of Sandwich, before they arrived at the islands of Amsterdam and Middleberg. Such was their reception at these islands (first discovered by Tasman) that Cook renamed them the Friendly Isles (Tonga). At one reception they were offered a drink made by the communal chewing of roots before the resultant mess was spat into a drinking bowl. Only Cook could bring himself to try it – 'the manner of brewing had quenched the thirst of everyone else'.

The return voyage to New Zealand was spent in increasingly poor weather. Upon reaching the vicinity of Queen Charlotte Sound the ships were driven back out to sea and it was a week before Cook could limp into the sanctuary of Ship Cove with a splintered mast and damaged rigging. The *Adventure* had been separated by the storms and now there was no sign of her.

Cook spent three weeks repairing his ship and preparing his men for another foray into southern waters. Contact was made with the natives and Cook was witness to a darker side to their life. A group of the natives brought a severed human head on-board and proceeded to cook it before slicing off parts of the flesh which were devoured in front of the ship's company. The sight caused many of the men to vomit over the ship's side. Cook could only accept the event by coming to the opinion that the natives only ate their enemies.

Having waited for as long as he could in the face of the approaching Antarctic summer, Cook sailed south on 26 November, having left a note for Furneaux in a bottle buried beneath a tree. Five days later the *Adventure* sailed into Queen Charlotte Sound and Cook's message was read. Like Cook, Furneaux's ship had suffered in the gales and it was vital that he carried out repairs before following in Cook's wake.

As the work was being carried out ten of his men rowed ashore in one of the ship's boats. Upon landing on the beach they were attacked by a large group of natives. Within minutes they had all been killed, stripped, and prepared for roasting over a large fire. The ghastly deed struck deep at the morale of Furneaux and his ship's company. After setting off in pursuit of Cook, the short-handed captain of the *Adventure* decided that neither his, nor his men's hearts, were in the venture. They set off for the Cape of Good Hope – and home.

Cook, in the meantime, was back amongst the loose ice of the Antarctic. He had sailed south from New Zealand until reaching the 60th parallel from where he continued south-easterly to the Antarctic Circle. Three days before Christmas they were stopped by the ice under weather that remained dark and forbidding, and under rigging draped with icicles. The ship hauled north and spent Christmas day contesting for ocean space with almost a hundred giant ice floes. Their situation did not stop them from enjoying the festivities. The elder Forster noted disapprovingly in his journal

> This being Christmas Day the Captain, according to custom, invited the officers and mates to dinner and the lieutenants entertained the petty officers. The sailors feasted on a double portion of pudding, regaling themselves with the brandy of their allowance, which they had saved for the occasion some months beforehand, being solicitous to get very drunk, though they are commonly solicitous about nothing else.

In early January 1774, Cook turned once again to the south and crossed the Antarctic Circle for the third time. Accompanied by whales, the *Resolution* threaded her way through the massive ice islands until, on the 30th, the pack ice brought her to a halt. They had reached 70 degrees, 10 minutes south. Ahead of them the ice stretched to the horizon and was so heavily studded with giant ice blocks that they resembled mountain ranges. Cook was now convinced that, even if there was land to the south, it would be quite impossible to reach. Should the impossible be achieved and the land attained, it would be wholly useless and of no benefit to the discoverer or his nation. Furthermore, Cook was now practically at the same longitude he had reached on his first voyage. He had, in effect, encircled the ice-bound mass to the south without a single sighting of land.

At this stage it would have been reasonable to have expected Cook to begin his journey home, but he knew that he had a ship's company in good heart and a ship capable of yet another sweep through the islands of the central Pacific. Accordingly, the *Resolution* headed north.

As they left the ice fields Cook fell ill and was nursed back to health by Surgeon James Patten. Johann Forster helped by sacrificing his pet dog, which was turned into a tasty broth to speed the captain's recovery.

The ship called at Easter Island and rediscovered the Marquesas Group – last seen by their Spanish discoverers in 1595 but unvisited since. Midshipman Alexander Hood had first spotted the islands and Cook rewarded the young man by naming the island after him.

Their next port of call was at the Society Islands where, in addition to the usual replenishment of stores, the chronometers were checked against the known longitude at Matavia Bay. The test proved, yet again, that Mr Kendall's instrument had not failed under the variety of conditions it had experienced.

Cook then returned to the Friendly Islands where he was baffled by being presented with an attractive young woman. When it became clear that he was expected to give something in return he thought he could escape the situation by pleading poverty. His hosts, however, assured him that he could 'retire with her on credit'. In the end he was forced to beat an undignified retreat to his boat whilst being berated by an old woman who loudly questioned his manhood.

Continuing westward, he found the island of Australis del Espirito Santos, first discovered by the Spanish in 1606. Cook renamed the place and its off-lying islands the New Hebrides.

The time had now come to turn southwards to return to New Zealand to see if the *Adventure* was waiting for them in Queen Charlotte's Sound. On 4 September, an unknown group of islands was encountered which proved to be a good source of pine trees – extremely useful for the production of masts and spars. Cook bestowed the name New Caledonia on his new discovery before leaving for New Zealand where he arrived at Ship Cove on 18 October.

There was no trace of Furneaux or his ship but, as the message he had left had been removed, Cook assumed that all was well and that the *Adventure* was probably on her way home. The natives proved to be friendly and Cook was presented with a chief's staff of office. An honour which he repaid with a suit of old clothes, much to the delight of its wearer – nicknamed 'Pedro' by the seamen. Nowhere was there a clue to the horror that the *Adventure* had endured.

New Zealand was quitted on 10 November and Cook headed eastwards towards Cape Horn. Christmas was spent off the coast of Tierra del Fuego and the humourless Forster was less than impressed with the two days of drunkenness which ensued. Even Cook's patience was tested to the extent that he loaded the drunken men into a boat and had them rowed ashore. They were left in the chilly open air surrounded by sea lions and penguins until they had sobered up.

The South Atlantic was reached on 29 December. A southerly course brought them to latitude 60 and Cook was tempted to continue further south, but decided against such a venture being 'now tired of these high southern latitudes where nothing was to be found but ice and thick fogs'. Two weeks later he came across a bleak land whose mountain tops were lost in the clouds and whose coasts were edged with ice-cliffs from which massive chunks broke off into the sea with the sound of cannon fire. So barren did the land seem that Cook could not see enough wood 'to make a toothpick'. The *Resolution* carefully coasted the seventy miles around what turned out to be a spectacularly dismal looking island. After landing to unfurl the national colours, Cook named the place the Isle of Georgia (South Georgia). Heading south Cook named his last sight of the island 'Cape Disappointment', his only pleasant memory of the place coming from the penguin meat he had tasted there – he found it to be like 'bullock's liver'.

Two days after leaving his latest discovery, Cook again reached 60 degrees south. He had now, in a single voyage, entirely encircled the southern ice. If there were land to the south it would be 'a country doomed by nature'. He now felt he could write with safety that 'no man will venture further than I have done and that the lands to the South will never be explored'.

The ship called at the Cape of Good Hope, St Helena, and Ascension before a last opportunity was taken at the Azores to check the chronometers. He arrived at Spithead on 30 July 1775, after being away for three years and eighteen days.

Within days of his arrival Cook had reported to the First Lord of the Admiralty – still the Earl of Sandwich – who introduced him to the king. So impressed was George III with his achievements that, on 9 August, Cook was promoted to post captain. Three days later he was appointed to be one of the distinguished captains who governed Greenwich Hospital – a palatial home on the banks of the Thames for seamen too old and unfit for life at sea, but who had given long service in the defence of their country on-board ships of the Royal Navy. Cook, by now forty-seven years old and exhausted through his work of discovery, could now afford to rest upon his laurels. Members queued to nominate him as a fellow of the Royal Society. His foot was firmly on the ladder to flag rank which could be achieved by simply rising to the top of the captain's list – a list that could be rapidly shortened by a moderately bloody war. But it was not in Cook's nature to sit back and enjoy the office he had earned among the grandeur of the Greenwich domes and columns. When writing to his old employer, John Walker, Cook declared 'I am going to be confined within the limits of Greenwich Hospital…whether I can bring myself to like ease and retirement, time will show'. It was not, however, time that was to bring his rest to an end, but the pull of icy seas – this time far to the north.

Cook had not been the only man to feel that pull. The honourable Daines Barrington, not himself made of the stuff of which explorers were made, had turned the 'pull' into 'push' the year following Cook's second departure to the south. He managed this through being well connected in the right quarters. One of his brothers, Samuel, was a distinguished naval officer who had jumped from lieutenant to post captain in two years and had been appointed as colonel of marines (an appointment which served only to increase the holder's salary). Another brother was the bishop of Durham. Barrington was a member of the Royal Society and also a friend of the First Lord of the Admiralty, Lord Sandwich. In early 1773 he declared one of his interests (along with studies into the biblical flood and in playing at the card table) to be the unknown Arctic regions. To this end he read the society a number of papers in which he supported the popular notion that the northern icy barrier encountered by whalers consisted merely of river ice that had floated out to sea. Once the barrier had been breached, it would be a simple matter to reach the Pole. It was not too difficult to engage the interest of the First Lord of the Admiralty in the idea of attempt to reach the North Pole by sea whilst Cook was showing the way south.

On behalf of the Royal Society and the Admiralty, the First Lord approached the king with the idea that an expedition should be raised to test the theory of the passable ice barrier. The king agreed and directed that the voyage 'should be immediately undertaken, with every encouragement that could countenance such an enterprise, and every assistance that could contribute to its success'.

Captain the Honourable Constantine Phipps, Royal Navy, had had a meteoric rise in the service. He entered the Royal Navy as a midshipman in his uncle's ship in 1760. Two years later he passed for, and was promoted to, lieutenant. After eighteen months he was commissioned as master and commander of HMS *Diligence*. Seven months later, having just reached the age of twenty-one, Phipps was promoted to post captain and given the command of the 24-gun *Terpsichore*. There was a short period of command in the *Boreas* before his career took an entirely different turn. In 1768 he was elected to the House of Commons as the member of Parliament for Lincoln where his friend and near neighbour was Joseph Banks, fellow of the Royal Society. As a result, when the proposed expedition was brought to his notice, the twenty-nine-year-old Phipps promptly put his name forward to the ready acceptance of the First Lord.

Although Cook had shown that the Whitby collier type of vessel could be used with success in polar waters, the Admiralty decided to use two 'Bombs' to go north. These ships were specially designed to mount heavy mortars (bombs) and required a solid bed on which the weapon could be seated. With the mortar removed and the bows strengthened with extra timbers the sturdy vessels appeared to have the ability to contend with ice. Phipps was appointed to HMS *Racehorse* which, prior to her conversion to a bomb, had been the French privateer (a privately owned and operated warship) *Marquis de Vandrevil*, captured sixteen years earlier. She had sailed up the St Laurence and taken part in the attack on Quebec under Saunders. Her consort was to be HMS *Carcass*, built as a bomb in 1759. Her command went to Skeffington Lutwidge who had held a commission as master and commander since 1771.

Both commanders were allowed to chose their own officers. One of the two midshipmen selected by Lutwidge was Horatio Nelson, transferred from HMS *Triumph* and, although only fourteen years old, had already experienced life at sea on a man-of-war and a merchant ship. The surgeon of the *Racehorse* was Dr Charles Irving who was to use the voyage to try out his new system of obtaining fresh water from seawater by the means of a condensating apparatus. The Board of Longitude recommended that the experienced astronomer Israel Lyon be carried on-board Phipps' ship and, when this was agreed, undertook to provide all the warm clothing needed for the expedition. Arnold's and Kendall's chronometers were supplied and Phipps wore an Arnold pocket watch as an extra check on the meridian (line of longitude). In case the ships were crushed by the ice, bricks and mortar were placed on-board in the hope that time would be found to erect a shelter whilst awaiting rescue. To assist with ice navigation, two whaling masters with Greenland experience were appointed to each of the ships as ice-pilots.

Serious problems were encountered in finding seamen to man the ships. A trickle of volunteers threatened to dry up completely when it was learned that a fleet of fifteen ships of the line was being fitted out in preparation for a possible war against the French and Spanish. It was on such an enterprise that prize money could be earned, whereas the promise of icy seas would add little to the pockets the men on the lower deck. The situation worsened when the Admiralty announced a bounty for men who volunteered to serve with the fleet. Twenty-one men promptly deserted from the *Racehorse* followed by three from the *Carcass*. There was, it seemed, no way of avoiding sending the ship's lieutenants out with press gangs until, almost at the last minute, word arrived that the threat of war had receded and men would not be needed for the warships. Phipps gained approval to allow the bounty to remain in force until his ships had been manned and was even able to extend the extra money to the men who had already entered with him before the bounty had been announced. Nevertheless, from then on, he insisted that, if his men wanted to go ashore for a drink, they could only do so under the control of the petty officers. One of the seamen on the *Racehorse* was a former African slave, Oloudah Equiano – probably the first black man to enter the Arctic.

The ships completed their victualling on 22 May 1773 and, on the following day, moved down-river from Deptford to Woolwich to collect their six-pounder cannon, cannon balls, and gunpowder. The ships had been designed to carry eighteen guns each but this number had to be reduced to eight with the intention that their use would be limited to signalling. Phipps, however, had heard that the French were also attempting to go north and he determined that, should he come across them, and they failed to pay the proper marks of respect to his ensign, he would open fire to insist on their paying the appropriate compliment. The problem with his intention was that, if the French were to make the attempt, they would be doing it with two frigates and a combined firepower of sixty-four guns. Not unreasonably, some of his officers expected to find themselves guests of the French until any hostilities had been sorted out.

In addition to his armament Phipps also received his orders. These told him to simply proceed northwards along the meridian until he was stopped by the ice. If he was able to penetrate the barrier he was to continue on until he reached the North Pole but, even if he should find the seas on the far side of the Pole to be clear of ice, he was to immediately return with the momentous news. The seamen, however, had their own views on the reason for visiting the Pole. For some it was believed that they were to carve a walking stick from the Pole itself for the use of the Prince of Wales. Others were convinced that the world was slowing down and they were being sent to scrape and grease the Pole to improve its turning ability.

On 4 June, having been delayed for several days by contrary winds, the ships left the Nore and headed up the east coast of England. They called in at Whitby to take

Captain the Right Honourable Constantine Phipps.

on livestock, water, and fresh vegetables before making their way to the Shetlands. By the 17th the light remained long enough to read all night and warm clothing (flannel jackets, waistcoats and breeches, and lambs wool stocking and mitts) was issued to the ships' companies. Three days later, Dr Irving's invention was tried out and proved to be a success. Up to forty gallons of fresh water was produced; an ample amount for the ship's company's normal requirements.

Letters were sent home via a snow (a small two-masted vessel) that was encountered whilst on her way to Hamburg, and the captain of the ship reported that a large body of ice had been seen to the north at about 72 degrees. Phipps pressed on whilst taking continuous measurements of temperature, depth, magnetic variation and dip. During the late evening of 28 June the jagged peaks of a far off land could be seen from the masthead. It was the southern point of Prince Charles Island, off the western coast of Spitsbergen.

The next day Phipps closed with the land and noted

> The coast appeared to be neither habitable nor accessible; it was formed by high, barren, black rocks without the least marks or vegetation; in many places bare and pointed, in other parts covered with snow, appearing even above the clouds: the valleys between the high cliffs were filled with snow or ice. This prospect would have suggested the idea of perpetual winter, had not the mildness of the weather, the smooth water, bright sunshine, and constant day-light, given a cheerfulness and novelty to the whole of this striking and romantic scene.

On the evening of the following day, a Greenland whaler, the *Rockingham,* came alongside, more out of amazement at seeing a man-of-war in those waters than for anything else. Her captain went on-board the *Racehorse* only to shake his head when told that their mission was to sail to the North Pole. He had just left the ice to the west and claimed it to be the worst he had ever known. Only six days had been free of fog and, to date, one English and two Dutch whalers had been 'nipped' (crushed) by the ice. He had, however, noted that the seas to the north-east were clear of ice. Phipps, nevertheless, decided to continue northwards until he met with the frozen barrier. As the land passed down his starboard side he took the opportunity to measure the height of some of the larger mountains, finding the highest to reach 'fifteen hundred and three yards'.

By now the sight of seals popping up to look at them had become commonplace and even the sight of whales blowing and thrashing the water with their glossy black tails was a regular occurrence. More whaling ships were met and one Dutchman proved very difficult to persuade that a war had not broken out, there being no other reason he could think of for a warship being in those waters.

Upon reaching a small bay whose shore could be reached by the ship's boats, Phipps went ashore with the astronomer, Lyon, to carry out observations and measurements. But, before they could set up their instruments, a thick fog descended and forced them back to the ship. Phipps was forced to keep firing his cannon to signal the *Carcass* (which had remained out at sea) before her answering fire brought them together. The *Rockingham* then re-appeared under his stern and her captain informed him that the ice was thirty miles off Hakluyt's Head, the north-west corner of Spitsbergen. He also brought up to date the list of casualties amongst the whaling fleet. By now seven ships, four Dutch and three English had been lost.

The next day, after passing a group of small islands, Phipps found loose ice and fog ahead of him. Shortly afterwards, as the fog thickened around the ships, a sound similar to waves beating against a shore could be heard. The *Carcass* came alongside and Lutwidge confirmed that he could hear the sound. Both ships cleared their lower decks, shortened sail, and prepared to meet whatever lay just ahead of them as the noise increased to a roar.

All eyes were straining to look ahead when the mist suddenly cleared. There, less than two hundred yards beyond the bowsprit and stretching from east to west, lay a vast, solid sheet of ice, against which the waves broke with thunderous force. The ships were just minutes from being driven hard against the ice. Phipps ordered the helm to starboard and the *Racehorse* tacked to the west followed by the *Carcass*. But the ships failed to pick up the wind required to give them way and found themselves still being driven onto the lee ice. Phipps hailed a warning to the *Carcass* that he was to go about. Again the helm went over and the ships turned away from the barrier to let the wind fill their sails and bring them back under control. Phipps commended his ship's company in the firm belief that the ships would have been lost 'had not the officers and men been very alert in working the ship'. Later that day, surrounded by fog, he heard the roaring sound once again and sent both ships well clear of the unseen hazard. A little caution had been introduced into Phipps' approach to the dangers from the ice.

The ships continued to claw their way to the east in the hope of finding a way through the ice. Ice poles were used to fend off chunks of ice where possible but the ships were often struck reminding all on-board of the risks they were undertaking. On one occasion, when the *Racehorse* collided with a large piece of ice, she was almost brought to a halt and the bowsprit of the *Carcass* reared over her taffrail. A collision between the ships was only narrowly avoided.

The whalers who used those seas rarely went to the east for fear that the ice would link up to the northern coast of Spitsbergen behind them, thus trapping them. Phipps reasoned, however, that if he could get as far as possible to the east he might find that the ice opened up to the north. If that failed, he would have the wind behind him to coast down the edge of the ice field towards the west thus being able to examine the barrier for navigable openings. After two days Phipps held a conference with the ice-pilots to discuss their position. It was agreed by all that there was little to be gained from continuing to the east. Phipps announced, therefore, that he intended to 'range along the ice to the northwest' in search for an opening. Unfortunately, things were not to be that straightforward. Whilst the officers and ice-pilots had been discussing what to do next, the *Carcass* had been surrounded by ice and was threatened from all quarters. Ice anchors were sent out at the bows and boats manned to try and pull the ship clear whilst men heaved at the capstan and lined the ship's side with ice poles. It took two hours before the vessel broke clear, 'The people in both ships being much fatigued'. There was to be little time to rest. The following morning provided little wind and the ships drifted towards the ice. There was no option but to lower the ship's boats and have them tow the ships clear.

Phipps was now able to make his run to the west, at the same time increasing the liquor ration of his men who had begun to complain of the cold. In an attempt to avoid being caught out as the *Carcass* had been, he organised his ship's company into 'gangs', each gang under a midshipman, to keep a watch open for threatening ice. An encounter with a whaler, *King of Prussia*, did little to help when her captain confirmed the impossibility of a passage to the North Pole.

After two day of crawling through thick fog, during which time the ships were frequently separated and the latitude 80 degrees, 36' was attained, Phipps found his passage to the west block by solid ice. Even as he pondered his position, the ice closed around him and he was forced to run up the foresail in order to charge the encroaching ice. The shock to the ship as it broke free knocked many of his men off their legs.

A repeated attempt to head eastwards ended with a collapse of the wind and more hauling the ships round with boats in an attempt to pick up the slightest breeze. On 13 July the threat of an approaching gale forced them into a small harbour know to the Dutch as Vogel Sang but, later, given the English name of Fairhaven. The harbour was already providing shelter for two Dutch and four English whalers. Much to the annoyance of the naval men, the whaler's crews had been ashore and had robbed all the seagull's nests of their eggs – a culinary treat that had been eagerly looked forward to.

Whilst in the shelter of the harbour the opportunity was taken to both top up the ships water casks and for the astronomer to set up a tent on Deadman's Island from where he could carry out a number of observations.

After five days in Vogal Sang, the ships weighed anchor and headed north-east towards the ice. They found that the ice now blocked their path both to the east and to the north leaving them no option but to head westwards. The edge of the ice led them into a number of openings to the north which raised their hopes of finding a passage in that direction but, in each case, proved to be nothing more than an ice-rimmed bay. Three days after they had set out to the west, the ice began to trend to the south and Phipps turned once again to the north-east in the hope of finding a way through in that direction. The *Racehorse* found itself in a stream of loose ice and collided with a floe so large that the ship was driven backwards by the blow. As no damage had been done and the strengthening of the bows proven to be up to the task Phipps felt that he 'could with the more confidence push through the loose ice, to try for openings'. He now came up with the idea that the only chance of success lay in the east. If he became trapped, the predominantly easterly wind could be used to get him and his consort out of trouble.

The temperature began to drop alarmingly as he rounded Hakluyt's Headland and icicles formed along the yards and rigging; their situation being made even more uncomfortable by a persistent icy rain. After fending off a mass of loose ice, Phipps saw that the sea to the north-east seemed open and offered 'the most flattering prospect of getting to the northward'. Soon they had sight of the low-lying Moffat Island. Finding himself becalmed, Lutwidge went ashore to explore the island and found the grave of a Dutchman buried two years earlier.

With the return of the wind, both ships pressed on eastwards meeting the edge of the ice once more and probing into every promising opening, but without success. On the 27th a Danish seaman serving on the *Racehorse* died of a 'Distemper' and was put overboard the following day, his body stitched into his hammock and weighted with cannonballs.

Continuing eastwards despite the concern of the ice-pilots, none of whom had been in that direction before – nor had any knowledge of anyone who had previously done so – the ships came across another large, low-lying island. Again the wind fell away so Phipps sent two officers in a boat in pursuit of a herd of 'sea horses' (walruses). Upon isolating one of the animals the officers opened fire but only succeeded in wounding their quarry. The walrus dived under their boat to re-appear seconds later accompanied by several of his companions who proceeded to launch an attack on the boat and its occupants. An oar was wrenched from the hand of a rower and, using their tusks as grapnels, the walruses seemed intent on overturning the small craft. Just when it looked as if honours were to go to the walruses a boat from the *Carcass*, under the command of Midshipman Nelson appeared on the scene and opened fire on the attackers driving them off.

The island itself was visited by Dr Irving who found evidence that it had been visited before but, by whom and when, he had no idea. A reindeer was killed and, upon being cooked, found to be 'fat and of high flavour'.

On the 30th the ships closed with a group of islands known as the Seven Islands. With no obvious passage in sight Phipps used ice-anchors to moor his ships to the ice field and sent his ship's master, John Crane, ashore to climb to the highest point to see if a way through could be seen. Lutwidge had arrived at the same idea and went ashore himself to join up with Crane. From the top of the highest available peak they could see that from the west, to the north, and on to the east, a great sheet of unbroken ice clearly barred any passage in that direction. To the south-east the ice continued on until it linked up with the Spitsbergen 'North East Land'. There seemed to be little chance of further progress to the north.

On their return to their boats Lutwidge and Crane found, despite the apparently warm weather, that the sea was beginning to freeze over to such an extent that they could not force their way through the new ice. To get back to their ships they were forced to find thicker floes over which to drag their boats to each patch of open water. If, however, such a task had been imposed upon them, they could not have found better conditions in which to do it. Phipps noted in his journal

> The scene was beautiful and picturesque; the two ships becalmed in a large bay, with three apparent openings between the islands which formed it, but every-where surrounded with ice as far as we could see, with some streams of water; not a breath of air; the water perfectly smooth; the ice covered with snow, low, and even, except a few broken pieces near the edges: the pools of water in the middle of the pieces were frozen over with young ice.

The picture was alluringly deceptive. Behind them the ice had closed up locking them into the bay. Phipps tried to break through but failed and was forced to put out his ice-anchors once again. In an attempt to appear unperturbed he had the ships fill their casks with water from the surface of the floe ('very pure and soft') and allowed the ships' companies to stretch their legs on the ice where they played leapfrog and other games. The ice-pilots were not fooled, however, and expressed great concern at their situation. Two days later the ice had completely surrounded the ships and pressure ridges began to rear up forcing piles of ice to the height of the main yard. Ice surrounding the ships was measured to be between 'eight yard ten inches in thickness at one end, and seven yards eleven inches at the other'.

By 3 August there was practically no open water in sight. Even the route they had taken from the west had now closed up. To make matters worse Phipps realised that his ships were drifting to the east whilst locked into their icy prison. The chances of being able to break out to any open water seemed, at best, remote. The ice-pilots suggested that the ship should be moved to the west to take advantage of a few small openings in the ice in that direction. Sheer-legs were rigged and ice-saws suspended from them in an attempt to cut through the twelve-foot thick ice that separated the ships from the patches of clear water. By the end of the day they had managed to move each ship no more than three hundred yards to the west whilst the current drove the ice even further to the east.

As if there was not enough tension in the air, Midshipman Nelson, along with another young man from the *Carcass*, set off in the early hours of the morning in pursuit of a polar bear that had been spotted from the ship. For a time, a veil of fog hid them from the ship causing some concern amongst the remaining officers, but such alarm was as nothing compared to what was felt when a lifting of the fog revealed the situation. Nelson and his companion were stood on one side of a crack in the ice whilst the polar bear, many times their combined size, stood threateningly on the other. A flag was run up ordering the young men to return but Nelson – not for the only time in his life – ignored the signal and, against the pleas of his companion, aimed his musket and pulled the trigger. He was rewarded solely by a click of metal and the fizz of burning gunpowder – his weapon had flashed in the pan. Now, to all intents and purposes defenceless, Nelson took his musket by the barrel and prepared to swing it at the beast. He was almost certainly saved by the loud bang of a cannon fired from the ship to scare the bear off. On his return on-board, the fourteen-year-old found himself in front of an extremely irritated Lutwidge who demanded to know what he thought he was doing going after a bear with neither support nor permission. 'Sir', replied Nelson, 'I wished to kill the bear, that I might carry the skin to my father.' His sense of obligation and duty prevented Lutwidge from judging the act to be little more than misguided enthusiasm and the matter was taken no further.

With the continued drift to the east rendering further attempts to saw their way out of difficulties a waste of effort, Phipps sent Midshipman Walden with two ice-pilots over the ice to a small island about twelve miles away (later named by Phipps 'Walden's Island') to see if any open water could be seen from its hills. They returned the following day with the news that, around the point of the island, the sea was open to the west. They also noted that the ships seemed to be sheltered from an easterly wind which could be felt on the island. Both items of news were welcome, but Phipps was well aware that they did little to resolve his immediate difficulties which had not improved upon his taking soundings and finding that he had less than fourteen fathoms beneath his keel. If the ice into which he was locked became

Nelson and the polar bear.

grounded, his immobile ships would almost certainly be nipped as the current forced the frozen mass down upon them.

It seemed to him that his options were limited to abandoning the ships and setting up an over-wintering base on one of the nearby islands, or of taking the ship's boats and setting out to the west in the hope of meeting open water and, eventually, one or more of the whaling ships. Both options had their problems. He did not have the resources for an over-wintering and, as the season was rapidly drawing to a close, there was every chance that the whalers had already set off for home. Phipps informed his officers that he had decided that their best chance for survival was to prepare the ship's boats for a journey over the ice. The boats were lowered over the side and fitted with a protective screen by securing a canvas strip to stanchions raised up on the gunwales. Eighty canvas bags were made to carry 25lb of bread each and two hundred joints of beef were cooked in readiness for the journey. A sail was cut up and made into belts and harness that could be used to drag the boats over the ice. As this was being done men were stationed at cracks in the ice to sound the depth in case the rate of shoaling should produce even greater urgency. When the launch had been prepared and the towing harness fitted, Phipps tried out the system by having

The Racehorse *and* Carcass *locked in the ice, 1773.*

Phipps' expedition preparing to abandon their ships.

fifty men tow the boat for two miles. The craft passed over the ice with no great difficulty, much to his satisfaction. As he was carrying out his trial he noticed that cracks had begun to appear in the ice to the west of his ships. Phipps immediately set his sails and, with the aid of a slight breeze from the east, managed to force his way slowly to the west with the boats being dragged along in his wake. This tiny success encouraged him to keep his sails set in case the combination of an easterly wind and breaking ice could continue to push the ship to the west.

Two ice-pilots and three men were sent further to the west to see if the prospects were encouraging but they returned after three and a half hours to say that there was no thinning or breaking up of the ice in that direction. Consequently, Phipps ordered that each man be issued with a musket, ammunition, and a thirty-pound bag of bread. He also insisted that, if the ships were abandoned, each man should take no more than the weapon and bread he had been issued with and the clothes he was wearing. Midshipman Thomas Floyd of the *Racehorse* promptly went below and

> put on me, two shirts, two waistcoats, two pairs of breeches, four pairs of stockings, a large pair of boots, a good hat, and stuck a pistol which I had into a canvas belt, which latter at the same time served to keep from falling the few sheets of my journal I had written on the progress of the voyage. The belt was to fasten to a rope to assist in dragging a boat. I likewise put in my pocket, a comb, a razor, a pocket-book full of letters, and some pistol shot, also a red woollen cap which I put on my head under my hat.

Floyd was clearly not going to let his circumstances be an excuse for letting his appearance slip.

Phipps set out with the launch again and his team of haulers managed to take her over three miles without any difficulty. On his return he found that the ship had not only inched even further to the west but that the ice itself had also drifted in that direction. The following day began with a thick fog which, upon clearing up at midday, revealed that the westward drift had continued. By the evening the launch had been passed and Phipps ordered it to be hoisted on-board. A westerly snow-bearing wind threatened to undo the distance that had been achieved and ice-anchors were sent out in an attempt to warp the ship forward.

On the morning of 10 August the sails began to flap under the influence of a wind from the north-northeast. Soon the ships had gathered way and were surging through the cracking ice. For several exhilarating hours the ships crashed through the splintering ice field taking several hard knocks and even snapping one of the anchors on the way. At midday the sound of ice grinding along the ship's side suddenly gave way to the gentle lapping of their natural environment. Against seemingly impossible odds, the *Racehorse* and *Carcass* had broken free of their icy trap.

After twenty-four hours sailing through almost ice-free seas the ships anchored amongst Dutch whaling ships in the shelter of Smeerenberg Harbour on the north-western coast of Spitsbergen. The next four days were spent, when the weather permitted, in making observations within sight of a spectacular glacier (known in Phipps' time as an 'iceberg') with a leading edge 300ft high and of 'a very lively light green colour'.

The ships left the harbour on 19 August, the advancing season being noted by 'an appearance of dusk' in the late evening sky. After a final visit to the western edge of the ice, Phipps turned for home just in time to run into a gale, the like of which, had been seen by no-one on-board. The bombs could not be described as good sea-craft and the *Carcass*, in particular, was an extremely sluggish sailer. Instead of rising to the waves both vessels ploughed their way through, shipping water with every plunge beneath the towering crests. Lower decks were cleared and pumps manned in a race against the water rising in the holds. Lieutenant Cuthbert Adamson and three men fought with the ship's helm in a desperate effort to keep her head to the sea – to have allowed her to have gone beam on to the waves would have led to a certain capsize. One monstrous wall of water toppled onto the ship and swept away three of the ship's boats hanging from booms. The same giant wave lifted a fourth boat from its housing and smashed it back down on the deck. Phipps had no choice but to order that it be broken up and heaved over the side in order to keep the upper deck clear. The deck itself began to split apart from the weight of the anchored cannons and two of the guns had to be jettisoned. The spare masts soon followed them. Of even more concern to Phipps was the fact that the coast of Norway was less than ten miles away and the gale was driving him fast in that direction. In an attempt to gain some control over the ship he ordered the mainsail to be set. It was instantly ripped to shreds. They were, quite plainly, at the mercy of the sea and weighed down with the belief that their consort had already been lost to the onslaught. But they were to escape that imagined terror when, after almost twenty hours of battering, the wind turned to the north allowing them to haul clear of the Norwegian coast. The *Carcass* had not sunk. Despite an equally terrible experience, she limped into view of the *Racehorse*.

Both ships arrived safely at Deptford and were paid off on 13 October. Skeffington Lutwidge was promoted post captain and went on to become a distinguished admiral and an ancestor of the creator of 'Alice in Wonderland'. Constantine Phipps, although having reached a record 80 degrees, 37 minutes, could not look for promotion as he was already on the lengthy ladder of promotion to flag-rank. After a period ashore, he inherited his father's title as Baron Mulgrave before being returned to the House of Commons as the member for Huntingdon and being appointed as one of the Admiralty lords in 1777. A year later he was given command of the seventy-four-gun *Courageux* and took a decisive part in Admiral Keppel's inconclusive battle against the French off Ushant. Keppel was later court-martialled on the word of his second-in-command, Cook's friend and mentor, Sir Hugh Palliser. Having given evidence on Palliser's behalf, Phipps was no longer employed at sea after Keppel became First Lord of the Admiralty in 1782. Much of the rest of his life was spent in politics and in assembling a magnificent naval library. He was elected a fellow of the Royal Society and took the lead in establishing a 'Society for the Improvement of Naval Architecture'. Raised to the House of Lords as Baron Mulgrave in 1790 he died two years later without leaving an heir. He is remembered by Phipps Island off north-east Spitsbergen and by the full Latin name for the polar bear 'Phipps's Ursus Maritimus'.

HMS *Racehorse* was refitted and sent on service against the rebellious colonists of America where she was captured by the American *Andrea Doria* in December 1776. A year later she was caught by ships of the Royal Navy in Delaware Bay whilst sailing under the Stars and Stripes – the third flag under which she had sailed. After a short engagement the tough old Arctic veteran was sent to the bottom.

The *Carcass* took part in the action off St Lucia under Daines Barrington's brother, Samuel, in December 1778. Six years later she was sold – probably for breaking up.

Midshipman Horatio Nelson continued his career in the Royal Navy until his death as a vice-admiral at the Battle of Trafalgar in 1805. Both his service and his death ensured an unassailable fame in his country's maritime history.

CHAPTER THREE

ICE BLINK

Samuel Hearn's early involvement with the Royal Navy proved to be something of a disappointment, but he was later to have such an effect that he helped towards the death of the most famous of the Navy's navigators. He was born the son of the secretary to the London Bridge Waterworks Co. and, on the death of his father, moved to Dorset where he turned out to be an indifferent scholar. His family connections, however, were just enough to have him taken into the Royal Navy as a 'captain's servant'. This was a pleasing fiction whereby a ship's captain took on a boy (sometimes his own son) and trained him to the level of an able seaman. Having proved himself in that rating, the boy could hope to be re-rated as a midshipman or as a master's mate. From the former he could aspire to sit the lieutenant's examination or, via the latter, obtain a Navy Board warrant as a sailing master. It was not at all uncommon for these 'young gentlemen' to move from midshipman to master's mate. A future commissioned officer needed to have the navigational and ship handling skills available to the masters in case they were later appointed as masters and commanders and be required to do their own navigation.

At eleven years old, Hearn was sent as captain's servant to Captain Samuel Hood on-board the new, twenty-gun, HMS *Bideford*. His career then spanned most of the Seven Years War during which time he fought the French in the Bay of Biscay and in the Mediterranean. When, in 1763, the war ended, Hearn found that his prospects in the service were somewhat less than promising. He had probably managed to be rated master's mate through experience and age, but his earlier failings to get to grips with the mathematics required for accurate navigation may have told against him.

Hearn then gained employment as a mate on the whaling ships of the Hudson Bay Co. He found time to improve his surveying skills under the direction of William Wales (the astronomer who was later to join Cook on his second voyage of exploration) and to fall out with his local employer – Moses Norton, the governor at the Prince of Wales Fort on the north bank of the Churchill River estuary. Norton, whose habit of taking possession of every attractive young woman in his region, had little use for a young Englishman who might be a threat to his personal harem of Indian girls. The company, however, came to the aid of the governor with a

Samuel Hearne.

request that someone be sent deep into the unknown country to the north-west to investigate a rumour that copper could be found. The search for the supposed metal could also be used to satisfy those in England who complained that the company was not undertaking that part of its charter which required it to search for a north-west passage. Norton had no difficulty in choosing whom he would send – it would be Samuel Hearn.

Quite unaware of what lay before him Hearn left Prince of Wales Fort on 6 November 1769, with two other Hudson Bay Co. men and two Cree Indians as hunters. As they left they were joined by a band of Chipewyan Indians who stayed with them until they had travelled two hundred miles to the north. At this point the Chipewyan turned on Hearn's party, looted all their supplies, and abandoned them. They were left with no choice but to return to the fort, boiling their leather jackets to provide soup as a meagre sustenance.

Setting off again the following year Hearn, accompanied by his Indian guides, reached the edge of the Barren Lands by the beginning of June. The absence of game forced them into eating berries and gnawing on old deer hide. Little help came from large parties of Chipewyan who began to gather around him. Soon, almost six hundred of the natives had come together, and his Indian guides were keen that they should winter alongside the Chipewyan rather than try to keep heading north-west. The question of the immediate future was, however, decided by the Chipewyan who stole Hearn's belongings. They then, accompanied by Hearn's guides, left him abandoned and alone in the bleak emptiness. Once again he turned his steps back to the far-off Fort. But this time he had no shelter, no snowshoes, no warm clothing, or food, and the first iron chills of winter were feeling their way from the north. For three days he walked doggedly southwards, merely putting off the inevitable cold and lonely death to which the natives had committed him. Just when it seemed that the time had come to lie down and accept his fate a movement caught his eye. Against almost incalculable odds, he could see the tall figure of an Indian striding across the bleak landscape towards him. The stranger turned out to be a Chipewyan chief named Matonabbee who had been born and brought up at Prince of Wales Fort. Taking command of the situation, Matonabbee clothed and fed the Hudson Bay man and led him back to the Fort.

During the long journey the two men established a working rapport and Matonabbee offered to lead Hearn to the region where the copper was said to be found. Less than two weeks after their return to the Fort they set off northwards once again – the Indian taking his eight wives and nine children for company. Before long other Chipewyan joined them and Hearn found that to survive he had to learn to live like one of the natives. He soon came to terms with the Indian food, even such delicacies as raw caribou brains and still warm unborn buffaloes and beavers ripped from their dying mothers. He had difficulty however, in accepting the way the Indians treated their women. Not only were they regarded as little more than pack animals, they were always at the mercy of their husbands (who could reject them totally with little ceremony) or to other males who were free to abuse them at their will. A woman in discomfort or pain was worthy of little attention and Hearn noted one woman who took over fifty hours to give birth yet was still expected to carry a load through freezing water and haul a sledge the following day.

Most of the winter was spent dragging a sledge over the snow, stopping only to chop tent poles and collect birch bark to make into canoes for later river crossings. As they pressed on to the north-west they were joined by a new band of natives. These were Copper Indians who, in the late spring, began to take over the direction of the march. By June, a river flowing over rapids had been reached (the Coppermine River) and the bank followed northwards against driving snow.

On the late evening of 17 July 1771, the Indians signalled Hearn to remain where he was whilst they crept forward with painted faces and hair tied back. Alarmed that he might be left behind, Hearn stayed in touch with the natives and became a witness to an event that stunned him with its brutality. The Indians had discovered that, just ahead of them, about twenty Eskimos lay asleep in their tents. Within minutes they were all dead, fallen to the knives and spears of the laughing Indians. One young woman ran to Hearn in the hope of safety as he stood to the side watching the awful sight. As she flung her arms around his legs, two Indian spears were thrust through her and Hearn had to plead with her attackers to put her out of her misery. The last to die was an old woman, probably deaf, who had continued fishing just out of sight of the camp and was unaware of what had happened. When there was no one left to kill the Indians mutilated the bodies and destroyed the camp. For the first time a white man had witnessed the age-old hatred between the Indians and the Eskimos that had grown from the competition for the scarce resources of the vast Barren Lands and the Arctic emptiness.

Their terrible deed completed, the Indians moved on from 'Bloody Fall' towards the mouth of the river, less than eight miles away. Across the delta's mudflats Hearn saw a northern sea, speckled with drifting ice floes, that stretched beyond the east and west horizons. His were the first European eyes to see the great waters that lapped against the northern American coastline during the brief summer and locked them in an icy grip for the dark winter. But, to Hearn, there seemed little cause for celebration. Not only had his achievement been soured by the savage events of the day before, but any plan that the Coppermine River could have been used as a north-western highway to the interior of the Hudson Bay Co.'s territory were dashed by the shoals that barred the entrance to the river. These, combined with the falls and rapids he had seen on his way down the Coppermine, would prevent all but the smallest canoes from using the waterway.

Having used an ancient quadrant to find his position, Hearn turned to retrace his steps. Further disappointment came when, three days later, he arrived at the site of the much-desired copper deposits. At the end of a search of some hours all he had been able to find was a modest chunk of the metal. More might have been available, but the Indians were keen to get back to their camps to the south – winter was on its way.

It took the best part of a year for Hearn to return to the Prince of Wales Fort. He had found it difficult to keep up with the natives and had left a trail of bloody footprints across the Barren Lands and the frozen waters of the Great Slave Lake as he limped in their wake. His round journey of 3,500 miles came to an end on 30 June 1772 – to a welcome that was less than overwhelming. Given a reward of £200 from the company for his endeavours, he was then returned to his previous job as mate on a whaling ship. He remained with her for eighteen months until his superior, Norton, died after bellowing at one of his wives 'Goddamn you for a bitch! If I live, I'll knock your brains out!'

In 1774, Hearn was sent to establish the company's first inland post in an attempt to stem the expansion of the rival French-controlled North West Co. Cumberland Fort was set up by the Saskatchewan River and rapidly proved to be a success. The following year he led a convoy of thirty-two canoes laden with furs back to York

Prince of Wales Fort painted by Samuel Hearne.

Factory via Lake Winnipeg and the Nelson River. At long last he was rewarded for his enterprise when the company appointed him as the Governor of the Prince of Wales Fort. He settled down to an agreeable life within the fort and even married a daughter of his hated predecessor, Norton. Sadly, everything came to an end when, as the mist cleared on the evening of 8 August 1782, he was stunned to see a seventy-four-gun French warship lying off shore.

The previous April, Rear Admiral Sir Samuel Hood (Hearn's old commander), had fought a battle against the French in the West Indies. Three of the enemy ships had escaped and made their way northwards under the command of the Conte de La Perouse. They entered Hudson's Bay with the specific intention of attacking Prince of Wales Fort. In the early hours of 9 August, French marines landed and advanced in silence towards the fort. Disturbed by the lack of opposition from within the ramparts, a drummer was sent forward accompanied by a messenger to request a parley. To their astonishment, as they came up to the fort, the gates were opened and a white flag broken out at the flagpole. Hearn had decided that his thirty-eight men, and a fort with no internal water supply, would stand no chance against the firepower of the French ships.

After taking all the men prisoner La Perouse sailed down the coast to attack York Factory whose governor surrendered after threatening to shoot any man who fired on the French. A sloop was commandeered by the French and their prisoners put on-board before being towed out of the bay. The French commander had taken into his possession Hearn's account of his journey to the Arctic sea and, when the prisoners were released, refused to return it until Hearn promised to have it published.

In the meantime, Hearn's wife, after fleeing north with the Indians, starved to death. Matonabbee, burning with shame at the loss of the fort, hanged himself, leaving six of his wives and four of his children to die of starvation.

After returning to Churchill to re-establish the run-down fort, Hearn left for England where he died five years later, in 1792.

The final entry in his diary as he ended his journey in 1772 read

> Though my discoveries are not likely to prove of any material advantage to the Nation at large, or indeed to the Hudson's Bay Company, yet I have the pleasure to think that I have fully complied with the orders of my Masters, and that it has put a final end to all disputes concerning a North West Passage through Hudson's Bay.

That may well have been the case, but there still remained the fact that he had seen and described a body of clear water on the northern lip of the continent. This solid fact, combined with further fancies of the, well-connected, Honourable Daines Barrington, kept the question of a north-west passage alive.

Barrington based his views upon the claims by a number of whaling captains and others that they had reached as far north as 84 degrees, 30 minutes, finding there 'but little ice'. All that was now needed was a reason to send an expedition in search of the passage. There was, however, a problem that had to be first overcome. The prize of £20,000 for the first to find the passage that had been offered by the Admiralty, and secured by a 1745 Act of Parliament, had excluded ships of the Royal Navy. Even worse, it had been offered solely for ships finding the route through Hudson's Bay. Accordingly, a new act was approved by Parliament which not only allowed his Majesty's ships access to the prize, but also laid down that *any* passage, in *any* direction, above the 52nd parallel would qualify.

The flimsiest of reasons to send ships into the Pacific then presented itself for the Admiralty's approval. When Furneaux had returned with the *Adventure* he had brought with him a young man from Otaheite named Omai. He had been presented at court, had adopted English dress and table manners, and had been taken to York races by Joseph Banks and Captain Constantine Phipps. But the time had come for him to return to his island home. The Admiralty decided that, not only should he be taken back by the Royal Navy, but two ships should be used. This, in turn, meant that the Admiralty had two ships virtually unemployed on the other side of the world once they had delivered their single passenger. Thus, to avoid any accusation of waste, it was decided that the ships would probe into the straits discovered by the Dane, Vitus Bering, thirty-five years earlier. Who then, could command such an expedition?

To solve the problem of command, the First Lord of the Admiralty, Lord Sandwich, invited the secretary to the Admiralty, Phillip Stephens, and Captain Sir Hugh Palliser to dinner to discuss the matter. To advise them in their deliberations, the First Lord decided that there could be none better than Captain James Cook, and so he was invited to join them at the meal. It does not take an overly devious mind to reach the conclusion that Sandwich might have had more in mind for Cook than mere discussion. If that was the case, it succeeded. Cook left the meeting not only full of enthusiasm for the project, but had offered himself for the command – his only request being that, on his return, he could regain his position at Greenwich. Sandwich was happy to grant both requests. Two days later Cook was officially appointed as leader of the expedition.

HMS *Resolution* was available for Cook's new command, but the *Adventure* was being prepared for conversion to a fireship (eventually to be sold in 1783) and could not be re-commissioned. Cook returned to his favourite Whitby-built colliers for his second ship, choosing to buy Mr Herbert's *Diligence* and re-naming it HMS *Discovery*. He chose for his first lieutenant the American-born John Gore who had served him well on the *Endeavour*. His other lieutenants were James King – responsible for astronomical observations – and John Williamson. The ship's surgeon was to be William Anderson who, after demonstrating his abilities on Cook's second voyage, was also entrusted to be the ship's naturalist. The enthusiastic George Vancouver was accepted again as an able seaman (to be rated midshipman just after departure). As his sailing master, Cook chose a twenty-two-year-old with great promise in navigating and marine surveying – Mr William Bligh.

The command of the *Discovery* went to Charles Clerke. Promoted commander on his return with the *Resolution* the year before, he had also served on the *Endeavour* as a master's mate and with John Byron as a midshipman. His first lieutenant was James Burney, the second being John Rickman. The Board of Longitude appointed William Bayly – who had served in the *Adventure* – as astronomer in the *Discovery*. Joseph Banks sent along David Nelson, a gardener from the Botanical Gardens at Kew, to collect plant specimens.

Whilst Cook gathered his expedition together, HMS *Lyon* sailed from Deptford on 25 May, under the command of Lieutenant Richard Pickersgill. Pickersgill had served in the *Endeavour* as a master's mate and as a lieutenant in the *Resolution* (Cook had named Pickersgill Harbour in Dusky Bay after him). His voyage was, yet again, the result of the Admiralty using one purpose for the benefit of another. The official reason for the sailing was the threat to British whalers from American privateers who were becoming bolder as a result of a seething discontent in the American

Captain James Cook

colonies. Whilst he was engaged in these duties, however, it was felt that he might as well carry out a reconnaissance of the coasts of Baffin Bay – just in case Cook should later appear in those waters and need ready assistance. The Press were not so easily taken in; The *London Chronicle* reported that Pickersgill was 'bound on discoveries to the North-West Passage.'

Cook and the *Resolution* sailed from Deptford on 25 June and arrived at Plymouth five days later. There he found the *Discovery* waiting for him, but without her captain. Clerke had stood surety for debts on behalf of his brother, Captain Sir John Clerke. Unfortunately, the elder Clerke had vanished leaving his brother clapped inside a debtor's prison where he would have to remain until the debts were cleared. Cook decided to sail, leaving instructions for Clerke to follow as soon as he could.

After calls at Tenerife and the Cape Verde Islands, Cook arrived at The Cape of Good Hope. It had been decided that, instead of taking the Cape Horn route to reach the central Pacific, an easterly voyage would give them the advantage of the westerly winds of the 'Roaring Forties'.

As the *Resolution* was being re-caulked beneath Table Mountain, HMS *Lyon* returned to Deptford and an outbreak of acrimony. Pickersgill had arrived off the coast of Greenland ten days after most of the whaling fleet he was sent to protect had left for home. A passing whaler captain, wishing him luck on hearing that he

Captain Charles Clerke.

intended to go north, also suggested that he did not expect Pickersgill and his ship's company to survive the ice that lay ahead of them. When the ice was reached it came as a shock to the commander of the *Lyon* despite his experience with Cook at the edge of the southern ice fields. He found the glittering hazard that froze around his vessel 'almost beyond belief; what to do, I know not'. At 68 degrees, 26 minutes, he tacked and brought his bows around depressed by the approaching winter and the challenges it brought. Pickersgill then turned to the bottle for consolation and soon became detested by his officers and men. On their arrival back in England one of his midshipmen, Michael Lane, reported Pickersgill's conduct to the Admiralty. After a Board of Inquiry, Pickersgill was dismissed from the service. Probably entering the Merchant Service on less arduous duties, he was to die by drowning forty years later.

The *Discovery*, leaking badly but still commanded by the now debt-discharged Clerke, arrived at the Cape on 10 November and the two ships left in company three weeks later. Heading south-west and pushed along by a westerly gale, Cook arrived at a group of islands earlier discovered by the French. As their original discoverers had omitted to give the islands names, Cook named them Prince Edward Islands after the king's fourth son. The two smallest islands were named Marion's and Crozet's Islands after the French navigators who had first seen them.

The ships then sailed eastwards along the latitude of the islands discovered by another Frenchman, Yves-Joseph de Kerguelen-Tremarec four years earlier. Kerguelen had named the main island La France Austral and returned to France to declare that his discovery would not only supply his country with wood, minerals and precious stones, but also open a new French route to the orient. His speedy return to the island revealed the true nature of the island. Bitterly cold, barren and windswept, with none of the promise of which he had persuaded himself, Kerguelan renamed the place 'Land of Desolation' (Kerguelen's Land).

On 24 December a small island was spotted from the masthead of the *Resolution* – named by Cook 'Bligh's Cap' after his young sailing master – followed almost immediately by a much larger one, Kergeulen's Land. Fog delayed any landing for a day and so it was Christmas Day before they stepped onto the desolate shore of the bay Cook named in honour of the celebration. The British flag was broken out amidst inquisitive penguins and seals whose curiosity got the better of them and

Penguins watch as Cook arrives at Kerguelen's Land.

provided easy prey for the ship's butchers. Leaving six days later, they set their course through almost continuous fog towards Van Dieman's Land (Tasmania) where they arrived at Furneaux's Adventure Bay on 26 January 1777.

The natives of the place came as a surprise to the visitors. The men, totally naked, and the women, shaven-headed and with a kangaroo skin over their shoulders, seemed to have little interest in the gifts offered to them. They spurned metal objects and appeared to have no organised system of obtaining food. Although they lived by the sea, they had no means of catching fish and had no canoes – an aspect of their life that convinced Cook that Van Dieman's Land was part of the southern coast of Australia.

On completion of checking the magnetic variation, recording the tides, and fixing the latitude and longitude of their anchorage, Cook left for New Zealand and Queen Charlotte's Sound. They arrived to an atmosphere of distrust and fear. These were the natives that had killed and eaten the *Adventure*'s landing party and, although they came out to meet the ship in their canoes, they refused to go on-board for fear of retribution for their terrible deed. Cook, however, took great pains to put aside their fears, getting the Tahitian, Omai, to tell them that he meant them no harm. At the same time he sent Lieutenant Burney to the spot where the outrage had taken place. Little more than a few bones were found.

Despite his efforts to show that he meant no harm to the natives, Cook ensured that all shore parties were either well armed or escorted by marines.

After a fortnight the ships were ready to continue their voyage and Cook, leaving New Zealand for the last time, sailed on a northeasterly course towards the Society Islands. The passage was slowed down by a succession of head winds which caused him to work wide of his intended track. As a result he came across a number of small islands (the Cook Islands) whose natives were friendly but whose coral-edged coasts made landing extremely difficult. After hazardous visits to the beaches by Lieutenants Gore and Burney, and the surgeon, Anderson, Cook headed for the Friendly Isles in search for fodder for the livestock carried on-board.

Delayed yet again by contrary winds, it became clear to Cook that he would not reach the north-west corner of the Pacific before the summer season had begun to decline. Any attempt to breach a north-west passage that year would be, therefore, impracticable. Cook decided to spend time cruising among the islands giving his ships' companies a chance to recuperate, and the artists and scientists a chance to examine in greater detail the life of the islands and their people.

As before, the welcome from the islanders was overwhelming. The King of Tonga held banquets in Cook's honour whilst dusky young beauties installed themselves below decks and provided other comforts for the men. A diplomatic game of trying to impress the other side broke out when the natives demonstrated their skills at dancing and singing. Cook retaliated by having his marines give a display of drill and marching. This was followed by native wrestling and boxing matches in which some of the contestants were women. Cook brought the light-hearted contest to an end with a firework display that so amazed the islanders that they withdrew with honour. The only difficulty came from the persistent stealing carried out at every opportunity by all the natives from the chiefs down. At first Cook resorted to flogging the offenders, but finding this to have little effect, acted upon Clerke's suggestion and shaved the heads of those caught thieving. This harmless humiliation rapidly reduced the number of thefts but brought unwarranted native suspicions on those among Cook's own seamen 'whose heads were not overburdened with hair'.

The Friendly Islands were left on 17 July and Otaheiti reached just over three weeks later. Anchoring in Ohetepeha Bay, Cook found a warm welcome from the natives and evidence that they had been visited by other westerners since his last visit. A wooden cross had been raised and inscribed with the words *Christus vincit. Carolus III. Imperat 1774.* To put this rather mild invasion by Spanish priests into its proper place Cook had carved in the other side *Georgius Tertius Rex. Annis 1767, 1769, 1773, 1774, 1777.*

One of the difficulties Cook could see in the future lay in the limited supplies of rum and brandy available for his ships' companies. The year's delay in getting to the north had left the supplies short and Cook was keen that the spirits should be saved for the colder conditions that could be expected. Mustering his men, he explained to them that if they were successful in finding a passage across the top of North America they would be well rewarded with parliamentary prizes, but such achievements would be put in jeopardy if there were no spirits available to help them face the cold. This argument won the day rather than his offering coconut milk in lieu. A tot of grog was to be allowed on Saturday evenings to toast the health of wives and sweethearts.

Cook moved his ships to Matavai Bay twelve days after his arrival and found a ready welcome from the local chiefs. Most of the livestock (including a peacock) was landed as gifts. One of the chiefs responded by sending his mother, three sisters and eight other women to massage away the rheumatic pains that had been causing Cook some discomfort. Unfortunately, the visit was marred slightly by Cook's refusal to get involved in a war that had broken out with a neighbouring island. A further shadow was cast when Cook found himself present at a human sacrifice during a religious ceremony. The site of the deed was littered with a total of forty-nine skulls, some clearly belonging to recent events. At this sight, Cook decided that the time had come to move on.

The ships sailed from Otaheiti on 30 September and arrived on the same day at coral-ringed Maurua (Moorea), the most westerly of the Society Islands. The natives, now no longer so impressed by their European visitors, launched upon a series of thefts that was only halted when Cook had a number of houses and canoes destroyed. After eleven days they departed for Huaheine (Huahine) where they dropped anchor at Owharre. It was there that Omai, the much-travelled native of Otaheiti, had decided to settle. Carpenters were sent ashore to build him a house and a garden was planted with citrus fruits, vines, pineapples, melons and vegetables. Whilst this was being done a sextant was stolen. Cook was incensed at the loss of this vital instrument and, when the thief was caught, and the sextant returned, the unfortunate native had his head shaved and his ears removed.

The next port of call was the island of Ulietea (Raiatea) where the local attractions proved to be too strong for a number of men who promptly deserted. One of them, a marine, John Harrison, was easily found in the arms of two women. His claim that he had been enticed away by the women only ten minutes before he was due to be relieved on watch was accepted by Cook and he was only lightly punished. Another two, however, had slipped away from the *Discovery* and taken a canoe over to another island, Bolabola (Bora Bora). Cook believed that this could only have been done with native assistance. He responded by kidnapping the chief of Ulietea's son, daughter and son-in-law and refusing to return them until the deserters were returned. The tactic worked, but Clerke and Gore both narrowly escaped being captured by the natives in retaliation.

The last of the Society Islands to be visited was Bolabola where Cook negotiated the trading of an anchor that had belonged to one of the ships under the command of the French explorer, de Bougainville. Because of the extra year's delay in getting to the north much of the iron used for trading with the natives had gone. The anchor, Cook felt, would give him an extra supply once his blacksmiths had broken it down into useable pieces.

Seventeen months after he had left England, Cook at last headed north, crossing the Equator on 22 December. Two days later he came across a low, barren, island which he named, inevitably, as Christmas Island. On 18 January 1778, more islands were seen. These were large green and hilly islands that had not been recorded on any previous chart. When natives paddling canoes nervously made their way out to the ships from Atooi (Kauai) it became clear that no white man had ever landed on their shores. At this, Cook decided that the islanders should receive as little contamination as possible from contact with his ships and men. He ordered that boat crews were not to include any known troublemakers, and even that those selected to man the boats would not be allowed to land except where it was unavoidable. Equally, no women were to be allowed on-board.

Shortly after their arrival at anchor off Atooi, Cook sent three boats ashore under the command of Lieutenant Williamson who had orders to search for water. Just as he was about to step onto the beach, a large crowd of natives charged into the water and surrounded the boats excitedly, grabbing at every metal item including muskets. Williamson, alarmed for the safety of the boat's crews opened fire, instantly killing one man. The natives immediately fled. Now fearful of Cook's response to his action, Williamson ordered his men to keep quiet about the matter and his captain did not learn of the incident until the ships had left the island.

The next day Cook went ashore in the company of the surgeon, Anderson, and Webber, the official artist. He was amazed to find that wherever he went the natives prostrated themselves full length in his presence and would only rise upon his insistence. An amicable system of trading was set up and the natives provided willing help in supplying the ships with water. It was also noted that, in common with others on the Pacific Islands, the people of Atooi resorted to cannibalism.

Other islands were visited and Cook named the whole group in honour of his friend and patron, the Sandwich Islands (Hawaiian Islands), before turning his bows northwest on 2 February. For over a month the ships headed into a squally northwesterly wind until land was sighted. A cape of hills and wooded slopes was the first sight of 'New Albion' that presented itself to Cook and his ships' companies. Naming the feature Cape Foul Weather he pressed on northwards. Cape Blanco – first seen, and named, by the Spanish in 1603 – was located before Cook's hopes were raised by, what seemed to be, a promising inlet. His hopes, dashed by a barrier of low land, led to him naming the spot Cape Flattery.

Continually troubled by strong winds threatening to drive him onto a lee shore, Cook stood off for a week before a favourable wind allowed him to close in once again. On 29 March, he sighted a land that was very different from that he had last seen. High, snow-capped mountains rose above thickly-wooded valleys that flooded down to the shores of a wide bay containing an island.

As the ships drifted to an anchorage, three canoes bearing eighteen Indians came out to look at the newcomers. They were clearly unafraid of the visitors and their 'mild, inoffensive' manner encouraged Cook to allow them on-board. Before long, the trading of metal objects for furs was well under way. Cook decided to carry out repairs to his ships in the shelter of the bay and went ashore to select a tall sturdy pine to replace the *Resolution's* mizzenmast. He also charted the wide inlet giving it the name King George's Sound. Later, however, he adopted the native name – Nootka Sound. The island in the centre of the Sound was named Bligh Island after the *Resolution's* master. Cook seems to have been unaware that the Spaniard, Martinez, had discovered the Sound four years earlier. Martinez had not landed, but a casual trade had been established with the natives and two silver spoons, presumed stolen by the Indians, were recovered during Cook's visit.

The natives were found to live in communal timber houses which Cook found to smell offensively of fish, seal oil, and smoke. They soon developed a skill in stealing anything they could get away with and, because they had iron-bladed knives, were especially adept at cutting free items that had been secured by ropes or were part of the rigging. Cook decided to take a mild view of such activities and tried to control theft by the stationing of sentries. Far worse, in everyone's eyes, was the native habit of turning up with human skulls and bones in the hope of trading them for metal – the seamen, sensibly, preferring furs, especially the skin of the sea-otter. On one occasion several canoes came out to the ships and their occupants began to sing, beating time with their paddles against the sides of the canoes. On another, a chief received a small gift from Cook and gave a beaver skin in return. Cook felt that the chief had got the worst of the bargain and gave him yet another gift. At this, the native leader presented Cook with a cloak made entirely from beaver. The trading was finally closed when Cook gave the chief a brass-hilted sword and the man went away clearly happy with his day's dealing.

Almost four weeks after their arrival, the *Resolution* and the *Discovery* made their way out of Nootka Sound and continued north-west in the foulest of weather. For much of the time they were forced clear of the coast, able to return only when the weather moderated. They found a rugged tree-clad coastline with numerous inlets, but few that offered any hope of a passage to the north-west. Where appropriate Cook bestowed names on prominent features and Mounts Edgcumbe, Fairweather, and St Elias found they way onto his charts along with Cross Sound and the Bay of Islands. After Cross Sound the land tended further and further to the west. Cook, concerned about serious leaks appearing in the *Resolution*, began to look for a protective harbour in which he could carry out repairs. He called at a small island but could not find the refuge he was looking for. Whilst he was there, he left a bottle containing a paper with the names of his ships and the date of the discovery. The bottle also contained two silver two-pence coins bearing the date 1772. These had been given to him by the Reverend Dr Kaye, the dean of Lincoln, and Cook named the place Kaye's Island in his honour.

The following day a large island-guarded bay, which suited Cook's purposes admirably, appeared on the starboard bow. This inlet was to be named Prince William Sound after initially being named Sandwich Sound. Cook soon had the *Resolution* heeled over to have her gaping seams caulked with pitch and oakum to restore her watertightness. The natives of the area came to trade and were noted to have a close resemblance, both in appearance and in their kayaks and weapons, to the Eskimos of Hudson's Bay and Greenland. An attempt to penetrate far inland up a north-eastern arm of the bay ended after two hundred miles amidst a barrier of snow-covered mountains.

Once the carpenters had completed their work, Cook set off to follow the coast as it began to trend towards the south-east. The ships had not sailed for more than a few days when a large opening appeared which appeared to offer the most optimistic hope of a passage towards the north-east. Cook took his ships over two hundred miles up the inlet before it ended in two shorter arms and an un-navigable river. Lieutenant King was sent ashore to claim the land in the name of his sovereign

Resolution *and* Discovery *in Prince William Sound.*

and bury another bottle containing a paper and more silver coins. In his annoyance at the time wasted in probing this dead-end, Cook omitted to name the waterway. It was later to be honoured by the name Cook River (Cook Inlet) by his friend and patron, Lord Sandwich.

Two weeks after their departure from the disappointing inlet, the ships were off Shumagin Island when Cook was alerted by three cannons being fired from the *Discovery*, the signal for Clerke wishing to meet him. On boarding the *Resolution* Clerke told Cook that he had been approached by natives paddling kayaks, one of the men had stood up, bowed, and removed his hat after the style of a European. When his kayak had reached the *Discovery* he had handed up a small wooden box before paddling off. The box contained a written note in a language that no one could understand but the dates 1776 and 1778 were plain enough. After some consideration, Cook decided that the paper was probably a message between Russian traders. The natives, he felt, had assumed that his ships were Russian, and so had passed it on. Two days later another man paddled his way from the Alaska Peninsula and approached the ships. Dressed in a black cloth jacket and green breeches he, like the earlier visitor, stood up bowed and raised his hat. But his reward was to be little more than a few waves and curious stares – Cook had little time for social niceties with the season rapidly advancing.

On 27 June, a day after narrowly missing rocks in a particularly thick fog, Cook decided to stop at one of the most easterly of the Aleutian Islands, Oonalashka (Unalaska). Once again a note was delivered by a politely mannered native who bowed low upon receiving gifts from Cook. All that could be deduced from these overtures was that the natives had been subjected to some form of western culture – almost certainly Russian.

The ships rounded Oonalashka and headed north-west where, after two weeks, a large promontory was sighted. Cook sent Lieutenant Williamson ashore with a note in a bottle to take possession of the country in the king's name. The officer was also ordered to climb the highest hill he could to see how the land trended. Williamson reported back that the coast seemed to lead directly northwards. Cook named the point Cape Newenham before leaving to follow the barren, rocky coast.

As the treeless land slipped by to starboard, the *Resolution*'s surgeon and amateur naturalist, William Anderson ('an agreeable companion, well skilled in his profession'), died of tuberculosis. He was buried on a small island named by Cook Anderson's Island in his memory. The surgeon's mate of the *Resolution*, David Samwell, was sent over to the *Discovery* to replace her surgeon, Dr Law, who, in turn, was appointed to take the place of Anderson.

After naming a wide bay Norton Sound in honour of the speaker of the House of Commons, Cook sailed on until he reached the most western extremity of Alaska which he named Cape Prince of Wales. From this point he was less than forty miles from the most eastern cape of Asia. Crossing the Bering Strait he made contact with the Russian coast where he found the local people 'very fearful and cautious'. There was no time to study these natives or to improve relationships. It was already 11 August and the short Arctic autumn was already upon them, soon to be followed by winter. Returning to the Alaskan coast at a place named by Cook Mulgrave Point after his Arctic co-explorer, Captain Constantine Phipps, the ships set off north and north-east.

On reaching 70 degrees, 33 minutes north on the 17th amidst 'sharpness of the air and gloominess of the weather' Cook's attention was called to 'a brightness in the northern horizon like that reflected from ice, commonly called the blink.' It was indeed, 'ice blink', nature's warning to seamen that ice lay ahead. In less than two hours the ships came up to a sullen barrier that ranged up to 10ft high at its edge. It was obviously no mere fringe to a navigable polar ocean, nor was it ice that had collected from the outflow of rivers. The ship had not been built to force its way through the field of ice that stretched beyond the northern horizon. Like Phipps before him, all that remained to Cook was to sail along the edge of the ice in search of a way through. As his aim was to find a way across the top of Northern America he tacked eastwards. Before long the Alaskan coastline began to loom up on the starboard beam and the gap between the ice and the shore grew narrower. Eventually, as a promontory reached out from the shore towards the ice, Cook feared that to press on would inevitably lead to his ships being trapped in the merging ice and coast. He was now some 300 miles beyond Bering's Strait and in temperatures at times 'very little above the freezing point and often below it, so that the water vessels on deck were frequently covered with a sheet of ice'. Naming the land formation Icy Cape, Cook turned about and sailed along the edge of the ice to the west to see if any way could be found through to the north in that direction. None appeared and, as he was quite aware that the ice was heading southwards, thus reducing any chance of a northward passage, he decided that he had done enough that season. He would come back next year.

By 2 October the ships were back at Oonalashka where Cook sent one of his marines, American-born Corporal John Lediard, to try and make contact with any Russians in the area. Two days later Lediard returned with three men who had set

Resolution *and* Discovery *in pack ice north of Bering's Strait.*

up a trading base after sailing from Russia in a 30-ton sloop. Although neither side could understand the other, friendly relations were established and bottles of rum and wine swapped for furs.

Whilst this bout of local diplomacy was in full swing, Cook decided on his future plans. He would leave Oonalashka and head for his newly-discovered Sandwich Islands where he would spend the winter recuperating and studying the islands and their inhabitants. The following spring would be spent reaching Kamchatka on the Asian Russian mainland prior to a further summer assault on the problem of a passage across the top of North America.

The island of Mawee (Maui) was sighted on 26 November and Owhyhee (Hawaii) two days later where Cook was astonished to see two snow-capped peaks rising to almost 14,000ft. The ships' companies were less taken with the scenery than by the sight of scores of canoes carrying flower-bedecked women coming out to greet the ships as they coasted round the islands in search of a suitable anchorage. The days dragged by slowly into weeks and it was not until 16 January 1779, that William Bligh, sounding the depths from one of the ship's boats, found a safe harbour known as Karakakooa (Kealakekua Bay). The next day the *Resolution* and the *Discovery* were surrounded by canoes in their hundreds bearing natives in their thousands. Many more lined the shores whilst others swarmed around the ships 'like shoals of fish', all expressing their delight at the arrival of the newcomers.

Over the next few days contact was made with the local chief and gifts were poured on Cook and Lieutenant King who had gone ashore to pay their respects. Huge quantities of vegetables and many pigs were handed over. Parcels of cloth were piled on the ground in front of them and Cook was presented with a magnificent cloak and helmet made from red and yellow feathers. As these gifts were being bestowed the word 'Lono' kept being spoken. The natives, it seemed, were treating Cook as a god whose arrival on the island had been long-predicted by their priests.

For the following week, officers and men from the ships were treated as honoured guests and given the freedom to roam over the island. The natives put on dancing and wrestling matches. They, in turn, were enchanted by firework displays. When William Watman, a gunner's mate died, thousands turned out to honour his funeral with promises that the grave would always be cared for. Cook, however, unwilling to outstay his welcome, decided that the ships would leave on 4 February. The parting was as warm as the welcome with canoes following the ships far off shore. Other canoes joined in the procession as the ships made their way along the palm-fringed coast. Two days after their departure a gale sprang up and a number of natives had to be rescued when their canoes overturned. The wind had also damaged the foremast of the *Resolution* so Cook now turned about and headed back to Karakakooa to return the natives and carry out repairs. Unfortunately, the priests had not told the people that the god, Lono, would return for a second time.

The welcome for the returning ships was much more muted than before and, although a relationship was re-established with the natives, the atmosphere was different. Insolence took the place of greetings and thieving became commonplace. On one occasion, when Cook was ashore with King and Midshipman Vancouver, he heard the sound of musket fire from the direction of the *Discovery*. A canoe was being paddled furiously away from the ship – clearly some form of theft had taken place. Cook and the others raced along the beach in an attempt to cut off the canoe but arrived too late while the occupants of the craft laughed and mocked at his efforts to catch them. Thomas Edgar, the master of the *Discovery*, who had followed in the *Discovery*'s pinnace was driven off by stones when he attempted to take the canoe that had been used in the theft.

The next morning Cook learned that the *Discovery*'s large cutter had been stolen. He promptly sent out ship's boats to stop canoes from leaving the bay. He than left the *Resolution* with Lieutenant Molesworth Phillips, the marine officer; two NCOs; and seven marines. The pinnace crew, under the command of Midshipman Henry Roberts, was also armed. As they approached the shore, Cook ordered Lieutenant John Williamson – stationed at the western end of the bay – to join him with the launch. His plan was to take the local chief hostage until the cutter was returned.

As he stepped ashore the natives reverted to their earlier act of prostrating themselves as he passed. On arrival at the chief's hut Cook sent the marines in to bring the old man out. When this had been done Cook explained to the chief that he would like him to return on-board with the party where he would be looked after until the boat was returned. The chief did not object to this turn of events and, after some delay, went with Cook and the marines. As they left they noticed that the natives were beginning to arm themselves and putting on the thick matting which they used as armour. A crowd of some hundreds began to gather and surround the party as it made its way to the beach. The marines forced a lane through to the point where the boats waited. Just as the chief was about to climb into the pinnace, one of his wives flung her arms around his neck and implored him not to go. At this the chief sat down on the sand, apparently confused, as the crowd began to press around Cook and the marines. Phillips saw a native draw a knife and raised his musket to shoot but Cook forbade him to open fire. As the native advanced towards Cook, Phillips hit him with his gun sending him reeling back. Another native attempted to snatch the sergeant's musket and Phillips struck him also. At this point Cook could see that there was no point in continuing with his attempt to detain the chief and was about to give the order to release the man when a native charged down on him with a spear. Cook was armed with a double-barrelled musket with one barrel loaded with shot, the other with ball. He fired shot at the man to try and keep him at a distance, but the matting armour protected the native and merely slowed him down for a moment. Cook, reluctant to use ball unless absolutely necessary, swung

The death of Captain Cook. Cook can be seen holding his hand up to prevent the boats closing with the shore just before he was struck down.

his musket and sent his attacker to the ground. He then began to shout at the crowd, telling them to stand back whilst at the same time urging the marines to abandon the chief and to get on-board the boats. Another native raised his spear in an attempt to throw it at Cook who opened fire with his remaining barrel. A man to the side of the would-be spear thrower fell dead as the sergeant shot the original attacker. The natives fell back for a moment but returned with a shower of thrown stones. At this, the marines opened fire with a volley that was followed by more firing from the boats offshore. Cook raised his hand to stop the firing from the boats and ordered them to come close inshore to allow the marines to board. Midshipman Roberts promptly gave orders for his crew to pull for the beach but Lieutenant Williamson, who seemed to be aghast at the drama being played out just a few yards from his boat, actually steered the launch away. As the marines tumbled into the pinnace the natives attacked them. Four were knocked down and killed, Phillips was wounded. Now Cook was left alone at the water's edge with the launch, under Williamson's command, barely a few yards off. Surrounded by natives, he was hit by a club on the back of his head – the blow causing him to stagger a few paces before dropping on to one knee. As he attempted to rise he was stabbed in the back of the neck and fell into the sea. A final blow from a native club killed him as he reached out towards the over-laden pinnace.

His body was dragged up the beach onto some rocks where the frenzied natives competed to stab and mutilate it. Some order had been obtained in the pinnace and volleys of musket fire drove the natives back. This created an opportunity to rescue the body of their captain and several of the midshipmen present urged Williamson to be allowed to so, but he ordered the boats back to the ships.

So died the greatest navigator the Royal Navy had ever known – a man who had led the way through Antarctic gales to the south, and through Arctic fogs to the north. He had set the standard for all subsequent hydrographers with charts that were still in use 150 years later. From humble birth he had risen to prominence with no other influence than that which he created for himself, yet never failed to encourage the deserving who served with him. As was written about him when his death became known in his native land:

> If public services merit public acknowledgements; if the man, who adorned and raised the fame of his country, is deserving of honours, then Captain Cook deserves to have a monument raised to his memory by a generous and grateful nation.

The plea was not to be in vain, and not just made by his own nation. Throughout the world, monuments, statues, inscriptions, and natural features all bore witness to his achievements and recorded his fame for posterity.

Six days after the tragedy, a priest handed over Cook's skull, arm and leg bones and his hands. They were committed to the deep off shore from where he had so bloodily met his end. With Cook's death, the command of the voyage had fallen upon the ailing Commander Charles Clerke. On hearing of the events on the beach, Clerke at first intended to take 'a stout party ashore, make what destruction among them I could, then burn the town, canoes etc.' He did not carry out his intentions and, apart from the occasional revenge attack on natives and their property, it was generally felt that Cook's memory would be better served by leaving the place and continuing with the expedition's aim.

On 23 April, five weeks after leaving the Sandwich Islands, the ships arrived off the east coast of the Kamchatka Peninsular with their rigging festoon with icicles. Entering Awatska Bay the officers searched for the town of Petrapavlovsk. All they could see was 'a few miserable log houses, and some conical huts raised on poles, amounting in all to about thirty.' Much to their disappointment, the humble collection of buildings *was* the eagerly anticipated port.

A boat was hoisted out and Lieutenant King was ordered ashore to make contact with the Russians and request that provisions be made available for the ships. Before long the simple mission had degenerated into farce. As the boat approached a half-mile wide strip of ice lining the shore, the settlement – which until then had appeared to be asleep – suddenly broke into a frenzy of activity. Soldiers armed with muskets rushed onto the beach and two artillery pieces were wheeled around to the front of the most substantial of the log houses. King, determined not to be put off by this show of strength, stepped from the boat and strode out across the ice followed by the boat's crew who brought with them their boat hooks, their experience of Pacific natives putting them on their guard against the theft of metal objects. With the best traditions of his service as his guide, King walked sternly towards the soldiers – only to disappear through the ice as it gave way beneath him. Pulled from the freezing water by his men, the soaked and shivering lieutenant gritted his teeth and continued on towards the waiting party. On coming up to them he found that there were about thirty soldiers under the command of a sergeant who, on seeing that the strangers were offering no threat, took them back to his house. There they were treated to an excellent meal and King was warmed and given dry clothes. Everything, however, had to be done to a series of smiles and bows as no one knew the other's language. It was, nevertheless, made clear that the sergeant had sent a message to the Governor of Kamchatka on behalf of the visitors in order that their wishes could be complied with.

Petrapavlovsk.

When the time came to return to the ships, an individual dog-sledge and driver was provided for King and each of the seamen. Much to the merriment of the visitors a further sledge was furnished for the sole use of the boot-hooks.

Three days later, a reply was received from the Governor of Kamchatka expressing his regret that, with Petrapavlovsk's entire stock of cattle amounting to no more than two heifers, the town would be unable to supply the ships. Clerke decided to send Lieutenants Gore (now in command of the *Discovery*) and King overland to meet the governor personally in order to stress the need for supplies. The journey, by both canoe and dog-sledge brought them to Bolcheretsk, the capital of the region, where they were treated very well. Not only were the supplies provided, but the governor refused to accept any payment and even included an extra 400lb of tobacco when he learned that the ship's seamen were running short of the commodity. When this particular news reached the ships, the seamen on both vessels voted to forego a day's ration of rum which they sent on to the garrison at Bolcheretsk in their appreciation of a comradely gesture.

The ships sailed from Awatska Bay on 16 June to the salute of a volcano erupting on the northern shore. Following a run up the coast of Kamchatka they once again penetrated Bering's Strait with the intention of sailing between the 68th and 69th

Lieutenant King advances across the ice towards the troops at Petrapavlovsk.

parallels until they struck the coast of Alaska but, two days later, they encountered a vast sheet of ice which edged them further and further to the south until they found that it was locked on to the American shore without a single opening to the north. Clerke then returned towards the Asiatic shore along the ice edge probing into every lead that presented itself. On two occasions the *Discovery* was forced broadside onto the ice and eventually had to furl sails and retreat to a small opening where she was secured by ice-anchors to escape further battering. With a change of wind she was able to escape with the loss of much of her sheathing and an alarming increase in leakage.

When the weather allowed, hunting parties were sent out on to the ice and a number of walruses were killed along with two polar bears. The meat of the latter was tested on the ships' companies and was found to be better than their salted meat despite a pronounced fishy taste.

On 27 July Clerke decided that there was simply no hope of obtaining a way through the ice. His fellow officers thought that to continue to try and find a north-west passage would be 'impracticable, and that any further attempts would not only be fruitless, but dangerous.' The best he had achieved was 76 degrees, 33 minutes – fifteen miles short of the record reached the year before. He now decided to return to Awatska Bay.

Three days later, as the ships passed through Bering's Strait, Clerke began to feel the effects of the tuberculosis he had been ignoring for some months. The death of Cook had pushed his mind beyond his ailing body and, despite being wracked with a bloody cough, he was determined to carry on the work of his dead leader. By 17 August he could no longer stand and was forced to remain in his bunk. On the 22nd, the day after the coast of Kamchatka was sighted, the thirty-seven-year-old Charles Clerke died. He had entered the Royal Navy at the age of fourteen and served throughout the Seven Years War. Towards the end of the conflict he had been on-board HMS *Bellona* when she captured the French warship *Courageux*. Clerke had been stationed in the mizzen-top when a broadside from the enemy brought the mizzenmast toppling over the side. He had survived the hundred-foot fall with only minor injury. His Royal Society paper on the Patagonian 'giants' had brought him to the attention of the right quarters and he was appointed to serve with Cook on all his voyages of exploration. When, during the first voyage, Lieutenant Hicks died of tuberculosis, Clerke was appointed, not only to the late Hick's position, but also his cabin.

Clerke was buried in a valley on the north shore of Awatska harbour. The spot was chosen because the local priest was intending to build a church on the site. The church, however, was eventually built some distance away from the grave and willow trees planted by the seamen around the site remained the only reminders of the distinguished British explorer who lay beneath the frozen soil.

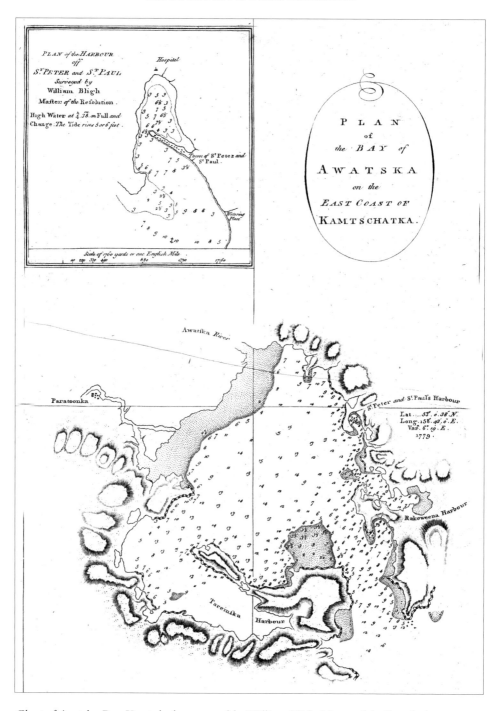

Chart of Awatska Bay, Kamtschatka, surveyed by William Bligh, Master of the Resolution, 1779.

Men from the Resolution *and* Discovery *hunting walrus.*

The command of the voyage now fell upon Lieutenant John Gore who moved to the *Resolution* and placed the *Discovery* under the command of Lieutenant King. Both ships required considerable repair to the damage done by the ice and it was not until 9 October that they were ready to sail. Just as the anchor of the *Discovery* was about to be weighed it was discovered that the marine drummer had deserted. A party was sent ashore to the house of a local woman with whom the drummer was known to be friendly and, before long, a crest-fallen and chastened young man was returned to his ship just in time to catch the tide.

After an attempt to survey the islands north of Japan and frustrated by incessant gales, Gore intended to follow the expedition's instructions and survey the east coast of Japan itself. But yet again the foul weather forced him from the shore and prevented anything but a fixing of the position of Mount Fuji.

A voyage across a sea encrusted with floating pumice stones from a recent volcanic explosion brought them to the port of Macao. There it was discovered that America, allied to France and Spain, was at war with Great Britain. This was a particularly difficult position for Gore, an American. At first the ships were prepared for action but word soon reached Gore that all the enemy ships had been issued with a recommendation from Benjamin Franklin that Cook's expedition, if encountered, was not to be attacked, but was to be treated with 'all Civility and Kindness'. He, therefore, decided that he and his command would endeavour to remain neutral and not engage any of the enemy ships.

Another effect of landing at Macao was to prove even more bizarre. The clothes worn by the officers and ships' companies had long worn out and consisted of little more than fur-patched rags. Before long a brisk trade was underway with the skins they had brought down from the north. Soon, even the most junior man on-board was dressed in the dazzling silks and cottons of China.

Macao was left on 12 February 1780, and Cape Town reached two months later. 12 June saw the crossing of the equator and the coast of Ireland was sighted within eight weeks. An attempt to land at Port Galway was frustrated by the weather and Gore was forced to press on until he could anchor off Stromness. Lieutenant King was sent ashore with the instructions to make his way to the Admiralty to report the arrival of the expedition as Gore brought the ships southwards again in the teeth of head winds. It was to be another five weeks before the ships reached the Nore. They had been away from England for four years, two months, and twenty-seven days.

Within its aims the voyage could not be counted a success. The attempt to find a passage across the top of North America from west to east had been thwarted by the great ice barrier, and a navigator to rank with Columbus, Magellan, and Vasco da Gama had been clubbed to death on a far-off rocky beach. Nevertheless, the surviving officers had, for the most part, maintained the leadership required on such an extended voyage and the seamen, with the exception of a few desertions, had done everything their country could have expected of them.

John Gore was promoted captain on 2 October for his work in bringing the ships home safely and was given the post held for Cook at Greenwich Hospital. He was to die ten years later having had little opportunity to further enhance his reputation as a competent seaman. The day after Gore's promotion (the delay probably to grant Gore an appropriate seniority) James King received his promotion to captain. The following year, King was appointed to HMS *Resistance* and given the job of escorting five hundred merchant ships to the West Indies. Such was the intense anxiety that his responsibilities brought about in him that, on his return, his hair had turned grey. His declining health forced him ashore where he worked upon Cook's journal of his third voyage. His 'Astronomical Observations' were published by the Board of Longitude and earned him a fellowship of the Royal Society. Four years after his return with the *Discovery* he died in the south of France where had been forced to live by his continued illness.

The most surprising of the promotions that were granted on the expedition's return was that of John Williamson. His appalling behaviour when Cook was under attack seems to have been overlooked or ignored and he was promoted to the rank of commander on 3 October, and to captain two years later. Ignominy, however, was to catch up with him when in command of HMS *Agincourt* at the Battle of Camperdown, 11 October 1797. Whilst other captains were being knighted for their exploits in the battle Williamson was being court-martialled for 'cowardice, negligence or disaffection'. He was dismissed from the service. What must have made this outcome extra galling was the fact that William Bligh, the sailing master of the *Resolution* – and thus a mess-mate of Williamson's – was also present at the battle as the captain of HMS *Director*. Bligh had distinguished himself by cannonading down the enemy line until he could give help to the sorely pressed Admiral Duncan, his action contributing much to the ultimate victory.

Bligh had waited for a year after his return before gaining a commission as a lieutenant. His acquaintanceship, through Cook, with Sir Joseph Banks led to his being appointed to the command of the *Bounty*. Although one of the best seamen the Royal Navy ever produced, he suffered from a demanding nature and sharp temper which led, almost inevitably, to the infamous mutiny. He was to die as a vice-admiral in 1817.

Banks was also to be instrumental in having David Nelson, the gardener from Kew who had served in the *Discovery*, appointed to the *Bounty* under Bligh. Nelson was to join Bligh in the *Bounty's* boat and suffer the rigours of the long voyage only to die on reaching Timor.

On his return to England, the marine corporal, John Lediard, who Cook had sent to make contact with the Russians at Oonalsashka, set out in an attempt to cross Russia. He aimed to reach North America via the Bering Straits and set up as a fur-trader, and had obtained sponsorship from Banks for the purpose. On reaching Siberia, however, he was arrested by the Russians, transported to Poland, and forbidden re-entry. Thwarted in his northward ambition, Lediard then headed towards Africa and died in Cairo eight years after leaving the *Discovery*.

HMS *Resolution*, having served her country well through two distinguished voyages, was captured by the French whilst being employed in the East Indies in 1782. Her companion, HMS *Discovery*, was sold within a year of her return.

Two of the midshipmen from Cook's final voyage went on to earn their place in the annals of their service. One – Edward Riou – set his country alight with his deeds but was to be forgotten with the passage of time. The other – George Vancouver – remains firmly on the map despite a catalogue of misfortune.

The monument built to honour Captain Cook at the site of his death.

CHAPTER FOUR

'I HAVE DETERMINED TO REMAIN IN THE SHIP'

Edward Riou never again took part in polar exploration but, nevertheless, underwent a horrifying experience which exemplified the danger faced by ships when they found themselves up against ice. He had served in the *Barfleur* and the *Romney* before joining Charles Clerke as a midshipman in the *Discovery*. On his return from Cook's final voyage, he passed his lieutenant's examination and was promoted to that rank eight days later at the age of twenty-two. He saw service in the *Scourge* in the West Indies, the *Ganges* at Portsmouth, and the *Salisbury* at Newfoundland before, in April 1789, being appointed to the command of the forty-four-gun HMS *Guardian*.

As if to justify her name, the *Guardian* was to transport convicts and their overseers to Australia. In addition, she was to carry £70,000 worth of government stores, seeds, plants, farm machinery, and livestock. Of considerably greater responsibility to the ship's commander was the appointment to the *Guardian* of Midshipman Thomas Pitt, the son of Lord Camelford, and close relation of the Prime Minister and the First Lord of the Admiralty. Altogether there would be three hundred people on-board.

The ship sailed in August and had an un-remarkable voyage to the Cape where yet more livestock and plants were taken on-board. Whilst at the Cape, Riou met the *Bounty's* commander, Lieutenant William Bligh, who had just arrived from Timor where he had landed after his momentous open boat voyage of 3,618 miles.

Picking up the westerlies at the Cape, Riou headed south of east towards his New South Wales destination. Twelve days out from Table Bay; on 24 December, at 44 degrees south, 41 East; a vast 'ice island' was seen. Instead of steering clear of the hazard, Riou welcomed the chance to use the ice to replenish his fresh water casks which had been severely depleted by the large amount of plants and animals he had in his care. Positioning himself beneath the soaring ice cliffs, Riou sent away his boats to collect the ice. By the time the task was completed night had fallen and, just as the final boat was hoisted in, a bank of fog rolled across the grey sea and covered the *Guardian*. The situation in which Riou now found himself was dangerous in the extreme. He was in darkness, blanketed with fog, and with a vast wall of ice to leeward. Lookouts were positioned at the bows and in the rigging as the ship was edged forward, taking her further and further away from the peril. Before long the ice had been left behind and it seemed that Riou's calm handling of the situation had brought them clear of the threat. But, just before nine o'clock, a shout from the forward lookout brought everyone's eyes to a strange pale glow in the darkness ahead of them. Riou instantly ordered the helm to starboard and brought the ship into the wind. For a few breathless moments it seemed as if the ship had been saved. A wall of ice, towering above the masts, silently glided past the ship's side when, with an appalling crash, the *Guardian* struck an underwater projection from the iceberg. The ship reared up and, urged on by a savage burst of wind from an approaching gale, pivoted completely around to face in the opposite direction. Now it was the turn of her stern to receive a battering that was to wrench off her rudder, shatter her stern-frame, and rip open her hull.

Riou, remaining calm, ordered the sails to be set so that he could use them to steer clear of the ice. With this achieved safely, and with her head kept to the wind, Riou took stock of his situation. He had 2ft of water in the hold and water continuing to pour in, a gale was blowing and the sea was rising. The pumps were manned continuously but, by midnight, the water in the hold had increased to 6ft. With the dawning of Christmas day, Riou organised the preparation of an oakum-packed studding sail to be lowered over the side to stop, or at least reduce, the in-flow of water. By eleven o'clock the vigorous pumping had reduced the water in the hold to 19in, only for the pumpers to be defeated yet again as the sail beneath the hull ripped apart and water flooded into the ship.

At this, a number of seamen approached Riou and requested permission to take their chances in the ship's boats. Using all his powers of leadership, the captain persuaded them to stay at their posts. Another sail was sent under the hull, but parted immediately under the pressure of the water. As light faded, the water in the hold reached 7ft with the ship lolling violently – each roll bringing more water pouring over the ship's side. With the seamen and convicts toiling in teams at the pumps, Riou led the chaplain, purser, and two men in ditching overboard the animals, stores, and guns. As he helped to clear the bread room in order to get at a leak, a cask fell and crushed his left hand, the pain and injury forcing him to stop. With the light of the following morning, everyone on-board was in a state of exhaustion. The sails had been ripped to rags by the gale and the ship was settling by the stern with the sea rushing up the rudder-case. Again the seamen, now supported by the convicts, approached Riou to put their case that they should be allowed to take to the boats. This time Riou consented. There could be little reason to prevent those who wished to from leaving, even if he could. But there were only five boats, not nearly enough to take all the people on-board. After agreeing to let the boats go, Riou announced 'As for me, I have determined to remain in the ship, and shall endeavour to make my presence useful as long as there is any occasion for it'. He then busied himself in preparing the boats for the hazardous voyage that faced them. When they were ready, he took pen and paper and wrote a letter to the secretary to the Admiralty –

Sir,

If any part of the officers or crew of the Guardian should ever survive to get home, I have only to say their conduct after the fatal stroke against an island of ice was admirable and wonderful in everything that relates to their duties considered either as private men or on his Majesty's Service.

As there seems no possibility of my remaining many hours in this world, I beg leave to recommend to the consideration of the Admiralty a sister who if my conduct or service should be found deserving any memory their favour might be shown to her together with a widowed mother.

I am Sir remaining with great respect

Your ever Obedt & humble servt,

E. Riou

Some of the crew and passengers taking to the boats after HMS Guardian was struck by an iceberg.

The note was handed to Mr Clements, the master of the *Guardian*, who was to take command of the ship's launch. A total of 259 people chose to abandon the ship and packed themselves into the *Guardian's* five boats. With sails set, the small craft headed off into the heavy seas in the hope of reaching safety. There now remained on-board sixty-two people – Riou, three midshipmen, the surgeon's mate, the boatswain, the carpenter, three superintendents of convicts, Miss Schafer (a daughter of one of the superintendents) thirty seamen and boys, and twenty-one convicts.

The water in the hold had by now reached a depth of 16ft, all the ballast had fallen through the holes in the hull, and water was breaking over her sides. On investigation, however, Riou found that the large number of casks that had been secured in the hold had broken free and were bumping against the underside of the lower gun-deck. It was almost certainly this unexpected aid to buoyancy that was keeping the ship from plunging to the bottom of the southern Indian Ocean. Seizing his chance Riou had the lower gun-deck hatches sealed and caulked, thus effectively making the deck the ship's bottom. Once again a sail was sent under the ship in an effort to stem the water whilst the pumps were continually manned.

For nine weeks, under the barest threads of sails, Riou urged both the ship and his companions onwards in the direction of the Cape until, on 21 February 1790, land was sighted. Rarely had the Cape of Good Hope so earned its name. When the *Guardian* was spotted from the shore, two whalers were sent out to help tow the stricken ship into Table Bay and safety. The ship was run ashore in an attempt to prevent her sinking at anchor, but a raging gale struck the coast and completed the destruction which had been started by an iceberg over two thousand miles out at sea.

Once the news reached England, the First Lord of the Admiralty drove in a carriage and four to give the news to Lord Camelford. The family of Midshipman Thomas Pitt had been in a state of alarm at the news which had been delivered by the sole survivor of the ship's boats. The *Guardian's* launch had witnessed the sinking of the jolly boat and had lost contact with the two cutters and the long-boat before it had been fortunate to fall in with a French merchantman on passage to Table Bay.

On his return to England in September Riou was promoted to commander and, nine months later, captain. After service in the West Indies and command of the Royal Yacht he was appointed to HMS *Amazon* in July 1799 and found himself under the leadership of Nelson off Copenhagen. The admiral gave him overall command of the frigates and smaller craft with the instructions to use them to the best advantage whilst the larger ships took their place in the line of battle. The battle began badly for the British. The three leading 74-gun ships – the *Agamemnon*, the *Bellona*, and the *Russell* all grounded. A quarter of Nelson's squadron were rendered helpless without a shot being fired. The remaining seventy-fours could take on the Danish ships, but the great Trekroner batteries with their massed 24- and 36-pounder guns supported by a pair of two-deck blockships remained unopposed.

Riou, who had placed himself opposite the northern end of the Danish line, saw that the Trekroner batteries were unmolested and gave orders that his small fleet of lightly-armed vessels should take on the task. For two and a half hours Riou's ships withstood the massive fire power of the enemy whilst taking great casualties. Among those wounded was Riou himself who was struck on the head by a splinter. Unable to stand for long he seated himself on a displaced gun-carriage from where he continued to direct the firing of his cannons.

At just after one o'clock Admiral Hyde Parker, the commander-in-chief, with signals of distress flying from the grounded ships, and in the belief that Nelson was meeting greater resistance than had been expected, ordered the signal 'Discontinue action' to be flown from his flag-ship. Nelson acknowledged the signal, but ignored it with 'Leave off action! Now, damn me if I do!' His second in command, Admiral Graves also ignored the signal, but repeated it. Flying from the maintopsail yardarm of Grave's ship, the signal could be seen from the nearest of Riou's small ships, HMS *Alcmene*, who repeated it before cutting her cable and standing out of the fight. She was followed by HMS *Blanche* in obedience to the signal leaving the *Amazon* alone in the forefront of the fight against the forts.

With the withdrawal of the *Alcmene* and the *Blanche,* the thick cannon smoke which had helped to hide the *Amazon* from the enemy gunners was dramatically reduced thus giving the Danes a clear field of fire. The *Amazon* stood her ground for a further half hour before Riou was forced to retire. With the words 'What will Nelson think of us?' he gave the order to cut his cables. The ship's head swung round to present her stern to the batteries guns. With a final roar the 36-pounders opened fire and a hail of iron hurtled along the upper deck of the *Amazon* cutting Riou almost in two.

When Nelson heard of Riou's death he declared that 'the country has sustained an irreparable loss'. Parliament voted a monument to Riou in St Paul's Cathedral and the poet Thomas Campbell included in his ballad 'The Battle of the Baltic' the lines –

> *Brave hearts! to Britain's pride,*
> *Once so faithful and so true,*
> *On the deck of fame that died*
> *With the gallant, good Riou.*

Captain Edward Riou.

CHAPTER FIVE

'EVERY HARDSHIP FATIGUE AND HUNGER COULD INFLICT'

Whereas time has seen the fading of the name of Edward Riou, another of Cook's midshipmen, George Vancouver, remains proud upon the map despite the malignant efforts of one of Riou's midshipmen, Thomas Pitt.

The life of George Vancouver was visited by great sweeps of glorious fortune liberally sprinkled by rotten luck. His good fortune took effect early when the connexions nurtured by his father – a Kings Lynn customs official – led to the fourteen-year-old Vancouver being appointed to HMS *Resolution* in January 1772. Under the critical eye of Captain Cook, Vancouver learned the demanding skills of an able seaman whilst retaining the privileges of a 'young gentleman'. He was described by one of the ship's midshipmen as a 'Quiet inoffensive young man' and proved adept at learning to manage the sails, steer the ship, and use small arms. His bad luck emerged when, after scrambling to reach the end of the *Resolution's* jib-boom to proclaim himself the most southerly man in the world, his moment was soured by the ship's Swedish botanist, Andreas Sparrman, who claimed to have been in his cabin at the *Resolution's* stern and, as the vessel swung round to head northwards, had found himself fractionally further south than Vancouver.

When, in July 1776, Cook sailed once again for the Pacific and the search for a western entrance to a north-west passage, Vancouver was appointed to HMS *Adventure*, Cook's accompanying ship commanded by Captain Charles Clerk. He entered as an able seaman but, shortly after sailing, was advanced to midshipman as a result of completing three years of training. On Friday 13 February 1779 – the day before Cook's murder at the hands of the natives – Vancouver was in a boat pursuing natives who had stolen some items from the *Discovery* when the boat ran aground. At this moment the boat and its occupants came under a stone-throwing attack by natives. The *Discovery*'s master, Thomas Edgar jumped out of the boat in an effort to push it clear when a native ran at him swinging a broken oar. Unaware of the threat, Vancouver, stepped out of the boat to help Edgar and 'received the blow, which took him on the side and knocked him down.'

Twelve days after the return from his second voyage around the world, Vancouver took and passed the examination for lieutenant. Two months later he was sent to the West Indies where he took part in the capture of a Spanish ship, but missed Rodney's engagement at the Battle of the Saintes. He returned to England in June 1783 and had to endure eighteen months on half-pay before returning, once again, to the West Indies. Whilst in Jamaica, Vancouver was ordered to carry out a survey of the harbours of Port Royal and Kingston. His training under Cook proved to have held good and, when the charts were printed and first used, they were considered to be 'very correct'.

Vancouver left the West Indies for home in 1789. He had advanced to be the first lieutenant of the station's flagship, HMS *Europa*, and had earned the respect of the commander-in-chief, Commodore Sir Alan Gardner.

As a result of the work done by Cook and other voyagers to the south, the whaling industry in that part of the world had expanded rapidly and a need for bases from which the whalers could operate had arisen. It was decided by the government that an expedition should be raised to explore the region. On completion of its work in the South Pacific, the expedition was then to sail northwards to carry out a survey of the north-west coast of America – the area that Cook had sailed past in his attempt to find a western entrance to the Polar Sea. Gardner, by now occupying a seat on the Admiralty Board, suggested to the Earl of Chatham – the First Lord of the Admiralty – that Vancouver might be found an appointment on the expedition. Accordingly, Vancouver entered a newly-built HMS *Discovery* as first lieutenant under the command of Captain Henry Roberts (who had also served under Cook) on 6 January 1790. They were to be accompanied on their voyage by HMS *Chatham* and the two ships spent the next two months being fitted out and provisioned for the great adventure that lay ahead of them.

But it was not to be. Cook's voyages had not only led to the creation of the southern whale fishery, but also to the wealth of fur-bearing animals to be found on America's north-west coast. This information had led to a number of commercial enterprises (some led by officers who had served under Cook) to Nootka Sound with the intention of setting up a base from which to start a trade in sea-otter furs. The situation was further complicated by the fact that the Spanish had visited Nootka Sound four years before Cook, but had not landed. Cook, on the other hand, had landed, raised the British flag, and claimed the area for the British crown. In addition, both the British and the Spanish were concerned that the Russians were slowly extending their territory eastwards, towards Alaska. The Spanish – who considered the entire pacific coast of the Americas to be their private domain – had responded to the attempt to set up a fur-trading station at Nootka Sound by sending ships from Mexico. On arrival at the sound, the Spanish captain, Esteban Jose Martinez, set about building a fort. The work had hardly begun when three British trading ships sailed into the sound under the command of one of Cook's *Resolution* officers, Captain James Colnett. Martinez, instead of simply ordering the British back to sea, arrested Colnett and his ships and sent them as prisoners to Mexico.

Once news of Martinez's action reached the British government they mobilized a large fleet (the 'Spanish Armament') and cancelled the *Discovery*'s voyage to the Pacific. Vancouver was re-appointed to HMS *Courageux* under the command of Gardner who had surrendered his Admiralty position to get into the forthcoming conflict. After five months of energetic gesturing by the British, and with a lack of assistance from the revolutionary French, the Spanish retreated from their insistence that the eastern Pacific was their sole territory and allowed Britain the freedom of exploration along the coast of north-west America anywhere to the north of the point where Spain had already established posts. Unfortunately, this northern limit was not clearly defined and may have even included Nootka Sound itself. Furthermore, the Spanish agreed that the territory in Nootka Sound claimed to have been established by the fur-traders before Martinez's arrival would be restored, although the extent of this claim was vague in the extreme.

With the signing of the Nootka Convention, the government's eyes once again rested upon the north-west coast of America. The lands in Nootka Sound would have to be received from the Spanish by someone representing the government and the area firmly secured by a British presence. The obvious choice was the expedition under Captain Roberts that had been cancelled at the outbreak of the Spanish threat. The *Discovery* and the *Chatham* had been used during the alarm as 'receiving' ships to hold men taken up by the press gangs and Roberts had remained in command throughout.

Captain George Vancouver.

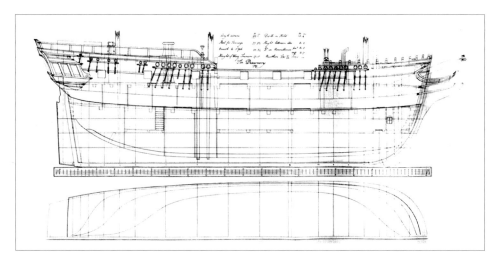

Sheer plan of HMS Discovery.

Vancouver was ordered to the Admiralty on 20 November 1790. He was told, no doubt to his great delight, that he was to be promoted to master and commander and to have command of the *Discovery*, as Captain Roberts was to be appointed to another ship. He was also, at the age of thirty-two, to be in command of the expedition.

As was the custom at the time, Vancouver was able to select the officers who were to serve with him. He chose his three lieutenants from officers who had served with him in the *Europa*. The first lieutenant was to be Zachary Mudge. Just twenty years old, Mudge had convinced the lieutenant's examining board that he was older than he really was and had passed his examination the year before. He had been in the service since the age of ten and was a protégé of Admiral Sir John Jervis (later Earl St. Vincent). Lieutenant Peter Puget had entered the service at the age of twelve years and had seen service in the West Indies, Mediterranean, and on the India Station. The third lieutenant was Joseph Baker. For his sailing master, Vancouver chose Joseph Whidbey who had been his companion during his surveys of Jamaican harbours and had served alongside him in the *Courageaux*. The command of the *Chatham* went to twenty-eight-year-old Lieutenant William Broughton who had been taken prisoner during the American War of Independence, had been present at several notable engagements off India under Admiral Hughes, and was serving on-board HMS *Victory* during the Spanish Armament. His first lieutenant was to be the recently promoted James Hanson. The sailing master of the *Chatham* was James Johnstone, an experienced seaman who had served under Captain Colnett in the Pacific and on the north-west coast of America. He had also served with the expedition's botanist, Archibald Menzies. Menzies had been a naval surgeon and had expected to join the expedition as the *Discovery*'s surgeon, but Vancouver was wary of Menzies sponsor – none other than Sir Joseph Banks. He was well aware of the problems caused to Cook by Banks before the start of Cook's second voyage and, already, Banks had made his influence felt by arranging to have a twelve by eight foot glass frame built on the *Discovery*'s quarterdeck. Menzies was clearly Bank's man and so, in order to reduce his effect upon the voyage, Vancouver appointed Dr Alexander Cranstoun as the surgeon of the *Discovery*. Dr William Walker was appointed as surgeon of the *Chatham*. A lieutenant of marines was carried in the *Discovery*, along with a corporal and fourteen privates.

Discovery's complement allowed for six midshipmen and three master's mates. However, a further six 'young gentlemen' were carried as able seamen to serve under Vancouver in the same capacity as he had served under Cook. The qualification for such young men to enter a ship rested, in general, in the 'interest' and connexions they had. One to enter the *Discovery* was the son of an earl; another the friend of a Marquis; two were nephews of Vancouver's old captain, Sir Alan Gardner; and another was the son of Vancouver's Navy agent (who looked after his financial affairs during his absence). The best connected among them all, however, was the Honourable Thomas Pitt, the son of Lord Camelford, cousin to the Prime Minister and to the First Lord of the Admiralty. During his time with Vancouver, his sister was to marry the First Lord and he was to succeed to the title of Lord Camelford on the death of his father. Through the influence of another cousin, Captain (later Admiral Sir) Sidney Smith, Pitt had been appointed to the HMS *Guardian* under Edward Riou. Despite having survived the perils of the *Guardian*'s collision with the iceberg, and having remained with the ship until its running ashore at the Cape, Riou was later to refuse to sign Camelford's recommendation for promotion to lieutenant as 'his conduct was such as not to entitle him to it.' At the other end of the social scale was Edward Roberts who had been recommended to Vancouver by William Wales, Cook's astronomer on his second voyage. The captain, probably with his midshipman's mess full to overflowing, packed Roberts off to live with the seamen.

The ship's company of the *Discovery* numbered 100 (including a 'widow's man' – a non-existent seaman borne on the ship's books whose pay could be used to provide an income for a widow's fund, despite the fact that the ship's gunner was the only married man on-board). The *Chatham* carried forty-five officers and men. There was one passenger, a native of Hawaii named Toworero, who – according to Vancouver – had not 'benefited by his residence in this country.'

The voyage did not have a very auspicious beginning. The *Chatham* was delayed in an attempt to improve her sailing qualities (her master, Johnstone, referred to her as a 'dung barge'); the *Discovery* lost a seaman overboard whilst making her way down the Channel and had much of her ship's head washed away requiring a visit to Portsmouth for repairs. At Falmouth, sixteen men deserted from the *Discovery* and five from the *Chatham*. Unusually, each of the ships lost a warrant officer. The *Discovery*'s boatswain failed to return to the ship and a close examination of the boatswain's stores exposed a number of deficiencies. The *Chatham* lost her carpenter who seems to simply have had second thoughts about the enterprise ahead. All had to be replaced before the voyage could continue.

The two ships finally left the shores of England in the early dawn of 1 April 1791, and set a course for Tenerife. On passage, Vancouver encountered weather that allowed him to test his chronometers, finding they 'agreed exceedingly well together.' He also learned exactly how slow and erratically the *Chatham* sailed and used the time waiting for her to catch up by washing his storerooms down with vinegar and 'smoking' the ship with a mixture of vinegar and gunpowder to get rid of pests.

On arrival at Santa Cruz, the capital of Tenerife, Vancouver took some of his officers with him – all but one wearing civilian clothing – to pay his respects to Senor Don Antonio Guitierres, the Governor General of the Canaries. The governor apologised for not being able to entertain the visitors for dinner as he had was extremely short of supplies and refused Vancouver's suggestion of an exchange of gunfire salutes on the ground that he did not have enough gunpowder. The party then went on to have dinner with a Mr Rooney – an Irish gentleman.

Before leaving for his official engagements, Vancouver had given permission for a number of men from both ships' companies to go ashore. At some stage an argument between *Discovery*'s midshipmen and members of *Chatham*'s ship's company led to a brawl breaking out. A Spanish soldier tried to intervene but had his musket wrenched from his hands and hurled into the water. He promptly left the scene in search of re-enforcements. Just at that moment, Vancouver and the officers arrived. The fighting was brought to an end and the officers were supervising the men getting into the ship's boats when the Spanish Guard arrived on the scene under the command of an officer who was determined to take prisoners. The Spanish soldiers promptly attacked the seamen who, putting aside their own differences, turned to defend themselves whilst Midshipman Pitt and others leapt into the water to escape. The master of the *Discovery* had a close escape when two Spanish soldiers ran at him with their muskets levelled. Trapped against a wall he stepped aside just in time to see the bayonets break on the bricks behind him. Lieutenant Baker, the only officer in uniform, was badly beaten about the head, several others received wounds. The greatest indignity, however, was reserved for Vancouver himself. He was grabbed by a number of Spaniards and, in the struggle, toppled off the wharf into the water to be rescued by one of *Chatham*'s boats. Heavily outnumbered, the officers ordered the boats to lay off in order to avoid being captured as the seamen retreated to the water's edge and jumped in to escape the well-armed soldiers.

Apart from a large number of cuts and bruises, the shore parties had seen a lucky escape. On returning to his ship Vancouver wrote a strongly-worded letter of complaint to the governor. In his reply, Senor Guitierres, announced that disciplinary action would be taken against the Guard, but pointed out that the fracas had been started by the seamen and that Vancouver and most of his officers had not been in uniform. Governor Guitierres was later to achieve his own small role in history when, in 1797, Santa Cruz was attacked by Nelson at the cost of his right arm. The governor was the first person to receive a letter – thanking him for the way he had treated British wounded seamen – to be written by Nelson using his left hand.

The voyage towards the Cape of Good Hope provided an easy passage, yet the head of the *Discovery* was still prone to damage and the ship's company's 'heads' (lavatories – or 'seats of ease' as the carpenter referred to them) were washed away. Another problem was the slow sailing rate of the *Chatham*. Eventually, the frustrated Vancouver signalled his consort that he would press on ahead and she was to follow as fast as she could. It was with some surprise therefore that, as they reached the Cape, they found the *Chatham* waiting for them having arrived the day before.

The five-week stay at the Cape was longer than Vancouver had intended. Worse, however, was the fact that the delay was long enough for them still to be in harbour when a Dutch merchantman arrived bearing dysentery. Soon other ships at the anchorage – including the *Discovery* and the *Chatham* – were infected. Vancouver sailed as early as he could in the hope that the disease could be shaken off but, before long, the symptoms of the disease began to show. The situation was made even worse when the surgeon, Cranstoun, suffered a stroke. Three weeks later both ships were in the grip of the dysentery and a marine, Private Neil Coyle, died as a result.

Before leaving the Cape, Vancouver had given instructions to Lieutenant Broughton that contained a list of rendezvous in case the ships should be separated. He also informed him of his own instructions regarding the events at Nootka Sound and the route he intended to take. He had also decided that he would have a close look at the position of two islands – Amsterdam and Saint Paul. Cook had fixed the island's position, but Lieutenant Bligh – reaching them in the *Bounty* – believed the position to be incorrect. Unfortunately for Vancouver, the *Discovery* and *Chatham* sailed between the islands without spotting either.

His next intention was to follow the leads given by Dutch ships in charting the coast of western New Holland (Australia). The Dutch had reported sightings of a coast but, seeing no commercial possibilities, had not stopped to chart or explore the lands they had sailed down.

High seas were met as they cruised eastwards from the Cape and a threat to the *Chatham* occurred when one of her stern windows was driven in by the sea during a powerful thunderstorm. An alarming amount of water flooded into the ship before the breach could be blocked whilst the *Discovery* failed to see her distress signals. On the *Discovery* herself, the light in the binnacle was blown out and Lieutenant Puget claimed to have been blinded for ten minutes as a result of the lightning.

Land was spotted on the evening of 23 September but could not be approached due to the weather. Three days later, in calmer seas, the land was seen once again, resembling, to many, the coast of Cornwall. A further two days brought them to a fine harbour which Vancouver named King George the Third's Sound (King George Sound) after displaying the national colours and drinking His Majesty's health.

Altogether, twelve days were spent anchored in the sound. Evidence of human habitation was discovered but no people were seen. Menzies, the botanist, rambled over the land collecting plants, black swans were spotted, and the ships watered. Vancouver, however, had no wish to stay for longer than necessary. He had already abandoned plans to find out whether or not Van Dieman's Land was an island and, on sailing, headed directly for New Zealand and Dusky Bay (Dusky Sound).

The voyage to Dusky Bay went without incident apart from the *Chatham* being in collision with a whale before Van Dieman's Land hove into sight. On arrival, however, they found themselves subjected to violent storms which threatened the safety of both ships. For a time the ships were separated, much to the distress of the midshipmen who looked upon the social events that took place between the young gentlemen as providing much welcomed breaks in the day-to-day routine.

After completing the survey work started by Cook, the ships sailed into a storm and were soon separated. Vancouver was not duly alarmed as Broughton was aware of the next point of rendezvous – Matavai Bay on Otaheite (Tahiti). A month after sailing, with still no sign of the *Chatham*, land was sighted. It turned out to be Rapa Island and the natives, shy at first, came out to greet the visitors in their canoes. Soon they had scrambled on-board and began to help themselves to anything that was not bolted down (after the foremost among them had rubbed noses with Vancouver). They appeared to have no understanding of weight and became very frustrated at their inability to make off with the blacksmith's anvil or the ship's guns. Attempts were made to persuade Vancouver to land, but he remained off-shore deterred, according to some rumours, by the sight of hill-top fortifications that could have been constructed by the mutineers from the *Bounty* – he had no wish to be delayed by attempts to engage and capture Fletcher Christian and his fellow mutineers.

At this stage of the voyage Vancouver's relationship with his young gentlemen began to go seriously awry. One of the midshipmen, who had the responsibility for keeping the chronometers wound, fell foul of one of the lieutenants. As a result, the midshipman refused to continue with the duty. In consequence of this action, Vancouver called Able Seaman Edward Roberts on to the quarterdeck. This was the same Roberts whose recommendation by William Wales had failed to achieve him a place with the officers. He was, however, well educated and quite capable of undertaking the responsibility for the chronometers. Vancouver ordered him to take over the duties and to move in with the midshipmen. The young gentlemen, on the other hand, had other ideas and refused to admit Roberts to their mess. Vancouver's response to this insubordination was to tear down the canvas screens that separated the midshipmen's mess from the seamen.

Just over a week after leaving Rapa Island they arrived at Matavia Bay to find that they had been beaten, yet again, by the *Chatham*. Vancouver's consort had found an island of her own which Broughton had named *Chatham* Island in honour of the First Lord of the Admiralty. A landing had been made and John Sheriff, a master's mate, had volunteered to go and meet the natives that had come down to the beach. Cautious at first, the natives began to show hostile intent and tried to detain Sheriff. Shots were fired and one native was killed. After taking formal possession of the island in the name of the king, Broughton returned to his ship, naming the landing place Skirmish Bay.

Vancouver now prepared to make his fourth landing on Tahiti. He had been there on three previous occasions with Cook and, taking the example of his old captain, issued a set of orders to cover his ship's company's dealing with the natives. They could barter for any curiosities, but only in small amounts, only after the ship's trading requirements had been met, and not in a manner that would devalue the use of iron, or beads, etc. They could not deal with anything that would disturb the balance of arms that existed between the different islands. They should 'cultivate a friendship with the different indians, and on all occasions treat them with every degree of kindness and humanity'. Any arms or tools that were lost by carelessness to the natives would be charged to the individual concerned and anyone found trading in any of the ship's stores would be disrated and would suffer any other punishment thought appropriate. A separate order was issued, no doubt bearing in mind the experiences of Lieutenant Bligh and the men of the *Bounty*. Only officers, the sick and those on duty were allowed ashore.

Among those frustrated by the order forbidding shore leave were the midshipmen, led in their discontent by Master's Mate the Honourable Thomas Pitt. Whilst in Dusky Bay the midshipmen had taken an old hen coop and bent it into a shape that would serve as a barbecue for use on beach parties. This item happened to be at hand when an attractive young native woman, who had gone alongside the *Discovery* in a canoe, suggested to Pitt that he might be able to share in her favours in return for a small gift. The master's mate promptly handed her the iron griddle and was spotted in doing so. Vancouver ordered him to 'kiss the gunner's daughter' – that is, to be taken to the great cabin, tied down over a cannon barrel, and to be given twenty-four strokes with a cane in the presence of the other young gentlemen. After Pitt had received twelve strokes, the first lieutenant, Zachary Mudge, stepped forward and offered to speak to the captain on his behalf if he promised to behave better in the future. Pitt replied that he did not want to be 'begged off' and suffered the final twelve strokes. Shortly afterwards, a drunken midshipman, the Honourable Charles Stuart, approached Vancouver, produced a cut-throat razor from his waistcoat pocket, and waved it under the captain's nose with the words, 'If Sir, you ever flog me, I will not survive the disgrace. I have this ready to cut my throat with.' Stuart spent much of the remaining voyage at the masthead where Vancouver lost no opportunity to send him for even the most trifling offence.

Events off the ship, however, went reasonably well until the third week of their stay. The natives had been granted the job of washing the officers' clothing and, before long, shirts began to disappear in large numbers. The *Chatham*, in particular, began to suffer. The master lost several shirts; the surgeon, six; and the captain, twelve. As bad, or even worse, was the loss of four axes that Vancouver had loaned to native chiefs for the cutting down of wood for the ships. Three were returned upon his demand, but the fourth remained hidden away. Finally, Toworero, the native due to be returned to Hawaii, absconded with the daughter of a chief whilst taking with him the personal property of one of the ship's gunners. Unless these problems were sorted out, Vancouver threatened to burn down the native villages and destroy all their canoes. This threat resulted in the retrieval of the missing axe and the return of Toworero along with boat loads of fresh fruit in compensation. Toworero's punishment was to be ejected from the gunner's mess, and to be left to fend for himself among the seamen. The missing shirts were never recovered, so Vancouver cancelled a promised firework display, much to the distress of the natives.

Vancouver also continued to cause distress among his midshipmen. They had been given six pigs by the natives and were, no doubt, looking forward to enjoying fresh pork over the coming weeks. The captain, however, had other ideas and confiscated the animals, had them killed, and served them out to the entire ship's company, thus saving a day's rations.

The ships sailed from Otaheite on 24 January 1792, and reached the Sandwich Islands (Hawaii) on 1 March. A pause was made off Karakakooa (Kealaekua Bay) in memory of Cook's death on its beach before the ships were surrounded by scores of canoes bearing pigs, salt, and fresh fruit to trade with the newcomers. Soon contact was made with the local chief who offered to take Towerero into his service. In exchange, Vancouver agreed to take on-board a young Hawaiian named Tarehooa. Having already visited the north-west coast of America, Tarehooa (who much preferred to be called 'Jack') had served on an American ship as an interpreter and Vancouver felt that he had 'a probability of being made useful.'

The stay lasted only a few days and Vancouver moved his ships first to Waikiki Bay on Wahoo (Oahu) and then to the island of Attowai (Kauai) where the local prince was noted as answering only to the title 'King George'.

Whilst hunting duck on Attowai, Vancouver displayed an irrational streak that caused consternation among his officers. A number of large fires were seen burning on the surrounding hills and Vancouver took these to mean that they were about to come under attack by the natives. Despite being assured by the botanist, Menzies, and others that the fires were merely lit to burn off the old grass, Vancouver demanded an immediate return to the ships. The *Discovery's* pinnace was waiting off shore and Vancouver, disregarding the heavy surf that was pounding the beach, insisted on getting into a native canoe and ordering it to take him and the officers out to the pinnace. The canoe had not gone far when it was overturned and two midshipmen were nearly drowned. Vancouver, believing the incident to be an attempt upon his life, ignored pleas to return to the canoe and swam out to the pinnace. The following day, Vancouver was visited by local chiefs who put his mind at rest – there had been no threat against him or any of his ship's company. To the delight of the natives he made amends by providing a firework display.

The two ships sailed from the Sandwich Islands on 16 March 1792, and were soon heading north-eastwards towards the coast of America. It was not a particularly happy voyage despite reasonable weather. The foretopgallant yard was damaged and when brought to the deck was found to be beyond repair. The *Discovery's* carpenter, Henry Phillips, was ordered to manufacture a replacement. When the new yard was completed, Vancouver inspected it and found it not to be 'agreeable'. Something about the captain's attitude towards his workmanship triggered off an abusive response from the carpenter which resulted in Vancouver ordering him to be confined in his cabin as a prisoner awaiting court martial. Midshipman Pitt probably did nothing to help the captain's temper when, whilst 'romping' with another midshipman, he broke the glass protecting the binnacle compass. This action earned the midshipman another flogging over the barrel of a cannon. He was to earn yet another public beating for an un-recorded offence later in the voyage.

The coast of America was reached on 17 April at a point, some 115 miles north of San Francisco Bay, named Cape Cabrillo. Turning northwards the ships passed Cape Mendocino and headed along the coast. At Cape Orford (Cape Blanco) they came to anchor and a number of canoes appeared bearing natives who were eager to trade. Vancouver noted how difficult it was to give them presents as they insisted on exchanging the gift for an item of clothing.

Three days later he arrived at Deception Bay, so-named by one of Cook's former officers, Lieutenant Meares, whilst trading for furs in the area. To Vancouver, the bay was well named. Although it had the appearance of the outlet of a large river, a line a breakers around its edge clearly showed there was no passageway for his ships. So 'not considering this opening worthy of more attention' Vancouver continued northwards towards the Strait of Juan de Fuca. The straits had earned their name through a story told by an Englishman, Michael Loc, who, in 1596, claimed to have met a man named Juan de Fuca who had described to him a voyage he had made up the western coast of America. At 47 degrees north he had found a wide strait which led in a north-eastern direction. The strait had been entered and was found to widen as it proceeded. On the shore, men were seen wearing furs. After twenty days sailing beyond the straits, de Fuca returned to the entrance having 'well discharged his office.' In 1787, a British merchantman under the command of Captain Charles Barkley came across a wide inlet that appeared to head in a north-easterly direction. Convinced that this was the straits described by de Fuca, Barkley named the entrance 'Straits of Juan de Fuca' and so it appeared on subsequent maps. Vancouver had been told by the Admiralty before his departure that an American sloop, the *Washington*, had entered the straits in 1789 and had emerged further along the coast, north of Nootka Sound. His orders included an authorisation to survey the straits to see if it led, as de Fuca had suggested, to the north – perhaps even as far as the Polar Sea.

On 29 April 'a very great novelty' occurred. A ship was spotted standing inshore. Vancouver's astonishment was even greater when Lieutenant Puget and Menzies returned from the ship (named *Columbia*) with the news that the captain, Robert Grey had been the captain of the *Washington*, the ship that was supposed to have entered the Straits of Juan de Fuca. What was more, the captain denied the exploit accorded to him and told his visitors that he had only penetrated fifty miles up the straits. The reason behind the mis-information was that Grey had met Meares whilst undertaking the same fur-trade. Meares had boasted that he had secured a great haul of sea-otter skins. The American, not to be outdone and 'knowing the North West passage to be the Hobby horse of his opponent in Commerce, reports his discovery of it…dressed up in language with a chart…that points out the track of the Vessel with fanciful precision.' Nonetheless, Grey warned Vancouver to be on his guard with the Indians. A native of Hawaii on the *Columbia* had made an agreement with the Indians that he would dampen the gun-powder in loaded fire-arms that were kept ready in case of native attack. The plan, however, was discovered and the assault foiled.

Led by the *Chatham*, the ships rounded Cape Flattery and entered the Straits of Juan de Fuca, making their way along its southern shore. After seventy miles Vancouver dropped anchor in a wide bay (Discovery Bay). From this point he decided that the only way to avoid missing a possible route to the north would be to examine every foot of the shore line. And the only way to carry out such a survey was to send the ship's boats where the ship itself could not go. On 7 May 1792, five boats, led by Vancouver in the *Discovery's* pinnace set off for the rocky shore.

After travelling a few miles to the east the party came across a large inlet (Admiralty Inlet) which led, in turn, to a complex series of waterways. Returning to the *Discovery*, Vancouver sent the *Chatham* north to look at a group of islands (the San Juan Islands) whilst he took the *Discovery* into Admiralty Inlet. An inlet to the south-west was named Hood's Canal and the waterway on which the *Discovery* was continually heading south was named Puget Sound after the ship's first lieutenant. On 19 May the *Discovery* anchored off a point of land on the western side of Puget Sound and fired a seventeen-gun salute to commemorate the restoration to the British crown of Charles II in 1660. The land to the west was named Restoration Point.

From the time of anchoring in Discovery Bay, contact had been made with the local native peoples. Vancouver had been horrified to find that the natives were not only keen to trade in bows, arrows, and clothing (many of which were later to end up in the British Museum), but were also eager to sell their children. Human heads were found rammed onto pointed stakes and the native dwellings gave off a stench that Puget described as 'intolerable'.

Almost as intolerable was the fact that a supply ship, *Daedalus*, which was expected to be found waiting in the area, had not been seen and Vancouver was forced to reduce rations by a third.

The *Chatham* joined *Discovery* at Restoration Point and was sent by Vancouver to investigate a wide inlet that branched north-eastwards from northern Puget Sound whilst he, Whidbey and Puget surveyed to the south.

The boats were armed with small swivel guns and Puget was forced to fire one of them in a demonstration against natives who had all the appearances of turning hostile. He was astonished to find that the loud report of the gun had no affect whatsoever on the natives who only turned friendly when they discovered that Puget had more men with him than they had originally thought.

Vancouver, in the meantime, had come across a group of friendly natives, two of whom joined his party as they were about to eat venison. The natives looked at the meat closely, and then reacted with expressions of horror and disgust. It took considerable work by Vancouver to persuade his guests that the meat was not human flesh and that he and his party were not cannibals.

With the waterways at the bottom of Puget Sound surveyed, Vancouver returned to the *Discovery* and followed northwards in the track of the *Chatham*. A lamp shining from her masthead fixed the *Chatham*'s position in a wide sound and the ships settled down for the night. The following day the *Chatham* led the ships up the sound only to find herself run aground in the afternoon. The grounding came about because a seaman, David Dorman, instead of taking soundings as he had been ordered, had simply made them up and mislead the officer of the watch. Dorman was awarded three dozen lashes for his carelessness and the opportunity was taken to repair the *Chatham*'s copper sheathing which had been damaged by her anchor.

Vancouver spent two weeks surveying the area and, on 4 June, gave his ships' companies a double ration of rum to drink the king's health as he went ashore to formally take possession of the lands and waters in the king's name. He named the waterway Possession Sound and the island to the west Whidbey Island (the *Discovery*'s master, whilst exploring the island's coast, had been forced to bare his chest to convince the natives that he had not painted his face and hands white).

The following day Vancouver left the sound and, passing though Admiralty Inlet, headed northwards into the island-speckled waters he had named Gulf of Georgia (Strait of Georgia). The ships anchored off an island named by Vancouver Cypress

Island after the large number of trees of that type that could be seen on its shores. During this operation the *Chatham* lost one of her anchors and, when Broughton reported this fact to Vancouver, he was rewarded by having a request for oil with which to make yellow paint being refused. This resulted in the *Chatham* having one side painted yellow, the other black.

The anchorage provided little in the way of victuals ('a few wild onions and leeks') so Vancouver continued his way north until he found a bay where the botanist, Menzies noted a large number of black birch trees. In consequence the bay was named Birch Bay and Vancouver decided to establish a base on its shores for continuing his exploration of the coast by boat.

Sending Whidbey south to link up with the earlier boat explorations Vancouver left the *Discovery* at four in the morning in the ship's yawl accompanied by Lieutenant Puget in the launch. After surveying the coast of a large bay they arrived at its northern arm which Vancouver named 'Point Roberts' after his 'esteemed friend and predecessor in the *Discovery*'. North-west from this point, shoaling waters prevented the boats from closing with the coastline but Vancouver could make out 'two openings' through the low-lying land. These, he considered, could 'only be navigable by canoes'.

Further to the north, around Point Grey (named after 'my friend Captain George Grey of the Royal Navy') the boats sailed into a wide inlet where native Indians came alongside in canoes and traded fish and their weapons for any objects of iron. Finding nowhere to pitch their tents, the majority of the crews spent the night sleeping on the boats. The midshipmen, on the other hand, decided to sleep on a stony beach and were rewarded by a soaking from the incoming tide for their trouble.

The following day, having decided that the waterway was unfit for shipping, Vancouver crossed to the northern side of the inlet where snow-covered mountains reached down to the water. The inlet was given the name 'Burrard's Channel' (Burrard Inlet) in honour of one of Vancouver's friends from his days on HMS *Europa*. On leaving the inlet, the boats were aided by a strong southerly wind up a passage (Howe Sound) lined on its south-east shore by tall mountains down which thundered mighty waterfalls of melted snow. A break in the gloomy weather allowed a sighting to be taken off Anvil Island before Vancouver proceeded up an easterly-tending arm where a camp was made. Once again contact was made with the Indians and more trade carried out.

For the next two days, Vancouver sailed his boats further up the eastern coast of the Strait of Georgia to a point well over a hundred miles from his ships. With his rations running low, despite obtaining fish from the natives and the occasional bird brought down by the officer's muskets, he had little choice but to make his way back. On the way south he probed into an inlet he named Jervis Channel (Jervis Inlet) only to find it to be yet another dead end. Whilst up the inlet, Puget joined

Vancouver in the yawl leaving the launch under the command of Thomas Manby, a master's mate from the *Discovery*. Unfortunately, the boats became separated as they left the inlet and Manby and his crew were left to make their own way back to the ships without rations or compass, thus suffering 'every hardship fatigue and hunger could inflict.'

As Vancouver approached Point Grey on Friday 22 June 1792, (Vancouver's 35th birthday) he was surprised to see two large sailing vessels a short way off the point. At first he took them to be the *Discovery* and the *Chatham* but then saw that they were flying Spanish colours. The brig *Sutil* and the schooner *Mexicana* had been sent to survey the coasts in much the same manner as Vancouver had been ordered.

Given a civil welcome by the Spaniards, Vancouver learned that they had already spoken to Broughton and Whidbey on-board the *Chatham*. He also learned, much to his disappointment, that the Spaniards had surveyed the entire length of the Strait of Georgia. His hosts went on to inform him that Senor Juan Francisco de la Bodega Y Quadra, the Spanish commander-in-chief on the west coast of America was waiting for him at Nootka Sound. The two sides came to an agreement that, as they proceeded north on their way to meet Quadra, they would operate together in carrying out further surveys.

The haul from Cape Grey to Birch Island had to be done in the face of a stiff south wind and incessant rain. Vancouver and his boat's crew were exhausted on arrival. The first to feel the brunt of Vancouver's tiredness was Manby who was roundly abused in a 'language I will never forgive' for loosing sight of the yawl.

To cheers from all vessels, the four ships joined up and sailed northwards, passing – in Vancouver's case for the third time – the low area between Point Roberts and Point Grey with its shoaling waters and two shallow exits. The combined flotilla passed through a narrow channel (Malaspina Strait) and anchored at the entrance to a waterway Vancouver named Desolation Sound. More boat surveys were carried out with Puget and Whidbey probing into an east-tending waterway (Toba Inlet) and James Johnstone, the master of the *Chatham*, sailing northwards to test the continental shore. Vancouver had been at pains to persuade the Spanish to survey the islands to the west whilst his boats explored the eastern coastline in an effort to find any inlet that could link him to the north. This almost led to conflict when Puget entered his inlet only to find a Spanish boat on its way out. The Spaniards told Puget that they had surveyed the inlet's entire length and had found it closed off. Puget, nevertheless, proceeded with his own survey, an action that led to the Spaniards complaining to Vancouver that his men were not treating their allies with 'the greatest confidence'. Vancouver managed to control the issue by replying that his orders insisted that he 'saw it all for himself'.

Johnstone, in the meantime, after surveying another eastern channel (Bute Inlet) discovered a rapid tidal flow coming from the north. Shortage of provisions forced him to return but he set off again immediately to push his survey even further. At a distance of about one hundred miles from the ships, Johnstone found himself with a clear view of a wide waterway (Queen Charlotte Strait) that was clearly an arm of the sea. To the south of him, Puget had rounded a point of land (Cape Mudge) and found a channel heading northward (Discovery Passage). With all the boats safely back on board, Vancouver bid farewell to his Spanish allies (who continued northwards in the track of Johnstone), rounded Cape Mudge, passed through Discovery Passage and the newly named Johnstone Strait, to enter Queen Charlotte Strait. The grand procession was marred somewhat when the *Discovery* ran aground in fog and was left on her side when the tide retreated. Fortunately, the ship lifted off with the returning tide – only to see *Chatham* go aground. This second grounding, however, was not so severe and the *Chatham* soon broke free. Whilst the *Discovery* was aground a rope parted and a seaman, John Turner, broke his arm. It was never to mend properly and prevented Turner from fully carrying out his work. As a result Vancouver later awarded him twenty-four lashes with a cat-of-nine-tails for 'neglect of duty'.

The fog caused Vancouver to miss a number of deep inlets that entered the northern side of the strait before he arrived at Port Safety, a steep-sided inlet on the east coast of Calvert Island (Vancouver was to change the name of the inlet to 'Safety Cove'). Again the ship's boats were sent out in cold rain and fog. To the south, Smith Sound; to the east, Rivers inlet; and to the north-east, Burke Channel; were all surveyed by boat crews described by the botanist, Menzies, as being of 'persevering intrepidity and manly steadiness.'

A week later an English brig, the *Venus* appeared at the entrance to the cove. She was on a commercial expedition in the search for sea-otter skins, but her captain had news for Vancouver. Quadra was waiting impatiently at Nootka Sound and the expedition's supply vessel, HMS *Daedalus*, had arrived. This was excellent news for Vancouver. He had been hoping for the *Daedalus* arrival before he met Quadra in case she carried further instructions for his meeting with the Spaniards. There was also news of a tragedy. The commander of the supply ship, Lieutenant Richard

Discovery on the rocks in Queen Charlotte's Strait.

Hergest; William Gooch, an astronomer intended to join the expedition; and a seamen, had been murdered by natives on the Sandwich Islands. Hergest's death was a particular blow to Vancouver as he had been a close friend who had served with Cook on the *Resolution*. Two days later, the *Discovery* and the *Chatham*, sailed for Nootka Sound.

Following a journey hampered by fog which caused the ships to separate, the *Chatham* – true to form – arrived at Nootka ahead of the *Discovery*. There she found the Spanish brig *Activa* flying Quadra's broad pennant. Vancouver arrived a few hours later. In passing Cape Scott, to the north of Nootka Sound, Vancouver became the first person to circumnavigate the large island that lay off the mainland. He had done it in two parts, the western coast with Cook, and the eastern at the head of his own expedition. Three days after his arrival, the Spanish ships *Sutil* and *Mexicana* sailed into the sound – the first vessels to do the circumnavigation in a single voyage.

Once the formalities of gun-salutes and introductory dinners were out of the way, Vancouver and Quadra set about the problems of returning the possessions which had been in British hands before they had been seized by the Spanish in April 1789. Despite Quadra proving to be friendly man who warmed to Vancouver, serious problems blocked the way to smooth agreement. Not only was the right to the assumed possessions challenged by the Spanish, they also intended to set up a base at the entrance to Juan de Fuca Strait. Vancouver had no instructions in how to deal with these matters, and none had arrived in the *Daedalus*. Matters were not helped by the fact that the only person who had any expertise in the other side's language was one of Quadra's servants. But, whilst he could manage a number of words in English, he could not read or write in the language. Eventually, it was discovered that Midshipman Thomas Dolby, who had arrived in the *Daedalus,* had a tolerable command of both written and spoken Spanish. Vancouver had him transferred to the *Discovery*. He also put Lieutenant James Hanson of the *Chatham* in command of the *Daedalus* and promoted James Johnstone, the master of the *Chatham*, to lieutenant in place of Hanson. One of *Discovery's* master's mates, Spelman Swaine was promoted to be the *Chatham's* master.

The talks dragged on for three weeks with no side being able to act as their orders intended. It became clear that the only answer was to refer the matter to the British and Spanish governments. Before this was done, the two leaders decided that the island on which Nootka Sound was situated, and which had been so recently circumnavigated for the first time, should be named 'Quadra and Vancouver Island' (Vancouver Island).

There were more changes to be made among the ships' companies before the *Daedalus* left for Port Jackson. The health of Alexander Cranstoun, *Discovery's* surgeon, had broken down and he was transferred to the store-ship for the voyage home. He was joined in her by the boatswain of the *Discovery*, William House, and the carpenter, Henry Phillips, on his way to a court martial as a result of his insolence towards his captain. Puget and Baker were advanced to be first and second lieutenants of the *Discovery*, and Swaine promoted to be third lieutenant. Thomas Manby was now appointed as master of the *Chatham*. These latter changes came about as a result of Lieutenant Mudge being sent home by Vancouver with letters and charts to inform the government of the latest situation. Mudge sailed in a Portuguese vessel for China on 30 September 1792, armed with a letter requesting the aid of the East India Co. in getting him back to England.

Vancouver sailed south from Nootka Sound on 12 October, and arrived at Deception Bay where, in April, he had been prevented by breakers from entering a large river that was supposed to meet the sea at that point. Both ships now attempted to cross the bar, but only the *Chatham* was successful, the *Discovery*, with her deeper draught, being forced to retreat. To his surprise Broughton found a small English trading vessel, the *Jenny*, anchored in a bay on the south side of what was clearly the entrance to a wide river. Coming to anchor, Broughton took the ship's cutter and launch more than a hundred miles up the river, naming his furthest limit Point Vancouver and a nearby site Possession Point after he had taken formal possession of the land in the name of the king. He named the waterway as 'River Oregon' (Columbia River).

Meanwhile, the *Discovery* had pressed on southwards and suffered both gales and an outbreak of scurvy before she entered San Francisco. Vancouver and his ship's company were offered the hospitality of the Spanish settlers and the officers were loaned horses and a bodyguard for a ride to a Christian Mission south-east of San Francisco. On arrival all the naval officers were limping painfully and Lieutenants Baker and Johnstone promptly took to their beds. They had been ill-informed that the journey was to be eighteen miles – it actually turned out to be eighteen leagues (fifty-four miles).

Eight days after the arrival of the *Discovery*, Chatham sailed into the harbour and took on-board the first fresh greens since they had left the Cape of Good Hope, 'a matter that gave the Jacks no small satisfaction.' Both ships sailed for Monterey three days later, arriving on the following day.

Among the ships at Monterey was the *Daedalus*, already being warmly entertained by Senor Quadra. The storeship was given orders to proceed to Port Jackson via Tahiti and New Zealand taking with them cattle and sheep provided by the Spanish to help the colonists of New South Wales. Lieutenant Hanson was then ordered to take the *Daedalus* to Nootka Sound the following autumn to replenish Vancouver's ships. The *Discovery* and the *Chatham* were themselves delayed for almost three weeks by a fruitless search for two deserters from the *Chatham* and did not sail until 15 January 1793. Puget was placed in temporary command of the *Chatham*. Her commander, Lieutenant Broughton, with an American-born able seamen, John Campbell, as his servant, was to take passage on a Spanish ship in order to carry letters and charts home to England, and to return with further 'guidance' for Vancouver.

During the wintering at the Sandwich Islands, Vancouver was called upon to use his political skills during a lull in fighting between the islands, noting with regret that the introduction of fire-arms to the natives accounted for much of the hostilities. He also tried to persuade the king of Hawaii to cede the island to Great Britain. In this he failed, but did manage to have the murderers of Hergest, Gooch and the seaman, tried and executed.

The *Chatham* had scraped against some rocks in her departure from Nootka Sound and native Hawaiian divers discovered that there was considerable damage to the false keel and to the copper sheathing. The tidal range at the Sandwich Islands was too small for the ship to be beached for repairs so Vancouver ordered Puget to return her to Nootka Sound where the damage could be repaired. Puget took just twenty-two days to reach land to the north of Nootka Sound. A gale forced him to seek shelter and the *Chatham* narrowly escaped destruction as Puget found himself being driven by a tidal race through an opening 100ft wide. An anchor was lost as he tried to control the headlong race and his starboard mainyard ripped branches from the trees lining the water's edge. It took two days before the tide relented enough to allow the ship to proceed on her way to Nootka.

After repairs to the hull and false keel, the *Chatham*, following Vancouver's orders, left Nootka to continue the boat surveys from the point where they had been broken off the year before.

Two days after the *Chatham* left the sound, *Discovery* sailed in after a 'long and tedious' voyage of fifty-two days. With such a loss of time, Vancouver was eager to catch up with Puget and, once the formalities had been carried out with the Spanish authorities, and with a few sightings taken to check the sound's longitude, he left Nootka and found the *Chatham* at the entrance to Burke Channel. The two ships moved up the channel a few miles to Restoration Bay and an observatory was set up ashore as the boat surveys got under way. The work was to be much the same as the previous year, but lessons had been learned. Now, instead of being completely exposed to the weather, the crews could be protected by awnings of painted canvas. Bags of the same material were supplied to the crews to keep their possessions dry as they rowed along the cold, wet, shores. Extra 'portable soup' was provided in order that they could have at least two hot meals a day. Additional food could be obtained off the land and bear, eagle, and mussels all added to the diet. The latter food, however, proved in the case of Johnstone's boat party, to be deadly. An American-born midshipman, Robert Barrie, and three seamen were poisoned by the molluscs and one of the seamen, twenty-four-year-old John Carter, died as a result. He was buried on the nearby shore and the place was given the name 'Carter Bay' in his memory. Nearby features were named 'Mussel Inlet' and 'Poisoned Cove'.

On the western coast of Revillagigedo Island, Vancouver found himself under attack by natives whose canoes fell upon his boat when he had become separated from Puget. In the stern of the canoes, old women sat and screamed encouragement to their Indian braves who pressed home their attack until Vancouver was forced to give the order to open fire. Vancouver's first instinct was to pursue the natives with the object of destroying their canoes but, as two of his seamen had been wounded, he decided that their needs were of greater importance.

Vancouver's ability to attract indifferent luck continued. On the night of 4 June 1793, his boats parties had camped at the entrance to Elcho Harbour, an inlet reaching north-westward from Dean Channel. Eighteen days later, Alexander Mackenzie painted on a rock close by the entrance the words 'Alexander Mackenzie, from Canada, by land, the twenty-second of July, one thousand seven hundred and ninety-three.' Mackenzie, on behalf of the North-West Co., had made the first crossing of North America north of Mexico. Vancouver was looking for a sea-route from the Atlantic to the Pacific; Mackenzie had found an overland route. Had they met, it would have been a meeting that would have echoed down in history. As it was, Mackenzie turned to make his way back overland, and Vancouver's seamen rowed him northwards.

By September, the *Discovery* and the *Chatham* had sailed north into Sumner Strait as it curves around the top of Prince of Wales Island only to find bad weather driving them into a shallow inlet Vancouver named Port Protection. This, it seemed to Vancouver, was the end of the exploring season for 1793. He had failed to find any waterway that would take him to the north to link up with the Polar Sea discovered by Hearn, and now the weather was clearly deteriorating. At 'Cape Decision' he turned southwards to return to Nootka Sound.

Between May and October Vancouver's surveys had covered little more than 300 miles of the North American coast, but the arduous task of entering every inlet, scouring every bay, and probing every channel had increased that distance many times. During one twenty-three-day expedition Vancouver had travelled over 700 miles, but had accounted for a mere sixty miles of coast.

On arrival at Nootka, Vancouver stayed for just three days before heading south. No letters containing instructions regarding the political problems surrounding the port had arrived for his guidance, and the store-ship *Daedalus* was not, as he had hoped, waiting at Friendly Cove.

The welcome at San Francisco was much more muted than at their last visit. Rumours had been circulating that Vancouver had plans to attack Monterey or San Diego. Shore leave was restricted to official calls, and the local commandant visited the ships at night to avoid giving the impression to his superiors that he was being over-friendly. From the number of guns being set up on the shore it was clear that the port's defences were being strengthened.

Right: *Map of Vancouver Island and the adjoining coast showing the complexity of Vancouver's survey.*

Far right: *Map of part of the coast of North America north of Vancouver Island, again illustrating the complexity of Vancouver's survey.*

The ships sailed after five days and, one day out, met the *Daedalus*. For a while the three vessels sailed in convoy, but bad weather forced the *Chatham* to separate. True to form, she arrived at Monterey ahead of the other two ships. Yet again it was a cold welcome that awaited Vancouver and his expedition. This time, however, he decided that the onus was no longer on him to try to maintain the good relations he had established and, much to the approval of his officers, refused to salute the local governor. Four days after they had arrived, the ships sailed out under the cover of darkness and headed for San Diego despite Vancouver being warned by the governor that he would not be welcome at that port.

After a brief call at Santa Barbara – where the local commandant proved to be friendly, even allowing the midshipmen an opportunity to go ashore – the ships arrived at San Diego. The commandant, although aware that he was supposed to place restrictions upon Vancouver, provided as much help as he could and offered to send dispatches to London on behalf of the expedition.

Vancouver intended to complete a survey of the coast south from San Diego and used a Spanish chart as he left the port. He soon found the chart to be a very poor representation of the coastline and took great pleasure in naming features that had remained un-named on the Spanish document after those Spaniards who had proved welcoming and helpful during his time in their company.

With his survey completed Vancouver arrived at Hawaii twenty-four days after he had left San Diego. At last he was able to transfer the stores the *Daedalus* had brought out and allow his ships' companies an opportunity to rest. When the transfer of stores was completed the *Daedalus* was to be sent back to New South Wales. Vancouver took the opportunity to rid himself of some of the problems that had constantly caused him difficulties since the beginning of his voyage. Chief amongst these was the well-connected Midshipman the Honourable Thomas Pitt, whose early canings had done little to improve his behaviour and attitude towards his captain. In addition to having been flogged on at least two occasions, Pitt had also been placed in irons

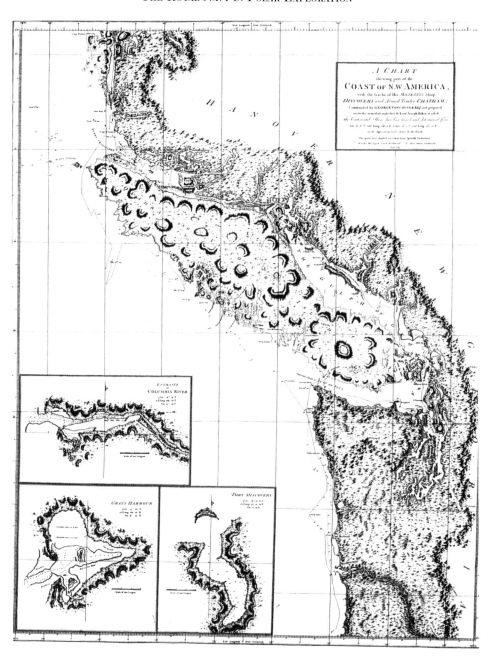

Vancouver's chart of Vancouver Island and the adjoining coast.

for sleeping on watch. Another midshipman, Augustus Boyd Grant of the *Chatham*, had also been flogged and had been 'excluded from the Society of Gentlemen'. Even worse, – according to Puget – he had taken up with 'one of the foremast people with whom he lived, and whose habits he had contracted in a most shameful Manner.' Another of the *Discovery*'s midshipmen, Thomas Clarke, had also been flogged for misbehaviour and joined Pitt and Grant in being sent home.

Even more important than ridding himself of a few undesirables, Vancouver pressed home his plan to take the Sandwich Islands under the protection of Great Britain. The king – Kamehameha – was persuaded that he should cede his lands to King George III who, in turn, would look after his new subjects. The treaty was signed in Vancouver's cabin on 25 February 1794, with both King George and his nation unaware that they had gained important new territories in the middle of the Pacific Ocean.

Vancouver returned to the coast of North America in early April – having been separated from the *Chatham* en route – and sailed north to reach Cook's River (Cook Inlet) on the 12th. He had been instructed to take his surveys to the 60th parallel, a line of limit that passed through his destination. Great hopes rested on the survey of the river as it was felt that the waterway was connected to a series of known lakes which could be used as a trade route. As he entered the river, Vancouver unknowingly passed the *Chatham* which had taken refuge in an inlet (Port Chatham) to escape bad weather and had remained there to carry out minor repairs and to take on wood and water.

Discovery's voyage northwards up the river was hazarded, not only by shoals and shallows, but by ice floes drifting south as a result of the spring break-up.
Before long, the *Discovery* had reached Cook's 'Turnagain River' and Whidbey was sent to survey its length taking ten days rations. In the event, the survey required only two days. 'Turnagain River' was nothing more than an eastern inlet of Cook's River, and Vancouver altered the charts to read 'Turnagain Arm'. With Whidbey's return Vancouver set out to survey the northern continuation of the river. This survey took even less time than the one carried out in Turnagain Arm. It did not require a full day to reach its end and Vancouver was forced to the conclusion that 'Cook's River' was, in fact, a deep inlet with no navigable link to the interior.

The following day the *Chatham* was discovered anchored close by. She had sailed northwards along the western shore and had visited a Russian trading post.

With the inlet offering no hope of a passage to the north, Vancouver left and headed south-east for Prince William Sound. The sound had been visited by Cook, but had only received a cursory examination as Cook had been keen to reach beyond the 65th parallel. With the *Discovery* in need of repairs, Vancouver anchored at Port Chalmers on Montague Island and sent Whidbey to survey from the south-west entrance of the sound (Cape Puget) to Cook's anchorage at Snug Corner Cove.

Johnstone was to survey from Snug Corner Cove to Kayak Island at the south-east entrance to the sound.

Whidbey's survey of the winding passages and scattered islands had been brightened by the discovery of a large number of glaciers that advanced towards the heads of the inlets, and the sight and sound of an avalanche which thundered down less than a hundred yards of the boat party's camp. By the time he returned to the *Discovery* after nineteen days, Whidbey had surveyed over 400 miles of coastline.

Johnstone had a more difficult time in his survey. At Port Fidalgo, east of Snug Corner Cove, he had an axe stolen by natives, an act which he responded to by making the men on watch at the time suffer extra watches. Continually troubled by rain and high winds, Johnstone came ashore (Orca Inlet) to find ten Russians living under an upturned skin boat. The Russians were not alone, and Johnstone and his party spent a nervous night with 200 natives in the very close vicinity. The following day it became clear to Johnstone that the proposed survey route would leave him exposed to the open seas. Consequently, he returned to the *Chatham* at Port Chalmers and Vancouver ordered Puget to continue the eastern survey using his ship. On completion he was to join the *Discovery* at Yakatut Bay. As usual, however, the *Chatham* arrived at the bay first.

On the *Discovery*'s eventual arrival, wind conditions made it impossible to enter the bay so she moved on to the next rendezvous, Cross Sound, arriving on 7 July. As she sailed down the coast a sail was seen which proved to be the trader *Jackal*. From her, Vancouver learned

> not only of the melancholy intelligence of the death of Louis XVI and of the anarchy which existed in France, but likewise her declaration of war against England, and of the attempts which the discontented were making in Great Britain, by the promulgation of French doctrines, to subvert our inestimable constitution.

The *Chatham* arrived at Cross Sound the day after the *Discovery* and no time was lost in sending Whidbey and Menzies to survey the northern shore. Ice proved to be a problem and the boats were continually threatened with being trapped and crushed between drifting ice floes. From the eastern end of Icy Strait Whidbey turned northwards into a long waterway (later named 'Lynn Canal' by Vancouver after his birthplace) where he met a group of natives. They had appeared to be friendly but, after a night sleeping in their boats, Whidbey's party were awoken the following morning to find several canoes bearing down upon them. Fumbling about in an attempt to get at their weapons, the seamen could not prevent an Indian from the lead canoe leaping into Menzies' boat. He was pushed out, others prevented from entering, and the canoe fended off without casualties. With their attack repulsed, the Indians then resorted to waving otter skins as if trying to trade. But Whidbey gave orders to row themselves clear of the threat and, after a few miles the Indians gave up the pursuit.

The party, on leaving the entrance to Lynn Canal, found themselves in a southerly-bearing waterway (Stephens Passage) which Whidbey took to be nothing more than an inlet. Once again the natives appeared in a threatening manner and the party were forced to row all night to escape their attentions. In doing so they passed around a point of land at the entrance to Lynn Canal which Vancouver later (and rather ungraciously) named 'Retreat Point'. Again they found another broad southerly-bearing passage (Chatham Strait) which Whidbey explored until the coastline turned eastwards (Point Gardner). At this point Whidbey could see the open sea directly to the south but, by now, his boats crews were exhausted and he decided to return to the ships anchored in Cross Sound.

On Whidbey's arrival, Vancouver took his ships south passed Cape Edgecombe and rounded Cape Ommaney to anchor in a small bay just beyond the cape. Whidbey, accompanied by Lieutenant Spelman Swaine, was sent off once again with two boats to carry on his survey from Point Gardner, and Johnstone and Midshipman Barrie set off for Cape Decision to survey northwards from the final point of the previous year's work.

Returning down Stephens Passage, Whidbey rejoined the waterway at its southern entrance and continued to explore its northern coast. Once again the natives approached in canoes and only left after a musket had been fired at them. Shortly afterwards, the party landed to cook a meal but Whidbey felt uneasy about the circumstances and eventually ordered everyone back into the boats. They had only just cleared the shore when a large number of Indians burst from the trees. With their quarry having narrowly escaped, the Indians took to their canoes and set off in pursuit but promptly retreated when Whidbey's boats were reinforced by the sudden, unexpected, appearance of Johnstone's party.

Johnstone had made his way northwards from Cape Decision and had been exploring the southern shore of the same waterway as Whidbey when the two parties met. The day of the meeting happened to be the birthday of Prince Frederick, Duke of York, which later led Vancouver to name the waterway 'Prince Frederick's Sound' (Frederick Sound). Whidbey took the occasion, with all the formality he could concoct under the circumstances, to take possession of all the land and waters they had surveyed in the name of King George III of Great Britain.

Vancouver first learned of the final completion of his task when, through pouring rain, he saw his four boats enter the bay from the north. At last he was able to note that his work had enabled the removal of

every doubt, and set aside every opinion of a *north-west passage*, or of any water communication navigable for shipping, existing between the North Pacific, and the interior of the American continent within the limits of our researches.

From the Strait of Juan de Fuca to Cook Inlet he had demonstrated that there was no commercially viable waterway to link up with the trading companies to the east, and no passage to the Polar Sea. He could feel satisfied with his achievement, despite sailing at least three times past the mouth of the mighty waterway that was later to be named the 'Fraser River'.

The enterprise did not end on a note of celebration. Bad weather delayed the departure from Port Conclusion and the ships almost ran aground on Cape Ommaney. Boats had to be lowered to tow the *Discovery* clear of the rocks and one of the cutter's crew, Isaac Wooden, was lost overboard. A rock off the cape was named 'Wooden's Rock' (Wooden Island) in his memory.

The delay in departure caused a frustration amongst the ships' companies that was worsened on reaching Nootka Sound. There it was discovered that no instructions had arrived for Vancouver's unfinished negotiations over the handing over of sovereignty (not only were the ships' companies eager to go home after being away for so long, they were also missing the chance of prize money now that war had been declared). After six weeks, even Vancouver's patience with 'this infernal ocean' ran out and he sailed for Monterey. Not long after sailing, the ships were separated in fog and, yet again, Vancouver found the slow-sailing *Chatham* waiting for him at the port. He also found that he was to be replaced as British commissioner for the negotiations over Nootka Sound. Fortunately for his pride, Vancouver did not learn until later that he was to be replaced by a marine lieutenant whose sole qualification for the role was his ability to speak Spanish.

Vancouver had expected to find Lieutenant Broughton waiting for him at Monterey having returned from England, but there was no sign of him and Puget was confirmed in his command of the *Chatham*.

During his voyage south, Vancouver checked the position of a number of islands to confirm the accuracy of his charts and to take the opportunity to provide water and provisions for his ships. On leaving the Galapagos Island, he became impatient with the sailing qualities of the *Chatham* and ordered Puget to join him at Juan Fernandez Island. Bad weather, however, held the *Discovery* back and, by a month later, the *Chatham* had caught her up.

An outbreak of scurvy, and damage to the *Discovery's* mainmast and yard, convinced Vancouver that, despite his instruction being to the contrary, he had to call in at a Spanish South American port. Valparaiso was chosen, and the British ships found a warm welcome. Whilst the work on the *Discovery* was being carried out Vancouver found time to visit the Governor of Chile – the Irish-born Don Ambrosio O'Higgins. During his stay with the governor, Vancouver was appalled at the lack of cleanliness of every building from the peasant's hovels to the palace itself. The rooms he and his officers had been given had floors so covered in rubbish that it would 'rather have required a shovel rather than a brush for its removal'.

Both ships took a battering as they rounded Cape Horn, but the weather improved as they headed north to St Helena. During the passage the ships lost contact and as the *Discovery* prepared to sail into St Helena Bay, two months after leaving Valparaiso, she, yet again, found the *Chatham* waiting for her. On his arrival, Vancouver discovered that, in addition to the conflict with France, Great Britain was now at war with Holland. To his great joy, the following day, a Dutch ship – the *Macassar* – sailed into the harbour, unaware that Holland had declared war. Vancouver achieved her capture by the simple expediency waiting until she was secure in the harbour and then sending Lieutenants Baker and Swaine on-board to announce to the amazed captain that his ship was now a prize of the Royal Navy. Seventeen seamen were put on-board and Lieutenant Johnstone was put in command to sail her to England.

No doubt much to the annoyance of Puget and his ship's company, Vancouver ordered them to take dispatches to the Brazilian port of San Salvador where British forces were waiting, before they were to make an attempt to secure the Cape of Good Hope for Great Britain. Puget's orders were tempered with the (probably un-necessary) instruction that, once the dispatches hand been delivered, he should use his 'utmost exertions, for the purpose of immediately proceeding to England.'

The *Discovery* reached Ireland two months after leaving St Helena. Placing her under the command of Lieutenant Baker for the voyage to Deptford, Vancouver left for the Admiralty. On arrival he not only found out what had happened to Lieutenants Broughton and Mudge, he also found that he was to be placed on half-pay – despite learning of his promotion to post-captain in August 1794, and his nation being engaged in a desperate war. Perhaps just as disappointing, was the reaction to his news that he had obtained valuable islands in the centre of the Pacific for his sovereign. With the war presenting pressing needs in all quarters, no-one was interested. The news was ignored and, instead of ending up as a Pacific jewel in the British Empire, Hawaii was destined to become a state of the United States of America (retaining the Union Flag as part of her state flag).

William Broughton had arrived home safely with the charts and letters from Vancouver via Mexico and Madrid. Within three months he had been promoted to master and commander and appointed to command HMS *Providence*, the same ship used by Bligh on his second bread-fruit voyage. He was to rejoin Vancouver and assist in the completion of the survey, particularly of the south-western coast of South America. Zachary Mudge had arrived home with his parcel of charts after a voyage from China in an East India Co. vessel and was appointed as the *Providence's* first lieutenant. Unfortunately, the ship did not sail for another fifteen months and, after a somewhat leisurely voyage, arrived at Nootka Sound eighteen months later to find that Vancouver had sailed for home. Following a visit to Monterey (sailing just before the arrival of news of the Spanish entry into the war on France's side), Broughton and his officers decided to survey the Asian Pacific coast. At Macao he purchased an 87-ton schooner to act as tender to the *Providence* – a sensible act as it turned out. A month after leaving the port, the *Providence* hit a reef and sank – only the presence of the tender preventing loss of life. Sending Mudge and most of his seamen home, Broughton continued his survey. The following year he was promoted to post-captain and appointed as commodore in the East Indies. In 1809 he launched an attack against the Dutch in Java, but was to be accused of showing too much caution. As a result he was replaced the following year by a rear admiral, a move which so incensed Broughton that he applied to have his successor brought to a court martial for 'behaving in a cruel, oppressive, and fraudulent manner unbecoming the character of an officer, in depriving me of command of the squadron.' The court martial was denied and Broughton removed 'to the great relief of all in the fleet and army.' At the end of the war he was made a companion of the order of Bath, appointed as a colonel of marines three years later, and died in Florence in 1821.

Mudge was promoted to post-captain in 1800 and five years later, carrying Nelson's dispatches in the West Indies, fell in with a superior French force. With his ship sinking under him he had no choice but to strike his colours. However, at his court martial, he was commended for his 'very able and gallant conduct'. After service in two further ships Mudge returned to shore where, in due course, he was promoted to admiral before dying in 1852.

Following his promotion to post-captain in 1797, Peter Puget had an active career at sea before being appointed as commissioner of the navy at Madras in 1810. His health broken by the Indian climate, he was rewarded by being made a companion of the order of the Bath. He retired to the city of Bath where he was promoted to rear admiral the year before his death in 1822.

Lieutenant Spelman Swaine had two ships wrecked under his command, but survived to be promoted to rear admiral at the age of seventy-seven. He died six years later in 1852.

After promotion to post-captain and narrowly escaping death from yellow fever, Thomas Manby was also promoted to rear admiral after returning home early from fishery protection duties 'in consequence of ill health from the effects of yellow fever and the cold of Greenland.' He died on his Norfolk estate in 1834.

James Johnstone had been confirmed in his rank of lieutenant when he returned home and was promoted to post-captain in 1806. In 1811 he was appointed commissioner of the navy at Bombay returning to England in 1817. He died six years later.

Joseph Whidbey was promoted to master attendant on his return. Whilst serving in that capacity at Woolwich he was sent to Plymouth to help plan the building of a mile-long breakwater for the protection of Plymouth harbour. With construction under way, Whidbey was promoted to resident superintendent at Plymouth. He died in 1833, eight years before the breakwater was completed.

Archibald Menzies gave up botany and qualified as a doctor. He established a practice in London until his death in 1842.

Whatever happened to his officers, none of them suffered quite in the way that George Vancouver did on his return. Living on half-pay and building up debts whilst waiting for the Admiralty to approve his pay for the four-and-a-half years he had been away, Vancouver settled down with his brother, John, to write his account of the voyage. The peace and quiet so desired by Vancouver was shattered when a letter arrived from Midshipman the Honourable Thomas Pitt – now Lord Camelford. The contents of the letter challenged Vancouver to a duel in Hamburg. Camelford had even enclosed a money order to cover Vancouver's expenses. The letter, however, had arrived a fortnight after the date of the rendezvous – not that Vancouver had any intention of meeting Camelford on the duelling ground. A reply was sent stating that Vancouver was happy to have his conduct examined by any flag officer. This resulted in Camelford making an appearance at Vancouver's house where he raged and demanded personal satisfaction for the treatment he felt he had suffered at Vancouver's hands. Vancouver promptly asked for the protection of the court but, as he was waiting for a decision, he was making his way down London's Conduit Street

The Caneing in Conduit Street. Vancouver is attacked by Midshipman Pitt.

with his youngest brother, Charles, when Camelford appeared on the other side of the road. Crossing the street Camelford immediately began to aim blows at Vancouver with his walking stick. At first he was driven off by Charles and a subsequent attack was thwarted by both brothers using their sticks. 'The Caneing in Conduit Street' became the subject of a famous James Gillray cartoon which showed Vancouver in a very poor light. Camelford then promptly challenged Charles to a duel, which was eventually accepted but was unable to be carried out as Charles was ordered by the court to keep the peace. Promoted lieutenant about the time of the assault in Conduit Street, Camelford was sent out to the West Indies where he had a disagreement with Lieutenant Charles Peterson over the question of their respective seniorities. When Peterson refused to accept his orders, Camelford shot him dead. Despite his important connections, his continued bad behaviour ensured that Camelford was removed from the navy two years later as a 'Superannuated Commander'. He was to meet his death in a duel with Captain Thomas Best in 1804.

Vancouver and his brother, John, pressed on with his account of the voyage whilst fending off rumours that there had been a mutiny in the *Discovery* and fighting off other claimants for the prize money accruing from the capture of the Dutch ship at St Helena. He did not receive his pay for the almost five years he had commanded the *Discovery* until two years after his return. Even then he was only awarded six shillings and sixpence a day and had to plead to have the rate put up to eight shillings a day to bring him level with the pay awarded to Lieutenant Bligh of the *Bounty*. None of this helped his already failing health and he died, leaving his book to be completed by his brother, John, in April 1798. He was forty years old.

George Vancouver did not die without leaving his name to posterity. Within decades the 'Island of Quadra and Vancouver' became known simply as 'Vancouver Island'. A trading post on the Columbia River was named 'Fort Vancouver' and eventually became the American city of Vancouver, Washington State. When a name was sought for the western terminal of the Canadian Pacific railway the general manager of the company decided that it should be named after the best-known feature in the area. Thus Vancouver Island gave its name to the splendid new city of Vancouver, British Columbia. Mount Vancouver rises in the Yukon and Cape Vancouver, the Vancouver Peninsular, and Vancouver Rock in Australia commemorate his discovery of King George Sound. In New Zealand, Vancouver Arm leads off Dusky Bay.

HMS *Discovery* was refitted as a bomb-vessel in 1799 and served under Nelson at the Battle of Copenhagen and during the attack on the Boulogne invasion flotilla in 1801. In 1818 she was converted into a convict ship and was broken up sixteen years later. HMS *Chatham* survived in service with the Royal Navy until she was sold off in Jamaica in 1830.

CHAPTER SIX

'A PROUD SIGHT FOR ANY ENGLISHMAN'

With the end of the Napoleonic wars, as so often happens in peacetime, the Royal Navy became an expensive burden on the state's finances. At the close of hostilities the navy could number more than ninety ships of the line and 130,000 officers and men. Two years later the numbers had dropped to thirteen ships of the line and 20,000 officers and men. The Impress Service had been closed down and the pressed men freed to return to their homes. Unwanted seamen had been paid off and many were forced to beg on the streets. Those officers who were not put on half-pay could expect little in the way of promotion – twenty-five years after the war there were still 200 commanders and 1,450 lieutenants serving in the same rank they had held in 1815. With no enemy on the sea, and no threat to the nation, it was difficult to justify even the rump of a once powerful force. To one man, however, the navy did not need an enemy or a threat to find a useful role in the nation's cause.

John Barrow was born of humble parentage in a thatched cottage near Ulverstone. Showing early promise in mathematics, science, and navigation Barrow worked at an iron foundry before joining a whaling ship for a voyage off the Greenland coast. In addition to learning the skills of a seaman during the voyage, he also took a close interest in the use of the thermometer, compass, and barometer. On his return he taught mathematics for three years before obtaining a post on the staff of the British ambassador to China studying the country to such depth that he was later able to advise the British government on negotiations with the Chinese. He then lived and worked in South Africa carrying out a topographical survey of the country and acting as an intermediary between the warring natives and Boers. Whilst serving in South Africa, Barrow had become acquainted with General Henry Dundas and, when Dundas (as Lord Melville) was appointed First Lord of the Admiralty, he, in turn, appointed Barrow as second (i.e. permanent) secretary. With a single short break, Barrow was to remain in that office for the next forty years.

In 1815, even before the war had ended, Barrow had conceived the idea of using the skills and abilities of the Royal Navy in the field of exploration. He wrote

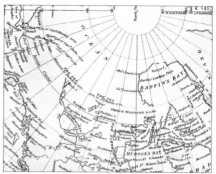

Above: *An 1818 map of the Arctic. Between Cook's Icy Cape and Baffin's Bay only two points are known on the Arctic coast – the mouths of the Coppermine and MacKenzie rivers.*

Left: *John Barrow, 2nd secretary to the Admiralty.*

To what purpose could a portion of our naval force be, at any time, but more especially in time of profound peace, more honourably or more usefully employed than in completing those details of geographical and hydrographical science of which the grand outlines have been boldly and broadly sketched by Cook, Vancouver and Flinders, and others of our own countrymen?

His eagerness attracted the attention of the aged Sir Joseph Banks who wrote to Barrow

If anything will cure the gout it must be the pleasure I derive from finding our Ministers mindful of the credit we have obtained from Discovery, and willing to continue and to increase and enlarge the only splendid source of honour which Peace allows of.

The first effort to match the fine words ended in disaster. In 1816 an expedition under Captain James Kingston Tuckey was sent to sail up the River Zaire (River Congo) with the sloop HMS *Congo* and with HMS *Dorothea* acting as store ship. By the time the *Congo* had reached 200 miles up the river, all the officers, all the civilian scientists, and most of her ship's company were dead, felled by the diseases endemic to the area.

The following year provided an impetus for a change in direction. The 1817 whaling season had been remarkable in that the seas off Greenland had been more free of ice than at any time within memory. One of the whaling captains, William Scoresby, had caught Bank's attention and the president of the Royal Society, under the guidance of Barrow, wrote to his friend the Prime Minister via the First Lord proposing that expeditions should be raised

> To endeavour to correct and amend the very defective geography of the Arctic Regions, especially on the side of America. To attempt the circumnavigation of old Greenland, if an island or islands as there is reason to suppose. To prove the existence or non-existence of Baffin's Bay; and to endeavour to ascertain the practicability of a Passage from the Atlantic to the Pacific Ocean, along the Northern Coast of America.

Barrow had a proposal ready should the Prime Minister give his support. There would be a western and an eastern expedition. Two ships would penetrate Davis's Strait and survey Baffin's Bay in the hope of finding a passage to the west, two more ships would follow Phipps' track and try to reach the Pacific via Spitsbergen and the North Pole. After having Barrow's plan approved by the Royal Society, the Admiralty gave their permission to proceed.

The vessels commissioned for service among the ice fields were the sloop, *Isabella*, a hired whaler; the hired brig *Alexander*, the ex-store-ship from Tucky's expedition; *Dorothea* (hired originally but purchased shortly afterwards); and the sloop, *Trent*, another hired whaler. All were to be double-planked, internally strengthened, and given iron sheathing at the bows.

The first of the expedition commanders received his letter of appointment in December, 1817. He was Commander John Ross, a bluff, red-haired, Scotsman who had seen considerable action against the French. He had first been borne on a ship's books at the age of nine and went to sea three years later. Advised that service with the merchant marine would provide good experience, he was bound apprentice on a merchantman for four years, visiting the West Indies and the Baltic. Ross was then taken on by the East India Co. for five years before returning to the Royal Navy in 1799 as a midshipman. During his training in merchantmen, Ross had found time to study astronomy under the guidance of William Wales, Cook's astronomer on his second voyage. Promoted lieutenant in 1805, Ross was appointed to HMS *Surinam* under the command of Captain William Broughton – the former captain of HMS *Chatham* under Vancouver. In the same year, he took part in the cutting out of a Spanish ship from under the guns of the forts at Bilbao and left the scene of the engagement with two broken legs, a broken arm, internal damage caused by a bayonet thrust, and three sword cuts to the head. On his recovery, Ross was appointed to HMS *Victory* and saw service in the Baltic where a command of the Swedish language (probably learned during his time with the merchant marine) proved so useful that he was eventually created a knight of the Swedish Order of the Sword. He was promoted to commander in 1812 and given command of the ten-gun sloop *Briseis*. Four months later he launched an attack against a merchant vessel which had recently been captured by the French. Under the leadership of his first lieutenant – Thomas Jones, with one midshipman and eighteen seamen, the ship was recaptured (twenty-two years later Ross was to take Jones's daughter as his second wife). Later the same year, with the *Briseis* disguised as a merchantman, Ross captured a French privateer and prevented an attack on a convoy he was guarding. In 1815, in command of the sixteen-gun HMS *Actaeon*, Ross compelled a forty-gun French frigate to stop; handing her captain over to an English frigate that had been chasing the enemy.

By the end of the war, Ross was comfortably off from the prize money he had earned, and was receiving pensions for the thirteen wounds he had suffered. He had spent winters amongst Baltic ice, had been trained in astronomy by Cook's astronomer, and had acquired surveying skills from Vancouver's second-in-command. His achievements were tested in 1815 when his determination of the latitude and longitude of the dockyard at Archangel (reached by the use of Jupiter's satellites) was compared to that of the Russian global circumnavigator, Admiral Krusenstern. The readings proved to be barely distinguishable.

Ross was appointed to command the western (Davis's Strait) expedition and selected the *Isabella* as his ship. His second-in-command, Lieutenant William Edward Parry, chose the *Alexander*.

Parry was a tall, handsome man of Welsh extraction. Born in Bath in 1790 as the son of a distinguished doctor he had entered the Royal Navy thirteen years later on the books of HMS *Ville de Paris*. Following service in the Baltic he was promoted to lieutenant in January 1810, and commanded a gunboat in action against the Danes. Parry then served on whale-fishing protection duties off Spitsbergen, using opportunities as they arose to survey the coasts of Denmark, Sweden, and the Shetland Islands. In 1813 he was sent to the North America station where he wrote a treatise entitled 'Nautical Astronomy by Night'. The work was passed around the other officers on the station and was published by his father three years later. Parry returned to action in April 1814, when he commanded one of six boats that were rowed and sailed ten miles up the Connecticut River. Off Pettipague Point they attacked and sank twenty-seven American vessels. In all, the attack destroyed over 5,000 tons of enemy shipping. After, (fortunately for him) failing to be selected for Tuckey's expedition to Africa, Parry heard about the proposed attempts on the north-west passage and the North Pole. He wrote to a friend of his father that he was ready for anything 'hot or cold' and the letter ended up in the hands of John Barrow along with a copy of Parry's book. A meeting was arranged and Barrow immediately took to the young officer and introduced him to Sir Joseph Banks. A further introduction was made to Sir George Hope, one of the lords of the

Admiralty, who would be responsible for selecting the leaders of the expeditions. Barrow may have been making the case for Parry as one of the leaders, but Sir George had already decided upon John Ross. Instead, Parry was to command the *Alexander* and sail as second-in-command to Ross on the western expedition.

The leader of the eastern expedition was to be Commander David Buchan who had come to the Admiralty Board's attention through his exploits in Newfoundland. Promoted lieutenant in 1806 and to commander ten years later, Buchan had been serving on the Halifax Station in command of the schooner HMS *Adonis* when he was sent to explore the interior of Newfoundland and to make contact with the natives should any be found. The party of twenty-four seamen and three local guides set off in January 1811, and made their way along the bank of a frozen river. After travelling some 130 miles he came across a native village with about seventy-five inhabitants. At first it seemed that the Indians were intent on establishing good relations so Buchan – using sign language – persuaded the chief and three others to accompany him and his party back to their campsite of the night before, where gifts would be available for them. Two of his men requested that they may be allowed to remain in the village whilst the party returned to the campsite, and Buchan, with no reason to expect any aggression from the natives, agreed. The four natives accompanied the party for about six miles when the chief took one of the Indians and returned to the village. Just as Buchan's party was about to reach their overnight camp one of the two remaining natives fled, but the other stayed and collected the gifts Buchan had brought with him. The party then made their way back to the native village. On their arrival they found the place to be deserted, much to the consternation of their accompanying Indian. After a night spent sleeping in the deserted tepees they pressed on under the guidance of the native until they had reached about a mile from the village. At this point the Indian – walking ahead of the main party – suddenly gave a yell and sprinted for the cover of nearby trees. Buchan walked forward until he had a clear view of the frozen river. There, on the ice, bristling with arrows, lay the headless, naked bodies of the two men he had allowed to remain with the natives. Thus ended the first attempt to establish good relations with the natives of Newfoundland. Buchan's party arrived back at the *Adonis* less than three weeks after they had set out. It was this experience and his proven skills as a surveyor that caused Buchan to be chosen to captain the *Dorothea* and command the eastern expedition.

The command of the *Trent* went to Lieutenant John Franklin. Franklin was the son of a Lincolnshire trader who discovered his love of the sea when he paid his first visit to the county's coast. His father, reluctant to let him go to sea and in an effort to remove the idea from his head, sent Franklin on a voyage in a merchantman from Hull to Lisbon. Instead of dissuading Franklin, the voyage confirmed his desire to go to sea and so, once the usual family and friends connections had been made, the fourteen-year-old joined HMS *Polyphemus* as a first-class volunteer. A year later the *Polyphemus* sailed as part of the fleet under Admiral Sir Hyde Parker and, within weeks, took part in the Battle of Copenhagen. Returning unscathed from the engagement Franklin learned that a cousin by marriage, Lieutenant Matthew Flinders, was about to set sail on a voyage of discovery to inquire into the nature and range of the Australian coastline. An appeal to his father set the family links in motion and Franklin was accepted on Flinders' ship, HMS *Investigator* as a midshipman.

The survey of Australia took up where Vancouver had left off. Flinders surveyed the previously unknown Great Australian Bight and the whole of the southern coast before reaching Port Jackson where the *Investigator* underwent a refit. This was followed by a survey of the east coast and a passage through Torres Strait into the Gulf of Carpenteria. At that stage it became clear that the *Investigator* was in a very poor condition and she was beached in order that her hull could be examined. It was soon discovered that much of her timber was rotting away at an alarming rate to such an extent that if she was to encounter a strong gale she would be almost certain to founder. Flinders was faced with two practical options: he could take her back along the east coast with the risk of her grounding on the Great Barrier Reef, or he could continue westwards along the north coast, sail down the western side of the continent, retrace his wake along the southern coast, and then head northwards to Port Jackson. He chose the latter route and arrived at the port eleven months later as the first circumnavigator of Australia.

The *Investigator* was beyond repair on her arrival and Flinders and his ships company transferred to the store-ship HMS *Porpoise* for the voyage home. Less than a week later the ship hit a reef and was wrecked. No lives were lost thanks to a nearby sandbank where the survivors mustered with the few stores they had managed to save. Flinders took one of the ship's boats and with thirteen others sailed off to Port Jackson, 750 miles to the south, to get help. Six weeks later he returned with three ships – the merchantmen *Rolla*, and two naval sloops. Taking two of his officers and eight men, Flinders remained on one of the sloops, HMS *Cumberland*, as she was sailing directly to England and he had to get his charts back to the Admiralty. Tragically, however, his ship called in at Mauritius only to find the island in the hands of the French. The ship was taken and Flinders spent almost seven years as a prisoner of war. By the time he was released his health had been broken and he died on the day the account of his voyage was published in 1814.

Franklin sailed in the *Rolla* to Canton where he managed to obtain a berth as a signal midshipman in the East India Co. vessel *Earl Camden*. Two weeks after sailing for home, the *Earl Camden* was part of a convoy under the command of Commodore Dance when they ran into a French fleet in the Malacca Straits. What should have been a British route was reversed when Dance unexpectedly formed line of battle and ran up the signal 'Bear down in line ahead and engage the enemy'. After a brief engagement the French stood off in the belief that they were somehow being tricked. At this, Dance ran up the signal 'General Chase' causing the French to cram on sail and to leave the scene after being pursued by Dance for two hours.

On his return home, Franklin was given six weeks leave before being appointed to HMS *Bellerophon* and a year of blockading duties. The following year the *Bellerophon* was part of Nelson's fleet at Trafalgar and had a very hot time of it. Engaged on both sides, both her captain and her master were among the early casualties. The main and mizzen masts went by the board and French boarders had to be repelled. On the quarterdeck, out of forty-seven officers and men, only seven escaped death or wounding. Among the lucky few was Franklin who, nevertheless, suffered damage to his ears from the continuous cannonading.

On completion of repairs to the battle-damage, *Bellerophon* returned to blockading duties and Franklin remained with her until 1807 when he was transferred into HMS *Bedford*, firstly as a master's mate and, shortly afterwards, as an acting-lieutenant.

The *Bedford* was employed for the next two years in escorting the Portuguese royal family to Rio de Janeiro and remaining on that station as their guard-ship. This was followed by a further two years of blockading duties before being sent to the West Indies.

In September, 1814, the *Bedford* moved north towards the mouth of the Mississippi as part of a fleet under Admiral Cochrane. In the following January it was decided to attack the city of New Orleans with the Royal Navy opening the way with an assault on five gunboats anchored at the head of Lake Borgne – an inlet from the sea. To carry this out, forty-five ship's boats had to be rowed thirty-six miles upstream carrying 1,000 officers and seamen. Inevitably the reception was hot with the American commander issuing possibly history's most un-inspiring naval signal to his men 'Sink the enemy or be sunk yourselves.' Despite the heavy fire from the gun-ships, the attack was pressed home and, at the end of the day, the Union Jack could be seen flying from each of the enemy gunboats. Among the wounded was Franklin with a shoulder injury. The severity of the wound may be judged, however, by the fact that, within days, he was part of an assault that captured an American gun-battery. The battle of New Orleans was, nevertheless, to be lost, and the loss of life on all sides rendered particularly tragic when it was revealed that a peace treaty had been signed before the battle had begun, but the news had failed to reach the commanders in the field.

With his rank confirmed, Lieutenant Franklin, was appointed as first lieutenant in HMS *Forth* on his return to England in 1815. But, with the cessation of hostilities after the battle of Waterloo he, like hundreds of other officers, was placed ashore on half-pay with little hope of further employment. His appointment, however, as second in command of the Eastern Expedition under Buchan possibly came as a result of his having remained in contact with Robert Brown, Flinders' naturalist in the *Investigator*. Brown was on excellent terms with Sir Joseph Banks.

The only reservation Franklin had was an article Barrow had published in the Quarterly Review concerning the forthcoming expeditions. He wrote to his friend, Captain Cumby (who, as Lieutenant Cumby, had taken command of the *Bellerophon* on the death of her captain at Trafalgar),

> I think it calculated to make the Reader form too favourable anticipations – they will not, I fear, be prepared to receive any accounts of failure and consequently feel the greatest disappointment in the event of such a misfortune.

In the same letter, Franklin went on to bemoan the lack of a scientist for the voyage:

> You will be surprised to learn there has not yet a scientific man full qualified offered for our branch of the expedition and that it is more than probable we shall sail without any. We must all become collectors and gatherers........the absence of a scientific man is more to be regretted in an Astronomical point of view – the observations which may be made are most important and interesting. We shall be well supplied with instruments – most of them new, provided by the Royal Society; it may perhaps be amusing to know what they are – I will enumerate some of them – The Pendulum, Variation Transit – Transit Instrument; Repeating Circle; Dipping Needle – Compasses of several kinds, many of them with great improvements; Hydrometer – Cyanometer; Barometers Sea and Mountain; Thermometers plain and register – An Artificial Horizon to be used at sea on the principle of a Spinning Top (made by Troughton); and last though by no means least useful an instrument proposed by Captain Kator for taking altitudes without an horizon – the principle of the old Astrolabe – which instrument, if it answers our present expectations, will be most valuable in those Northern icy latitudes where the atmosphere is so continually dense and foggy. There is also an Electrometer invented by Sir Humphrey Davy for experiments principally on the Aurora Borealis. He, I believe, is of opinion contrary to Dr. Franklin that there will be found Electric Poles in some part of the Arctic Circles. I think you will say, to make ourselves acquainted with even the instruments, will be a work of no slight difficulty – how we shall get on in the observing without the assistance of some Professor, I cannot tell!

The four ships completed their preparations for the voyages in March, 1818, and were inspected by HRH the Duke of Clarence; Lord Melville, the First Lord of the Admiralty; and the comptroller of the navy, Sir Thomas Byam Martin. As they toured the ships, crowds on the shore were entertained to a demonstration of kayak paddling by John Sacheuse (pronounce 'Sackhouse' by the seamen), a Greenland Eskimo who had been taken on-board by Ross as interpreter for his expedition. Also joining Ross was his nephew, James Ross. Known to his contemporaries by his full name of James Clark Ross to distinguish him from another naval officer and settler of the Coco (Andaman) Islands, James Clunies Ross, Midshipman Ross had served with his uncle since he had entered the service in 1810. By co-incidence the sons of two famous artists were appointed to the expeditions, Lieutenant Henry Hoppner sailed with Ross, and Lieutenant Frederick Beechey served as Franklin's first lieutenant. An unusual addition to the *Isabella's* ship's company was Captain Edward Sabine of the Royal Artillery. Sabine had written to Banks to inform him that he was studying zoology and was taking a keen interest in the compass and Captain Kater's pendulum (by which it was hoped to describe exactly the true shape of the Earth). Although, in fact, unqualified in any scientific discipline, Sabine's enthusiasm earned Banks's support and the recommendation of the Royal Society.

To compensate for the general lack of experience of sailing in ice, an 'Ice Master' was appointed to each of the ships. These were experienced whaling captains who could be depended upon to be alert to the dangers of northern waters. One of these appointments had been offered to William Scoresby, whose original report on the ice-free state of the Greenland seas had been chiefly instrumental in promoting the expeditions. Scoresby, however, had wanted to be in command of one of the ships – an idea unacceptable to the Admiralty – and he declined the opportunity.

For the ships' companies, not only was there to be an issue of warm clothing, but each man was to receive double pay, a welcome development that was to be repeated on all subsequent polar expeditions to the beginning of the twentieth century.

The four ships sailed from the Thames on 25 April 1818, and reached Lerwick in Shetland where the commanders had a final conference before separating. Ross's orders were that his ships should 'proceed together by the north-west through Davies' Strait'. Buchan was to go 'in a direction as due north as may be found practicable through the Spitsbergen seas'. If either was successful, they could return by the route they had already taken, or continue into the Pacific and return by one of the capes.

The call at Lerwick gave Franklin an opportunity to attend to a serious leak that had developed in the *Trent*. The ship was beached and some damaged planking found, but, when they sailed northwards they found the leak undiminished, a situation that required half the time spent on watch being dedicated to manning the pumps to keep the flooding waters at bay.

Two weeks after leaving the Shetlands, the *Dorothea* and the *Trent* reached Bear Island. They had crossed the Arctic Circle days before and were now in the zone of permanent daylight with its harsh bright light and deceptively blue seas. The ships were separated by a gale shortly afterwards, but both made their way up the mountainous west coast of Spitsbergen to the appointed rendezvous at Magdalena Bay. Heavy snow had fallen during the voyage and, with each dip of the bow into the waves, the spray froze to the bowsprit. Eventually the accumulated weight threatened to break the projecting spar and the ice had to be chopped off with axes. Ice that gathered in the rigging was cleared by beating the ropes with sticks.

From the anchorage at the mountain-ringed Magdalena Bay a solid mass of ice could be seen to the north, its edge stretching far to the west. Buchan reasoned that the best he could do was to wait to see if the ice would break up enough to allow him a northwards passage. The ships' entry into the bay had revealed herds of walrus, a living harvest for a group of Russians who were living in a hut and collecting walrus hides and tusks.

On one side of the bay several glaciers met the sea and the frequent, thunderous, sound as they 'calved' rang around the mountains and snow-covered valleys. Franklin and Beechey were examining the face of one of the glaciers from one of the ship's boats when a huge section calved and fell into the sea. The mass of ice disappeared beneath the surface of the water in a boiling mass emerging some seconds later to rear up at least 100ft into the air before settling down. The succession of rolling waves caused by this incident put the small boat at grave risk, but skilful handling kept them afloat. The newly-born iceberg was calculated to be a quarter of a mile in circumference with 60ft showing above the water. Its weight was in the region of 425,000 tons.

A group including Beechey attempted to climb the nearby Rotge Hill. At 2,000ft the ascent became so dangerous that they marked the position with a red flag and began to make their way down. The conditions, however, in particular the loose rock on which they found themselves, forced them to make their way across to a ledge leading to a bank of snow. The only way this could be achieved was by hammering in the 'tomahawks' (boarding axes) they had carried for use when encountering ice. The axes were employed as footholds as they made their way safely to the more secure ground, but had to be abandoned when their recovery proved to be too dangerous.

After a few days in the bay, Buchan decided to have a closer look at the edge of the ice. Before them lay a vast field of ice that stretched to the northern horizon. No way of entering the pack could be seen and, even worse, the wind suddenly failed leaving the ships at the mercy of a heavy swell which threw them repeatedly against the ice. The night was spent in great anxiety as the ships' sides were hammered and scraped by the solid mass. Luckily, in the early morning, a slight breeze blew up which enabled them to haul clear and repair the damage the repeated collisions had caused.

Buchan now decided to try heading to the west in order to see if a way through the ice could be found but, after twenty-four hours without a break in the ice, and by learning from the captains of whaling ships that there was no northward trending opening in the ice to the west, he decided to return to the coast of Spitsbergen. Reaching Cloven Cliff on the north coast, Buchan was delighted to find a wide lead running between the land and the main body of the ice. With this opportunity to make their way to the north, Buchan took the ships into the gap. They had not proceeded far when the ice closed in, trapping both ships in almost the same place where the ice had caught Phipps forty-five years earlier. The great danger that faced them was the increasing pressure from the ice. If they were to be 'nipped' (i.e.

Right: *HMS* Trent

Below: *HMS* Dorothea, *with HMS* Trent *on the extreme left, being driven into the ice pack. 30 July 1818.*

Walruses attacking one of the Trent's *boats off Cloven Cliff.*

crushed) by the great weight of ice pressing on either side of the ships, there would be nothing they could do except hope to survive long enough to get ashore. Six days after they were trapped, the *Trent* was suddenly lifted several feet by the pressure of ice beneath her keel. To the relief of all, the ship slowly settled back into her previous position. An anonymous writer on the *Dorothea* noted that when looking about him he:

> never failed to experience sensations at once solemn and astonishing, for there was something in my breast which for ever associated itself with the possibility, nay, probability, of never being able to extricate ourselves.

The time spent in the ice was not, however, to be without its benefit. The surgeons' assistant on the *Trent* was relaxing below decks when he heard the sound of water rushing into the ship. On this being reported the sound was located and the inner-bulkhead of the spirit-room was torn down to reveal a cascade of water. This, at last, was the source of the water that had proved to be such a burden to the *Trent's* ship's company. On examination it was discovered that a hole, intended to take a bolt, had been merely covered over with pitch. With a wooden bung hammered into the hole the leak was brought to an end, much to the relief of all.

Thirteen days after they had been trapped, the ice relented and the ships were sailed undamaged into open waters. Now free of the ice, a party of seamen was given permission to hunt among a herd of 'sea-horses' (walruses) that could be seen basking on a nearby ice floe. The first fusillade of musket-fire caused the animals to panic and rush into the water. Once in their natural element, the walrus turned

A romanticised view of HMS Dorothea *and HMS* Trent *in the ice off Spitsbergen.*

upon their attackers and charged the boat, attempting to turn it over and puncture it with their tusks. Using oars, harpoons and axes, the men desperately fended off the onslaught in, what seemed to be, a one-sided battle. Luckily, one man managed to load his musket in the violently rocking boat and fired down the throat of the lead bull animal. At this, the now-leaderless herd withdrew and the party managed to make their escape back to their ship.

The following day Buchan took the ships into Fair Haven, an anchorage that afforded protection from winds from the south and west, and from where the ice pack could be watched for any sign of breaking up. Reindeer were spotted in the surrounding hills and, before long, forty had succumbed to ship's muskets (as did one of the *Dorothea's* midshipmen – accidentally shot through the knee by the ship's purser whilst in pursuit of the deer). Hundreds of incautious eider duck were captured and also used to supplement the ship's provisions.

The ships put to sea again on 6 July and closed once again with the ice-barrier, reaching 80 degrees 15' north before coming to a halt. They now found themselves surrounded by large ice floes that dealt the ships several large blows before they could get clear.

On the following day it seemed that the expedition was about to have a change of luck. The vast ice field began to split apart revealing many wide leads. A number headed directly north and it was down one of these that Buchan led his ships. But, within hours, the open channels had closed up and both ships were, once more, rigidly beset in the ice. In the succeeding days, attempts were made to haul the ships to the north. Ice anchors were sent out and attempts made to warp the ship forwards. Ice saws were used in an attempt to cut a passage. Not only was the work desperately difficult, it also proved to be pointless. No matter how far the ships advanced northwards, the drift of the ice to the south more than reduced the advantage gained.

The pressure of the ice against their sides affected both ships. The *Dorothea*, in particular, with her almost vertical sides, suffered to the degree that some of her deck planks were split fore and aft and her frame timbers could be heard cracking with loud reports. The *Trent*, despite her sloping sides, was, in some ways even worse off. The ice pressure had concentrated on her quarter with the result that the ship was being twisted. Cabin doors were flung open and the false sternpost moved 3in. Once again the cracking of timbers could be heard throughout the ship.

Three weeks after being beset, the ice broke apart and the ships limped out to open waters. Whilst in the ice, Buchan had reached the highest latitude the expedition was ever to achieve. When Buchan and Franklin compared their readings, the mean position reached was 80 degrees 37'.

Having failed to find a way through to the north and east, Buchan turned his bows once more to the west. He had not gone far when a strong gale blew up and threatened to force the ships onto the pack ice. Both ships were consequently forced to act in a manner that would be resorted to only in absolute desperation – probably on the advice of the ice masters. Outside the pack – now a heaving mass of ice floes – the ships would stand no chance of survival, they would be driven onto the broken ice. If, however, the ships could be got into the pack, the ice, acting as a succession of breakwaters, would calm the water. Only within the quieter waters of the pack itself would survival be possible.

On the *Trent,* lengths of rope were cut to hang over the sides to act as fenders, and iron plates and walrus hides were hung over her bows. The standing rigging – the stays and braces – was strengthened by extra ropes and all the hatches battened down. At last the orders were given and the ships ran before the gale straight at the mass of seething breakers which lined the edge of the broken pack. The outer line of floes was swept aside by the rush of the vessels that then ran hard onto the solid pack itself. Everyone was thrown to the deck by the concussion and all eyes looked up to see if the masts had survived the collision. The *Trent's* extra rope work had served her well and, although the masts had whipped forward alarmingly, they remained unbroken. She rolled violently from side to side as she was forced broadside to the wind, her bell ringing with each roll. Collision after collision rocked the ships as they staggered out of control among the ice floes and all that could be done on-board was to hang on for dear life. Gradually, however, extra sails were put out and the ships urged deeper into the pack where the water was calmer.

The gale lasted for four hours before subsiding and allowing the battered ships to return to open waters. They made for Fair Haven where the extent of the damage sustained was revealed. The *Trent* had suffered damage, but not to the extent that the *Dorothea* had. Her port side had been stoved in and many of her frame beams had been sprung. It was quite clear that, for the time being, her usefulness in ice-strewn waters was at an end. And there was no guarantee that the crippled ship could be brought safely home.

Despite the state of his vessel, Franklin urged Buchan to be allowed to continue the attempts to breach the ice barrier, but it was quite impossible. Buchan's ship was in such an un-seaworthy condition that it would be unthinkable to allow it to attempt the voyage home without an escort. Whilst those repairs that could be effected were carried out, Fair Haven was closely surveyed, its position fixed, and magnetic observations carried out.

The homeward voyage began on 30 August. Both ships had to be nursed through the sometimes challenging sea and they did not reach Deptford until 22 October – almost exactly six months after they had started out.

The expedition proved little beyond what was already known. The ice north of Spitsbergen was impenetrable, and no passage for ships through to the North Pole existed in that direction. Neither Buchan nor Franklin produced a published record of the voyage and the public had to wait for twenty-five years before the first lieutenant of the *Trent* – by then Captain Frederick Beechey – published his account.

Commander David Buchan was promoted to captain five years after his return from the ice fields. He died, still young, in 1839. One of his descendants was the author John Buchan ('Thirty-nine Steps') who, as Lord Tweedsmuir, became Governor General of Canada. Franklin, Beechey, and one of the *Trent's* master's mates, George Back, went on to further fame in the cold waters of the north.

The *Dorothea* was sold out of the service in 1819 and the hired *Trent* was returned to her owners.

The first icebergs to be encountered by the western expedition were seen by John Ross on 26 May 1818, two days after he had passed Cape Farewell – the southern tip of Greenland. Three days later snow fell as they made their way up the eastern shore of Davies' Strait and soon streams of ice drifting south provided entertainment and hazard for the ships' companies. June the 3rd saw the crossing of the Arctic Circle and the following day a toast to the health of King George III before the *Isabella* and the *Alexander* were moored alongside a grounded iceberg. While some of the seamen amused themselves sliding down the ice, the officers took pot-shots at circling birds or checked the chronometers, compasses and dip circles. Eskimos clambered onto the iceberg from the shore and were given gifts.

Captain John Ross.

Passage through the ice, June, 1818. A watercolour by John Ross. The Isabella *and the* Alexander *are accompanied by whalers.*

Before long, whalers were sighted and contact made. They were on their way north and Ross joined them as they headed towards the mountains of Disco Island. There they found more than thirty other whaling ships held up by the ice barrier that curved to the west from the Greenland shore. As Ross's ships sailed in amongst the whalers the air rang with the cheers of the whaling men – it was, as Parry noted in his journal, 'a proud sight for an Englishman'. The time spent with the whalers was spent in practising cutting docks in ice and watching as whales were stripped of their blubber and baleen 'whale-bone' (many of Ross's seamen, however, were well-practised Greenland whaling men who would have found little novel in the activity around them).

The interpreter, John Sacheuse, made contact with Eskimos ashore and returned to the ship with a number of them paddling their kayaks. Ross persuaded them to part with a sledge and some sledge-dogs in return for a musket. As a further reward they were given coffee and biscuit, had their portraits sketched, and were taught Scottish reels by the seamen.

A wait of almost a month had to be endured before the ice relented and a passage opened up between it and the shore. Accompanied by a few whalers, the

A remarkable iceberg. 19th June, 1818. A watercolour by John Ross.

ships reached the steep slopes of Sanderson's Hope where whales were to be had in plenty. Using this last opportunity to get letters to England, Parry wrote to Barrow informing him that the compass variation (the difference between magnetic and true north) was an amazing 89 degrees to the west. In other words, they would shortly find themselves north of the north magnetic pole.

With the whaling ships behind them, the *Isabella* and the *Alexander* made their way into a huge, mountain-edged bight that Ross named Melville Bay in honour of the First Lord of the Admiralty. The ice or lack of wind frequently halted progress and the ship's company were forced to walk ahead on the frozen surface towing the ships to tunes provided by the ship's fiddler. Whales abounded in the open waters and, on one occasion, Midshipman James Ross was sent out to chase one. He came back with a forty-six-foot specimen that provided thirteen tons of blubber to be held in reserve for fuel should the expedition be forced to winter in the ice.

On 7 August, the ships were surrounded by loose masses of ice that forced them to collide with each other. The collision crushed one of the ship's boats and tore away chain-plates. For a short time it even looked as if the masts were threatened, but the ice drifted apart leaving two of the bow anchors locked together in a deadly tug-of-war. Eventually, the *Alexander's* anchor cable parted and the ships, reeling upright, were allowed to separate and attend to their damage.

Three days later, as the ships made their way along the edge of a wide shelf of ice fast against the shore, figures were seen waving on the ice. The ships were stopped immediately and ice-anchors used to secure the ships to the ice edge. Ross had taken the strangers to be seamen in distress. But, when attempts were made to approach the fur-clad figures they made off in a hurry on dog-drawn sledges. Realising that these people were natives of the area, Ross left out presents and sent off one of his dogs after them with beads around its neck. Halfway between the ship and the shore a flag was erected which had on it representations of the sun, the moon, and a hand holding a sprig of heather. At ten o' clock the next day the Eskimos appeared again and Sacheuse went out to meet them. He found the natives to be a tribe that had no contact with either others of their own race, or with white men. In accordance with a well-established naval tradition of courtesy towards newly-met representatives of a foreign nation, Ross and Parry put on their dress uniforms with swords and cocked hats and made a strange, gallant, sight as they crossed the ice to meet the Eskimos, their silk-lined coat-tails flapping in the Arctic breeze.

Sacheuse, managing to make himself understood by the Eskimos, learned that they thought the ships were living creatures that had come from the moon or the

Isabella *and* Alexander *with their anchors hooked, gust 1818.*

Captain John Ross and Lieutenant William Parry meet the Eskimos. In common with naval tradition, both are wearing full uniform upon meeting foreign visitors.

sun (an intelligent interpretation of the designs on Ross's flag). Persuaded to go on-board, they were terrified of a pig but sneered at the ship's terrier. Exhibiting a trait common amongst the natives of far warmer climates, they tried to make off with as many of the ship's items as they could – including the unliftable ship's anvil. Once again portraits were sketched and gifts given to repeated nose-pulling gestures of appreciation before the Eskimos returned to the ice for the excited journey back to their summer tents. Ross decided to name the area 'The Arctic Highlands' (Thule) and the natives 'Arctic Highlanders' (Etah Eskimos).

The arrival of a southerly wind broke off any further contact and, just over a week later, the ships arrived off a rocky promontory that Ross named Cape York. On the slopes of the cape he was amazed to see snow that was coloured deep crimson and sketched this 'red snow' for the benefit of the inevitable disbelievers at home (the red snow was actually the result of an algae – *Chlamydomonas nivalis*). Baffin's Cape Dudley Digges was reached and passed as was his Wolstenholme Sound. At Whale Sound, with its Hakluyt and Carey's Islands, Ross named the flanking capes after Parry and the *Isabella*'s first lieutenant, Lieutenant William Robertson.

The ships then set their course westwards with the ice-choked waters of Smith's Sound to their starboard. Ross decided that the sound was actually a bay and named its two capes after his ships. He had now reached his most northerly point – almost 77 degrees – and took a south-westerly course towards the rugged snow-covered hills now in sight. At the entrance to Jones Sound, Ross, once again took the inlet to be blocked off by land and followed the coast southwards until the land tended westward into, what was clearly Baffin's Lancaster Sound. On the evening of 29 August the two ships entered the wide waterway and bore away to the west.

For some, the clear sailing brought high hopes. Parry noted 'May this be the channel we are in search of!' but Sabine was of the opinion that there would be no passage to the west north of Cumberland Sound and noted the lack of current, driftwood and swell from the west in Lancaster Sound. Nevertheless, the ships' rigging and yards were hung with men eager to find a way through the sound's cliff-lined shores.

The progress continued the following day as church services were held on the two ships, and Parry quelled his impatience by taking sightings of the land and stars that were beginning to appear in the darkening sky. In the early hours of the following morning, Ross put on sail and soon had the slow-sailing *Alexander* nine miles in his wake. Eventually, Ross was forced to shorten sail in an effort to keep Parry's ship in sight as rain began to fall.

At about four o'clock in the morning, Ross was on deck when he saw land blocking his westward course. This was 'a high ridge of mountains, extending directly across the bottom of the inlet.' With a favourable wind he pressed on towards the land which soon became hidden behind a bank of fog. At midday James Beverley, the *Isabella's* surgeon, climbed to the crow's nest and caught a brief sighting of the land ahead. Ross now determined to land on the new coastline and carry out magnetic observations, all the time shortening sail to keep the *Alexander* in view.

A polar bear plunging off an iceberg. From a sketch by John Ross.

At about three o'clock in the afternoon, as Ross was eating a meal below decks, the officer of the watch informed him that the fog showed signs of clearing. Immediately repairing to the upper deck Ross was soon able to see 'the land, round the bottom of the bay, forming a connected chain of mountains with those which extended along the north and south sides'. Skirting the coast, and with its eastern edge seven miles from the ship, a great sweep of ice blocked the route to the new shores. Bearings were taken by Benjamin Lewis, the ice master; and a seaman, James Haig. Within a quarter of an hour the fog returned and obliterated the sight. Ross, now convinced that he had entered a bay, and seeing no possibility of getting through the ice to carry out his magnetic observations, tacked about and headed towards the pursuing *Alexander* – still eight miles astern. As he completed a sketch of the land he had seen, Ross gave the name 'Croker's Mountains' – in honour of the first secretary to the Admiralty – to the range he had seen sealing off the bottom of the inlet. A great bay that had arced away in the south-east was given the name 'Barrow's Bay' (thus both Admiralty secretaries would be kept happy with a view to Ross's future employment).

On-board the *Alexander*, however, not everything was quite as clear cut. The officer of the watch – Midshipman Bisson – claimed to have seen the land lining the western rim of the bay, but an anonymous officer (probably the surgeon, Alexander Fisher) was later to claim that 'we could not see anything like land at the bottom of the inlet'. If Parry was part of the 'we' he did not communicate his misgivings to Ross.

Just before the ships rounded the southern corner of Lancaster Sound (the headland being named Cape Byam Martin in honour of the comptroller of the navy) Ross sent Parry ashore with Midshipmen Ross and Skene to take possession of the land in the name of the king. Sabine also went ashore at 'Possession Bay' and, with Parry, collected natural history specimens.

Captain John Ross's sketch of his 'Croker Mountains'

Cartoon of John Ross's return. Ross has a false nose and many of his men have noses missing, apparently as a result of rubbing noses when greeting the Eskimos. Two seamen carry a barrel of red snow.

With Cape Byam Martin rounded, the ships headed south along a coast that Baffin had not been able to chart due to the presence of ice. No further openings of note were seen until they arrived off Cumberland Sound on 1 October. Warm clothing had already been issued to the ships' companies and Ross, although of the opinion that the sound offered a good chance of a passage to the west, decided that it was too late in the season to explore it and, rather than risk being frozen in, he would start back for home.

Off Cape Farewell the ships were separated by bad weather and the slower-sailing *Alexander* reached Lerwick on 30 October, some hours before the arrival of the *Isabella*. By a letter sent with the Lerwick packet Ross informed the Admiralty that he had arrived safely home and that there was no passage westwards from Baffin's Bay.

When the ships arrived at Grimsby, Ross handed over command to Parry and set off for the Admiralty taking with him the officer's logs and journals. Whatever was held in the report he made to John Barrow, the second secretary of the Admiralty, it contained something, or its manner of delivery suggested something, that caused Barrow great concern and irritation. Concern because, on reading the logs, Barrow had spotted discrepancies between different accounts of the land at the bottom of Lancaster Sound, and irritation that Ross had returned without (Barrow believed) trying hard enough to find a passage. Ross later noted that 'circumstances occurred which caused a personal altercation, and a rupture of our former friendly relations.'

Despite this breakdown between the two men, Ross was promoted to captain on 7 December 1818. Not that this ended his problems. They were made even worse when he discovered that Sabine was claiming the magnetic observations he had claimed to have been taken by his nephew, James. The artillery captain published a pamphlet stating his side of the case and Ross replied with a pamphlet of his own. With the affair out in the open, the Admiralty was forced to make a formal enquiry into the matter. Sabine's pamphlet also claimed that 'Croker's Mountains' did not exist and suggested, in support of the anonymous officer from the *Alexander*, that other officers felt the same way. Barrow then publicly waded in by anonymously responding to Ross's account of the voyage. It had been, according to Barrow, a farrago of exaggeration and failure to pursue the aims of the expedition, indeed 'a mere voyage like his, round the shores of Baffin's Bay, in the summer months, may be considered as a voyage of pleasure.' Only Sabine's work on magnetism, on the pendulum, and on natural history (including the newly-discovered 'Sabine's Gull') had produced anything worthwhile.

Before the Board of Enquiry sat, Sabine had persuaded James Ross to sign a statement admitting that he had copied the magnetic readings and given the results to his uncle. This led to a clash between uncle and nephew at the enquiry despite James Ross writing to his uncle that there was not 'a single point in which I have said anything to your prejudice.' Nevertheless, John Ross told the board that 'James Ross was his greatest enemy'. A day later the board heard that 'Captain John Ross, being admitted, desires to state that he wishes to recall the observation he made yesterday against his nephew'. The whole affair, he now felt, was 'probably no more than the difference which arose from a Land Officer being embarked with the Sea Officers and produced no Injury to the Service.' The matter was thereupon closed as far as the board was concerned.

Above: *John Franklin as a captain.*

Right: *Surgeon John Richardson.*

Far right: *Midshipman George Back.*

John Ross had answered Sabine's pamphlet and deflected the question of the magnetic observations, but had earned the enmity of John Barrow. From then on the second secretary of the Admiralty made certain that Ross was never to be employed again by the Royal Navy.

If Ross was effectively removed from the Admiralty's mind, the possibility of a north-west passage was certainly not. Almost within weeks of Ross's return, Barrow had persuaded the Admiralty Board, and consequently, the government, that a new attempt should be mounted to try and settle the problem. As on the previous attempt, two expeditions would be sent out but, this time one of them would go overland.

Lieutenant Parry had managed to avoid getting deeply involved in the conflict between Ross, Barrow, and Sabine, although quietly claiming that he had no faith in the existence of 'Croker's Mountains'. William Beechey (the father of Lieutenant Beechey) had painted his portrait and he had managed to retain the support of Barrow. After Ross he was the senior naval officer with experience of sailing through the ice of Baffin's Bay. In January 1819, Parry was told that he was to lead the sea-borne arm of the attempt to find the elusive passage.

At the same time the leader of overland expedition was also appointed. He was to be Lieutenant John Franklin, recently returned from Spitsbergen. That a naval officer should have been appointed to lead an overland expedition would have come as no surprise. The project was instigated by the Admiralty, and was in search of a sea-passage across the top of North America. Naval officers were skilled in navigation, and accurate position-fixing in the unknown lands to the north would be vital to an expedition's success (many of the British Army's actions throughout the nineteenth century required naval officers to navigate their way to battle). Franklin had proved that he had all the qualities required for leadership, he had scientific skills, and he had remained a friend of Sir Joseph Banks. He was to be accompanied by Dr John Richardson, a naval surgeon who would act as the expedition's naturalist. Richardson was born at Dumfries and had known the poet Robert Burns. He had served on many ships and had seen action on a number of occasions including service in North America with the First Battalion of Marines. Placed on half-pay at the end of the war, Richardson studied botany and mineralogy before attempting to set up a practice as a physician in Leith. He had been in practice just a few months before being appointed to the expedition. At thirty-one he was a year younger than Franklin.

The twenty-three-year-old Midshipman George Back had entered the Royal Navy in 1806 and, whilst serving in HMS *Arethusa* off the coast of Spain, was captured by the French during a cutting out expedition. The then thirteen-year-old midshipman was so small that he could be carried in a mule pannier during the march across the Pyrenees on his way to the prisoner-of-war camp at Verdun. On release, five years later, he walked across France and returned to England where he was appointed to HMS *Akbar* in which he saw service on the North America station. When the *Akbar* was paid off, Back transferred to HMS *Bulwark* before being appointed to the *Trent* under Franklin's command. With the return of the expedition, Back re-entered the *Bulwark* before being sent to rejoin Franklin.

A year younger than Back, Midshipman Robert Hood was the Irish-born son of a clergyman and teacher. He had entered the Royal Navy in 1811 at the age of fourteen and had served on a number of ships during the war, but had seen very little action and had spent two years on half-pay before accepting an appointment to serve under Franklin. Both midshipmen were skilled artists whose sketches and paintings would record the natives, terrain, and animal life of the country through which they passed. As 'attendant', the officers were to be looked after by John Hepburn, a Scottish seaman who had begun his working life as a cowherd before taking to the sea as an apprentice seaman about 1810. An American privateer captured his ship and he was subsequently handed over to the Royal Navy. In 1818, he had joined Franklin in the *Trent* and so impressed his captain through his hard work, courage and honesty, that he was invited to accompany the expedition. Despite his Scottish birth Franklin frequently referred to him as an 'English seaman'.

Franklin's instructions from the Admiralty informed him that

> the main object of the expedition was that of determining the latitudes and longitudes of the Northern Coast of North America, and the trending of that Coast from the Mouth of the Copper-Mine River to the eastern extremity of that Continent.

He was also to 'amend the very defective geography of the northern part of North America' and to 'be very careful to ascertain correctly the latitude and longitude of every remarkable spot upon the route, and of all the bays, harbours, rivers, headlands, etc, that might occur along the Northern Shore of North America.' He could choose to go directly north from Fort Chipewyan and make his way westerly to the mouth of the Coppermine River, or journey down the river itself (following the route pioneered by Samuel Hearne in 1771) to its junction with the Arctic Sea. From there he was to head in an easterly direction until he reached the 'eastern extremity' of North America. He was to leave 'conspicuous marks' at places that could help the passage of a ship along the coast, and to leave any messages that might help Parry. Observations of temperature, meteorology, dip and variation of the compass, and the intensity of magnetic force were to be constantly checked. In particular, Franklin was to investigate any affect the Aurora Borealis might have upon the compass needle, and to see if the phenomena was 'attended with any noise'. He was also to see if there were any commercial possibilities in the supposed copper deposits from which the river obtained its name.

Agents of the Hudson's Bay Co. along the proposed route were ordered 'to promote, by every possible means, the progress of the Expedition' and the rival North-West Co. issued letter of recommendation to its people. It was through these sources that Franklin expected to obtain his native guides and supplies to see him and his party to the Arctic Sea, and to bring them back.

The stores and equipment he had already acquired were put on-board the Hudson's Bay Co. ship *Prince of Wales* at Gravesend and, on 23 May 1819, the party set sail for York Factory on Hudson's Bay. After delays caused by bad weather, the ship reached Great Yarmouth a week later. The chronometers were checked against the known position of Yarmouth Church to see if the change from lying on their backs in storage to being carried upright in the officer's pockets had any effect. No change could be detected. Shore leave was allowed whilst the weather conditions continued to be against them and Midshipman Back went to pay a visit to a house just outside of the town. Whilst he was absent, the wind veered around to the south-east and signal guns were fired to bring everyone back on-board in order to take advantage of the change. No sight was seen of Back and, eventually, Franklin was forced to leave a message for him with an officer of HMS *Protector* – that vessel remaining behind in the harbour. He was to take the next coach to the Pentland Firth and take a passage across to Stromness, where, it was hoped, he would find the ship waiting for him.

When Franklin first boarded the *Prince of Wales* he learned from some of the Hudson's Bay Co. employees that the chances of obtaining boatmen to take the expedition onwards from York Factory were, at best, slight. He, therefore, wrote to

Above left: *Silhouette of Midshipman Robert Hood.*

Above right: *Able Seaman John Hepburn.*

the Admiralty requesting permission to recruit boatmen at Stromness when the ship called at the Orkney Islands. On arrival, Franklin and his party were looked after by the local agent of the Hudson's Bay Co. who provided accommodation and posted notices on church doors announcing that boatmen were required. The agent held out little hope that there would be a great supply of these men available due to the increased requirement of the herring fishery. Ten men were sought, but the notices brought in just four. Even then, the boatmen who had responded, examined the expedition proposals in the greatest detail and demanded that they be sent home free of expense and to be paid up to the day of their arrival back in Stromness. How different, Franklin noted, to the 'ready and thoughtless manner in which an English seaman enters upon any enterprise, however hazardous, without inquiring, or desiring to know where he is going, or what he is going about.'

Whilst the expedition's instruments were being tested and the boatmen being recruited, the welcome arrival of Midshipman Back was announced. The first he had known of the ship's departure from Yarmouth was when he saw them sailing past Caistor beach. He immediately requested local boatmen to take him out to the ship but, when they saw the urgency with which he wished to get on-board, they raised their prices to such a level that even the agitated Back refused to pay. As a consequence, he was forced to make an uncomfortable nine-day coach journey with little rest to catch up with his ship. Nevertheless, despite the exhaustion brought on by such a journey, Back insisted on attending a ball on the night of his arrival.

On the afternoon of 16 June, the *Prince of Wales*, in company with the *Eddystone*, the *Wear*, and the Missionary brig *Harmony*, set sail bound for York Factory. Five weeks later they were at the entrance to Davies Straits where they learned from a whaling ship that the ice in the straits was the heaviest in the master's experience. It was fast on the western shore and reached almost across to Greenland. Several whalers had been 'nipped' by the ice and two had been completely crushed. There had been no sign of Parry's expedition.

A further two weeks brought the little convoy through streams of icebergs to the coast of Resolution Island, situated at the north of the entrance to Hudson's Bay. At this point, matters took a very serious turn. Fog prevented the coast from being seen by the ships and the breeze fell away leaving them at the mercy of the current and the floating ice. The *Eddystone* was seen to be drifting towards large icebergs and boats from the *Wear* and the *Prince of Wales* were sent to help haul her clear. But then the *Prince of Wales* found she had problems of her own. The fog parted for an instant to reveal that she was within yards of the jagged shore, beneath cliffs that towered high above her masts. Moments later the ship's hull ran upon a rocky spur. The rudder was jumped out of position and was only saved from being lost entirely by securing tackles. The current then forced the ship to run alongside the coast and drove it out of control into a small bay where it looked to all observers

The Prince of Wales *striking against the rocks.*

that it was bound to be dashed against the shore. Extraordinarily, the ship ran over a ledge of rocks, the concussion resulting in the rudder being replaced. With the onset of a slight breeze, this meant that steerage could be gained, but not before the ship collided once again with the base of the cliffs. Adding to the difficulties was the number of women and children who fearfully thronged the upper deck despite attempts to keep them below and away from the possibility of falling masts.

Eventually the ship clawed its way into the ice-strewn sea where the *Eddystone* could be seen under tow by three of her boats. Nothing of the *Wear* remained in sight. The *Prince of Wales* was leaking badly and the older women and the children were sent across to the *Eddystone*. The younger women, however, refused to go and lent their assistance in manning the pumps. A sail was lowered over the side to help block the inflow of water as they entered Hudson's Bay.

The ships arrived off Upper Savage Island on 12 August and the passengers and crew were soon busily trading with Eskimos who paddled out to the ships in their kayaks. Seal oil, walrus teeth, whalebone, fur clothing, boots, and model kayaks were happily swapped for knives, nails, saws and tin kettles. As the Eskimos accepted each item it was licked in approval of the deal. Attempts by the seamen to pronounce Eskimo words were invariably greeted by a great wave of hilarity.

York Factory was reached on 30 August and, to everyone's delight, the *Wear* was seen at anchor. The governor of the Hudson's Bay Co. post, Mr Williams, went on-board the *Prince of Wales* and told Franklin that he had been informed of his coming and was prepared to help as much as he could. Contact with the North-West Co. was to prove just as easy. The commercial war between the two companies had, however, almost reached boiling point and the governor of the Hudson's Bay Co. had detained the local officials of his rivals and they were being held at York Factory. Nevertheless, they proved willing to give their support to the expedition by providing letters for their agents along the route.

Problems, however, soon began to appear. It had been expected that an Eskimo interpreter would be picked up at York Factory, but it turned out that the Eskimos had left their camp at Churchill a month earlier. All that the governor could do was to promise that, in the following spring, he would send an interpreter to try and catch up with the expedition. Furthermore, the boat supplied by the governor proved to be too large to make a passage up-river with the small number of boatmen that Franklin had brought over with him, and too small to take all of the expedition's supplies. A steersman was supplied by the governor to help, and he further promised that those supplies that could not be carried would be sent on the following spring.

Franklin's plan was to take the boat up the Hayes River and follow a 600-mile chain of trading posts to the main depot on the Saskatchewan River – Cumberland House (originally founded by Samuel Hearn). From there a journey of about 1,200 miles would bring them to the Great Slave Lake.

The expedition left York Factory to an eight-gun salute on 9 September and, under sail, headed up the Hayes River. Only six miles had been achieved before the wind failed them and they were forced to resort to 'tracking' the boat by hauling it along from the bank. Far from resembling an English canal tow-path the banks of the river were steep, muddy, and littered with fallen trees; Franklin considered the work of tracking to be 'extremely laborious' and one which reduced the speed of passage to no more than two miles an hour. It was merely the start of a miserable journey.

Five days after they started out, three boats from York Factory covering the same journey joined them. An attempt was made to keep the four boats together, but Franklin's boat was so over laden that it soon fell behind. At this, Franklin suggested that the Hudson's Bay Co. boats help him by taking some of his cargo. Despite the note from the governor, his plea was ignored and the other boats pressed on. As a result, much time was wasted in following wrong channels although one of the company's clerks – perhaps through a stricken conscience – was found waiting with advice at particularly difficult stretches of the river. At one stage, the towline broke and the boat was swept broadside down the river. The situation was only saved by the occupants leaping out and holding the boat's head to the current as the towline was repaired.

At Rock House trading post on the Hill River, they learned that the rapids ahead of them were much worse than any they had passed. Consequently, they were forced to leave part of their stores at the post in the hope that they would be forwarded the following spring. The only way around such rapids was by 'portaging'. The boat had to be emptied and carried around the obstacle, then the cargo had to be retrieved and taken over the same route to rejoin the boat. It was backbreaking work from which no one was excused.

Snow had been falling for several days before they reached the Oxford House trading post on Holey Lake. Franklin had been deeply unimpressed by the drunken Indians he had encountered at York Factory, and had his first impression supported by the few disease-ridden Cree Indians he found at the post. His request to them for help in shooting ducks to supplement his rations was ignored.

Three days later, at White Fall River, the expedition came across their first sight of a route marker known as a 'lopstick'. This was a tall pine with its lower branches lopped off. Such markers were usually known by the name of the individual responsible for their production. To achieve such fame, all that was necessary was for a man to ply his comrades with rum whereupon they would carry out the required pruning and name the tree after him.

At the same site, Franklin was on his way to supervise his men when he slipped on wet moss and plunged into the river. The surging current forced him downstream towards a lower set of rapids as he tried desperately to find a handhold on the river's bank. Eventually, he managed to grasp a branch of an overhanging willow and was dragged ashore by two men. True to his nature, he was more concerned about the pocket chronometer he was carrying than his soaking in the freezing water. Handing the watch to one of his rescuers as he scrabbled up the bank, Franklin was mortified to see the man drop the instrument onto some rocks. The workings of the chronometer survived the experience, but the minute-hand was broken off.

Two days later, the governor of York Factory overtook the expedition. In turn, at Norway House trading post, just north of Lake Winnipeg; they caught up with a group of immigrants with whom they had shared the voyage across the Atlantic on the *Prince of Wales*. Amid the wild, bleak, landscape these people welcomed Franklin and his party 'in the light of old acquaintances'. From Norway House (where the manager replaced the broken minute-hand of Franklin's chronometer) the party headed across the northern edge of Lake Winnipeg in company with the Hudson's Bay Co. boats carrying the immigrants.

At the mouth of the Saskatchewan River, the routes of the Hudson's Bay Co. and the North-West Co. coincided and it was not long before evidence of the latter company's 'Voyageurs' were seen on the river's bank. This sight prompted the Hudson's Bay Co. men to prime their weapons and advance with great caution, so heated was the disagreement between the two commercial enterprises. However, all that was seen through the low-lying mists that coated the river, were small groups of sickly Indians suffering mainly from whooping cough and measles.

As they continued up the river, heavy snow began to fall and ice started to build up on the oars. Spray froze in air rendered more bitter by a stiff headwind.

Thirteen days after they had entered the Saskatchewan River, Cumberland House hove into view. It had been a close run thing. As it was, the oarsmen of the boat had to break the ice lining the shore before the boat could be brought alongside. Governor Williams, now removed from York Factory to winter at Cumberland House, informed Franklin that, as there was no possibility of his proceeding further, he and his team should accept his invitation to remain at the post until the spring. Accordingly, Franklin's men were put to completing an unfinished building that would serve them as accommodation for the coming months.

Two difficulties immediately became apparent. The Orkney boatmen had decided that they had had enough of travelling through such a country and demanded that they return at first opportunity to York Factory, and to the first ship they could find to take them home. To that was added the fact that Franklin had hoped to collect some Indian guides and hunters to assist him in his passage northwards. He found, however, that the Cree Indians, instead of supplying the depot with victuals, merely collected there in the hope of being given food. Such was their poor condition that rumours of cannibalism among the Indians was widely spread and accepted.

In addition to the Hudson's Bay Co. post, the North-West Co.'s buildings were situated a short distance away. Scrupulously trying not to be seen to be favouring one company over another, Franklin paid his respects to the manager, Mr Connolly, and was rewarded with an invitation to join him on New Year's Eve to dine on roasted beaver and to join the voyageurs and their women at a celebratory dance.

Just over a week later Franklin decided that, as guides and hunters for his journey were not to be available for hire at Cumberland House, he would press on to Fort Chipewyan on Lake Athabasca. There he expected to have better luck in procuring the men he wanted. He had already written to the manager at Fort Chipewyan, but felt no certainty that his letter would arrive. He would take Back and Hepburn with him, leaving Richardson and Hood to bring on the supplies with the spring thaw.

Both the Hudson's Bay Co. and their rival provided sledges and men for the journey to Fort Chipewyan. The party of ten men and seven dog-sledges set off on 8 January 1820, with the thermometer registering 42 degrees below zero, and the men of both companies grumbling about the weight on the sledges. Well protected against the harsh weather with fur hats, coats with hoods, and with moccasins laced to their legs, it was not the cold that provided the greatest difficulty for the British seamen, but the unaccustomed use of snowshoes. These vital accoutrements for passing through the winter landscape were between 4 and 6ft long with the leading edge turned up. Even without an accumulation of snow, the snowshoes weighed 2lb each and Franklin soon found that they chafed and caused blisters and swollen ankles. It was no use looking for sympathy amongst the voyageurs and company men for whom failing to keep up simply meant being left behind. Progress was made in 'Indian file' with the lead team, on being relieved, taking up the rearmost position.

On the first night, as they huddled beneath buffalo skin blankets and a covering of snow, the mercury in the thermometers froze.

The 263-mile journey to their first halting place, Carlton House Depot, took two weeks and was not without incident. Hepburn had supplies stolen from under his head by sledge-dogs whilst he slept, and Back, sleeping by the camp-fire, was abruptly awoken 'by an acute pain in my right foot, popped out my head and saw my right shoe and Buffalo skin on fire, made a sudden jump up to my knees in the snow… cooled my foot and went to rest'.

At Carlton House, Back rejoiced in 'cutting off the muzzle lashings' (shaving) and enjoyed the meal of buffalo steak provided by the depot manager. Pipes were continually smoked to fill up 'a vast vacancy in conversation' and Assiniboine (Stone) and Cree Indian buffalo hunters were met as they arrived to trade goods at the depot. Yet again Franklin was failed to be impressed by the tales he was told by the Hudson's Bay Co. men that the Indians frequently resorted to 'gross and habitual treachery' and the Stone Indians 'steal whatever they can'. Clashes between the traders and the Indians, and between different tribes were commonplace. Franklin was particularly affronted by the Indian's practice of attacking lone travellers, stripping them, and leaving them to fend for themselves regardless of the weather conditions. Any attempt at resistance was met by instant death. The casual approach to murder and its constant threat was exemplified when Franklin heard an elderly Cree tell the depot manager that the Stone Indians were talking of killing all the white people. The manager shrugged off the threat, but the Cree was annoyed enough to remark 'A pretty state we shall then be in without the goods you bring us.'

The party left Carlton House after ten days and travelled through deep snow and in temperatures so low that the thermometer was 'of no use'. Two days were spent at a small depot at Green Lake where, according to Back, 'The Indians were attacked with measles, the hunters had failed and the lake yielded no fish, the dogs had had nothing for five days and the inhabitants were little better.' When they left to continue their journey, the small population of the depot turned out to salute their departure with musket-fire – the women contributing most to the noise as their men were away hunting.

More musket salutes greeted them three days later as they arrived at the Hudson's Bay Co. fort on Isle-a-la-Crosse Lake. The lake had been so named from the Indians habit of playing the game of lacrosse on one of its islands and its waters provided copious supplies of excellent fish for the fort's inhabitants. Franklin's decision to travel to Fort Chipewyan proved to be well justified when he found that, at Isle-a-la-Crosse, he had caught up with his letter to the Governor of Fort Chipewyan. Despite many personal kindnesses he had received along his journey, he had now found evidence that the warring trade companies were not providing the whole-hearted support he needed if he was to be successful in his venture.

Far left: *The Indian chief Ekeicho and his son.*

Left: *Fort Providence.*

Bad weather delayed the departure from the fort until 5 March. On the following night, beneath a spectacular Aurora Borealis, Back recorded that 'Having a desire to hear the canoe songs we enlivened the spirits of the Canadians (i.e. French-Canadian voyageurs) with a dram which soon took effect, and they entertained us till midnight, the whole joining chorus.' The departure the next morning was delayed until hangovers were shaken clear.

Methye Portage was reached on 13 March. Twelve miles of carrying everything overland was eased by the spectacular scenery that so impressed Franklin that he camped early that night in order that Back could make a sketch of the deep valleys and rugged mountains. A week later the party arrived at the North West Co. depot at Pierre au Calumet where the manager, John Stuart, gloomily informed them that they would be unlikely to find any voyageurs to accompany them to the north as they were terrified of the Eskimos. Apparently a trading mission sent by canoe down the MacKenzie River had been murdered. Furthermore, the Indians at Fort Chipewyan had suffered badly from an illness that prevented them hunting. The inhabitants were forced to survive the winter on the few fish they could catch.

Despite this depressing news, Franklin declined an invitation to remain at Pierre au Calumet and pressed on towards Fort Chipewyan. Within a day's sledging of their destination, the party was held up by a blizzard. But, the following morning, it only took a short portage to enable them to reach the banks of the Athabasca Lake and see the log buildings of the fort.

Their journey had taken almost two and a half months through temperatures that rarely ascended to freezing point. In total they had travelled 857 miles across frozen rivers and lakes and, for the most part, slept beneath open skies. Snowshoes had been mastered and much learned about travel through an unforgiving land.

Fort Chipewyan belonged to the North West Co., and the day following their arrival, Franklin crossed over to a small island on Lake Athabasca where the Hudson's Bay Co. had its depot – Fort Wedderburne. Such was the antagonism between the two companies that, in order to discuss matters which affected both sides, Franklin was forced to erect a tent away from both forts to provide a neutral ground.

During his first days at Fort Chipewyan, Franklin met one of the North-West Co.'s half-breed interpreters who had descended the Coppermine River and, consequently, been able to draw a crude, but important, map of the route as he remembered it. As the map was being drawn, a Chipewyan Indian arrived and added the route along the northern seacoast he had used during an attack upon the Eskimos. He also told Franklin of two other rivers that flowed to the north coast east of the Great Slave Lake. One of these was the Fish River – later to be of great importance to both Franklin and Back.

Another new acquaintance to be of considerable help was Peter Warren Dease, a North West Co. employee who had spent a considerable time in the barren lands to the north of the Great Slave Lake. He proved to be most helpful in explaining the problems liable to be encountered, both in the country itself and in dealings with the Indians.

Less helpful, and infinitely more annoying, were the huge swarms of mosquitoes that arrived with the May melting of the snow and the break up of the ice. According to Back the insects 'ceased not to torment us night and day ...these creatures have no regard for decency'.

Even worse than the all-pervading mosquitoes, was the problem of raising men for the expedition. Both the companies had been requested to provide volunteers, but few names came forward, and those that did were demanding exorbitant wages that were beyond Franklin's purse. Relief came, however, from an unexpected source. A North-West Co. employee arrived from the Great Slave Lake with the news that an Indian chief had offered his help in raising men to act as hunters and guides. The chief was named Ekeicho (or 'Akaitcho', as Franklin spelt his name). He had, according to Back, told his men

I am your chief, but do not on that account follow me now. I do not wish to command you to do so. If I did I know you would cheerfully obey, but you must enter with a zealous warmth into this subject and recollect we are going to provide for, and defend if necessary, the chiefs that are coming.

Such noble sentiments 'proportionally elevated' the feeling of both Franklin and Back.

Their spirits were raised yet higher when Richardson and Hood arrived with two canoes on 13 July. During their journey, one of the canoes with two men in it had been overturned and swept away by a strong current. When news of this reached the remainder of the party, Hood jumped into the other canoe urging others to join him. He then shot the unknown rapids until he reached the upturned craft. One man had managed to make his way to the bank, but the other was never found.

They brought with them ten voyageurs who all showed a willingness to continue northwards with the expedition. Consequently, with more volunteers coming forward as a result of the news that guides and hunters had been found, Franklin was able to muster a total of sixteen voyageurs. Only a few gallons of spirit had been brought up due to shortages along the route, and the expected supply of pemmican (a concoction of pounded meat, fat, and berries) had proved to be so mouldy that it had been thrown away by Richardson. The Hudson's Bay Co. employees had eaten a supply of pemmican that Franklin had left for Richardson to bring on from Isle-a-la-Crosse.

Fort Chipewyan was 'cheerfully quitted' and the party, now consisting of twenty-seven people (four naval officers, one seaman, sixteen voyageurs, three voyageurs' wives and three children) in three canoes, headed down the Stoney and Slave rivers towards Fort Resolution on the south side of the Great Slave Lake. They had set off with little more than one day's food and for four days only a single fish was caught to add to the rations. However, on 22 July, several geese were shot and a buffalo brought down, but only after fourteen musket balls had been fired into its body. Three days later Fort Resolution was reached and the vicious jaws of the sand flies were added to the miseries of the mosquitoes.

At the fort, Franklin was able to add dried meat to his depleted supplies. He also took on the services of an interpreter to assist in his dealing with the Coppermine Indians waiting for him at Fort Providence, on the northern shore of the lake.

A river portage.

The fort was reached after a day and a half's journey from Fort Resolution. They were welcomed by Willard-Ferdinand Wentzel, the North West Co.'s clerk who was in charge of the fort. It was Wentzel who had arranged the Indian guides and hunters and was, in turn, expected by the Indians to accompany them on the expedition. This suited Franklin admirably as Wentzel would not only take charge of the Indians, but would also control the voyageurs. His ability to speak in the native Indian tongue was also an invaluable asset in keeping watch on the interpreter's transactions.

The following day the Indians returned from a hunting trip. Franklin and the other officers put on their uniforms and flew a silk Union Flag from their tent pole to greet them. The chief, Ekeicho, solemnly walked from his canoe and shook hands with Franklin who invited him to join them in smoking a pipe and taking a drink of watered spirit. Ekeicho, it seems, had arrived with some disappointment. He had heard that Franklin's party had with them a great chief with powers to raise the dead, and he had been looking forward to meeting some of his ancestors. Wentzel, however, had been forced to explain the limits of Richardson's medical abilities, and the chief complained that he now felt as if he had lost his relatives for the second time. Nevertheless, Franklin cheered the chief up by explaining that he was in his country at the wish of King George and for the benefit of all the people. Ekeicho then promised to guide the party until the expedition was over, and their hunters would 'do their utmost' to provide food. After discussions, Franklin abandoned his original plan to descend the MacKenzie River until he approached the Coppermine River, and decided to follow the Indian's advice to go directly north to the Coppermine via a chain of lakes.

The following night a dance for the voyageurs and the Indians was held at the fort. Hepburn did not attend the celebration and decided instead to place some burning embers in Franklin's tent so that the smoke would drive out the mosquitoes. Unfortunately, the seaman fell asleep only to wake in time to find the tent on fire. He dragged out gunpowder and other baggage, but could not save the tent or the flag. On learning of this, Franklin's main concern was that the Indians would interpret the incident as a bad omen and tried to keep it from them. Wentzel, on the other hand, knew that Ekeicho would find out, and insisted that the dancing continue to demonstrate that the matter was of no importance.

On the morning of 1 August, Ekeicho and his Indians were sent ahead to wait at the entrance to the Yellowknife River. This was done to get them out of the way whilst the baggage was being packed. Their automatic begging to be given things would, it was felt, hinder the operation of packing. Guns, powder, and ammunition were stowed along with knives, tools, nails, boat fittings, cloth blankets and fishing nets. Needles, mirrors, and beads were taken to give to the natives. The provisions included flour, 'portable soup', chocolate and tea.

The party had been strengthened during their stay at Fort Providence, not only by Wentzel, but also by a second interpreter and an additional voyageur. They set off in three canoes on the afternoon of 2 August. A fourth smaller canoe carried the women and children. Ekeicho's group was met at the entrance to the Yellowknife River; their numbers increased by more Indians who intended to escort the expedition for the first few days. In all, seventeen native canoes, many paddled by Indian women who spent much of their time loudly quarrelling, made their way up the river with Franklin and his party.

After a short portage, a lake was reached which Franklin named 'Lake Prosperous' – a perhaps unfortunate name for any prosperity which attached itself to the expedition did not extend to the supplies, and it was not long before the voyageurs were complaining about the lack of food. Back was able to help, whilst amazing the Indians, by catching fish with a feather and a hook, and a few more fish were trapped in the nets. Franklin instituted a system of keeping watch, both for any threat from strangers and to keep any eye on the Indians – an arrangement which impressed Ekeicho and saved the expedition when fire broke out among the tents in the early hours of the morning of 8 August. Four days later, lack of food brought the voyageurs to the verge of mutiny. They were only deflected from outright disobedience by Franklin threatening to make an example of the first mutineer by 'blowing out his brains'. Part of the problem was that the voyageurs wanted to get at the few remaining provisions to have as large a meal as possible. They appeared to have no understanding of the principle of rationing.

That night, the Indian hunters returned to the camp with enough caribou meat to keep the party fed for the next two days. A few paltry fish kept the party going until the 16th when, to everyone's delight, the hunters came in with the carcasses of seventeen caribou. Now that enough meat was available to see them through to their proposed winter camp, Franklin allowed Ekeicho to hunt caribou in order to provide his family with winter clothing whilst other Indians went on ahead to ensure food would be waiting when they arrived at the camp.

The site selected by the Indians for the winter camp was reached on the morning of 20 August. They had travelled 553 miles from Fort Chipewyan and 186 from Fort Providence. As it was a Sunday, Franklin celebrated the achievement by holding a church service. The expedition set up its winter quarters on a hill overlooking 'Winter Lake'. The site was well wooded with large spruce trees and Franklin soon had the voyageurs at work building a storehouse or helping the Indians bring in the caribou they had shot. The women began to cut the meat into strips ready for its preservation by drying, and Wentzel sent a party of hunters to set up a cache of meat on the bank of the Coppermine River.

Five days after their arrival the first signs of winter began to appear with ice forming on small pools of water. On the 25th, Hepburn had gone out hunting and had not been seen before fog fell upon the camp. Two Indian hunters, sent after him, failed to find him. The concern over Hepburn was added to when Ekeicho arrived at the camp with a mere fifteen caribou. He told Franklin that his brother-in-law had died and the recent days had been spent 'in bewailing his loss.' Even the winter clothing had not been obtained, and the party sent to cache food on the Coppermine had left to join in the mourning. Even worse, when Franklin told the chief of his plans to reconnoitre the route to the Coppermine, and to travel some distance down the river in company with the Indians before winter finally set in, Ekeicho promptly refused to go. He would, he said, send a few of his young men but would consider them to be dead from the moment they boarded the canoes. In the face of such obstruction Franklin was forced to reconsider his plans overnight.

The following morning saw the welcome return of Hepburn. He had been found by hunters a few miles from the camp carrying a caribou across his back. As he approached the camp one of the voyageurs offered to take the load from him, but Hepburn merely replied 'Never mind old boy, I can carry it'.

In view of the chief's refusal to help with the reconnaissance, combined with a threat to return to Fort Providence, Franklin ordered Midshipmen Back and Hood and seven voyageurs to make their way to the Coppermine by canoe. Ekeicho relented enough to send an Indian hunter along to help. They were to reach the river and even descend as much of it as they could if there was no risk of them being frozen in. They had eight days supply of food and were not to be away for more than a fortnight.

As Back's party left, Ekeicho took his hunters away to find enough meat to see the party through the winter. A few Indians remained behind to hunt locally including the family of an elderly Indian relative of Ekeicho named Keskarrah.

After ten days supervising the building of the log cabins at the camp, Franklin, Richardson, Hepburn and one of the voyageurs left Wentzel in charge as they set out to reach the Coppermine on foot. They were accompanied by the Indian, Keskarrah, who deeply impressed his European companions by stripping his clothes off every night and warming himself in front of the fire naked before retiring beneath a deerskin blanket. After a dozen miles, the trees began to thin out and soon the party was passing through 'a naked country' as a cold wind drove the falling snow around them. After three days, 'Point Lake', a widening of the Coppermine River, was reached. There being no purpose in remaining longer than was necessary, the party set out on the return journey the following day. The night of 13 September was spent sleeping sitting up with their backs against a bank of earth, but a sound sleep was had by all. Franklin, however, was bothered by a sprained ankle which slowed progress down but, on the 15th, the party covered nineteen miles and arrived back at the camp at sunset.

Back's party had returned to the camp the day after Franklin had set out. They had reached Point Lake (which Back doubted was actually part of the Coppermine River) with little difficulty beyond the poor weather conditions they experienced. Three days after they had set out, Back and Hood had set up their tent and retired for the night as the voyageurs slept out on the snow in the open air. During the night the wind blew so hard that the tent was blown down. As the two midshipmen got out to re-erect their shelter they looked around in amazement – it seemed as if all the others had vanished. In fact they were all buried several inches under a fall of snow.

It was probably at this stage that a quite unlooked for complication occurred. With their senior officers away, the two midshipmen became extremely friendly with a fifteen-year-old Indian girl named Greenstockings. Her father was Keskarrah, the Indian guide who was also absent with the Franklin party. Franklin himself noted that the already twice-married Greenstockings was 'considered by her tribe to be a great beauty' and Hood was to sketch her likeness – much to the distress of her mother who believed that when King George saw her likeness he would want to take her for his bride. It seems that Back gained the upper hand early in the contest to gain the girl's attention, but Hood was not to give up that easily.

With the building of the camp – now named by Franklin 'Fort Enterprise' – almost completed, the party moved into their 'house' during the first days of October. The building lay 50ft long by 23 wide and contained three bedrooms, a common room, and a kitchen. Although draughty, once a fire had been lit, it provided a comfortable shelter from the forthcoming winter.

A hunting party of Indians returned with a disappointing amount of meat claiming that their cache of caribou had been raided by Indians from the local Dog-Rib tribe. This did not trouble Franklin too much, however, as many caribou had been killed locally as they migrated passed the camp. Almost 200 of the animals had been shot and were stored in the camp or in caches close by. There were, nevertheless, serious shortages amongst their stores, particularly in ammunition and tobacco. Franklin decided that Back and Wentzel would return to Fort Providence to collect the stores that should have arrived from York Factory. The separation of Back and Hood might have been welcomed as their competition over Greenstockings may have threatened to turn into physical conflict. Perhaps inevitably, with Back away, Greenstockings moved to an even closer relationship with Hood. Franklin sent a party of voyageurs to take letters to Back for forwarding on to England. Amongst them was a letter to Back himself in which Franklin told him

> You will hear of the change that has taken place in family affairs, perhaps you were prepared to expect the pleasure of having a female companion in your room. Hood says he shall inform you of the circumstance, I need not therefore enlarge upon the subject.

Back was to learn that, as a result of Hood's ardent attention, Greenstockings was pregnant.

Fort Enterprise.

Ekeicho returned to Fort Enterprise a week after Back's departure and soon proved to be a severe drain on the expedition's supplies. With the knowledge that many caribou carcasses were held in the fort and in caches outside, the Indians could not be persuaded to go out hunting. They, in turn, blamed the lack of ammunition despite being skilled in traditional ways of trapping game. In desperation, Franklin had some pewter cups melted down to provided five musket balls for each of the hunters, but the result was a mere two caribou – both brought down by Ekeicho's marksmanship.

On 23 November, Belanger, one of Back's voyageurs, returned to Fort Enterprise with letters and the news of the death of King George III. A letter from Back reported that Nicholas Weeks, the clerk in charge at Fort Providence, had claimed that he was under orders to provide no more help to the expedition, and that Back was on his way south to Fort Chipewyan in an attempt to find more supplies. The Indians who had arrived with Belanger wasted no time in telling Ekeicho that Weeks was spreading the word that Franklin and his party were not naval officers at all, but mere traders who were intent in setting up in competition with the established trading companies.

One of the interpreters, St. Germain, was sent to Fort Providence with eight voyageurs to bring up the stores mustered there by Back. As they left they were followed by a wild dog, which had attached itself to Fort Enterprise. Franklin had hopes that the dog could be trained to haul a load but, much to his disappointment, the voyageurs killed and ate the animal on their first night away from the camp. Two weeks later, Franklin managed to persuade Ekeicho that his Indians were proving to be too much of a drain on the fort's resources and, at the cost of the remaining ammunition and a fishing net, the Indians departed leaving behind the old, the sick, – and Greenstockings.

The winter months settled down to a routine. Church services were held every Sunday with the Lord's Prayer and the Creed said in French for the benefit of the voyageurs. The main food staple was caribou meat with the occasional fish. Sunday mornings were enlivened with a cup of chocolate and special occasions were graced by sugarless tea. Candles were made from strips of cotton shirt and caribou fat. Hepburn became skilled in the manufacture of soap from salt, wood-ash and fat – a product greeted with some suspicion by the voyageurs. The new year was welcomed by an exchange of greetings and the supply of a little flour and fat to each man, but 'the feast was defective from the want of rum'. To help lighten the mood at the fort, Franklin introduced sledging down the banks of the river, the overturning of the officer's sledge providing the most amusement. The sport was not without its hazards – Franklin was thrown into the snow on one occasion when 'a fat Indian woman drove her sledge over me, and sprained my knee severely.'

In mid-January, the voyageurs returned from Fort Providence with two kegs of rum, 60lb of musket balls, some clothing and two rolls of tobacco. The journey had taken twenty-one days but, much to Franklin's annoyance, two of the days had been spent in a drunken stupor when one of the rum casks had been broached.

Two weeks later, Wentzel and the interpreter, St. Germain, arrived from Fort Providence with two Eskimo interpreters. The newcomers were Tattannoeuck ('belly') and Hoeootoerock ('ear'), but had acquired the English names of Augustus and Junius from their first arrival at Fort Churchill. Only Augustus spoke English. Immediately on their arrival, the Eskimos built themselves an igloo on the bank of the Winter River.

In early February, two Indians arrived from Ekeicho's hunting party with a demand for more ammunition. They also brought the information that the rumours spread by Weeks had reached the Indians, and that minor bills from Indians had gone unpaid at Fort Providence. The situation was not improved when Franklin sent St. Germain to Ekeicho with a request for two hunters to join a party he was sending to Fort Providence to collect the remaining stores. The interpreter, who was losing interest in the whole enterprise, spent much of his time supporting the ill-founded rumours.

More ammunition, sugar, and tobacco arrived at the beginning of March followed a week later by the return of Back. His journey of over 1,000 miles on snowshoes in pursuit of the expedition's supplies had cost him frostbite and a plunge through the ice of a lake. With the lack of supplies at Fort Providence, and with Week's severely uncooperative attitude, Back had been forced to travel as far south as Fort Chipewyan where he arrived to the astonishment of the Hudson's Bay Co. employees who had heard that the whole of Franklin's party had 'already fallen by the spears of the Esquimaux.' This misinformation, nevertheless, did not prevent George Simpson, the Hudson's Bay Co.'s senior representative, from turning down Back's request for supplies. He considered the midshipman to be 'impertinent' in his demands. The North West Co., on the other hand, helped as much as they could. On leaving Fort Chipewyan, Back was pleasurably surprised to find a line of women waiting to bid him farewell, and that custom expected him to embrace each one. Unfortunately, the moment was spoiled when he slipped on the ice and fell at the feet of an 'old squaw'.

Back also found that he had a score to settle with his companion, Hood, over the question of Greenstockings' pregnancy. When it appeared that a duel was in the offing, Hepburn quietly removed the charges from both midshipmen's pistols before some accord was returned to the young men's relationship.

Ekeicho returned to Fort Enterprise at the end of March to be met by his demanded shotgun salute and the flying of the Union Flag. He admitted to helping the spread of rumours that continued to be fed by Weeks at Fort Providence, but accepted Franklin's assurance that they were all false. The chief agreed to accompany the expedition to the north and to concentrate on getting as much caribou meat as he could before the journey's start. The return of the Indians yet again strained the fort's supplies and Franklin was distressed to see Indian women and children reduced to chewing on animal skin and breaking up bones before boiling them in an attempt to gain nourishment. Fortunately, the Indians returned to the hunt with the beginning of the thaw and the arrival of large numbers of caribou. By the beginning of May Richardson noted in his logbook 'A fly seen'.

On the 11th of the same month, Wentzel returned from a visit to the Indian camp where he had been supervising the preparation of the dried meat that would form the chief item of the expedition's provisions. Franklin took the opportunity to explain to the clerk his plans for the coming journey. He had decided that, once the mouth of the Coppermine had been gained, he would reduce the party to no more than enough to man two canoes. In effect, this meant that the Indians would return under the control of Wentzel as Franklin, the rest of the naval party, the voyageurs, and interpreters, would press on eastwards along the coast. The plan suited Wentzel well as he had requested that he might be allowed to return once the Arctic Sea had been reached.

By the end of May, Ekeicho was proving difficult once again, basing his complaints on the rumours spread by Weeks. He also complained of not being treated with the respect that should be accorded to a chief of his rank, on not being given new clothing, and the weakness of the rum he had been given. In a fit of pique, he refused all offers of presents and retired to his tepee. A change, however, was brought about when the other hunters began to accept the proffered gifts. The chief saw this action as an erosion of his authority and swiftly changed his attitude to one of desiring to please in order to regain his previous stature. He refused, nevertheless, to take his guides and hunters to the Coppermine River to set up a cache of food. The intention of all the Indians was to wait until the party had set off to see if they could get their hands on any stores that were left behind. To avoid this, and to keep control, Franklin decided to send Richardson ahead with the fifteen remaining voyageurs (two had been discharged earlier), two hunters, and all the expedition's baggage to establish a camp at Point Lake.

Richardson's party set off at four o'clock in the morning on 4 June. Each of the voyageurs was carrying a pack or dragging a sledge containing 120lb of supplies and personal belongings. Other stores were carried in three dog-sledges. Before they left, Franklin had another formal meeting with Ekeicho in the presence of Wentzel. He told the Indian chief that he was to ensure that supplies would be left at the fort before the following September in case the return route should pass that way. The chief agreed 'with a smile' that he would use his 'best endeavours to prepare provisions' and believed that 'if the animals are tolerably numerous, we may get plenty before you can embark on the river'.

Ten days later, Franklin and the remainder of the party set off from the fort taking the three canoes over the frozen river by sledge. The thin ice made the journey difficult and both Franklin and Back suffered a cold plunge as a result. At one stage, the ice of a lake was 2ft under water and contained many holes through which several of the party slipped. Back and one of the voyageurs separately succeeded in getting lost and were extremely fortunate in finding their way back to the main party. They arrived at Richardson's camp a week after starting only to find that Ekeicho and his hunters had used all their ammunition without bringing in a single animal. It later transpired that the chief had been supplying his close family with ammunition and pretending to have used it whilst hunting. Richardson, however, had kept two of the hunters with him, and had succeeded in obtaining 200lb of meat that had since been dried. In answer to Ekeicho's demand for more ammunition, Franklin issued a small amount and told the chief that further supplies of ball and powder would only be issued in return for supplies brought in. In the meantime, the voyageurs were employed in making sledges and pounding the meat to make pemmican for use on the journey along the Arctic coast.

At half past eleven in the morning on the 25 June 1821, the expedition at last began its journey down the Coppermine River, dragging their canoes and supplies over the ice of Point Lake. A camp was made early that day as the voyageurs had quickly become exhausted and, on the following day, it became clear to Franklin that the loads being carried by his men were too much. He decided, therefore, to cut the number of his canoes from three to two, caching one by the side of the lake for use on his return.

To feed the party, at least two caribou had to be provided each day by the hunters. This was proving difficult and soon the pemmican intended for use on the northern coast was being used to supply the expedition's needs. The voyageurs showed little concern over this for, with each meal of the preserved meat, the load they had to carry became lighter.

As they left Point Lake, an opportunity occurred to put the canoes into the running water of the river itself. Thus began several days of alternately using the open river and carrying the canoes and stores over stretches that remained ice-bound. Considerable concern was felt over the amount of pemmican that was being consumed due to the failure of the hunters to bring in enough fresh meat. At one stage, the Indians came across a dog that had escaped from the main party. They assumed that everyone had been killed by other Indians and fled southwards leaving the caribou they had shot that day. Fortunately, they ran into Ekeicho's personal slave who assured them that there had been no massacre. The meat, however, was lost. On the following day, amends were made when the hunters came in with the first musk ox to be shot.

At the base of a range of tall mountains, the party came across The Hook, an Indian chief they had encountered at Fort Enterprise. A rival of Ekeicho's, the chief lost no time in presenting Franklin and his people with so much fresh meat that there was enough to preserve some of it as pemmican. The Hook offered this welcome addition to the supplies by (according to Franklin) saying

> The amount, indeed, is very small, but I will cheerfully give you what I have: we are too much indebted to the white people, to allow them to want food in our lands, whilst we have any to give them. Our families can live on fish until we can procure more meat, but the season is too short to allow of your delaying to gain subsistence in that manner.

Even further, the chief agreed with Franklin to provide caches of food and leave signposts to his camp should Franklin be in need of either on his return journey.

It was at The Hook's camp that the last was seen of Greenstockings. She had accompanied the expedition thus far, but was now coming under the attention of one of the hunters who, despite her condition, decided to remain with her rather than continue downriver. Her aged father, nevertheless, stayed with Franklin. Both Franklin (who described the girl as 'fascinating') and Richardson mentioned the leaving of Greenstockings, but Back let the moment go unrecorded and Hood, the father of her expected child, left no surviving record.

Passing through Point Lake.

Three days after leaving The Hook's camp, the expedition came within range of Eskimos and the Indians began to show signs of nervousness at the prospect. Arrangements were made to see if contact could be made with the Eskimos and a guard was constantly kept whenever camp was made. Ekeicho offered to send two of his hunters ahead but Franklin, having doubts about the wisdom of this, sent, instead, the two Eskimo interpreters armed with both gifts and with pocket pistols hidden beneath their coats.

There followed several hours of intense anxiety. Franklin would not allow the Indians to roam far from camp in case they ran into hostile Eskimos, and the officers kept lookout from the nearest vantage point. Ekeicho insisted that the two interpreters had been murdered and that Eskimos were just waiting to attack the party.

Whilst the party waited, the officers climbed a hill to see the land ahead of them. All that could be seen was a range of blue mountains on the far north-eastern horizon. Richardson was left on the hilltop as he had the first watch for the night. Looking out into the darkening sky he heard a slight sound behind him and turned to find nine white wolves advancing silently towards him. The animals were ranged out in a crescent and their advance was clearly being made with the intention of driving him over the cliff edge. Rising slowly, Richardson saw them come to a halt and make way as he passed between them, fearing to fire his musket in case he alerted any hostile Eskimos. Later that night a caribou was driven over the edge by the same pack of white wolves.

With the two Eskimo interpreters having failed to return, Franklin decided that the officers and the voyageurs should make their way downriver to search for them. Before leaving, he made the Indians promise to remain where they were for, if they were to come into contact with the Eskimos without the officers present, a bloodbath could occur. He also instructed Wentzel to remain behind to ensure that Ekeicho's men did not try to advance.

That evening, the advanced party fell in with Junius, who despite being unable to speak English, managed to inform them that he and his fellow interpreter had come across an Eskimo camp close by Hearne's 'Bloody Falls'. Contact had been made, but the Eskimos had been reluctant to cross the river to receive the gifts which Augustus had proffered. Junius was sent back to join his companion accompanied by Hepburn who had orders to ensure that the advancing party's canoes did not come across the Eskimos unannounced. Just as they left, the Indians arrived, having ignored Franklin's and Wentzel's orders to remain where they were.

As the camp was being set up for the night, Richardson walked through a cloud of mosquitoes to the top of a nearby hill and became the second white man to gaze upon the shimmering ice of the Arctic Ocean at the mouth of the Coppermine River. The blue mountains that had been seen the day before, instead of being yet another barrier on their journey, could now be seen to lie beyond the ice. Franklin named the mountains 'Cape Hearne'.

The following day, leaving the Indians at the camp under the charge of Wentzel – and with the threat of withdrawal of their rewards should they leave the spot – the party reached Hepburn waiting for them at the head of Bloody Falls where the waters ran between red sandstone cliffs topped by tundra-clad slopes. The seaman informed Franklin that the Eskimos had been more relaxed in their approach, and had asked how many canoes of white men were coming. When told, the Eskimos even suggested a particular route the canoes might take through the rapids. Unfortunately, just at the moment when firm contact might have been established a group of voyageurs, who had been making their way along the bank of the river, revealed themselves to the Eskimos. At this, the natives took fright and fled.

Franklin visited the Eskimo's campsite. Much of the natives' food and property still remained, so he entertained the hope that they might return and contact could be re-established. Before leaving, he left small gifts of iron and trinkets in the abandoned canoes and made sure that the loaded fish-drying frames were protected from the dogs. Within a short distance of the native camp, Franklin and the others came across a number of human skulls and other bones, a grim reminder that this was the site of the massacre witnessed by Hearne. Richardson noted that the site had clearly been avoided for use as a subsequent campsite.

The next day, a party of voyageurs was sent upriver to collect dried wood for use as fishing floats whilst the canoes were being prepared for the short voyage to the sea. The voyageurs had not gone far when, much to the surprise of both sides they ran into a party of Eskimos. As the native women hid themselves the six men advanced towards the voyageurs and began to dance a few yards in front of them. The voyageurs replied by removing the hats and bowing, but neither side could muster the courage to step forward and make actual contact. Eventually the natives retired behind a small hill. When Franklin and the officers arrived with Augustus (followed shortly by Ekeicho and the other Indians), they found an abandoned campsite complete with dogs and a single elderly Eskimo who jabbed feebly with his spear at the Eskimo interpreter and the Indian chief. A gift of iron calmed the terrified man and he was soon talking freely to Augustus. From White Fox (for that was his name) the party learned that the sea was frozen, but a passage between the ice and the shore remained open, and that they could expect to meet small parties of Eskimos along the intended route who would give them meat in exchange for gifts.

The next day, another group of Eskimos was sighted. They, like the others, promptly fled, but their action did not encourage the Indians who were determined that they should leave the area as quickly as possible. The two Indian interpreters, St Germain and Adam, were also keen to leave, but Franklin would not let them go

The mouth of the Coppermine River.

as they had proved to be excellent marksmen and their skills would be needed in providing food for the party.

In the early hours of the morning of 18 July 1821, Franklin, in the presence of St Germain and Wentzel, reminded Ekeicho and the Indians of their agreement to provide a supply of food at Fort Enterprise. He 'received a renewed assurance of their attending to that point.' At five o'clock, the Indians set off south as Franklin and his party headed towards the mouth of the river. Wentzel accompanied the northbound party before he departed with four of the voyageurs, letters home, and instructions to see that the Indians were well paid for their efforts.

The Coppermine delta proved to be shallow and choked with numerous sandbars. Just beyond the river's mouth, several small, rounded islands could be seen whilst, to the east, an open lane of water between the ice and the shore could be seen exactly as the Eskimo, White Fox, had suggested.

At this stage of the expedition, it would not have been unreasonable for Franklin to have seriously considered his position. He was dependent for his return on supplies by natives who had frequently shown themselves to be undependable, and upon a fellow countryman in charge of Fort Providence who had proved to be no friend of the expedition. Ahead of him lay a journey in company with the voyageurs who had already stolen a bag of ammunition in order to provide themselves with food, and were terrified of both the sea over which they must pass, and of the Eskimos they were liable to meet. On the other hand, he had a core of naval men on whom he knew he could depend, whatever the circumstances. The two birch bark canoes were pushed off the banks of the Coppermine River just after noon on Saturday 21 July 1821, their bows headed towards the 'Hyperborean Sea'.

The easterly trending coastline proved to be both barren and rocky, many weather-eroded structures reminding Back of ruined Gothic castles. Out to sea, ice could be seen on the far horizon and stranded ice floes littered the shore. Off the coast, a series of islands helped to break up the waves and made the passage of the canoes easier. On one of the islands, a deserted Eskimo campsite was found and four sealskins taken for the repair of their footwear – a copper kettle, an awl, and some beads being left in exchange. The islands off the mouth of the Coppermine had been named by Franklin 'Couper's Islands' after a friend of Richardson, and the surgeon himself had a river to the west of the Coppermine named in his honour. Further to the east, Franklin named an island 'Hepburn' after the officer's loyal attendant who had frequently proved his value to the expedition.

After four days of deteriorating weather, Franklin found himself faced by a 'bold cape' which he named after John Barrow. Long poles were frequently resorted to in fending off loose ice which had been blown against the shore by a wind, a wind which also threatened to overturn the canoes, causing great consternation amongst the voyageurs. Cape Barrow was rounded safely, however, and 'Detention Harbour' was reached where the canoes were held up by wind-driven ice. An attempt to continue the journey and shake off the mood of depression that had settled on the voyageurs was made by carrying the canoes and stores a mile and a half across the eastern arm of the bay, but it failed when yet more ice was encountered. Almost exactly a week after they had left the mouth of the Coppermine, divine service was held on the beach at Galena Point (named after Richardson had discovered a small vein of the ore). Within an hour their prayers were answered as the ice began to break up, and a passage through made available for the canoes.

Before long, the coastline started to trend in a south-eastwards direction and, on 30 July, the party reached 'Arctic Sound' into which flowed a river that Franklin named after Midshipman Robert Hood. Land could be seen to the east, but it was not clear whether they were entering a large bay whose far shores they were sighting, or whether the land was yet more islands following the coast as it turned southwards. Franklin chose to follow the coastline. Within five days, and to his 'mortification' (and to Back's 'unspeakable chagrin'), he found that the route ended at a shoal-blocked river which he named after Midshipman George Back. Turning northwards in the hope of regaining an eastwards trending coast, the party reached a cape denoting the eastern tip of the bay. Franklin, no doubt remembering the trouble arising from John Ross's naming of a mirage, gave the name 'Cape Croker' to the clearly solid headland that marked his emergence from the large bay. The bay itself was given the name 'Bathurst's Inlet' after the secretary of state whose signature had sent the expedition on its way.

From Cape Croker, the canoes were paddled or sailed eastwards in rough weather that repeatedly threatened to overturn the frail craft. After passing a large bay, Franklin found himself, yet again, at the bottom of an inlet as the land turned first northwards then towards the west. The few sightings of land he had seen from the southern shore of the inlet had been taken to be small islands but now proved to be a low-lying shore. Another bay (which Franklin named after 'my friend Captain Parry') was reached before the party found themselves opposite Cape Croker – seven miles to their south. Franklin named the inlet 'Melville Sound' after the First Lord of the Admiralty.

From the point they had entered Bathurst Inlet to their emergence from Melville Sound, the party had covered over 300 miles and added almost nothing to their intended journey to Hudson's Bay. Franklin was forced to consider their situation very carefully. Less than three days supply of pemmican remained, and such hunting as had been carried out had added little to the stock – only one seal had been killed and the fact that it was blind made the voyageurs refuse to eat it although the naval officers were 'less nice'. The canoes were badly damaged with one of them in great danger of falling apart and the increasing wind velocity indicated that the

The canoes rounding Cape Barrow.

short Arctic summer was about to come to an end. Furthermore, the voyageurs had become much bolder in their complaints and had begun to voice their opinions loudly in the presence of the officers. With the agreement of his naval companions, Franklin informed the voyageurs that he had decided to continue only for as long as it took to confirm that the coast continued to trend eastwards and, if that trend failed to materialise, he would not continue for more than four days. For Franklin the greatest fear was that the route he had taken would prove to be nothing more than a huge inlet with no passage through to the east. Despite its obvious size, the opening found by Cook far to the west – and penetrated as far as Icy Cape – could yet prove to be another false passage on the coast of north-west America.

With the canoes held together by rope lashings, the party continued along the coast as it turned northwards, then north-east, around a cape named by Franklin after his unfortunate friend and captain, Matthew Flinders. Deterioration in the weather forced them to camp on the flat, muddy, shore and endure a night of savage winds that tore their tent down three times before the morning. The violence of the weather continued throughout the following day whilst the hunters managed to obtain a few geese to add to the food stocks.

On Saturday 18 August Franklin, Richardson, and Back set off to walk along the shore to see if the trend eastwards continued. After ten miles they had a clear view of the coast as it continued north-east to what appeared to be two small islands. Their experience suggested that the 'islands' were, in all probability, mere high ground on the continuing flatness they were crossing, and that the furthest 'island' was a cape which, Franklin felt, 'tended more to the east'. They named the spot on which they stood 'Point Turnagain' before making their way back to their encampment.

Franklin's original plan had been to return to the mouth of the Coppermine River and to make his way to Bear Lake where it had been arranged that the Indian chief – The Hook – would deposit caches of food, but the lack of hunting success along the coast, and the arrival of snow flurries, made him change his mind. Now, he reasoned, the best option available was to return to Arctic Sound and take the canoes down the Hood River for as far as it went in a south-westerly direction, completing the return journey to Fort Enterprise over the Barren Lands.

After three days of paddling and sailing though heavy seas, the mouth of the Hood River was reached. A large number of gifts for the local Eskimos were left in a conspicuous place and a Union Flag flown above the spot to attract both the natives and Parry's ships should they reach that far in their voyage through the supposed north-west passage.

They started their journey up the river by paddling between sandbars until they were stopped by a waterfall that fell 20ft. This was followed by a series of rapids that could only be passed by 'tracking' (towing) the canoes from the bank. The next day saw their way barred by an extraordinary sight. The river made its way through a narrow chasm with walls that reached 200ft in height. Into this chasm the water fell more than 100ft, the waterfall itself divided by a pillar of rock that soared 40ft above the foaming surface. Franklin named the spectacle 'Wilberforce Falls' out of his admiration for the great opponent of the slave trade.

From a nearby vantage point, the river could be seen to continue in a series of shallow rapids. Franklin decided, therefore, that the canoes should be broken down to produce two smaller craft that could be used for crossing any water barriers that may be met. From now on the bulk of the journey was to be on foot.

With the two small canoes having to be carried, the load of each of the voyageurs was now increased and the trek along the bank of the river was to prove difficult as falling snow, driven by a high wind, toppled the canoe-carrying men with resultant damage to the frail vessels.

Eventually, the river's western course began to lead the party from the south-westerly direction they needed to go and so, leaving its banks, they struck out into the Barren Lands. The following day, the last of the pemmican was served out and much of the next three days were spent shivering in tents, which were proving to be of little protection against the driving snow. On the third day, Franklin collapsed with exhaustion and had to be brought back to consciousness with a drink of portable soup. The fire used to heat the drink was fuelled by the remains of one of the canoes – the wind had blown the man over who was carrying it and it had broken beyond repair. A few ptarmigan were shot over the ensuing days and these were eaten with tripe de roche, a lichen which grew on the rocks which lay strewn in their path. Unfortunately, according to Franklin, tripe de roche was also effective in producing 'bowel complaints'.

The weather continued to deteriorate and, after all the party received a soaking in crossing the Cracroft River (named by Franklin after a prominent Lincolnshire family), their clothing froze and their boots could only be removed after thawing in front of a feeble fire.

On 10 September, to the joy of all, a herd of musk ox was seen and the hunters spent two hours approaching their target from down-wind as the rest of the party watched from a small hill. Eventually, the hunters opened fire and a cow fell. Within minutes, the animal had been skinned and butchered with the warm stomach contents and intestines being devoured without thought of preparation. A fire made of the stunted Arctic willow that poked through the snow gave the party the first real meal they had had for six days.

Within forty-eight hours, the last of the meat had gone and the party were reduced to eating tripe de roche and chewing on a piece of musk-ox hide. Their situation was not improved when, to Franklin's 'great mortification', they found their way barred by a large lake (Contwoyto or Rum Lake, so named from being the spot where Hearne opened a keg of rum to supply his accompanying Indians).

Gathering tripe de roche.

At first it seemed that some good might come out of this misfortune and Franklin ordered that the fishing nets be run out, only to discover that the voyagers had thrown away the nets and burned the floats. Realising that this action had come about because the voyagers were getting weaker and having difficulty in carrying their loads, he ordered the caching of all scientific instruments and books that were not required for their safe navigation.

Before setting out the following morning, the officers were sat around a small fire of willow twigs when St. Germain − one of the Indian interpreters − approached and gave each of them a small piece of meat he had saved from his ration. The act brought tears of gratitude to the eyes of Franklin and his companions. Even better, as they moved westward along the shores of the lake, they heard a musket being fired and discovered that one of the voyageurs, Credit, had shot a pair of caribou. One was devoured immediately and the other prepared for carrying.

Later that day they came across a wide river (Burnside River) which narrowed enough at a series of rapids for a crossing to be attempted. The remaining canoe was put into the water and Franklin and two of the men, St. Germain and Belanger, set off. At just about the halfway point the canoe overturned, plunging all three into the icy waters. Fortunately, they held on to the canoe as it was swept downstream until their progress was halted by a large rock projecting above the foaming surface. St. Germain and Franklin lifted the canoe clear of the river to empty the water out before getting back in. Leaving Belanger gripping the rock, they set off once again towards the opposite bank. Yet again the canoe overturned but, being in shallower water, they were able to safely reach the other side. To his great distress, Franklin found that he had lost the case containing his journal along with his meteorological and astronomical observations. Richardson's gun had also been lost in the waters of the river. After great difficulty, Belanger was rescued, stripped, placed between two other men and wrapped in blankets in an effort to revive him. In the meantime St. Germain returned with the canoe and the rest of the day, and the following morning, was taken up with transporting men and supplies across the river.

As they climbed the eastern slopes of the Willingham Mountains (named by Franklin after his brother), the next two days were made tolerable by the shooting of a deer, but their hunger soon returned. Snow fell heavily as they were reduced to chewing on singed deer hide and eating the gritty tripe de roche. The voyageurs began to faint from lack of food, and there was talk amongst them of dropping their packs and fleeing to Fort Enterprise. Only the lack of a guide prevented them from flight.

The desperate food situation was relieved only slightly when the party came across the remains of a long-dead caribou that had been partially eaten by wolves. Its bones were burned to make them edible, and the voyageurs accompanied this meal by eating the leather of their spare shoes – a source of food soon taken up by the officers. To his intense disappointment, Franklin learned that the voyageur responsible for the remaining canoe had broken it up and thrown it away rather than carry it any further.

As the snow turned to icy rain, causing them to shiver uncontrollably, they came across a herd of caribou and managed to kill five small deer. They were soon having their first meal of meat for eleven days. So hungry were they that, by that night, a third of the meat had already been eaten. The next day, to everyone's relief, they found themselves on the banks of the Coppermine River, their joy being completed by the discovery of the rotting corpse of a deer that had died wedged between rocks. To their rear, the officers had heard the sound of shooting from the voyageurs Michel and Credit and, when the two caught up with the party empty-handed, suspected that they had made kills, but had been eating their prey immediately rather than adding it to the common supply.

An attempt to cross the river by Belanger and another voyageur, Benoit, using bound bunches of willow twigs, failed when the wood proved to be too green to be buoyant. Richardson then decided to make an attempt. He removed his outer clothing and his boots and made towards the river bank. As he did so, he stepped on a knife, its blade cutting deep into his flesh. Undeterred, he entered the water with a line around his waist and began to swim. He had not gone far when his arms became numbed with the cold. Turning onto his back, he continued swimming just using his legs until, in turn, he lost all feeling in them and began to sink. He was hauled back to the shore by the line he had taken out, wrapped in blankets and placed before a fire to thaw out.

More twigs were gathered to make a raft but a strong wind rose up and prevented any attempt at crossing for that day. At this moment Back, who had been sent to reconnoitre the land to the south, returned with St. Germain. The Indian interpreter, seeing the problem presented by the proposed river crossing, decided to make a canoe of fragments of painted (waterproofed) canvas that was used to protect the voyageur's packs. Resin was collected from nearby pine tree to make the seams watertight. Three days of snow delayed the building of the canoe and the only food that could be found other than tripe de roche was the backbone and antlers of a caribou – all that remained of a wolf's meal. Again the bones were burned before being eaten and, to the joy of all, the spinal marrow still remained, although putrid.

The party eventually gathered on the river's bank to watch St. Germain launch his canoe, and it was with great relief, that he was seen to be able to control the fragile craft and make his way, towing a double line, to the far bank. By the end of the day, the entire party and their baggage had been towed across to the other side. The voyageurs, who until the crossing had appeared to be deeply depressed by their situation, suddenly cheered up and shook the officers by the hand. Sadly, however, Junius, one of the Eskimo guides, was nowhere to be seen and it was assumed that he had headed northwards in the hope of finding safety with the tribes along the northern coast.

It was now forty-one days since they had left the Arctic shore, and five days since they had eaten anything approaching a sustaining meal. It was time, Franklin decided, to send ahead for help. Midshipman Back was ordered to make his way to Fort Enterprise as quickly as he could where, not only would he find supplies of meat and other foods left by Ekeicho's Indians, but the possible whereabouts of the Indians themselves. Back was to be accompanied by St. Germain and two voyageurs – Solomon Belanger (unrelated to Jean Baptist Belanger who had been in the overturned canoe with Franklin) and Beauparlent.

Following Back's footsteps in the snow, the main party trudged southwards for the next two days on a diet of lichen and boiled moccasin leather. The stops for rest became more and more frequent until it was learned that two of the voyageurs, Credit and Vaillant, had fallen behind. Richardson, who had been helping the greatly enfeebled Midshipman Hood, turned and retraced his steps. After a mile and a half he found Vaillant exhausted and on the point of collapse. The doctor talked to the man in an effort to encourage him to make his way to the fire that had been built where the others were waiting but, after making no more than a few steps, the voyageur crumpled into the snow. Unable to lift him to his feet, Richardson then set out to look for Credit, but falling snow had obliterated the path and he was forced to return for his own safety. Vaillant remained where he had fallen and was unable to answer Richardson's attempts to rouse him. The doctor returned to the camp and, upon being told the situation, Belanger set off to see what he could do. Before long he had returned with Vaillant's pack having been unable to help the man himself. An appeal was made to the strongest of the voyageurs to go back and rescue their comrade, but the appeal fell on deaf ears. Instead they now demanded that Franklin allow them to abandon their loads and make a dash for Fort Enterprise. The officers discussed the problem and came to the conclusion that to allow the voyageurs to make their own way to the fort would, almost certainly, condemn them to death as they were incapable of working out the route. It was decided, therefore, that Franklin would go ahead with the voyageurs taking with him Adam, the Indian hunter; and Augustus, the remaining Eskimo guide. Richardson, Hood and Hepburn would remain behind. This would give Hood the rest he so desperately needed and allow for the possibility of Credit and Vaillant catching up.

On Sunday 7 October 1821, Franklin said prayers before leaving with the voyageurs. His load was to be restricted to his blanket and the officer's journals. The others shared the weight of a single tent between them. No food was available, so none would be carried. Most of the remaining ammunition was left with Richardson's party in the belief that it could be used to encourage the Indians they expected to meet in the Fort Enterprise area to return and collect the weakened men. Two of the voyageurs – Peltier and Benoit – agreed to return and bring food from Fort Enterprise and act as guides to any Indians they came across.

Most of Franklin's party had only managed to cover four-and-a-half miles through deep snow before they were forced to rest. They were joined a little later by the voyageurs Michel and Belanger who both claimed that their exhaustion prevented them from going any further. So weak, in fact, was the whole party that they did not have the energy to erect their tent and, consequently, Franklin agreed to have it cut up into pieces that individuals could use as covers. On the following morning, after a night of blizzards that prevented any sleep, Michel and Belanger begged Franklin to allow them to return to Richardson's campsite. He agreed and also sent back another voyageur – Perrault – who had collapsed twice as they tried to set off.

A small lake barred their path, but its frozen surface suggested to Franklin that it could be safely crossed. The strong wind, however, and its slippery surface made the crossing extremely hazardous and, as they reached the far bank, Fontano, an Italian voyageur, collapsed. No amount of entreaties from Franklin could persuade the man to rise and press on. Eventually, much to his distress, Franklin was forced to agree with Fontano's pleas that he be allowed to return to Richardson's camp. He now had three voyageurs remaining with him: Peltier, Beniot, and Samandre; and the hunter, Adam. Augustus had pushed on ahead and sight of him had been lost.

Over the next three days the party made their way through deep snow and over frozen lakes surviving on lichen and boiled shoe-leather. Despite their privations, they were buoyed up by the knowledge that they were approaching the fort with its ample supplies of meat and would be in the vicinity of Ekeicho's Indians.

As, at last, they made their way towards the fort, a degree of alarm made itself felt. There were no signs of Indians, and the buildings had a neglected and dilapidated air. Soon their worst fears were realized. The fort was empty. There was no cache of meat, not even the slightest morsel. All that remained from the supplies of the previous year was a small cask of salt. The door was open; the parchment windows of the building had disappeared and drifted snow lay piled against the inner walls. There was, however, a note from Midshipman Back. On finding the fort deserted and empty he had decided to continue southwards in the hope of finding the Indians, failing which he intended to press on to Fort Providence, 130 miles away on the shores of the Great Slave Lake.

For Franklin and his party, the discovery that they had been let down by the Indians, affected them so badly that they wept. The tears were not just for themselves but for Richardson, Hood, Hepburn and the others who were depending upon them for help. But tears would do nothing to help to keep them alive, and Franklin soon had his party boarding up the windows, gathering lichen to help supplement the scraps of caribou skin and bones that lay littered around the building, and collecting wood from the outbuildings for a fire. Once a fire was burning and the hide being singed the door opened and the missing Augustus walked into the room. He had taken a different route to the fort and had shown great skill in finding it.

Two days after their arrival, Solomon Belanger walked into the fort with a message from Back. The voyageur was in a dreadful state having fallen through the ice of a lake and had to be thoroughly warmed before his speech was restored. Back, it seemed, had found no trace of the Indians, was now heading for the site of their last summer's camp, and wanted Franklin's guidance on what to do next. Franklin's first thought was to order Back to meet him as he and his party made their way towards Fort Providence. The Indians would be heading in that direction and their slow movement with the women and children would allow him to catch them up. Belanger, however, pleaded against this idea as he was not sure where Back's party now was. Franklin, however, was not impressed and Belanger set off once again five days after his arrival with instructions for Back to meet Franklin at Reindeer Lake. It was not long before Franklin learned the truth of Belanger's reluctance in arranging for the parties to meet up. Not only had he feared that if Back's best hunter (St. Germain) brought down any game it would have to be shared amongst a greater number of mouths, but he had also tried to get Adam to return with him bringing the sole cooking pot that the Franklin party had. Such behaviour was beyond Franklin's comprehension and he put it down to the severe conditions 'warping the feelings and understanding' of Belanger.

As it was, Adam soon proved to be in no condition to move due to swellings on parts of his body. In consequence, Franklin changed his plans and decided to take

Benoit and Augustus in an effort to find the Indians. Using snowshoes they had made from parts of discarded broken ones, the three set off over the deep snow that led to the frozen surface of a lake. The ice was crossed without too much difficulty and they spent the night huddled together on the ground. Unfortunately, in the morning, Franklin's snowshoes were broken as he slipped and fell between two rocks. Finding it was quite impossible to keep up with the others without snowshoes, Franklin had no option but to return to the fort leaving the others to continue with notes for Back and the Hudson's Bay Co. man in charge at Fort Providence.

Finding the others at the fort incapable of looking after themselves, Franklin took on the task of cooking for the whole party, even though he was so weak himself that he had to ask Peltier to break up the bones they were eating.

As the days passed they became weaker still and found great difficulty in getting up from a sitting position. The collection of wood for the fire proved to be such a tiring task that it took three of them to bring the small pieces twenty yards from the adjoining building. As they searched for lichen – only to find it frozen to the rock – they could only watch as a herd of caribou passed within half-a-mile of them. None of them had even the strength to lift a musket, much less to go in pursuit of the animals.

As the dusk descended on that night – October 29th – the party were talking around the fire when Peltier suddenly motioned them to be silent. To their great joy they heard the sound of footsteps approaching the door of the building. In a moment the door opened and there stood the gaunt figures of Richardson and Hepburn. There was little said at first between them and Richardson produced a ptarmigan shot earlier in the day by Hepburn, In a very short space of time the bird was cut into pieces and shared out between them (the first flesh that Franklin had eaten for thirty-one days). After a reading of the scriptures from the prayer book and testament that Richardson had brought with him, the six men fell asleep.

Following a day of fruitless searching for caribou (and during which Richardson took charge of the accommodation – insisting that the sleeping blankets were rolled up during the day) Franklin could, at last, hear what had happened to Richardson and his party. And a horrifying story it proved to be.

When Franklin's party had left, Richardson settled down with Midshipman Hood and the seaman, Hepburn. As the result of a gift from Lady Lucy Barry, they had still retained a number of small religious books. Richardson determined that they would have morning and evening services supported by readings of the scriptures throughout the day. In this way, he felt the spirits of his companions would be raised enough to see them through the coming difficulties.

The following day, they were surprised to find that they were joined by the voyageur Michel (an Iroquois Indian) bearing a note from Franklin. He had, he claimed, made his way back with Belanger, but his companion had grown impatient and had left early, ahead of him. There was, however, no sign of Belanger. The following day, whilst moving to a better site, Michel produced a portion of meat which, he said, had come from a wolf which had been killed by a caribou's antlers. Richardson was extremely grateful as the meat was desperately needed for Hood who had grown weaker by the day.

Over the next five days, Michel disappeared during daylight on hunting expeditions but always returned empty-handed. He refused to allow anyone else to accompany him and grew more and more surly, eventually even refusing to cut wood for the fire. Richardson took the voyageur to the spot where he had last seen Vaillant and, the following day, Michel returned with a blanket and a bag containing two pistols.

The next morning, the voyageur refused to hunt and would not assist in getting wood for the fire even though the combined strength of Hepburn and Richardson could not bring to the fire a log they had found.

Again, the following day, Michel refused to go out hunting and remained by the fire cleaning his gun. Richardson left the camp to gather lichen and Hepburn went to gather wood noticing, as he left, that Michel and Hood were arguing. Whilst cutting wood a few minutes later, Hepburn heard the report of a musket and returned immediately to the camp. What he found made him bring Richardson to the scene.

When he arrived, the doctor found Hood lying dead by the fire, a copy of Bickersteth's 'Scripture Helps' lying open alongside him. Upon examining the body, Richardson soon found that the midshipman had been shot through the back of the head with a long-barrelled musket – a practically impossible way for Hood to have taken his own life. When Michel was questioned about the incident he claimed (at the same time holding a loaded gun) that he had left the gun he was cleaning to go into the tent. Whilst he was in there he heard the gunfire, but could not account for how it was fired. That night the hours were spent with Richardson and Hepburn keeping one eye open.

Two days later, with the drastic change in their circumstances, Richardson felt that Hepburn, Michel, and he, should attempt to reach Fort Enterprise. Michel was reluctant to go and frequently demanded that Richardson should go hunting with him in the woods. With the doctor's refusal, Michel began to turn on Hepburn, accusing him of telling lies about him. He then began to mutter aloud proclaiming his hatred of 'French' (i.e. 'white') people. Richardson became very concerned as the Indian was armed with a musket, two pistols, a bayonet, and a knife. Even without these weapons, his strength was such that he could have tackled both the others with little danger to himself. During the afternoon, Michel told Richardson that he intended to gather some tripe de roche and they should push on, he would catch them up in due course. This was the first opportunity Richardson and Hepburn had to talk together in private since the death of Hood. Both expressed their fear that their life was seriously under threat and that only the death of Michel would ensure their safety. Hepburn immediately offered to carry out the act, but Richardson, morally unable to allow a subordinate to bear the responsibility of such a dreadful deed, and, by now convinced that Michel was guilty of cannibalism in addition to at least one murder, refused. As Michel approached to rejoin them, Richardson raised his pistol and shot him through the head. Six days later the two men arrived exhausted and starving at the door of Fort Enterprise.

Three days after their return, Peltier, who had complained of a sore throat – probably brought about through eating too much salt – collapsed upon his bed. The others assumed that he had simply gone to sleep until a rattling sound alerted them that all was not well. By the time Richardson was by his side, the voyageur was dead. Before the night was through, the remaining voyageur – Samandre – was also dead. Unable to remove the bodies outside through weakness, the best that could be done was to drag them into a corner and cover them with a ragged blanket.

Richardson and Hepburn attempted on several occasions to shoot game but neither had the strength to lift a gun long enough to aim. Franklin was reduced to searching on his knees for fragments of bone and caribou skin that could be boiled or singed to provide the hope of sustenance. Their situation had passed being merely desperate, and they all realised they were on the verge of succumbing to an almost complete lack of sustenance.

Six days after the death of Samandre, on the morning of 7 November, Hepburn and Richardson were out gathering wood for a fire when they heard the sound of a musket shot followed by a shout. Looking up they were overjoyed to see three Indians making their way up the frozen river. When Richardson brought the news to Franklin, the expedition leader bowed his head in a prayer of thanks to the Almighty. The Indians, Boudelkell, The Rat, and Crooked-foot, had been sent to Franklin with supplies by Back who had discovered the Indian's camp some forty miles from the fort. They brought with them dried meat, caribou tongues, and some fat which Franklin, Richardson, and Hepburn devoured despite Richardson's own warning not to eat too much too quickly. As he had warned, they had reason to regret their haste in eating and were soon suffering severe stomach pains as a result. Adam, the Indian interpreter and hunter, fared better as, being unable to feed himself, he was gently spoon-fed by the Indians. Boudelkell, the youngest, was told to return to Back with a message from Franklin – more food was needed.

The two remaining Indians expressed deep discomfort at the idea of remaining in the building with the corpses of Peltier and Samandre still lying in the corner of the room, so Richardson and Hepburn – feeling stronger after being supplied with food – dragged the bodies for a short distance from the building and covered them with snow. Next the Indians turned their attention to the cleaning of the room before insisting that Richardson and Hepburn wash themselves and shave off their long

Surgeon Richardson reading from his prayer book to encourage the others at Fort Enterprise.

beards – a sight the Indians found offensive. For the following four days, with high winds and snow falling constantly outside, the Indians tended the fire, and caught fish for the weakened men. Then, almost without warning, they became despondent and refused to leave the building to hunt or fish. In the evening they produced a small amount of meat for each man and, taking up their belongings, left the hut. At first it seemed that the party had been abandoned, but Adam claimed that Crooked-foot and The Rat had feared that Boudelkell had failed to reach their tribe's campsite and had decided to go for help themselves. For the next two days food reverted to bone soup and singed caribou hide cooked by Franklin as Richardson and Hepburn dragged in wood for the fire. During the late morning of the third day, Hepburn was outside the building when he saw movement on the frozen river – it was Crooked-foot with two other Indians and their wives. Also with them was the voyageur, Benoit, with a message from Back. Brought back to fitness by the Indians, Back and the rest of his party were about to make their way to Fort Providence

With the southward movement of the caribou herds there was no time to delay in leaving Fort Enterprise. The following day – Friday 16 November – the party set off in pursuit of Ekeicho's camp. The Indians had given the white men their snowshoes and walked alongside them in support. They also hunted for meat and cooked food for Franklin and the others. Their kind treatment was only marred by one of the Indians ('The Fop') who frequently beat his wife – a girl aged about sixteen years. Consequently, there was almost a degree of pleasure when his gun exploded in his face causing him to press on ahead towards the rest of his tribe in order to have his injuries treated. His wife was left in a much more cheerful frame of mind as she pulled on her sledge loaded with provisions and the others were glad to be rid of his disagreeable behaviour.

Ten days after leaving Fort Enterprise, they caught up with Ekeicho. They found him waiting in his lodge and had to endure a lengthy period of silence – the native's way of showing sympathy for their sufferings. Franklin had clearly decided that to bring the Indian chief's attention to his failure in providing supplies at Fort Enterprise would be little more than an exercise in futility. Instead, he kept his opinions – and that of the others – to himself and accepted the hospitality the chief pressed upon them. Among the many curious faces that looked into the chief's lodge to see them was Augustus – the popular Eskimo interpreter had remained behind when Back had set off for Fort Enterprise.

Ten days after joining the Indians' slow journey southwards the voyageur, Belanger, arrived from Fort Providence in company with another man. They had brought two trains of sledge dogs, some rum and tobacco for the Indians, and a change of clothing for Franklin, Richardson and Hepburn. They also brought a message from Midshipman Back. From it they learned that Franklin was no longer a lieutenant. He had been a commander for almost a year with his promotion dated from the first day of 1821. Both Back and Hood were promoted to lieutenant, but Hood would never know of his promotion having been murdered forty-seven days earlier. Another item of news informed them that the North West Co. had merged with the Hudson's Bay Co. The problems caused to the expedition on its way north by the rivalry of the two companies would now be eased with the merger.

Franklin's party arrived at Fort Providence in the early afternoon of 11 December. They were welcomed by the clerk of the Fort – the same Nicholas Weeks who had proved to be, not merely unhelpful on their journey north, but had continually placed obstructions in their path (Back described him as a 'disgrace'). Once again, Franklin seems to have had no desire to have the clerk brought to account for his previous behaviour and, with the return of the party, Weeks was eager to be seen as a supporter of the enterprise. In the meantime, Back had pressed on to Fort Resolution, the Hudson's Bay post on Moose-Deer Island, in pursuit of goods that had been promised to the voyageurs and the Indians.

Whilst waiting to take his leave of the Indians, Franklin learned that Wentzel, who they had last seen heading down the Coppermine in the company of Ekeicho's Indians, had suffered greatly on the return journey. On one occasion he had been forced to survive for eleven days on the bowel-churning lichen, tripe de roche. He had, however, returned to Fort Resolution with the officer's journals and paintings safe in his pack. When they separated, the Indians had promised him that, once they had reached Fort Providence and obtained ammunition, they would return to Fort Enterprise and leave a cache of food – despite repeatedly insisting that they did not believe any of the expedition would survive. When they failed to do so, they gave the excuses that, not only had they failed to get any ammunition from Fort Providence, but also that three of their number had been drowned in a lake. As for Wentzel's own failure to leave a note, he claimed that he had no paper and had written a message on a wooden plank and placed it at the head of Franklin's bed. The fact that no such plank remained on Franklin's arrival was blamed on the Indians having removed it (nevertheless, Franklin recorded that he offered Wentzel paper, but the North West Co. employee had his own notebook and had only accepted a pencil from Back).

When Ekeicho and his Indians arrived at the fort, Franklin thanked them for the help they had given during the journey from Fort Enterprise and arranged with Weeks that they and the surviving voyagers should be properly compensated. He also arranged for the discharge of the interpreter, Adam, who had been re-united with his wife and now wanted to return to the Coppermine Indians. The party then moved on to Moose-Deer Island.

Back was the first to welcome them as they came through the gates of Fort Resolution. He was impressed by the progress they had made in regaining their health and shocked and saddened to hear the details of 'the lamentable death of my friend Mr Hood'. He was also able to inform them of his own journey after Franklin had sent him to lead an advanced party to Fort Enterprise.

Having resting for two days at Fort Enterprise, Back had set off in search of Ekeicho's camp. After little more than fifteen miles he found himself on the shores of a lake with his Indian hunter (St.Germain) not only having failed to bring down any game, but also unclear as to the possible whereabouts of Ekeicho. The voyageur, Belanger, had been sent back to Fort Enterprise to seek orders from Franklin. In the meantime, all that Back, St. Germain, and Beauparlent had to live on was lichen and the remains of caribou that had been abandoned by wolves. Three days

Midshipman Back welcoming Franklin and the other survivors of the party.

later Beauparlent was found dead, stretched out on the snow. Neither Back nor St.Germain had the strength to bury the body. The return of Belanger brought orders for Back to meet Franklin at Reindeer Lake, but they were all too weak from lack of food to make any immediate effort in that direction. In fact, it was to be another ten days of living on scraps of bone, skin and lichen before they discovered the remains of a caribou. This provided them with enough sustenance to allow them to set off three days later. Fortune smiled on them again the following day when they saw wolves and crows gathered on the ice of the lake and managed to obtain the shoulders and ribs of a caribou as their share of the wolf's prey. St. Germain continued to fail in his attempts at hunting and, by the time they had arrived at Reindeer Lake, Back was so weak that he could only walk with the aid of a stick. Nevertheless, with no sign of Franklin at the appointed rendezvous, the midshipman decided to press on in his search for the Indian's camp from where he hoped to send out help to Fort Enterprise.

The following day, footsteps marking the tracks of Indians were found and Back sent St. Germain to find the camp and bring back help. That evening, a young Indian appeared with a supply of meat and (much to Back's astonishment) a note from Franklin. The message had been brought by Benoit and Augustus who had arrived at the camp that day. When Back reached Ekeicho a day later he had to go through the ritual smoking of a pipe before he could impress upon the chief the urgency of sending aid to Franklin (Benoit and Augustus had tried to persuade Ekeicho to send aid the day before, but he had refused). On Boudelkell's return with Franklin's note, Back had more supplies sent to Fort Enterprise and ordered Benoit to accompany the Indians. Then, after great difficulty in getting supplies for himself and St. Germain, he struck out for Fort Providence. It was to be a slow journey. Despite access to more food he remained very weak and did not arrive at the fort until nine days after setting out. He remained only two days before alarm at the shortage of goods for the Indians prompted him to spend a further four days in reaching Fort Resolution and the warm welcome of the chief trader, Robert McVicar.

It took until the end of February before Franklin and the others had recovered enough to be able to walk any distance. They had met with much kindness during their stay at Fort Resolution and, under the care of McVicar, had been nursed back to almost full health. With the spring thaw well under way, it was decided that they would be able to leave on 26 May 1822, and, on the evening of that day, they boarded canoes to begin the journey back to York Factory.

It took them forty-nine days to reach the coast via Fort Chipewyan and Norway House. At York Factory they said farewell to Augustus – the loyal, cheerful Eskimo guide who had stood by them through the most difficult of times.

Their journey had taken them through 5,555 miles of Northern America. They had reached beyond the Arctic coast and charted many shores previously unknown to white men. The cost had been high. Of the eleven voyageurs that had started out with them from the mouth of the Coppermine only two – Benoit and Solomon Belanger – had survived the travelling. The expedition had suffered treachery, murder, and possibly, cannibalism. Against all this, Franklin, Richardson, Back, and Hepburn had survived through a combination of endurance, determination, and a firm belief in 'Providence'.

After a wait at York Factory of almost a month, the party embarked in the *Prince of Wales* – the same Hudson's Bay Co. ship that had brought them from England almost three and a half years earlier.

The Indian chief, Ekeicho, suffered greatly with the conclusion of the expedition. Despite his failing on numerous occasions to assist Franklin – especially his utter negligence in not providing supplies at Fort Enterprise – he had been well rewarded. As a result, his brave's hunting on behalf of the Hudson's Bay Co. had fallen off to the level where McVicar described their efforts as 'totally useless'. To make matter worse Ekeicho's tribe was attacked by the Slave Indians during the winter after Franklin's departure and suffered severe losses. Finally, the Hudson's Bay Co. closed down Fort Providence in 1823 leaving the Indians an extended journey to Fort Resolution in order to trade the furs they had managed to obtain.

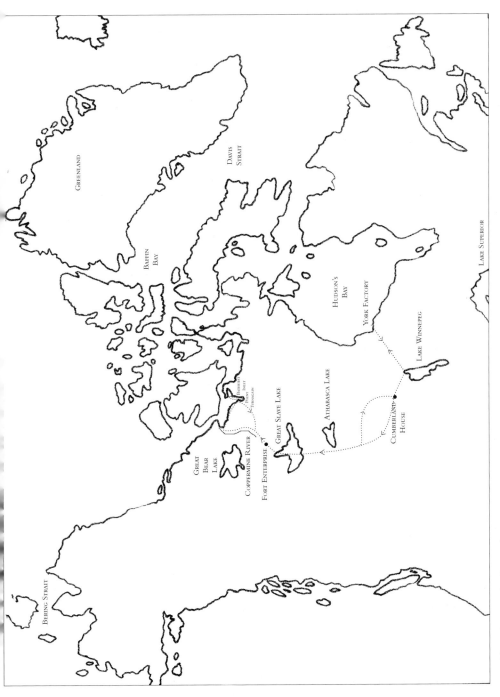

GREENLAND

DAVIS STRAIT

BAFFIN BAY

HUDSON'S BAY

LAKE SUPERIOR

YORK FACTORY

LAKE WINNEPEG

ATHABASCA LAKE

BELMONT POINT
TURNAGAIN
GREAT SLAVE LAKE

CUMBERLAND HOUSE

GREAT BEAR LAKE

COPPERMINE RIVER

FORT ENTERPRISE

BERING STRAIT

Franklin's first overland expedition 1819–1822

Midshipman Robert Hood shares a memorial with his brother, George, in St Mary's Church, Bury. It records that

> while engaged in the overland Arctic Expedition Under the command of CAPTAIN FRANKLIN, R.N. After having, with unshaken fortitude, endured unparalleled dangers and privations, AND, BY HIS SKILLS IN SCIENCE, Essentially contributed to the utility of the enterprise, was ASSASSINATED, by an IROQUOIS, October 20, 1821. Thus terminating, At the early age of four and twenty, A short but brilliant career, Distinguished by varied talent and steady determination, Which Were rapidly opening a path to the highest honours of his profession.

His brother, Lieutenant George Hood, died 'of a fever' at the same age two years later on an expedition to East Africa.

Franklin had learned of the results of Parry's expedition before he left Hudson's Bay. Now, on arrival in England, he found out that Parry had, once again, left for the north.

CHAPTER SEVEN

'NO COMMON MEN'

Lieutenant William Parry's instructions were simple and straightforward. He was to:

> ...advance to the northward as far as the opening into Sir James Lancaster's Sound.....use your best endeavours to explore the bottom of that Sound; or, in the event of its proving a strait opening to the westward, you are to use all possible means. ...to pass through it, and ascertain its direction and communications; and if it should be found to connect itself with the northern sea, you are to make the best of your way to Behring's strait.

Once through the strait he was to proceed to Kamchatka to hand copies of his journals to the Russian governor for overland carriage to St Petersburg. He could then refit his ships at the Sandwich Islands or Canton before a speedy return to England.

To carry out this task he was given command of HMS *Hecla* – a bomb vessel of 375 tons – and HMS *Griper*, a gun-brig of 180 tons. Both ships were barque-rigged (an arrangement of square-rigged sails that was easier to handle in the ice and required fewer men, consequently allowing the ships to work in three 'watches') and had their hulls double planked. Coal was used as ballast, a simple means of ensuring a supply of fuel which could be replaced by local stone during the voyage.

Command of the *Griper* went to Lieutenant Matthew Liddon, a friend of Parry's from his time in America. Liddon had been serving in HMS *Lily* as a midshipman when he was given command of a recently captured prize. Whilst endeavouring to bring his small vessel into port he fell in with a French privateer who captured the prize along with Liddon and ten men. They were taken to the Venezuelan port of Cumana as prisoners-of-war but had not been in captivity long before Liddon and his men used the dead of night to make their escape. Swimming over to an enemy schooner they scrambled over her gunwales and, after a struggle with its crew, captured the vessel and sailed it to the nearest port in British hands. Liddon took part in the storming of Montevideo in 1807 and was promoted to lieutenant four years later.

Many of the other officers had served with Parry in the *Alexander* or had experience of sailing in Arctic waters. His first lieutenant was Frederick Beechey who had been Franklin's first lieutenant on the *Trent* (and whose father, Sir William, was painting Parry's portrait as the expedition was being prepared). John Edwards had been surgeon in the *Isabella* and his assistant-surgeon was Alexander Fisher from the *Alexander,* as was John Allison, the 'Greenland' (i.e. ice) master. Among the *Hecla's* midshipmen was James Ross, no longer in conflict with his uncle, but still a firm supporter of Parry. One further figure from that conflict had also found passage on the *Hecla.* Captain Edward Sabine of the Royal Artillery had been appointed as the expedition's astronomer.

Liddon's first lieutenant was Henry Parkyus Hoppner, Parry's former first lieutenant on the *Alexander.* Charles Beverly – who had served in the *Isabella* as assistant-surgeon to Ross – was carried as ship's surgeon. George Fife, Franklin's ice master in the *Trent* was appointed to the same position in the *Griper.*

The officers provided an extraordinarily youthful leadership for the expedition. The oldest was Sabine who, at thirty, was two years older than Parry. None of the other officers was more than twenty-three years old.

Warm clothing was taken on-board the ships and a wolf-skin blanket provided for every officer and man. Recent experiments had proved the reliability of canned food and the ships received 12,000lb of carrots, 8,000lb of parsnips, 9,600 quarts of vegetable soup, and 5,000 cans of beef from Messrs Donkin and Gamble of Deptford (as the can-opener had yet to be developed, the cans had to be opened using an axe). Parry personally insisted that the lemon juice, to be carried as an aid against scurvy,

Captain William Edward Parry.

was obtained from fresh lemons, and – of at least equal interest to the ship's company – over 1,000 gallons of rum was taken on-board. Beer was to be made from essence of malt, hops and spruce. As usual, a large number of needles, knives, mirrors and other items were taken as gifts for any natives that should be met.

After a hectic social round in which the ships were inundated with visitors and dignitaries of all types, they were, finally, able to sail on 11 May 1819. It was not long before the poor sailing qualities of the *Griper* were revealed – 'utterly unfit for this service' according to Parry. The *Hecla*, however, proved to be 'a charming ship' of such qualities that, at times, the expedition could sail faster when the *Hecla* took the *Griper* in tow.

The voyage across the north Atlantic was met by the occasional westerly winds but Cape Farewell was reached safely on 15 June. Bottles were thrown overboard every day each containing a 'bottle paper', a printed request in six different languages asking the finder to return it to the Admiralty stating where and when it was found.

The ice was met immediately upon entering the Davis Strait. Within a week the ships were trapped with open waters four miles to the east of them and a sea of broken ice to the west. Unable to escape, they drifted over a dozen miles to the south, the frustration being only slightly relieved by the sight of whales breaching and plunging between the ice-floes and men from the *Griper* killing a polar bear that had been attracted by the smell of frying herrings.

On the fifth day of being frozen in, the ice around the ships began to break up and Parry was able to put out ice-anchors and warp his ship into the open waters. Three days later they crossed the Arctic Circle as a stream of large icebergs passed down their port side and Greenland loomed to starboard.

Parry was keen to get through the 'middle ice' that poured down the strait from Baffin's Bay rather than having to sail around the northern edge of the bay. But, with no immediate opportunity presenting itself, the ship's company set about increasing their victualling supplies by hunting the walruses that rested on the ice floes. Their experience told them that simply firing a musket at the animals rarely brought an immediate kill as the ball tended merely to flatten against the animal's skull allowing it to escape. Instead, sand was thrown into the walruses' eyes before dispatching it with a blow from an axe. In addition to the meat and oil which could be obtained from the animal, its tusks were popular amongst dentists for the manufacture of false teeth, and its hide could be used to prevent chafing of the ropes used in a ship's rigging. When cut into strips and plaited, the raw skin made excellent ropes for use with the ship's wheel. The killing of the walrus was, however, not without its risks as the animals, when under threat, would counter-attack by trying to overturn the boats. The boats were also at risk from polar bears who, on occasion, would try to climb aboard. Yet again, sand was carried to throw into the bear's eyes causing the animal to retreat, encouraged by jabs from a boarding pike. When seals were hunted,

HMS Hecla *in Baffin's Bay.*

the chief problem was that, when hit by a musket ball, they tended to sink very quickly. Consequently, birdshot was used to blind them first whilst they were still on the ice before being killed by an axe or spear.

A south-westerly wind pushed the ships along the edge of the ice until, on the 16th, they fell in with the Hull-based whaler *Brunswick* heading home with a full cargo of whale oil. The master of the whaler shouted across to Liddon that five days earlier he had left a large fleet of whalers to the north who were delayed at latitude 74 degrees by a barrier of ice.

Two degrees south of the whaling fleet, Parry attempted to force a way through the ice to the west but had to return to the open waters in the face of an impassable barrier of ice floes. A second attempt the following day resulted in the *Hecla* having to back out of the ice before returning to rescue the *Griper* by towing her clear.

At 73 degrees north, Parry found himself on the same latitude as Lancaster Sound and decided on one more attempt to cross the great stream of ice to the west. With a south-easterly wind coming to his aid, the ships bored into the ice before being brought to a halt by large ice floes. The ice, however, was mobile and cracks appeared opening up leads just wide enough for the ships to be hauled through by the ship's companies 'tracking' along on the surface of the floes. Eventually, the *Griper* was secured to the stern of the *Hecla* and her ship's company sent forward to assist in warping both

216

ships to the west. After progressing four miles in this fashion, fog descended and Parry ordered his men to rest on an extra allowance of meat and rum.

A further half-mile was gained the following day, but the effort was rewarded by the ice closing around the ships once again. At one stage Parry had sheerlegs rigged from which an ice-saw was suspended in an effort to cut themselves out of their predicament but, such was the nature of the environment in which they found themselves, that on 29 June, the ice parted of its own accord and they found themselves sailing westward through open waters. Two days later Parry was at the entrance to Lancaster Sound, his bold thrust across the middle ice having brought him to the area a month earlier than had been achieved by John Ross the previous year.

A westerly wind blowing directly out of the Sound prevented any immediate progress in that direction so Parry landed in Possession Bay with Sabine to take observations. The flagstaff that had been erected almost a year earlier still stood as a mute marker to Ross's passing. Around its base could still be seen the footprints of those who had raised it. A quarter of a mile from the sea, part of a sledge made from whalebone was found suggesting Eskimo activity in the area.

With the wind still from the west, Parry decided to cross the face of the Sound and look at the northern shore. The passage soon exposed yet again the poor sailing qualities of the *Griper* and, as the low, smooth shores of 'North Devon' loomed into view, Parry hailed Liddon with the instructions that the *Hecla* would sail to the west as soon as the wind permitted and the *Griper* was to make her own way to a rendezvous in the centre of the Sound at 85 degrees west. The breeze they had all been waiting for arrived on that evening, 2 August. With a clear view of the Sound on both sides and an open sea on the bow, the *Hecla* raced on towards Ross's 'Croker's Mountains'. Parry wrote 'We are now about to enter and explore that great sound or inlet which has obtained a degree of celebrity beyond what it might otherwise have been considered to possess, from the very opposite opinions which have been held with regard to it.'

In waters almost clear of ice, great whales spouted and plunged as officers and men took to the rigging in an effort to find an answer to the mystery of the barrier described by Ross. It was not long in coming. At a position just beyond 82 degrees west the *Hecla* sailed over Ross's mountain barrier – 'Croker's Mountains' did not exist. To compensate for the loss to the Admiralty secretary of his mountains, Parry named a bay to the north in his honour. Two inlets to the south were named after the Navy Board and the Admiralty.

After five days of heady sailing almost due west, the two ships came into view of two small islands just off the south coast. Parry named them 'Leopold Islands' after Prince Leopold of Saxe-Coburg. To the disappointment of all, a great sheet of ice stretched from the islands to the north coast, blocking the route west. To the south, however, an inviting opening appeared just beyond the Leopold Island and Parry, with an escort of white beluga whales shrilling like 'musical glasses', turned his ships in that direction.

For some time it had become clear that the ship's compasses were growing more and more sluggish. Now, with the new course, the compasses became quite ineffectual and Parry had them removed depending for the foreseeable future on astral navigation for his direction.

The ships sailed down the wide opening for 120 miles before being stopped once again by ice barring their path. Parry named the waterway 'Prince Regent Inlet' and the coast to the west 'North Somerset' (Somerset Island) before returning north. The capes at the entrance to Prince Regent Inlet were dedicated to royal dukes; that to the east, Cape York; and to the west, Cape Clarence. Returning to the Leopold Islands, Parry landed, climbed a hill, and looked westward through his telescope. All that could be seen was a glittering mass of ice with no possible chance of a way through. There was, however, no sign of any land in that direction. Although ice-bound, the channel continued in the directions of Parry's instructions. Before leaving, a bottle and message was placed beneath a small cairn of rocks on the top of the hill.

Whilst waiting for the ice to clear, the ships' companies amused themselves in pursuit of the unicorn-horned narwhals and the larger whales that foamed in large numbers around the ships. Parry named the strait in which he was delayed after John Barrow, the expedition's chief sponsor. Eager to continue his westward progress, Parry decided to take his ships across to the northern side of Barrow Strait rather than simply wait for the ice to break up. It was an inspired decision for, at nine o'clock that evening, after penetrating an area of loose ice floes, open water was found between the ice and the northern coast.

The next day (21 August) saw the open water continue and, when fog permitted, the ships made their way to the west. At the south-west corner of North Devon an island was named after Lieutenant Beechey and, just to the west, a wide, clear, inlet was named Wellington Channel in honour of the Iron Duke. Cornwallis Island, with its bald, brown hills, was named and passed, followed by Bathurst and Byam Martin islands. To the south a headland was seen and named 'Cape Walker'. To the north again, another low-lying island was named after Lord Melville – the First Lord of the Admiralty – and, to the whole archipelago, Parry gave the name 'New Georgia Islands' (later North Georgia, then Parry Islands) in honour of his sovereign.

On the following Sunday, after divine service, Parry announced that the ships had crossed the meridian at 110 degree West. They had earned a parliamentary prize of £5,000 for reaching that far. 'Three hearty cheers' greeted the news and a nearby promontory was named 'Bounty Cape' in honour of the event. Another feature was given the name 'Hearne Point' in memory of the man who had reached the Arctic Sea at that longitude.

Hecla *and* Griper *being cut into Winter Harbour.*

Further along the coast a landing was made and peat discovered on the shores of a small lake. Parry anchored and sent all the ship's boats away to bring in as much of the fuel as they could. Sabine used the time to set up an observatory ashore and found the position to be 74 degrees 46' north, 110 degrees 39' west. He marked the spot with another note in a bottle beneath a small cairn.

Whilst the party was ashore, tracks of musk-oxen had been seen and, as the ships were delayed by a strong northerly wind, Liddon sent his ice master, George Fife, ashore with six men to see if the animals could be hunted down. Snow fell heavily for much of the day and it was with some concern that the following morning arrived with no sign of Fife and the others. A search party was sent ashore but was itself only able to return in falling snow thanks to rockets fired from the *Griper*. The following day Parry had the *Hecla's* fore-royal mast removed, taken ashore, and erected with an ensign flying. A cache of supplies was buried at its base. With the land so low-lying, it was felt that the flag would be seen over very long distances and was less of a risk than sending more men ashore. After a third night, however, four parties landed carrying boarding-pikes surmounted by coloured flags. The men were sent in different directions to plant the pikes in lines leading to the flagstaff. From each pike a bottle was suspended containing a note informing the reader of the supplies left beneath the ensign. That evening, through the swirl of drifting snow, the missing men were seen assembling on the beach. They had become lost within hours of going ashore and had simply wandered about until the flag-staff was seen, Even then, Fife was of the opinion that they were looking at a different flag-pole, one that had previously been erected on the shore to the east, and had set off with two men in completely the wrong direction before returning to join the others. They suffered from exhaustion and frostbite but had survived by shooting ptarmigan. When asked how they had fared for food, one of the seamen, Peter Fisher replied 'The Duke of Wellington never lived half so well. We had grouse for breakfast, grouse for dinner, and grouse for supper, to be sure.' In gratitude for the safe return of his men Parry named a nearby promontory 'Cape Providence'.

The weather was beginning to deteriorate as Parry urged his ships still further to the west through an increasingly icy sea. Liddon had fallen ill at the same time as a large ice floe trapped the *Griper* between it and the shore. Seeing his escort's predicament and knowing the poor health of her captain, Parry anchored and sent a boat over to bring Liddon over to the *Hecla*. Liddon, however, was determined to remain with his ship and had a chair taken up to the quarterdeck. From his seat he managed to successfully extricate his ship from the danger.

There was, nevertheless, to be no further progress to the west that season. The temperature was dropping, ice was forming on the ship's rigging and on the surface of the sea. In consultation with Liddon, Parry decided to return eastwards to a sheltered bay just to the east of Hearne Point. With the cables frozen, considerable difficulty was experienced in weighing the anchors, and boats had to be sent out to chip ice from the rudders before they could be used. An open channel between the ice and the shore allowed a good run to the east before approaching darkness made the *Hecla* drop her anchor once again and the *Griper* seek the safety of a grounded floe.

The following morning, the ships reached beyond Hearne Point to find that the ice between them and the haven to which they were headed was several inches thick, and quite beyond the ability of the ships to sail through it. Under Parry's supervision, two parallel lines just wider than the *Hecla*'s beam were marked on the snow-covered ice and sheerlegs rigged with ice saws over each line. Once a cut of between 10 and 20ft had been made, a further cut was made at right angles between the lines. This left a rectangle of ice floating free. This slab was cut yet again, this time diagonally across and the two resulting triangular slabs were floated out to open waters. When the wind was in the right direction, masts were rigged on the floating ice and boat sails were used to drive the wedges out to sea. After nineteen hours of hard labour the ships were warped into the passage beneath a darkening sky that flashed with the lights of the Aurora Borealis. The work continued the next day but now, as the ships prevented the ice from being floated out, the sawn blocks were forced beneath the ice at the edge of the passage. At six o'clock that evening the *Griper* was secured to the stern of the *Hecla* and both ships' companies sent on to the ice to tow the vessels forward.

The next day, so proficient had the ships' companies become in sawing a canal through the ice, that they not only managed to achieve the same distance in four hours that had taken them the two previous days to complete, but also reached the spot where Parry decided that the ships should be secured for the winter. The entire length of the passageway was just under two and a third miles, cut through ice 7in thick. At half-past one on the afternoon of 23 September, the ships' companies began to haul their ships forward. An hour and three-quarters later, to three loud cheers, the ships reached the end of the cut. They were in the north-west corner of the bay, and a 'cable's length' from the shore (a cable was 600ft and was made up of eight shackles, each shackle being twelve and a half fathoms long, and each fathom 6ft). Parry noted '...our crews are composed of no common men: they do every thing cheerfully and well...' He named their berth 'Winter Harbour' and the length of curving coast in which they found themselves 'Hecla and Griper Bay'.

No-one had ever wintered before with ships at such a high latitude and Parry had to rely on a combination of practical seamanship, leadership, enterprise and commonsense to see his tiny flotilla safely through the severest winter any of them had known.

The first requirement was to have all the sails removed and the upper masts and yards taken down with the running rigging. These, along with spare spars, heavy stores and timber, were taken ashore and buried beneath the snow. Then the ship's boats were removed to the beach and, again, buried in snow. The lower yards were swung round to line up fore-and-aft along the centre line of the ships. In this position they provided a ridge over which a thick cover could be draped, its sides secured to the gunwales forming a tent-like protection for the upper deck. Around the ship, snow was banked up to the main chains to provide insulation and an ingenious system of stove pipes carried heated air below decks from the galley oven and from a stove set up amidships. As a safeguard against the threat of fire, a hole in the ice close by the main gangway was kept permanently open. The hole also served as a tide-gauge allowing tidal records to be kept.

But there was more to keeping the expedition's morale high than just securing the ships for the approaching winter. Both officers and men had to be kept in employment, had to be kept healthy, and had to be entertained through the morale-sapping darkness of the long winter months. Officers were reminded to keep an eye on their 'divisions' (forecastle, quarterdeck, between decks, tops, etc) to ensure that the men kept themselves and their clothing in good conditions. Lime juice, sweetened with sugar, was issued every day and (reluctantly) drunk under the supervision of the officers. The surgeons checked gums and shins once a week for signs of scurvy and Parry and Liddon carried out frequent inspections of their vessels to ensure all was well. After breakfast the ships' companies were sent ashore for exercise or, if the weather prevented leaving the ships, the men ran around the upper deck to the tune of an organ or to the rhythm of their own singing. Once the ships' routines had been established, the only serious problem remaining to trouble the expedition was the constant dampness inside the ships caused by condensation. Although Parry was keen that bedding should be aired on the upper deck it was found that as soon as the frozen blankets were brought below decks, the warmer, moisture-laden air soon made them too damp to use. Instead the bedding had to be hung between decks.

Beer was brewed whenever the temperature was warm enough to allow fermentation, and bread was baked with great success in the ship's oven. To keep the men busy between dinner and the six o'clock evening muster they were employed in manufacturing and repairing the rigging and any other jobs that could be undertaken below decks. After the muster they had supper and then amused themselves by singing and dancing until 'lights out' at nine o'clock. Amusement, however, did not include over-indulgence in drink – Parry had a seaman and a marine both flogged with thirty-six lashes each for drunkenness whilst in the ice off Melville Island.

About 700 yards to the west of the ships, Sabine had erected an observatory made from planks carried for boat repairs. Moss was packed into any gaps and the building heated by a small stove. The officers, working on a watch system, took Meteorological and magnetic observations. Many learned the hard way that, when subjected to extreme cold, bare metal would remove skin as easily as hot metal. Before long, the mercury in the artificial horizon froze solid. It was not just officers

Hecla *and* Griper *in their winter quarters.*

Parry's Rock, carved during his wintering at Winter Harbour (the '1851' was added by a later expedition).

Hecla *feeling the force of the ice as the* Griper *is threatened by the floe.*

who had to learn the dangers of bare metal. A Royal Marine private, John Pearson, who had served under Ross in the *Isabella*, went hunting on 10 October without wearing gloves. In gripping the barrel of his musket, his fingers froze to the metal and, by the time he was able to return to his ship, the damage to his hand was such that three of his fingers had to be amputated.

To reduce the risk of people getting lost in bad weather 'finger-posts' were erected on all the hills within three miles of the bay, their 'fingers' pointing to the ships. Between the observatory and the ships, whale-lines were strung supported by crossed boarding pikes. Should anyone become lost within this area of signposts and guidelines, guns would have to be fired and rockets launched – the cost of such signals being charged to the unfortunate offenders.

It was soon found that tight leather boots did little to prevent frostbite. To help reduce the problem Parry had boots made of canvas uppers and raw leather soles produced for everyone on the ships. Manufactured to a size larger than normally used, the new boots allowed two pairs of socks to be worn and air to circulate freely around the toes. The symptoms of scurvy appeared on the *Hecla*'s gunner, James Scallon. Parry helped cure the affliction by growing mustard and cress in a box above the heating pipes of his cabin. It was served as a salad with vinegar.

With his ships and immediate area secured, Parry turned his mind to producing a 'Plan of a Journey from the North coast of America towards Fort Chipewyan, should such a measure be found necessary as a last resource.' Sabine was given the task of editing a newspaper grandly entitled 'The New Georgia Gazette, and Winter Chronicle'. Contributors would hand in their article, essay, or poem to Sabine who then, if it passed his editorship, would copy it into a book which was then made available for all to read. A light-hearted threat by Sabine to prosecute all non-contributors was replied to by Parry's complaint

> that what with the time necessarily occupied in three regular meals, and two little ones per day, a two hours' nap after dinner, and another after coffee, with an occasional doze in the forenoon, together with the duties of his profession in those times of constant activity, he most positively deponeth that he hath scarcely been able to snatch his ten-hours' rest at night, much less employ any portion of his time in contributing to the general amusement.

Lieutenant Beechey was given the task of producing plays 'for the amusement of the Officers, and to divert the minds of the men during the tedious period of constant darkness.' His first production – 'Miss in Her Teens' – was performed on 5 November at the 'Theatre Royal, North Georgia', and a play was put on at fortnightly intervals throughout the winter. Parry took a leading role in the acting and the women's parts generally went to the midshipmen. When the few plays that they carried had been exhausted they turned to writing their own. The pinnacle of their own efforts was 'The North West Passage or Voyage Finished' in which Midshipmen Nias, Palmer, and Griffiths played seamen from the *Hecla*. Lieutenant Hoppner and the *Griper's* captain's clerk, Cyrus Wakeham took the parts of seamen from the *Griper*. The part of the landlord went to Midshipman Bushnan, and John Halse, captain's clerk on the *Hecla*, played the dual roles of 'James' and an 'Esquimaux'. The *Hecla's* purser, William Hooper, played 'Susan' and Midshipman James Ross gained the part of 'Poll'. William Marshal, who had been with Parry as an able seaman in the *Alexander*, played the part of a bear.

Much of the play's dialogue reflected the hoped-for outcome of the voyage. After news has reached England from the whaler *Brunswick* that the ships had been seen and that all was well, Poll remarks:

Delightful! And I warrant you they've got across the Bay, or else the other Ships must have seen 'em.

Susan replies

Aye that they have, and who knows but that they may succeed and come home by the South Seas: Oh! Poll, Poll, what a happy day that will be, my heart leaps for joy to think of it. Dear fellows! Covered with glory! Pockets filled with Prize-money – all the world coming to see them – oh there will be rare doings.

Thus was followed by Lieutenant Hoppner singing to the tune of 'Heart of Oak'-

> *At last, Brother tars, here we are at the Strait*
> *And the fam'd North-west passage is traversed complete.*
> *O'er blue rolling waves to the Southward we'll steer,*
> *And quickly arrive at the land of good cheer.*
> *In the ice of the North, British hearts were our own.*
> *Still seeking for Glory*
> *Famous in story*
> *We've gained for old England new yarns of renown.*

Much 'Huzzaing' followed this rendition and the production ended by three cheers and the singing of 'God save the King'.

An unexpected diversion happened in February when the wooden hut containing the scientific instruments caught fire. The blaze was only extinguished when the roof was pulled off and snow thrown onto the flames. Sixteen men suffered from frostbite whilst fighting the fire and one man lost part of four fingers as a result of picking up a metal instrument in his bare hands. The same month, however, also

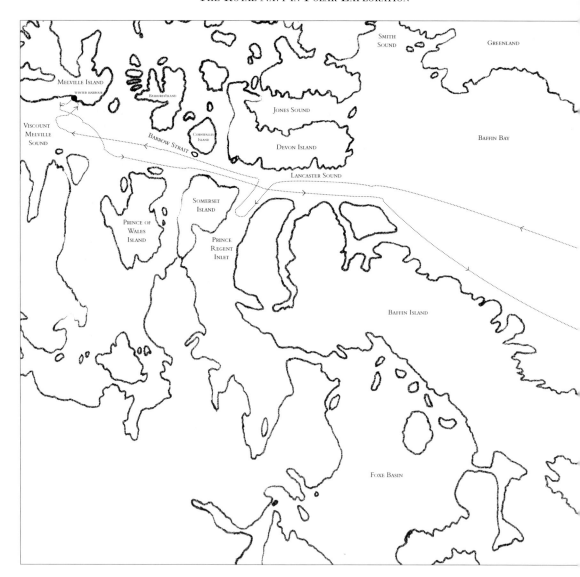

Parry's 1819-1820 voyage

brought good news. After nine days of watching from the rigging, the first sighting of the sun was made on 3 February and, four days later, the complete disk balanced for an instant on the horizon.

With the return of light – albeit for a brief period – work could commence on the outside of the ships to prepare them for their escape from the ice. Another task that required immediate attention was the replacement of the ships' ballast. Nearly seventy tons of coal had been used in the *Hecla* and a proportionate amount in the *Griper*. Parties were sent ashore and sledges and rocks were dragged to the beach where they were broken up and weighed before being taken to the ships. By the end of April, Parry was able to remove the deadlights from the stern windows of the *Hecla* and allow the first natural light below decks for seven months.

During the long, dark, winter, Parry had planned an inland reconnaissance of Melville Island, and the first appearance of rain in late May suggested that the time was right for such an expedition. To accompany him northwards Parry decided upon Sabine; Midshipmen Nias and Reid; the assistant-surgeon, Alexander Fisher; and seven men. A wooden cart had been manufactured on-board the *Hecla* to carry two tents made from blankets and supported by boarding pikes, food for three weeks, sleeping bags made of blankets, and chopped wood for fuel. Spare clothing was carried in knapsacks. The party set off on 1 June, using a compass to guide them over a featureless snow-streaked plain brightened only by the occasional purple-flowered saxifrage. They headed towards the 'Blue Hills' that could be seen from Winter Harbour, taking advantage of any wind by using a blanket on boarding pikes as a sail. After seven days they reached the edge of a level, frozen, expanse that reached the horizon. Parry had the ice chipped away using the pikes and the taste of salt water told him that he had reached the sea. On a nearby hill he named 'Point Nias', Parry erected a large cairn and enclosed within it a metal cylinder containing an account of the party and a number of coins. Observations gave their position as latitude 75 degrees, 26' north, longitude 111 degrees, 22' west. The return journey to the ships followed a more south-westerly course and led them to a frozen inlet that Parry named 'Liddon Gulf'. They crossed via a small islet ('Hooper Island') carrying all they could on their backs – the cart had collapsed when crossing the rough terrain south of Point Nias. Parry and his party reached the ships after an absence of fourteen days and a journey of 180 miles.

Less than two weeks after his return, Parry faced the first death in the expedition. An able seaman from the *Hecla,* William Scott, a man known for his over indulgence in rum and who had been ill for some time – probably with pneumonia – caught scurvy and died on 27 June. He was buried a short distance from the beach with full pomp and flags at half-mast after divine service the following Sunday. A tombstone was erected over his grave with an inscription stating his name, age, and the ship to which he belonged.

With the ships remasted and rigged, Parry was ready to sail when on 1 August – eleven months after he had entered Winter Harbour and the anniversary of his first entering Lancaster Sound – the ice cleared enough for a passage to be made westward towards Hearne Point. They set sail at one o'clock in the afternoon of that day making their way carefully past many ice floes. After eight days they found themselves, yet again, up against the same ice barrier that had blocked their passage westwards the previous year. A small passage remained between the great ice-sheet to the south and the land and Parry attempted to force his way through the narrow gap. It nearly led to his undoing when, anchored to an ice floe, it was seen that the great mass of ice to the south was advancing upon the *Hecla*. Fortunately, a great spur of ice projecting southwards from the floe took the brunt of the collision. With a thunderous roar the spur was forced up and back upon the flow itself. Shortly afterwards, another floe forced the *Griper* on to the shore cracking her rudder. The ships were finally halted at 113 degrees, 46' 43" west. Parry, Sabine and the surgeon, John Edwards, landed again on Melville Island and walked to the west to see if there was any hope of a passage, but none could be seen. They named the furthest point they could see to the west as 'Cape Dundas', after Lord Melville's family name, and an unknown land to the south 'Bank's Land' (Banks Island) after the president of the Royal Society, Sir Joseph Banks.

After consulting his officers, Parry decided not to risk another wintering in the Arctic. Instead he would head eastwards towards Baffin's Bay whilst looking for

Parry's men fighting a polar bear.

Hecla *and* Griper *at Parry's furthest.*

any possible route to the south. During an uninterrupted voyage no such passage revealed itself and Parry chose to sail for England. The ice-blocked opening of Admiralty Inlet was reached on 31 August and the entrance to Lancaster Sound the next day. The compasses were restored to the binnacles and all restrictions taken off fuel and victuals. The number of whales passed in Lancaster Sound seemed considerably reduced during their passage, and the reason why became clear two days after clearing the Sound. On 3 September the masts of three whaling ships appeared on the horizon and, two days later, they fell in with the Hull whaler *Lee*. Her master informed them that the country was now ruled by King George IV, that the previous season had seen the loss of eleven whalers, and that Parry's old ship, the *Alexander*, had been amongst those hunting the whale in Lancaster Sound. He was also able to tell them of Eskimos he had met at the River Clyde – an inlet named by John Ross in 1818. Parry decided to pay the natives a visit and, that evening, four kayaks were seen to be paddling out to the ships. The Eskimos showed no hesitation when clambering up the ship's side and were soon eagerly examining everything they could get their hands on. Of particular interest were the officer's shiny gilt buttons and a number were snipped off and given as gifts. The following day Parry went ashore and was met by natives offering him whalebone and sealskin clothing. Before long, a busy exchange of knives, axes, needles, and brass kettles was fully under way.

The Arctic Circle was crossed on 24 September and the last of the ice left behind two days later. Gales were met in the North Atlantic and the *Griper* was lost to the view of her companion. The *Hecla* suffered the loss of her bowsprit, foremast, and much of her mainmast. Jury masts had to be rigged to get her safely into the Shetland port of Peterhead where the *Griper* joined her the next day. Handing over the responsibility for the ship to Beechey, Parry immediately set off for London and arrived at the Admiralty on 3 November only to discover that the news of the expedition had preceded him. The master of the whaler *Lee* had delivered a set of dispatches that Parry had entrusted him with and, already the newspapers were full of his exploits.

John Barrow was cock-a-hoop that his differences with John Ross were – in his opinion – justified, and swept Parry into the presence of Lord Melville. Shortly afterward, John Croker presented him with a letter expressing the satisfaction of the lords of the Admiralty and the news that he had been promoted to commander (over the heads of 1,200 other lieutenants with greater seniority).

The expedition had been a splendid example of good luck combined with good leadership. Parry had discovered 850 miles of new coastline, wintered at a spot far beyond the known limits of the time, and, with a single exception, had brought all his men safely home. For crossing the 110 degrees west meridian he had earned £1,000, Liddon had £500, the lieutenants, ice masters, and Sabine received £200, senior midshipmen £30, and junior midshipmen £20. The seamen and marines were awarded £20 each.

Matthew Liddon received his promotion to commander the following year but he was never to receive an appointment to sea again. He was placed on the retired list as a captain in 1856 and died thirteen years later.

Parry was soon aware that his exploits had fuelled a keen interest in the north-west passage in all sections of society. The Russians, under the leadership of Lieutenant Kotzebue, had been nibbling yet again at the north coast of Alaska, nothing had been heard from Franklin's overland expedition, and the prize itself had yet to be grasped. The *Hecla* and the *Griper* had been paid off on 20 December, but Barrow, seizing the opportunity was able to tell Parry in the few remaining days of 1820 that he had been appointed to lead another expedition.

Parry's recent experience with the ice at the south-west corner of Melville Island had suggested that a practical passage through to the Bering Straits was, at best, unlikely. It seemed reasonable, therefore, to look to the south for a route. Seventy-nine years earlier, Middleton had penetrated Hudson's Bay and reached Repulse Bay through Sir Thomas Roe's Welcome, to the east of Southampton Island. He had been unable to voyage further north and an eastern exit was blocked by the ice of Frozen Strait, causing him to return the way he had come. To both Parry and Barrow the possibility of a passage leading to the west somewhere to the north of Repulse Bay offered the best hope of finding a way through to Bering Strait.

Parry was keen to have the *Hecla* with him once again and was happy to have her sister-ship, HMS *Fury*, commissioned as the second vessel. Not only had the 'bomb' proved herself in the northern ice, but two ships of the same class would allow for the easier interchange of spares. Taking the *Fury* for himself, the *Hecla* went to Commander George Francis Lyon who received his rank on taking up his command. Lyon had seen active service against the French and, in 1816, had fought at the Battle of Algiers on-board HMS *Albion*. He was still serving in her as a lieutenant at Malta when the Paris embassy secretary, a Mr Ritchie arrived on the island. Ritchie was on government business and travelling to Niger across the Sahara desert. He was to have been escorted from Malta by the naval author Captain Frederick Marryat but, when Marryat was delayed, Lyon volunteered to take his place. After four months learning Arabic at Tripoli the two men set off to the south at the end of March 1819. They travelled over desert for thirty-nine days and covered

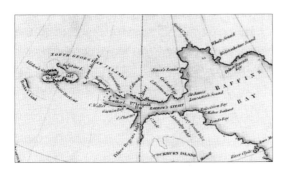

Left: *Parry's map of his 1819-20 discoveries.*

Below: *Lieutenant George Lyon in North African dress during his expedition to Niger.*

almost 500 miles before reaching Marzuq. There, Lyon went down with dysentery, followed rapidly by Ritchie. Over the next four months Lyon gradually improved but Ritchie worsened. The diplomat died on 20 November and Lyon was left weak from illness and with no funds. Undaunted, he continued southwards to the Niger border in an attempt to carry out Ritchie's mission but, on reaching it, was forced to turn back being without support and still enfeebled by dysentery. It took him three months to re-cross the desert to Tripoli where he arrived in March 1820, more dead than alive. He wrote an account of his adventures which led to his being selected to assist in a survey of the south-east coast of the Mediterranean. The illustrations to the book, however, all of which had been done by Lyon, caught the attention of Barrow and Parry and this useful skill, combined with his obvious qualities of initiative, led to his appointment to the *Hecla*.

Many officers and men from the previous expedition volunteered to take part and Parry was able to choose his officers with little difficulty. Nias and Reid – now both lieutenants – were selected for the *Fury* as were the purser Hooper and the surgeon Edwards. Midshipman James Ross was re-appointed and given the job of expedition naturalist. Among his new messmates Ross found a lifelong friend in the young Irishman, Midshipman Francis Rawdon Moira Crozier. Lieutenants Hoppner and Palmer were appointed to the *Hecla* and Fisher returned as surgeon. With Sabine being selected to carry out pendulum experiments on-board HMS *Pheasant,* the appointment of astronomer to the expedition went to the Revd George Fisher, an experienced scientist but newly-ordained cleric who had served as astronomer in the *Dorothea* under Buchan. John Allison moved into the *Fury* as ice master, George Fife taking the same post in the *Hecla*.

Whilst the expedition was being prepared, Parry found himself with a busy social schedule. The people of Bath presented him with a box made from the wood of HMS *Hecla* and he received a similar presentation from the people of Norwich. Not to be outdone, Bath gave him the freedom of the city and a silver-plate trophy in the shape of a vase supported by dolphins and engraved with the words 'Explorer of the Polar Seas'. The Bath and West of England Society for the Encouragement of Arts proposed to award him a silver medal, but changed their mind and gave him a gold one instead. In February 1921, Parry was elected as a fellow of the Royal Society. In addition to a busy life being rewarded for his achievements, Parry was also writing an account of the expedition and was understandably annoyed to learn that the surgeon, Alexander Fisher, had beaten him by having an account published before his own. Parry, however, did not press the issue as Fisher was serving in the *Hecla* and he did not want any open controversy to set in before the expedition had got under way.

The ships were victualled for a three-year stay amongst the ice. Canned food, which had proved to be successful during the wintering off Melville Island, made up an increased proportion of the supplies. Improved cold-weather clothing was taken on-board, each man being supplied with a thick, fur-lined, 'pea jacket' (the 'pea' was actually the 'p' of 'pilot' – 'pilot jackets' were used as cold-weather clothing by pilots when meeting ships before their entry into harbour). Woollen clothing was worn in layers beneath the pea jacket and pilot cloth was used to make trousers which were to be tucked into oversized soft leather boots which allowed two pairs of socks to be worn. On their heads, tarred (i.e. waterproof) straw hats were worn over red woollen caps.

Before the ships sailed, Lord Melville introduced Parry at court. Having congratulated Parry on his safe return, the king was introduced to Lyon by Melville who explained to his majesty that he was 'about to accompany Captain Parry.' 'Yes,' replied the king smiling at Parry, 'and to share in his honours.' As a final 'spree' the Fury's upper deck was turned into a ballroom and a hulk tied up alongside was cleared as a promenade for the dancers. Flags, bunting, and greenery decorated the rigging and the band of the Royal Artillery Regiment provided music.

Ten days later the ships were ready for sea but, as it was a Friday – a traditionally unlucky day to sail – Parry delayed the departure. For the next few days, the wind was contrary and the ships eventually had to be towed out to the Nore to begin their journey north.

On leaving the Orkneys, the two ships, in company with the Nautilus transport, had an uneventful Atlantic crossing. A week after meeting icebergs floating out of Davis's Strait, they were off the entrance to Hudson's Strait. The Nautilus's stores were transferred and the transport sent home with letters and dispatches. Keeping to the northern shore, the Fury and Hecla made their way westward through ice and mist. At one point contact was made with the natives, but Parry kept it short as the Eskimos clearly had previous contact with European ships (probably those of the Hudson's Bay Co.) and displayed the 'vices' which that contact had encouraged.

A month after entering the straits, Parry arrived off the north-east corner of Southampton Island. He now had to face the choice between a 450 mile-circumnavigation of the island to reach Repulse Bay through Sir Thomas Roe's Welcome, or to test Middleton's claim that there was a strait – albeit frozen – along the northern shore. He chose the latter and, with leadsmen continually sounding from the chains or from boats, eased his vessels ahead through fogs and ice. For almost three weeks the ships felt their way forward until, on 22 August, the fog lifted and Parry was astonished to find land ahead and on both sides. Without knowing it, and due to Middleton's errors in position fixing, he had sailed completely through Frozen Strait and now found himself in Repulse Bay.

No time was lost in getting the ship's boats out and surveys of the coast under way. Within days it was found that Repulse Bay had been well named and that no westward exit existed. Parry now began to explore the north coast as it trended eastward, following Vancouver's method by examining every tiny indentation, bay, and creek. Boats were victualled for a week or more and, as the ships lay off, the officers led the way through ice floes to search the coastline for a way through to the west. On completion of their allotted task, muskets were fired to attract the ship's attention and a blue light hoisted on the ship when the musket shot was heard. As the boats edged in a more north-easterly direction hopes were raised by the discovery of a wide inlet leading off to the north-west. But it proved to be yet another dead end terminating in a large lake. Parry named the waterway 'Lyon Inlet'.

With the season now well advanced, the hours of darkness lengthened and young ice began to form on the surface of the sea. Consequently, Parry searched for a safe haven to spend the winter and found it in a bay on the south coast of an island (inevitably named by Parry 'Winter Island') just to the north of the entrance to Lyon Inlet and just to the south of the Arctic Circle. Following the experience of Winter Harbour, little difficulty was found in preparing the ships for the approaching season. With his usual interest in maintaining the morale of his men Parry soon had theatre performances under way. The evident popularity of the plays led one of the officers to note:

> It must not be supposed that the pleasures afforded by these exhibitions arose from the great merit of the performers, and the excellence of the acting. The audience were a class ready to be amused by any novelty, and, in an especial manner, to be gratified by seeing the officers, to whom they were in the habit of looking up to with respect and obedience, voluntarily exerting themselves for their sole amusement.

The entertainment was not limited to the officer's acting. An anonymous lady had present the expedition with a magic lantern and accompanying slides, and the violin-playing Parry led 'a very respectable orchestra' in performances in his or Lyon's cabin with the cabin doors open so that the ship's company could enjoy the music. In addition to scientific and natural history research, a more practical means of passing the time was found by instituting classes of instruction to teach illiterates among the men to read. The aim of such instruction being that every man should be able to read the bible by the end of the expedition – an aim (much to Parry's satisfaction) that was achieved.

On the first day of February 1822, a new and unexpected diversion arrived upon the scene. A movement on the ice, when viewed through telescopes, proved to be a party of Eskimos walking towards the ships. Parry and some of the other officers immediately went out to meet them and found the newcomers to be an amiable group who carried strips of whalebone in the hopes of trading. So keen were they to barter that, when the officers expressed an interest in the design of the women's clothing, one of the women promptly began to disrobe despite the temperature being over twenty degrees below zero. The discomfort of the officers

Off Winter Island. The view from the Hecla *towards the* Fury. *A game of cricket is taking place in the foreground.*

was somewhat relieved when the woman proved to have another complete set of clothing underneath.

The Eskimos took Parry and the others to their community. It consisted of five igloos and about sixty people complete with dogs, sledges, and kayaks. For a while there was some bafflement amongst the naval people as to how the group could have been within range of the ships and not have been spotted previously but, when they eventually saw how quickly the Eskimos could erect their igloos, their question was soon answered. Both Parry and Lyon rapidly grasped that there was much they could learn from the natives and friendly relations were quickly established. The Eskimos were invited on-board the ships and thrilled to hear the sound of the ship's barrel organ and delighted when their songs were played back to them on a fiddle. Almost inevitably, thefts occurred and Parry had one Eskimo given 'two dozen moderately administered lashes' for the theft of an axe. Another Eskimo, who committed a 'trifling' theft was locked in the fore-hold where 'he fell into a sound sleep, which the poor fellow enjoyed with the luxury of lying upon coils of rope for his pillow.' Others bartered bladders of seal oil for empty portable soup tins. One item of native design was especially popular with both officers and seamen:

Spectacles are another of their articles which struck us as curious and well constructed. They consist of a piece of wood scraped thin, like a bandage, and perforated with two narrow horizontal slits, something like pig's eyes, where we would have glass; a rim, about an inch broad, projects in the same direction as that of a hat would; and this simple mechanical process, tied about the head, protects the eyes from the drifting snow and speculae, and improves the sharpness of the sight.

A native woman, Iligliuk, proved to be highly intelligent and was able to draw a map of the region for Parry and the other officers. Using a pencil and paper she continued the coastline in a northwards direction, then – to the surprise of all – she traced a coastline that turned abruptly westwards before bringing it southwards to within a few miles of the western end of Repulse Bay. Her map, if correct, suggested that the land to the west and north of Winter Island was a peninsular and, at the point where the coast swung to the west, lay the north-east corner of continental America.

With such a chart at their disposal, Parry and his officers were eager to test its effectiveness but were forced to wait until the beginning of July before they were released from the ice's grip. Channels were cut to reach the open water where a passage was found between ice still fast on the shore and large ice floes drifting out in the Fox Channel. The passage was fraught with danger. At one stage the ships collided and one of the *Hecla*'s boats was demolished by the *Fury'* anchor. On another occasion, whilst their passage was blocked by ice and they were waiting for it to clear, the ships used ice-anchors to secure themselves to an ice floe. The *Hecla*, however, found herself trapped by another ice floe which forced her stern out of the water. The friction caused by the hawsers as the ice-anchors tried to restrain the ship caused the bitt-heads to catch fire.

The detailed search of the coast had been abandoned as they clawed their way northwards, but they were halted by the discovery of a river. It proved, however, to offer no passage to the west, but gave Parry the opportunity to name a feature after the expedition's chief sponsor. From Barrow River a clear run was made to the north through herds of walrus resting on ice floes until, on rounding an island (Igloolik), Parry was presented with a wide opening that showed all the possibility of being the point at which Iligliuk's map turned to the west. Unfortunately, the opening was blocked with ice. There was no chance that the ice would clear in what was left of the short summer so Parry decided to winter at Igloolik in the hope that the following summer might see the opening of the passageway which he named the 'Strait of Hecla and Fury' (Hecla and Fury Strait). Before the winter set in, Parry led an overland expedition to the tip of a promontory he named 'Cape North-East' (Northeast Cape) from where he could see along the full length of the strait. He was in no doubt that he was looking westwards towards an open sea and, when the water at Cape North-East proved to be salt, he celebrated by building a cairn of rocks, giving 'three hearty cheers', and issuing an extra allowance of rum.

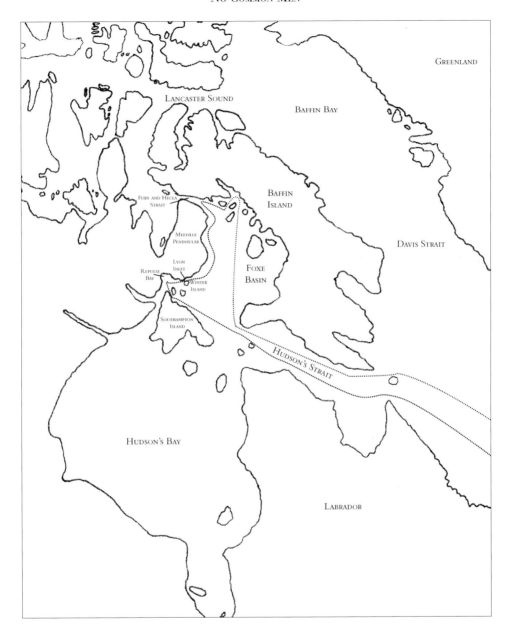

Parry's 1821-1823 voyage

Life on-board followed its, by now, well-accustomed course enlivened by cricket matches on the ice and frequent contact with the local Eskimos, many of whom they had met during the previous winter. Whilst patches of water remained open, Parry and Lyon experimented with the native kayak and later purchased dogs and sledges from the Eskimos. Before long – under the tuition of the natives – both were able to drive a dog team with a modicum of success. Lyon, in particular, took great interest in the life and customs of the Eskimos, studying their language, dances, and clothing. In June 1823, he attempted to cross the Melville Peninsular with two men using dogs and a sledge but was prevented from success by melting snow. He returned after thirteen days, the first naval officer to attempt a long journey by dog-sledge.

By the end of the winter, Parry had decided that he would send the *Hecla* home whilst he would attempt to breach the ice-bound strait. In this way he would face the obvious dangers himself, reduce the numbers of others exposed to risk, and inform the Admiralty of his situation. Stores were transferred between the ships and Parry wrote to his parents

> I am determined…with the continued assistance of Providence, to show that perseverance has not been wanting in this enterprise; and no consideration shall induce me to relinquish it, while a reasonable hope of success remains. Whatever the event may be, our efforts shall be worthy of our country, and our return, I trust, at least not inglorious.

But 'reasonable hope' was dashed just a few days before the ice cleared around the ships – George Fife, the *Hecla's* ice master and the leader of the shore party that had lost its way on Melville Island in 1819, died of scurvy. The disease was also detected in other men.

In addition to his surgeon's advice that he should return home with both ships to avoid further spread of scurvy, Parry could also see that the ice in the Strait of Hecla and Fury showed no sign of breaking up in the summer. In fact, the season proved to be late – and, therefore, short. Thus, 'with a passing sigh for the Polar Sea, which lay at the western gates of his newly discovered strait', Parry saw he had no other option than to return home with both ships.

During the voyage through the Foxe Basin the ships were swept along with a tide of ice floes and were constantly at risk from being caught between the giant blocks of ice and crushed, or from being forced ashore. The short season also placed them in danger of being iced-in for a third winter, and it was with great relief that they achieved open water to the north of Hudson's Straits.

The Shetlands were reached in the second week of October and the inhabitants of Lerwick illuminated the town, rang the church bells, and flooded down to the docks to see the ships' arrival. Before a service of thanksgiving in the local church, Parry opened the letters waiting for him. From Barrow he learned that, in his absence, he had been promoted to captain and that a relief expedition had been ready to sail if he had not returned safely that summer. Another letter reduced Parry to tears of relief as it bore the signature of John Franklin and brought congratulations for all that had been achieved on both voyages. A letter from his mother, however, caused Parry to weep tears of deepest sadness. She told him of the death of his father the previous March. The news depressed him to the extent that he completely lost his appetite and was soon taken to bed with a fever. The gravest concern was expressed at his condition before his eventual meeting with his mother and his consequent recovery. To make matters worse, a gentle pursuit of a Miss Browne, a niece of Sabine, foundered on the two-and-a-half years' separation and the lady had cast her ambitions elsewhere. Parry's response to this news gave rise to a popular piece of doggerel that went the rounds.

> *Parry, why this dejected air?*
> *Why are your looks so much cast down?*
> *None but the Brave deserve the Fair,*
> *Any one may have the Brown!*

John Barrow accepted Parry's inability to breach the ice of the Strait of Hecla and Fury with his usual energetic fever to secure the north-west passage for his country. Cook had taken his ships through Bering's Strait as far east as Icy Cape, Franklin had confirmed that the Polar Sea was an open waterway during the Arctic summer, and Parry had shown that there was no route for ships through Hudson's Bay but had noted that there was a possible route south from Barrow Strait through Prince Regent Inlet. With this information Barrow decided on another concerted attack upon the problem. This time there would be four expeditions.

CHAPTER EIGHT

'GREAT THEREFORE WAS OUR DISAPPOINTMENT'

Captain John Franklin had not been merely fêted and honoured on his return from the Barren Lands. In August 1823, he had married Eleanor Porden, an attractive young woman with a lively mind and a taste for poetry that had earned her the honour of being the first woman to be elected a member of the French Institute. She was sixteen years old at the time of her election – and France an implacable foe. An example of her style and interests may be glimpsed from an extract of a poem she penned after visiting the *Trent* in 1818, just before Franklin sailed for Spitsbergen under Buchan:

> *Sail, sail, adventurous Barks! go fearless forth,*
> *Storm on his glacier-seat the misty North,*
> *Give to mankind the inhospitable zone,*
> *And Britain's trident plant in seas unknown.*

Nine months after the marriage, Eleanor gave birth to a daughter and the family settled down to live in Devonshire Street, London. But Franklin had lost none of his taste for the north and the adventure and glory that still lay untapped among the ice. He was also, like others, concerned about the Russian presence on the north-west corner of the American continent. A frenzy of diplomacy had led to a treaty which limited the boundaries of Russian expansion overland to the east and south and had secured the right of passage for British ships along the Alaskan coast. There still remained, however, the possibility of Russian probing into the western end of the supposed north-west passage. Franklin forwarded a proposal to Barrow suggesting that an overland expedition should descend the MacKenzie River from the Great Slave Lake and, once the Polar Sea had been reached, head westwards to link up with Icy Cape. Such an enterprise would ensure British priority throughout the length of the passage. Once Icy Cape had been reached there existed the possibility of a ship meeting the overland expedition to take it home. Barrow lost no time in bringing the idea to the attention of Lord Melville, the First Lord of the Admiralty, 'To give up the attempt before this point be tried, would indeed be to have opened the door, at a great expense and labour, for some other nation to reap the honour and glory, and to triumph over us who have for two Centuries and a half endeavoured in vain to accomplish it.'. The Admiralty agreed.

Parry, once over his distress at the loss of his father, was keen to demonstrate his desire to keep a grip on the eastern end of the problem. Franklin's proposal was all very well with its political and diplomatic overtones, but the pressure on the north-west passage from the east should not be forgotten. He wrote to Lord Melville

> The information lately obtained makes it less advisable than ever for England to make the attempt from any but the Atlantic side; because it is obvious, that any difficulties of a more than ordinary nature should be encountered at first, while the resources are complete, the ships uninjured, and the energy of the crews wholly unimpaired.

He pointed out that the field of exploration had narrowed down considerably since the early days. Any route through Hudson's Bay was blocked by the ice of the Strait of Hecla and Fury, and the passage between Melville and Bank's Island was equally blocked. All that remained was the southwards-trending Prince Regent's Inlet. Again their lordships agreed and instantly nominated Parry to lead such an expedition

> The confidence which we are justified in placing in your judgement and experience, determine us to authorise and direct you to pursue the course which you consider most promising, namely, through Prince Regent's Inlet.

Not only did Melville have 'confidence' in Parry's abilities, he also thought enough of him to appoint him to the position of hydrographer to the Admiralty. Normally such a distinguished office would have prevented Parry from taking command of an expedition, but the First Lord assured him that it would remain his in readiness for his return – a privilege that would lift the threat of half-pay on completion of the voyage.

Hudson's Bay, however, was not to be entirely forgotten. The ice in Prince Regent's Inlet might bring Parry's progress to a halt as it had done in 1819. But there was still the possibility of a western route across the Melville Peninsular from the head of Repulse Bay to the coast (named by the natives as 'Akkoolee') that had been sketched out by the Eskimo woman, Iligliuk. With Akkoolee achieved, there was every chance that a western-trending coast would lead to Franklin's Point Turnagain.

Few would have been surprised that the command of the overland and River Mackenzie expedition should go to Franklin, and that Lyon – by now promoted to captain in recognition of his service under Parry – was chosen for the crossing of the Melville Peninsular. All that remained was for the ship to meet Franklin at Icy Cape.

The vessel chosen was the sloop HMS *Blossom* and her command went to Commander Frederick Beechey who, as a lieutenant, had accompanied Franklin to Spitsbergen in the *Trent* and Parry to Melville Island in the *Hecla*. Beechey had also taken part in an overland survey of the North African coast and had published an account of his adventures under the title 'Proceedings of the Expedition to explore the Northern Coast of Africa from Tripoli eastward, in 1821–22; comprehending an Account of the Greater Syrtis and Cyrenaica, and of the ancient Cities composing the Pentopolis'.

Lyon, despite Parry's earlier disapproval of the use of gun brigs for Arctic work, was given command of the Arctic veteran *Griper*. She had increased her experience amongst the ice by being taken to the coast of Greenland in the summer of 1823 by Commander Douglas Clavering to allow Sabine to carry out scientific experiments. Clavering, who had been a midshipman in the *Shannon* during her famous victory against the American *Chesapeake,* was lost at sea four years later whilst in the pursuit of slave traders.

Lieutenant Peter Manico was appointed as the *Griper*'s first lieutenant. He had seen service under Admiral Collingwood against the French, but had no previous Arctic experience. Edward Kendall, an experienced master's assistant (a new rank created to replace the 'master's mate' and to avoid confusion with the newly-created rank of 'mate' – a senior midshipman undergoing the navigation studies necessary for promotion to lieutenant) was appointed as assistant surveyor.

The *Griper* sailed from England on 6 June 1824, and reached Hudson's Bay without incident. They anchored off Coat's Island (believed at the time to be part of Southampton Island) and Lyon had himself rowed towards the shore. With still a mile to go they saw the strange sight of an Eskimo paddling towards them sitting astride three inflated sealskins with his sealskin boots dangling in the water. As the native approached, it could be seen that not only were his teeth chattering with fear but '…himself, and the seal-skins trembled in unison.' Lyon felt that such courage should be rewarded and threw a string of beads to the man. He, in turn, was rewarded by being thrown a couple of pieces of dried fish and a flint arrowhead. Soon the native was persuaded to enter the boat and the floating seal skins were towed astern – an arrangement nearly upset by Nee-a-Kood-loo (for that proved to be his name) continually standing up and energetically gesticulating by waving his beads to a small group of natives who had gathered on the shore. After accepting more dried fish and offering gifts, Lyon returned to the *Griper*. He now found himself with the same choice that had faced Parry – to attempt to reach Repulse Bay through Frozen Strait, or to go the long way around Southampton Island and approach the bay through Sir Thomas Roe's Welcome Sound. He chose the latter, and suffered the consequences. On reaching the sound, the *Griper* found herself in the teeth of a violent storm that threatened to dash the vessel against a reef. The ship's anchors were thrown over and held the ship whilst Lyon led the men in prayers. In time their pleas were answered and the savage winds abated. Lyon wrote that 'Noble as the character of the British sailor is always allowed to be in cases of danger, yet I did not believe it to be possible that among forty-one persons not one repining word should have been uttered.' He was to find, however, that the effect of the prayers was short-lived. Within days they were at the mercy of another storm which caused serious damage to the ship's hull and the loss of all the anchors. Lyon consulted his officers and all agreed that the expedition should be abandoned. They arrived home in November with little more to show for their efforts than Lyon's account of the voyage 'A Brief Narrative of an Unsuccessful Attempt to reach Repulse Bay through Sir Thomas Rowe's Welcome, in H.M. Ship Griper in the year 1824'.

The Admiralty was unimpressed and Lyon was never to serve at sea again despite Parry blaming the *Griper* as being of 'such lubberly, shameful construction'. Lyon married into the aristocracy and worked as a mining commissioner in Mexico for two years – suffering shipwreck on his return. A new mining venture in South Africa was cut short by failing eyesight. Returning to England for medical assistance, he reached Buenos Aries where he died in October 1832.

The *Griper* remained in service with the Royal Navy until she was transferred to the Coastguard in 1836. She became a target-vessel in 1865 and survived long enough to be sold to the breakers in 1868 after a total of fifty-five years service.

Parry, who had no time for gun-brigs such as the *Griper* in polar work, was to make his attempt to find a north-west passage through Prince Regent's Inlet by using his old ships *Hecla* and *Fury*, returning to the former for the command of the

Captain Lyon's Griper *riding out a storm in Hudson's Bay.*

Captain Lyon leading his men in prayer for their preservation.

expedition. His first lieutenant was John Land Wynn who had been Clavering's first lieutenant in the Greenland expedition. Joseph Sherer, a former midshipman in the *Hecla* under Lyon and now a lieutenant, was appointed as second lieutenant. The appointment of assistant surveyor (and unofficial astronomer) went to Lieutenant Henry Foster, an extremely talented young officer who had served as a midshipman under Clavering. The result of his work as Sabine's assistant had earned Foster a fellowship of the Royal Society. The *Hecla*'s ice master was to be John Allison – his third voyage with Parry. The *Fury* went to Henry Hoppner who had been promoted to commander whilst in the *Hecla* under Lyon. His first lieutenant was to be Horatio Thomas Austin – an officer with experience against the Americans under Nelson's flag captain, Sir Thomas Hardy. The *Hecla*'s second lieutenant was James Ross, recently made a fellow of the Linnaean Society for his scientific and natural history work under Parry in Hudson's Bay. The ice master was George Crawford, his fourth naval expedition into Arctic waters.

No doubt swayed by the success of his previous sending-off party, Parry ordered an even larger event, this time on both ships. Over 300 guests danced beneath coloured lights hung in the rigging, attended a concert on the *Hecla*, and listened enthralled to the singing of 'Madame Pasta'. Two weeks later the ships sailed from the Nore.

The first ice was met a month after leaving and, shortly afterwards, Parry was given an opportunity to demonstrate his response to danger. Conducting divine service below decks one Sunday, he was interrupted by the quartermaster who dropped hastily down a ship's ladder and whispered something in his ear. Parry told the man to return to his watch and continued the sermon. After making the blessing Parry raised his hand and said 'Now, my lads, all hands on deck, – but mind, no bustle!'. A fog they had been sailing through had suddenly lifted to reveal land dead ahead. Armed with the quartermaster's report, Parry had correctly judged the time he had before he needed to take action, and had used the time to complete his religious service. The Almighty, however, proved to be not always so helpful and, after visiting the Greenland port of Disko, two frustrating months were spent in trying to break through the middle ice of Baffin's Bay before their efforts achieved success. Their trials, nevertheless, were not over and, just as the entrance to Prince Regent Inlet came into view, they were trapped in young ice and forced back out towards the entrance to Lancaster Sound. Fortunately, a gale broke the ice up and, despite headwinds, they managed to struggle into the great waterway and find refuge in the tiny, cliff-lined, inlet of Port Bowen on the eastern side of Prince Regent's Inlet. Parry knew it from a survey he had carried out there in 1819.

It was clearly too late to press on further to the south that season and so the ships were prepared for the winter. A stove, newly developed by a Mr Sylvester, had been installed at the bottom of the ships' holds and the resulting warm air rose through pipes to all inhabited parts of the ships. There still remained, however, the important question of maintaining morale where, for many, the novelty of a wintering in the Arctic had worn off, and there were no natives to provide a diversion. As Parry noted in his journal,

> Whichever way the eye is turned, it meets a picture calculated to impress upon the mind an idea of inanimate stillness, of that motionless torpor, – of anything, in short, but life. In the very silence there is a deadness, with which a human witness appears out of keeping. The presence of man seems an intrusion on the dreary solitude of this wintry desert, which even its native animals have, for a while, forsaken.

William Hooper, the *Hecla*'s purser, set up a school of reading to which came, not only those who needed basic instruction, but at times the entire ship's company. On Sundays, the church lesson was used as the reading material followed by yet more prayers. There was still the need, nevertheless, for some form of light-hearted entertainment. The idea of continuing to perform plays was discarded as being 'threadbare' and a new form of novelty was sought. The answer came from Commander Hoppner. A 'general masquerade' (fancy dress party) was organised to take place in the *Fury*. For days prior to the event much effort was put into producing a wide variety of costumes. A tavern was erected on the *Fury's* lower deck to be known as 'The Fury, No.1, Arctic Street', and tickets for beer were sold before the event. On the first night, the most keenly awaited fancy dress was that to be worn by Parry. He crossed over the ice to the *Fury* wrapped in a long cloak and clutching his violin. On reaching the 'masquerade hall' he threw off the cloak to reveal himself dressed as a one-legged marine begging for halfpennies. To complete the picture he scraped on his fiddle and implored the watchers to 'Give a copper to poor Joe, your honour, who's lost his timbers in defence of his king and country.' He was joined by men dressed as Quakers, chimney sweeps, Turks, and rag-and-bone men all 'footing it' to music. At four bells in the first watch (ten o'clock in the evening) the shrill whistling of boatswains calls and the shouts of 'Away there, Heclas!' brought the festivities to an end. The event had been such a success that it was repeated monthly on alternate ships throughout the long winter.

There was, of course, much more serious work to be done during the dark months. Parry (when not affected by the rheumatism which had begun to afflict him) took part in experiments in gravity and geomagnetism assisted by Foster and Ross. It was noticed that the variation between 'true' and 'magnetic' poles had increased by 9 degrees since 1819 and studies were made of an increased meteor activity in December and the effects of the Aurora Borealis. Foster carried out experiments in sound and discovered that, in calm weather and over a stretch of ice, he could easily converse with another person over a distance of more than a mile. Ross was kept busy with lunar observation and the preservation of the rarely seen animals and birds that had been caught.

In the late spring of 1825, Parry sent two sledge expeditions out. One, to the north, was under the command of Ross. With four men he kept to the ice just off the coast and reached Cape York, seventy-five miles from Port Bowen. On his return he was able to report that Barrow Strait was free of ice and open water had reached to within twenty-two miles of the ships. A southern party sent out under the command of Sherer achieved sixty miles before turning back at the northern edge of a wide bay. Sherer gave the name of the southern point of the bay 'Cape Kater' after a distinguished scientific naval officer.

The ships broke free of Port Bowen's icy grip on 20 July and Parry headed towards North Somerset on the western side of Prince Regent's Inlet. This was now the real start of the expedition and all eyes eagerly sought for a gap in the tall cliffs of the western coastline. At first the ships were prevented from closing with the shore by ice that lingered on the western side of the inlet long after it had disappeared on the east, but gaps did appear and Parry sailed between the ice and the rubble-strewn beaches that lined the bases of the cliffs.

The manoeuvre proved to be a grave mistake. Parry soon found himself under threat from the ice itself as the wind pushed it towards the shore. The blow came off a low-lying beach just as the coastline curved westwards. Both ships were forced aground, the *Fury* just narrowly missing a collision with the *Hecla*. High tide allowed them to be floated free, but it was soon evident that the *Fury* had received serious damage to her hull. Her ship's company manned her pumps and worked to the point of exhaustion. The damage, however, was too great and the flow of water could not be stemmed. Consequently, a dock was cut in the ice lining the shore to allow the ship to be 'heaved down'. This involved strengthening the masts so that blocks and tackles could be rigged between them and the shore. Then the ship could be hauled over to expose the damaged part of the hull in order for it to be repaired. But, with the preparations under way, a gale struck and destroyed the ice dock. All that could be done was to have the *Hecla* tow the *Fury* clear with the crippled ship's sails lowered over the side to reduce the rush of water into the hold. After four days of dodging the ice the *Fury* was driven ashore once again. She was now stranded well beyond the help of any high water and at the mercy of wind and ice. The exhausted ships' companies were put to work unloading the stricken vessel, piling the stores on the beach as Parry and Hoppner examined the damage closely. It did not take long for both officers to come to the conclusion that the *Fury* was in no state to return to sea and that her ship's company would have to transfer to the *Hecla*. The arrival of another gale forced the *Hecla* out to sea and drove her far to the south through waters as clear of ice as any Parry could have wished for. Clawing their way back to the fated beach they found the *Fury* lying on her side and her damage confirmed as being beyond any hope of recovery.

With the *Hecla* packed with two ships' companies, and with much of his stores piled on 'Fury Beach', Parry knew that he had no other option but to abandon both the *Fury* and the expedition. He gave the orders and, with the depressing sight of invitingly clear waters beckoning to the south, the *Hecla* turned northwards to Barrow Strait and Lancaster Sound.

Parry arrived at Peterhead in October and travelled overland to make his report to the Admiralty. There was little that could be said. About ninety miles of new coastline had been added to the map at the cost of two lives and a ship. The question of whether a passage existed through Prince Regent's Inlet was still unresolved. Barrow – rather unkindly – noted that Parry had left the problem of the north-west Passage 'precisely where it was at the conclusion of his first voyage'.

One item of business that had to be completed soon after the expedition's return was the formality of Hoppner's court martial for the loss of the *Fury*. Held on-board HMS *Gloucester* at Sheerness, the trial attracted a large crowd of naval officers and civilians. Extraordinarily, however, there were not enough qualified captains to make up a full board and Parry found himself taking a seat in judgement of a case in which he held ultimate responsibility. But, as was usual in such cases, the charge against Hoppner remained little more than a formality and he was acquitted of all

The Fury *thrown against the base of the cliffs. From this position she was towed by the* Hecla *to the beach where she was abandoned.*

negligence and, both he and Parry, heard the court lavish great praise on their recent endeavours.

Hoppner was promoted to captain three months later, and died at Lisbon in 1834.

The attempt to find a way to the south through Prince Regent's Inlet proved to be Parry's last search for a north-west passage. As generous in spirit as ever, he wrote that he would be 'happy' to make another attempt but, if that was not to be, 'May it still fall to England's lot to accomplish this undertaking, and may she ever continue to take the lead in enterprises intended to contribute to the advancement of science, and to promote, with her own, the welfare of mankind at large.' Parry now turned his thoughts to making a success of the hydrographic department, marriage, and the possibility of an assault on the North Pole itself.

HMS *Blossom* had sailed from Spithead under Commander Frederick Beechey on 19 May 1825 – a few days ahead of Parry. His first lieutenant was George Peard, the eldest son of a vice-admiral. The second was Edward Belcher who was to act as assistant surveyor to Beechey. Belcher was the grandson of a Governor of Halifax, Nova Scotia, and the great-grandson of Joseph Belcher who had been the Governor of Massachusetts, New Hampshire, and New Jersey. He had twice seen action and had been invalided home from the Africa station. John Wainwright, the son of a distinguished captain and lieutenant-governor of the Royal Naval College, was appointed as the third lieutenant. Midshipman Richard Beechey, the captain's younger brother, was also appointed to the ship. He had already served in five ships and had seen action at the blockade of Algiers, taking part in a number of 'cutting out' expeditions. The *Blossom*'s master was Thomas Elson, and Charles Osmer was appointed as clerk. George Tradescant Lay received the Admiralty appointment as expedition naturalist.

Beechey's instructions ordered him to investigate the existence – or otherwise – of a number of South Pacific islands before making his way to the Bering's Straits. He had to arrive there by the autumn of 1826 for the purpose of meeting Franklin's party as they made their way westwards from the mouth of the MacKenzie River. If no contact was made with Franklin, Beechey was to return to the same area at the same time the following year for a further attempt to meet Franklin. At all times, he was to be aware of the possibility that Parry might arrive in the area and require assistance. Particular attention was to be made to the checking of longitude by use of the ship's chronometers, and the naturalist was to collect 'rare and curious specimens'. Should war break out during his absence he was, on no account, to engage in any hostile acts with the enemy, and hope to avoid enemy action against himself by the declaration that he was only at sea 'for the purpose of discovery and science'.

Cape Horn was doubled with little difficulty and stores were taken on at Concepcion and Valparaiso before surveys were carried out on a number of small islands and coral reefs off the South American coast. At Easter Island, the natives proved to be hostile and water could be obtained only at the expense of minor injuries to the shore party.

Pitcairn Island was reached on 5 December. Off its steep shores the *Blossom* was greeted by a ship's whaler under sail and, much to everyone's surprise, they were soon welcoming on-board the sixty-two-year-old John Adams who, under the name Alexander Smith, had taken part in the mutiny in the *Bounty*. Adams, however, had nothing to fear from his actions of thirty-seven years earlier and faced nothing more than eager questions about the incident. They learned how the mutineer's leader, Fletcher Christian, had met his end by being shot in the back by a Tahitian. A violent death had been the reward of many of the mutineers and the natives who had accompanied them. Adams was the sole survivor of the mutiny but a number of descendents – including those of Christian – were still living.

Just before the close of the year, the *Blossom* reached the Gambier Group of islands (Mangareva Group) where they found themselves yet again under attack from the natives. The ship's master, Thomas Elson, was forced to defend himself with a cutlass before a musket-ball wounded his attacker. For some time after this, the natives restricted themselves to rubbing noses with the newcomers and stealing anything they could get their hands on (the first lieutenant of the *Blossom*, rather ungallantly, noted that the 'women are ugly'). The peace, however, was precarious and, as the shore party was returning to their boats, one native grabbed Lieutenant Wainwright as another jabbed at him with a spear. He broke free and ran towards the beach calling out for help. Lieutenant Belcher heard his cries and ran forward to his aid as the marines aimed their muskets (a risky action by Belcher as the marines 'were notoriously bad shots'). Both officers survived at the cost of the life of one of the natives. It was believed that the natives of the islands were cannibals, and Beechey wrote in a letter that he would 'be sorry to be cast upon their islands, even in Lent time.'

Tahiti was reached in mid-March 1826. To the surprise of the *Blossom*'s ship's company they found everyone at prayer despite it being a Saturday. It turned out that the reason was that the missionaries who had descended on the islands had arrived from the west and, consequently, were a day ahead of anyone arriving from the east. Christianity had been broadly accepted once the king had embraced the religion, but the natives resented the missionaries' attempts to abolish their dancing. Before long, however, it was discovered that a liberal supply of rum would keep the missionaries both happy and at a distance as the natives gyrated to the throb of the island's drums. This interest in dancing extended to visitors and, whilst the *Blossom*'s rigging was undergoing a refit, a ship arrived from New Zealand. Amongst the newcomer's crew were a number of Maoris who laid on a demonstration of their war dance – the 'HaKa'. The sight of the yelling Maoris, stamping the ground and sticking their tongues out whilst grinning hideously caused the Tahitians to flee in

Above left: *Captain James Ross.*

Above right: *Captain Frederick Beechey.*

Left: *HMS* Blossom.

terror 'no doubt, congratulating themselves that there was so wide an expanse of water between their country and New Zealand.'

A month after her arrival at Tahiti, the *Blossom* sailed for the Sandwich Islands and Hawaii. Within days of being at sea, Midshipman John Crawley and the captain's steward, William Must, both died from dysentery. On arriving at the town of Onorooroo (Honolulu) on the island of Woahoo (Oahu) the island was found to be over-run by cattle, all descending from those left there by Vancouver (the beasts had escaped slaughter when Vancouver – to save the stock from being wiped out – had suggested that their meat be solely a royal prerogative). Ten days later, the sixteen-year-old, King Tamehameha paid the *Blossom* a visit wearing a gold-laced coat, a cocked hat, and gold epaulettes. His escorting party – one of whom, at least, had visited London – swaggered in his rear in western clothing 'and would not have disgraced Bond Street'. After taking on stores, the *Blossom* sailed north. Two weeks later Private William Fairbrass of the marines died of 'an inflammation of the stomach'.

On reaching the snow-streaked coast of Kamchatcka, the ship hauled into the port of Petrapavlovsk. The call of the cuckoo reminded the officers of home as they paid a social call on the local governor in his timber-built house. In the grounds of the building lay the body of Captain Charles Clerke. Above the grave, a stone honouring a fellow explorer had been erected by the French explorer, La Perouse, the same man who ejected Samuel Hearn from the Prince of Wales fort in 1782.

A message for Captain Beechey brought the disappointing news of Parry's failure to find a way through Prince Regent's Inlet. It meant, however, that there was every chance that they could meet up with Franklin and return home that year. Only three days were spent at Petropavlosk before the *Blossom* sailed for Bering's Straits, calling on the way at Bering's Island where a brisk trade in souvenirs was carried out with the islanders.

The straits were passed in mid-July and Chamisso Island, to the north of Kotzebue Sound, was reached on the 22nd – just five days after the date previously agreed by Beechey and Franklin. A frisson of excitement was produced by a man-made cairn of rocks on the summit of the highest hill on the small island but, when the feature was investigated, it gave no clue to having been erected by Franklin.

An astronomical observatory was set up on the treeless mainland close to where a few friendly natives were met and an abandoned village discovered. Those who made the trip ashore were, however, glad to return to the ship to escape from the swarms of mosquitoes that attacked any exposed skin. On the tiny islet of Rurick Island, just to the west of Chamisso, Beechey had a cairn of stones erected and buried a bottle containing a message for Franklin. The bottle's position was indicated by the painted instructions on the cairn 'Three feet magnetic north'. A large rock close-by was painted with the message 'Six feet North' to disclose the position of a buried barrel of flour.

The *Blossom* made her way around the northern edge of Kotzebue Sound and began the north-eastern voyage towards Cook's Icy Cape. As they felt their way along the dark, low-lying coast, messages in bottles were buried on the shore and contact made with the natives. The ship's barge, under the direction of Thomas Elson, kept close in to the shore searching for any sign of Franklin or his party.

Beechey, observing that pack ice could be seen stretching along the northern horizon, left the barge in his wake and pressed on through open waters to a point thirty-six miles beyond Icy Cape. The ice had now disappeared and clear water lay ahead to the north-east. The ship's officers, including Beechey, were sorely tempted by the perfect conditions to make an attempt on the north-west passage. But, not only was the barge several miles to their rear, Beechey's instructions prevented him from risking his ship being frozen in. Lieutenant Peard noted in his journal 'Great therefore was our disappointment when we bore up and made sail to the South Westward…'. The day was made worse when an anchor was lost in shallow waters off Icy Cape and the ship's master at arms, Patrick Giblin, died of a liver complaint.

The barge was met the following day and Beechey ordered Elson to take the small vessel as far to the north-east of Icy Cape as he possibly could in an attempt to find the Franklin party. The ship's master began his voyage on 18 August, as the *Blossom* turned to sail back to Kotzebue Sound.

Elson's vessel had been especially built at Woolwich for inshore exploration. She was schooner-rigged and had a crew of ten men including her commander and her second-in-command, William Smyth, one of the ship's mates. The *Blossom*'s master soon found that the wind was directly on his bow and it was with great difficulty that he beat his way north-eastwards towards Icy Cape. Another problem lay in the constant pestering by the natives who rowed out to the barge in their skin-hulled 'baidaras'. Capable of carrying up to twelve men, the native craft would have been welcome, particularly for the trading of food, had it not been for the continual guard necessary against theft. Three days after separating from the *Blossom,* the barge reached the point where Beechey was forced to turn back. Through falling snow, Elson clawed his way past a succession of offshore islands he named 'Point Good Hope' (Seahorse Islands) until he reached a low, ice-cluttered, point of land that projected almost due north. Beyond the shallow peninsular a wide bay curved away to the east. Elson was now six days away from the *Blossom* and both nature and the natives began to combine against him. Not only had the wind swung round to the south-west but a strong current had also set in from the same direction. The ice – held off by the wind – hovered menacingly out to sea, and armed Eskimos patrolled the shore preventing Elson from landing to leave a message for Franklin. At midday on 23 August, he turned his bows and headed south-west after giving the low spit of land the name 'World's End'. After four hours of battling against wind and tide, the current had pushed him back to the point he had started from. In an effort to get into slacker water, Elson had his men row the barge closer to the shore only to find that hostile natives were following his progress. By vigorously pulling on the oars, the barge's crew managed to haul themselves clear of the threat. A night at anchor was followed by a seemingly friendly wind which filled their sails and drove them westwards along the shore. Unfortunately, it also brought in the ice and the barge was struck many times by heavy ice floes. To make matters worse, the wind then swung around to the south and Elson found himself surrounded by ice and with a headwind. His crew, however, when the danger of their situation was explained to them, simply 'gave a cheer' and began to haul the barge along from the shore. With an extra ration of rum to encourage them, the crew managed to tow the vessel at a rate of two miles an hour before help came from a most unexpected quarter. A native village came into view and, after receiving gifts of beads and tobacco, the Eskimos joined in and helped to tow the boat beyond the settlement. But it looked as if all the effort was to be of no avail. The ice closed in around the barge and drove her ashore. Soon there was no open water to be seen and the gaps between the ice floes began to freeze over.

In considering his precarious position, Elson came to the conclusion that the barge would not be freed in time for them to reach Kotzebue Sound that year and began to prepare for his only alternative. Using canvas from the spare sails the men made themselves knapsacks and covers to protect the locks of their muskets. Skin boots were traded from the natives and the men prepared to walk the 450 miles around the coast to reach the *Blossom*.

Aware of the daunting task that lay ahead of them, Elson decided to wait by the grounded and trapped boat for one week just in case the weather might turn in his favour. After two days, clear water was seen about a quarter of a mile ahead and a passage was cut through the ice to reach it. Yet again the natives helped tow the craft along the shore until a barrier of ice blocked their way some two miles beyond their starting point. That evening the wind shifted to the south-east and a sleepless night was had by all as they prayed for the ice to drift northwards. With the light came their answer – the ice had broken up and the barge could make its way through the scattered floes.

Two weeks of snow-laden gales followed causing sails to split and the bowsprit to be carried away. Elson noted in his journal 'No one in the boat ever experienced the like of this before.' But, for the most part, the wind remained in their favour and, at midday on 10 September, twenty-four days after their departure, Elson dropped anchor close by the *Blossom*. He had not found any evidence of the Franklin party, but had extended the knowledge of the coast for almost 500 miles and had reached the highest latitude on the coast of northern America west of the MacKenzie. Wisely, Beechey did not accept Elson's naming of the promontory marking his furthest point as 'World's End', giving it the name instead, of 'Point Barrow'. The ship's master was, however, to be rewarded for his efforts. Beechey named the bay Elson had seen curving away to the east beyond Point Barrow as 'Elson Bay'. A small headland to the south-west of Point Barrow was named 'Cape Smyth' in honour of the expedition's second-in-command – the mate, William Smyth.

With the thermometer already showing well below freezing, Beechey found another incentive to examine his position. On 8 October, James Woodford, a private in the marines died of dysentery and was buried on Chamisso Island. With signs of scurvy beginning to be seen in several of the men, he called his officers together and asked their opinion. On the 13th, a further barrel of flour was buried on Rurick Island and the message '*Blossom* sailed on 14th October' painted on a rock. As they sailed southwards the following day, ice began to form along the barren shores all were happy to leave in their wake.

With a fair wind astern, the *Blossom* reached San Francisco three weeks after leaving Kotzebue Sound. Beechey found the local Spanish missionaries 'worthy and benevolent' yet 'very bigoted'. They were always keen to trigger off an argument over religion, and one priest with whom Beechey dined found additional amusement by hurling pancakes at the open mouths of his Indian servants. Fresh meat, eggs, cheese, milk, and flour were purchased ashore and 6,000lb of biscuits was bought from visiting whaling ships. An observatory was erected and leave was granted to the ship's company – most of whom spent their leisure time careering about on hired horses. The visit also saw the death of marine private Joseph Bowers who drowned after getting out of his depth in a duck pond whilst attempting to recover a downed bird. After two months, Beechey took the *Blossom* to Monterey where he took on-board cocoa, sugar, salt beef and potatoes. No doubt much to the delight of the ship's company, the purser also managed to obtain 920 gallons of rum from a visiting American merchant ship.

Four days after their arrival at Monterey, the ship sailed for the Sandwich Islands, arriving off Onorooroo after twenty days at sea. The king and his formidable mother (acting as Prime Minister) were dined on-board after a welcoming twenty-one-gun salute with the yards manned. A firework display completed the formalities. At the king's request, the ship's marine sergeant gave instruction in arms-drill to the native men. So popular did this become ('completely a mania') that small boys would be seen shouldering sugar-cane sticks to the shout of 'shoulder ump!' and, on one occasion, the purser's steward – assumed by the natives to be equally efficient at drill as the sergeant, yet was unlikely to have ever handled a musket in his life – was forced to flee from their demands to train them.

From the Sandwich Islands Beechey headed for the Portuguese settlement at Macao. The welcome they found was rather muted and, whilst Beechey was ashore doing the rounds of local dignitaries, a boat came alongside the *Blossom* and demanded that customs officers be allowed on-board. Having been sent on their way with a dusty answer from the first lieutenant, a letter arrived two days later at the office of the senior local official of the British East India Co. The missive came from the head of the Chinese customs and insisted that the *Blossom* be sent packing immediately. The 'Peih-che (Beechey) Cruiser' was to 'go away and return home, she is not allowed to linger about.' Above the signature of the emperor of China an edict furiously stated that the *Blossom* 'will not be allowed to make glossing pretexts for her lingering about and creating disturbance which will implicate them in crime. Let the day of her departure be reported. Haste. Haste. A special Order.' The letter was dated '7 Year – 3 moon 24 day (19 April 1827) and was, according to the *Blossom*'s first lieutenant, 'treated with the disregard and contempt it merited.' His view was probably coloured by the merchant who provided the ship with provisions. He was a Chinaman who paid the local Mandarin for the privilege and was then 'allowed to cheat you as much as he pleases.'

Beechey then sailed north and visited Napakwang (Naha) on Okinawa in the Loochoo Islands (Ryukyu Islands) where it was noted that the people tended to blow their noses on handkerchiefs made of paper, which were then disposed of. The ship was watered and more stores brought on-board as the officers attempted to master the use of chopsticks as they attended a dinner given by the chief Mandarin.

Their next call was at the Bonin Islands which Beechey took formal possession of in the name of the crown despite the fact that the islands had been known to the Japanese for many years. His claim was made even weaker by the discovery on one island of two shipwrecked seamen, one Norwegian, the other German, who, with their shipmates having already been rescued, decided to stay. All they asked for was a few old clothes to supplement their rags.

The coast of Kamchatka was reached on 2 July and Beechey dropped anchor off Petrapavlovsk the following day. The *Blossom* was refitted for her return to Arctic waters as the officers underwent a hectic round of social engagements concluding in a ball given on the ship's quarterdeck. Eighteen days after her arrival the *Blossom* sailed for the Bering Straits.

The ship's barge was put over the side south of Kotzebue Sound and Elson again given orders to survey the coast and look out for signs of Franklin. He was to rejoin the ship at her anchorage off Chammiso Island. On his return after four days, Elson was able to report the discovery of a harbour formed of shingle banks to the south-east of Cape Prince of Wales. Putting Lieutenant Belcher in charge of the barge with orders to follow the course northward laid down by Elson the previous year, Beechey took the *Blossom* southwards to have a look at Elson's harbour.

The new discovery turned out to be as fine as Elson had suggested. Ringed by low cliffs and shingle banks with fresh water lakes on shore, the haven suggested a possible base for future expeditions in the area. Beechey named the site 'Port Clarence' after the lord high admiral. Returning to Chamisso Island, Beechey experienced tragedy and a brush with disaster. John Dray, a young ordinary seaman, was aloft on the foremast adjusting the sails to meet squally weather when he fell into the sea. He remained afloat long enough for a ship's boat to be launched but, almost within reach of his rescuers, Dray sank out of sight and was never seen again. Two days later the *Blossom* ran aground off Cape Blossom (named after their first landing the previous year). Attempts to haul the ship clear by warping failed, but a high tide arrived and lifted the vessel clear. The run of bad luck, however, was to continue.

As the *Blossom* arrived at her anchorage off Chamisso Island, a small group of men was seen standing on the Choris Peninsular just to the north of the island. Above them flew an inverted ensign. The ship's boats were sent out immediately and returned with the news that the barge had reached Icy Cape, but had been forced to return when the ice barred their further progress. On reaching the peninsular, a high wind drove the barge ashore and two able seamen and one boy seaman had been drowned. The survivors were then placed under threat by the local natives who came down to loot the wreckage and were only driven off when Belcher grabbed the largest of the men and held him prisoner until the arrival of the *Blossom*.

Other natives proved troublesome on the island when a watering party was sent ashore. Attempts at theft led to weapons being drawn. Just along the coast, two seamen, digging a grave for one of the barge disaster casualties, were attacked and had a knife stolen. Such behaviour led to Beechey ordering Lieutenant Wainwright ashore with the ship's marines to clear the island of Eskimos. A few days later the natives returned and, after lingering offshore and ignoring Belcher's demands that they get well clear of the island, he fired a musket just astern of their boat. Instead of making the natives leave, this action caused them to paddle furiously to the shore. On reaching dry land they let fly with their arrows, wounding one of the seamen in the thigh from a distance of over a hundred yards. One native was slightly wounded by the return musket-fire before the group reached the top of the cliff-lined beach. From there they were chased away by two rounds fired from the *Blossom*'s cannon. The sergeant and four marines were sent after them only to fall into an ambush in which only one marine came out un-injured. To make matters worse, two of the marines had their bayonets poorly fitted to their musket and, on firing their weapons, saw the bayonets shoot away to fall into the hands of the natives. At this point the ship's master, Elson, arrived on the scene and fired a combination of ball and lead shot at one of the Eskimos before himself retreating. Beechey, by now realising that the natives would not be removed without the risk of considerable loss of life, ordered his men to withdraw and bring the native's boat with them to the ship. Two days later the boat was returned to the beach with beads and tobacco in payment for three knives and two bows that had been found in her and retained on-board the *Blossom*.

All this activity had taken place amid icy rain and a plunging thermometer. The first few days of October had seen the temperature fall below freezing, the onset of westerly winds brought the threat of ice, and there had been no sign of Franklin or his party and little chance that they would be seen so late in the season. After consulting his officers, Beechey decided that the time had come to leave for home. The *Blossom*'s bows finally turned southwards on 5 October 1827.

Within three weeks scurvy appeared in four of the ship's company, but a double ration of vegetables had the problem under control before they arrived at Monterey. With water difficult to obtain in the port, and with firewood having to be purchased from local dealers, Beechey pressed on south to San Francisco where an American whaler carried away the *Blossom*'s spritsail yard and damaged other rigging. Whilst waiting for the manufacture of a new yard the ship's surgeon, Alexander Collie, used his time to amputate the leg of an English seaman who had been injured on-board

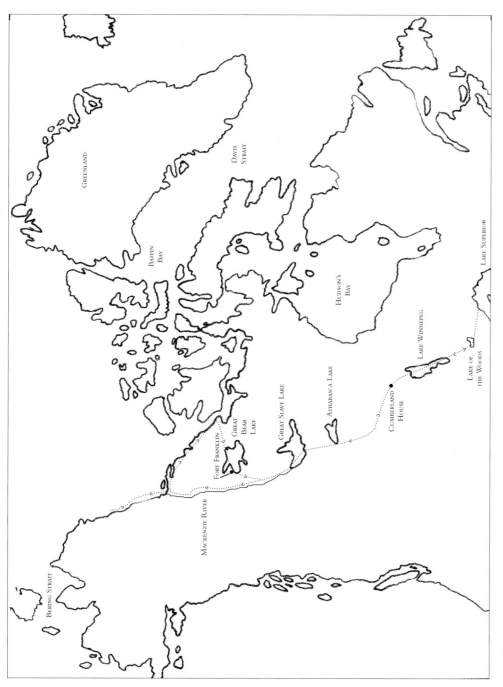

Franklin's second overland expedition 1825-1827

another American whaler. He was, however, unable to save the life of one of the marines, James Bailey, who died of 'liver complaint' and was buried on the shore of Whale Bay (Richardson Bay).

Their next port of call was at San Blas on the Mexican coast and English newspapers were obtained dated as recently as September. It was, however, an American newspaper that gave them the news that a rumour had been picked up in Montreal that Franklin had returned to the Great Bear Lake in September the previous year. The article also went on to suggest that, when Elson was at his furthest point in the barge, Franklin was within three days journey. Three weeks later, still at San Blas, confirmation was received from a two-month-old Liverpool newspaper. Franklin had returned to the port on 29 September.

After a call at Acapulco, the *Blossom* arrived at Valparaiso where the welcome news was received that Beechey had been promoted to captain a year earlier. The first lieutenant, George Peard, was promoted to commander and William Smyth, the mate who had accompanied Elson to Point Barrow, had been promoted to lieutenant.

The *Blossom* returned to England in October 1828, after a voyage of 73,000 miles. She was paid off at Woolwich on the 12th of that month and her captain repaired to the hydrographer's office to supervise the amendments of the Admiralty charts resulting from his voyage.

Two months after his return, Beechey married the sister-in-law of the bishop of Oxford and began work on his account of the voyage. He remained an active surveyor and commanded HMS *Sulphur* (from which Belcher eventually relieved him) in a survey of the coasts of South America. He later commanded three steamships in a survey of the Irish coasts. Beechey never lost a keen interest in the polar regions and forwarded a proposition to the Admiralty that he should lead an expedition to the Antarctic, but failed in the face of continuing pressure to breach the north-west passage. He kept in close contact with Franklin and Richardson for the remainder of his life, always pressing for more effort in polar exploration against the economies that led 'to the detriment of laudable discovery and even to our naval establishment'. He was never, however, to return to the Arctic. After twenty-seven years in the rank of captain, Beechey was promoted to rear-admiral in 1854. He died in November 1856.

The *Blossom's* first lieutenant, George Peard, published his journal of the voyage under the title 'To the Pacific and Arctic with Beechey'. He was never employed again at sea and died in London in February 1837.

HMS *Blossom* was reduced to a hulk four years after her return and was finally broken up in 1848.

So what had happened to Franklin?

CHAPTER NINE

'MOTIVES AS DISINTERESTED AS THEY ARE ENLIGHTENED'

Armed with the experiences of his first overland expedition, Franklin had planned his journey in great detail. His intention was to reach the mouth of the MacKenzie River and there divide his party into two groups. One group would head westwards towards Icy Cape, thus linking up with James Cook's furthest point. The second would go eastwards along the coast to the mouth of the Coppermine River. If successful, it would mean that the entire coastline from Franklin's Point Turnagain westward would have been be surveyed. The eastward party would return up the Coppermine and make their way across the Great Bear Lake to the expedition base which would be established on the lake's western shore. On reaching Icy Cape, the western party could either retrace their steps to the base or, with luck, fall in with Beechey and HMS *Blossom*. It was also possible that both parties would meet up with Parry if he was successful in finding a way through from Prince Regent's Inlet.

For his party, Franklin turned once again to the surgeon, John Richardson, 'a really good man in every sense of the word'. Although appointed as surgeon to the Chatham division of the marines, the First Lord had promised Richardson the next staff vacancy that arose at any of the naval hospitals. But he was still keen to go with Franklin, and leave of absence had been approved with any hospital post safeguarded until his return. Lieutenant George Back had suffered in his promotion due to his lack of sea experience and, having been appointed to service afloat in the West Indies, Franklin felt it better for his career to leave him where he was. Instead, he applied for the services of Lieutenant John Bushnan who had served under John Ross in the *Isabella* and under Parry in the *Hecla* and the *Fury*. Although appointed, Bushnan died as the expedition was being prepared. Franklin was then left with no real choice other than to ask for the services of Back, 'a fine young officer and full of zeal'.

New to the party was Edward Kendall, a mate who, in the same rank, had served as assistant surveyor under Lyon in the *Griper*. A further addition was a naturalist, Thomas Drummond, who would accompany the expedition only as far as Lake Athabasca before setting off to explore the Rocky Mountains.

Surgeon John Richardson.

Lieutenant George Back.

One man who was desperately keen to join the party was John Hepburn but, although his reliability and enterprise had shone throughout his first overland expedition, Franklin reluctantly refused to take him. Hepburn had done well since his return and had obtained a position as commander of a buoy-vessel in the Firth of Forth. Franklin wrote to a friend 'I cannot think of taking him from his situation as I could only hope to obtain a similar one for him on my return.'

Hepburn's contribution, and his own experience, led Franklin to insist that, apart from Indian hunters and Indian and Eskimo interpreters, his party would be made up of British seamen and marines. Among those he chose to go with him were able seamen William Duncan and Robert Spinks, both of whom had served under him in the *Trent*.

With the amalgamation of the rival trading companies, the problems of supply that had bedevilled the first overland expedition were swept away. Not only was Franklin able to ensure his supplies, but also was able to send out stores that stood a reasonable chance of arriving safely at their destination. He also obtained the services of Peter Dease – formerly of the North-Western Co. but now a chief factor with the Hudson's Bay Co. – to help with any negotiations with voyageurs and Indians. He had first met Dease at Fort Chipewyan where he had proved to be a stalwart and trusty helper.

Franklin's experience of birch-bark canoes in the first expedition led him to design a more rugged form of sailing-boat that could be used with safety on rivers and lakes and on the Arctic coastal waters, yet be light enough to be carried over portages. Three such boats were to be built – one of 26ft and two of 24ft. The overseeing of the construction of these boats at Woolwich Yard was taken in hand by Captain Buchan, Franklin's expedition leader on the Spitsbergen voyage who now lived close by the dockyard. Another innovation was a wooden-framed canvas boat designed by Colonel Pasley and known as the 'Wallnut Shell'. It was 9ft in length, 4ft, 4in in beam, and weighed 85lb. The canvas used was of the new type invented by Mr Mackintosh and the boat could be broken down into six separate parts for ease of transportation. During trials on the Thames this fragile craft carried six passengers – three of whom were ladies.

Although preparations for the expedition continued to progress satisfactorily, Franklin was put to great worry by the frail health of his wife. Never a strong woman, Eleanor had been weakened by the birth of their daughter and was frequently required to take to her bed in order to recover her strength. She remained, however, both cheerful and courageous, on one occasion writing to her sister-in-law:

> I am getting stout and well, and mean soon to be strong enough to look better after your brother, and to try and keep him in some sort of order. I suppose the newspapers have told you how the ladies pulled him to pieces at Captain Parry's ball. He was in such request that I wonder they left a bit of him for me. Such a flirt he is! The like was never known.

Some stores were sent ahead to Dease in March 1824, and the party of seamen along with the boats and other supplies sailed in a Hudson's Bay Co. ship three months later. Their orders were to make their way up the Saskatchewan River to Fort Cumberland where they would spend the winter. With the arrival of the thaw, the men were to follow the rivers and lakes as far as possible towards the Great Bear Lake until the officers overtook them.

Franklin, Richardson, Back, Kendall and Drummond, accompanied by four marines – Corporal Robert Hallom and Privates George Wilson, William Money, and Shadrach Tysoe – sailed for New York in the American packet *Columbia*. On arrival, they were inundated with hospitality and the eight days they spent in the city checking their chronometers and scientific instruments were enlivened by social events and visits to museums and private collections. Franklin, however, was appalled to find that American men kept their hats on in theatre boxes, despite being seated next to ladies.

The British consul, James Buchanan, offered to accompany the party as it journeyed through New York State and introduced them to the state governor, the Honourable de Witt Clinton, on their arrival at Albany. He, in turn, assured them that had the consul not been available to escort them, he would have done so himself. The border into Canada was crossed at the Niagara Falls, the sight of which had Franklin standing 'wrapt in amazement'.

The group travelled on until they reached Lake Huron where they picked up large canoes and a number of voyageurs to help them with their stores. Their halt on the lake was at the Royal Naval base at Penetanguishene under the command of Lieutenant Douglass. It was whilst staying with the commanding officer that Franklin received the painful news that his wife had died. He noted, '7pm. The distressing intelligence of my dear wife's death has just reached me.' However sad the news may have been, it was not unexpected and, in the knowledge that his daughter would be looked after by his sister, Franklin continued his journey to the north taking with him the silk Union Flag that Eleanor had made for him to fly on the Arctic coast.

The officers caught up with the seamen and the boats on 29 June 1825 at the Methye River portage. With the party, Franklin found the sturdy, reliable, Eskimo interpreter Augustus who had brought along a friend, Ooligbuck.

The ten miles of the portage – always a difficult time for all involved – was passed with one of the boats being carried, the second being dragged, and the third being placed on a 'truck' (a wheeled carriage). The latter mode of passing over the rocky path was entirely novel and had been Franklin's idea. So well did it work that Franklin had his carpenters make extra trucks on his return journey and recommended the same system to the fur traders in order to save their voyageurs from 'much fatigue and suffering'.

After a call at Fort Chipewyan, the party reached Fort Resolution on 29 July. Despite a warm greeting from two of the Indians who had acted as hunters on the first expedition, Franklin found, yet again, that the arrangement he had made with the Chipewyan Indian chief, Ekeicho – to supply his party with meat – had fallen through. This time the reason given was that the Dog-rib Indians had fought a war with the Chipewyan and the Copper Indians, and Ekeicho was refusing to go into Dog-rib territory. Peter Dease had been partially responsible for arranging a truce and Ekeicho was now claiming that he would not cross the enemy border so that peace could be maintained whilst the Franklin party was making its way north. The best that Franklin could do was to leave the Indian chief a silver medal and a message that he should continue to observe the peace. As for hunters, he was forced to trust that the local Indians at the Great Bear Lake would provide hunters. In any case, knowing that the lake abounded in fish and that Indian braves generally proved to be less expert than their claims, he ensured that he had plenty of fishing nets to try and catch enough fish to see them through the winter. Two days after their arrival at Fort Resolution, the party set off down the MacKenzie River.

With sails set and with favourable winds and current, the 570 miles to Fort Norman were completed in just five days. At the point where the Bear Lake River branched off towards the lake, Franklin put into operation a plan he had been considering for some time. Instead of preparing immediately for the approaching winter, the remaining few weeks before the arrival of the ice could be used to reconnoitre the routes planned for the following year. Accordingly, Richardson – at his own suggestion – was to take a boat across the Great Bear Lake to the point where it nearest approached the Coppermine River. Once the spot had been established, it would provide a fixed destination for the return journey from the Arctic coast. Franklin was to continue down the MacKenzie to investigate the state of the sea, the trend of the coast both east and west, and – if natives were to be encountered – their attitude towards strangers. Back was to join Dease (already at the base site on the Great Bear Lake) to oversee the construction of the fort and to organise the Indian hunters and the fishing activities.

Taking the largest of the boats (already given the name *Lion*) Franklin, Kendall, Augustus, and six seamen set off downriver. They took with them a voyageur from Fort Norman who, it was claimed, would show them the way to the most northerly of the Hudson's Bay Co. forts – Fort Good Hope. He turned out to be, however, 'altogether ignorant' of the route. With sails bent on to its two masts, the *Lion* made extraordinarily good speed and covered the 312 miles to the fort in just two and a half days. The few occupants of the place had not expected to see any strangers and took some time to get over their shock at finding a distinguished naval captain and explorer on their doorstep. A welcome meal was provided and the useless voyageur 'exchanged' for the fort's Indian interpreter who wished to go north to stay with an Indian chief.

Despite a tendency to fall asleep at every opportunity, the new interpreter proved to be of great value as the journey was resumed and several Indians were met. Wary at first, the natives soon showed themselves to be friendly once contact had been made. Also, as peace had been made with the Eskimos, Augustus was also made welcome, his presence reinforcing the good will shown to the expedition party.

As they approached the mouth of the river, several large mountains could be seen and Franklin was soon bestowing names upon the most marked features. Richardson, Fitton (after the president of the Royal Geological Society), and Cupola mountains were named before the party reached the open waters of the Arctic Sea on 16 August – just over 1,000 miles from the Great Slave Lake. Following a delay caused by fog, Franklin steered towards an island some miles offshore and reached it just as the sun was setting. He named the place 'Garry Island' after the deputy governor of the Hudson's Bay Co. and gloried in the sights around him. Not only was the water clear of ice, 'many seals, and black and white whales were sporting on its waves'. The soil with its appearance of 'frozen mud' glowed with the flowers of purple saxifrage and inquisitive Arctic foxes trotted over to see the newcomers. Over all, Franklin hoisted the silk Union Flag sewn by his departed wife as his men cheered and drank the rum he had supplied them for the occasion. On the following day, he had buried a message for Parry beneath a blue and red flag and had a waterproof box put into the sea with the hopes that it would drift to the east to be picked up by his fellow explorer.

The arrival of gales from the north-west signalled that the time had come to make their way to the Great Bear Lake. Difficulty was experienced in getting the *Lion* through the many shallow channels at the river's delta and the boat had frequently to be hauled over sandbars before they reached the wide, clear water of the river itself. On their passage they came across a recently deserted Eskimo campsite and left a kettle, axe, knife, file, red and blue cloth, and some beads as gifts.

Vast flocks of birds flew south beneath cheerless skies as the party made their way upriver. That night the water in their kettle froze. More Indians were met before the party reached Fort Good Hope where they learned that a rumour had come upriver stating that the entire Franklin party had been massacred. On leaving the fort, the wind swung round into their faces and the party spent most of the following five days hauling the boat against the stream. This fatiguing work was made worse when three of the men went down with dysentery. The Great Bear River was entered on 1 September and, after contending with another fifteen miles of rapids against which the boat had to be towed, the camp was reached four days later.

The winter quarters, named 'Fort Franklin' in their leader's honour, had been built on the site of an old North-West Co. fort and consisted of three buildings;

Fort Franklin.

the officer's quarters, the men's mess, and a store room, surrounded by a wooden stockade. Within its snug walls, Franklin met Richardson who had made a successful journey across the Great Bear Lake and had established a return destination at the lowest rapids on the Dease River just before it flowed into the lake.

As the winter began to set in there were fifty people living in the fort. Four officers; Dease; twenty-eight seamen, marines, and voyageurs (the latter brought by Dease to help transport the stores); two Eskimos; four Chipewyan hunters; three women and seven children. Occasional visits were made by sick Indians who required temporary medical assistance.

Everyone was allotted a task to spread the load of the work that had to be done to see them through the winter and to prepare for the following summer. Franklin and Kendall worked on the charts and observation that had been taken thus far. Back was given charge of the naval men and remained the official artist. Dease had responsibility for the voyageurs and Indians. Richardson was not only the medical officer, but also the expedition naturalist (Drummond had left the party to search among the Rocky Mountains). The officers also took turns to teach the men reading, writing and arithmetic three nights a week. Some of the men looked after the fishing whilst others helped to bring in deer killed by the hunters or collected wood for the fires. Two of the voyageurs, skilled in the use of snowshoes, carried messages and letters to forts as far away as the Great Slave Lake.

Divine services were held twice on Sundays and weekday evenings were spent in games or dancing to the bagpipes of Marine Private George Wilson. Once the flagstaff had been erected, Franklin held a parade at which a salute was fired, three cheers given, and Wilson led a march-past before a health was drunk to the king and to the success of the expedition. The only note of trouble happened when the voyageurs asked if the Scotsmen in the party came from the same country as the English. When told this was not so, but that they were 'natives of the mountainous lands', the voyageurs took to calling the Scots 'Montagnards'. Unfortunately, this term was also used by the voyageurs to describe the Dog-rib Indians and a fight soon broke out after the voyageurs began to use their new name for the Scots and the latter took exception. The officers stepped in to stop the commotion and sent everyone to bed. In the morning the Scots had the meaning of the word *montagnard* explained to them and peace was restored.

Warm clothing was issued with the arrival of snow in October and, shortly afterwards, the lake was available for ice-skating. By December it was too dark for the hunters and so they were employed in fishing using nets beneath the ice of the lake. Regrettably, however, the Indians found it easier to steal the fish from the nets set by the seamen and Franklin was forced to threaten the withdrawal of rations if the practice did not cease. Other Indians, nevertheless (from the Hare, Copper, and Loucheux tribes), did arrive with a welcome supply of dried caribou.

Christmas was spent feasting beneath paper decorations and playing 'snap dragon' (grabbing fruit from a bowl of lighted brandy using only the teeth). During the evening, a ball was held at which English, Gaelic, French, Inuktatuk (Eskimo) and various Indian dialects competed for attention. Similar celebrations saw in the new year. On 16 January 1826, a welcome package arrived from England having been posted the previous June. Inside were letters and copies of the 'Quarterly Review', the 'Edinburgh Philosophical Journal', the 'Literary Gazette', and the 'Mechanics Magazine'. This immensely cheering package had almost been lost when it had been stolen by an Indian south of the Hudson's Bay Co. post at Cumberland House. When he realised that the parcel had no value the thief had thrown the contents away. The letters, etc. had been found by a group of voyageurs and returned to Cumberland House (Franklin later ensured that these men were rewarded for their good deed).

By February, the rations had become dangerously low due to the assistance given to Indians who looked to the fort for help and Franklin was forced to send to Fort Norman for some bags of pemmican he had left there for the use of the expedition. The situation was saved before the arrival of the pemmican by the shooting of a moose by three of the voyageurs, and by the discovery of a supply of fish by the Dog-rib Indians. When Franklin asked Able Seaman Robert Spinks what he thought of the difference in the food when compared to that on-board ship, Spinks replied 'Why, Sir, we never minded about the short allowance, but were fearful of having to use the pemmican intended for next summer; we only care about the next voyage, and shall all be glad when the spring comes, that we may set off.'

With the arrival of the much anticipated season, preparations began to get under way for the forthcoming expedition. Franklin had an additional boat built and named it *Reliance* (he had intended to give that name to the fort before it was named after him). With the *Lion* already named, the two other boats were named *Dolphin* and *Union*. Richardson and Kendall set off to complete the survey of the Great Bear Lake on foot and returned having named its five great bays or arms Keith, Smith, Dease, MacTavish and MacVicar after officials of the Hudson's Bay Co. By late May, those awful harbingers of summer, the mosquitoes, began to appear and annoy their victims.

On 14 June Richardson set off by canoe along a small channel the melting ice had opened up on the Great Bear River with the intention of collecting specimens of plants from its banks. He would rejoin the expedition at Fort Norman. Franklin tried out the boats on the lake and found them to be satisfactory under both oars and sails. He issued warm clothing and the newly designed, sky-blue coloured, waterproof suits made of MacIntosh's canvas (instantly recognisable if stolen by the natives) to the men. The officers wore their uniform tailcoats and the newly issued 'round hat' – similar in style to a top hat with a black cockade on the right-hand side. Two volunteers were asked for from amongst the voyageurs to bring the western party up to fourteen men. All offered their services, and Franklin chose Francois Felix and

Alexis Vivier on the grounds that they did not ask for an increase in their wages as a result. A stiff westerly breeze pushed the ice clear of the lake bank on 21 June and the four boats were pushed off leaving Dease in charge of the fort.

It took them three days to reach Fort Norman. Delays had been caused by large blocks of ice remaining wedged in the Great Bear River and, where the boats had to be towed, the banks were found to be soft mud. Clouds of mosquitoes harassed the party every foot of the way. Extra gifts for the natives were picked up at the fort, Richardson rejoined the party, and the boats, with flags and pennants flying, left to the cheers of the occupants. The spring floods and heavy rain raised the water of the river – and especially the rapids – to a level where the risk of grounding was much reduced and the boats made good progress reaching Fort Good Hope after three days. They arrived to a gun salute from the local Indians, and the news that relationships between the Indians and the Eskimos had recently come close to breaking down.

The manager of the fort had arranged for two Indians to accompany Franklin as guides and interpreters, but they soon proved to have little knowledge of Inuktatuk, an even worse knowledge of the mouth of the MacKenzie, and expected to bring the families with them. Franklin declined their services. This led to a lot of shouting and threats which Franklin bore for several hours until he realised that the aggressive display was merely an attempt to obtain gifts. Once a few trifling items had been handed over, the natives left in the best of humours.

The fort was quitted on the early evening of the following day and the night was spent camped on the riverbank. Franklin issued each man with a gun, ammunition, and a knife as 'vigilance and precaution are never to be omitted in intercourse with strange tribes'. The next day, on reaching the river delta, Franklin divided the stores between the two parties. Richardson took charge of the *Dolphin* and *Union*, Colonel Pasley's 'wallnut shell' portable boat, and twenty-six bags of pemmican along with arrowroot, macaroni, and portable soup. Franklin retained in the *Lion* and the *Reliance*, thirty-two bags of pemmican and a proportionate amount of the other stores. The supplies were intended to last for eighty days, but if put on two-thirds rationing would last for a hundred.

That evening Franklin reminded Richardson of his orders. He was to take charge of Kendall and the ten men and survey the coast between the mouths of the MacKenzie and the Coppermine Rivers. The latter waterway was then to be ascended until the party reached a position closest to the Great Bear Lake. He was then to make his way to the point on the Dease River already decided upon, where he should meet a group of Indians waiting for him with canoes. They would then take him across the lake to Fort Franklin. Unfortunately, two of the three chronometers supplied to the expedition had suffered broken mainsprings and Franklin could only give Richardson a pocket-watch. Kendall, however, was a skilled marine surveyor and would be able to use the watch with lunar distances to find the longitude.

Much of the rest of the night was spent in a last meal and drinking a bowl of punch. At six o'clock in the morning of the 4th, the boats parted company at a position Franklin named 'Point Separation'. On Richardson's insistence, Franklin left first and, after an exchange of cheers, soon disappeared from view around a point of land.

Richardson took command of the *Dolphin* with Able Seaman Thomas Gillet as his coxswain. Kendall had the *Union* coxed by John McLeay. 'Determined not to abandon the enterprise on light grounds', the party made its way north and east through channels carved out of low-lying marshes. After three days, a party of Eskimos was discovered and an attempt at trade was made but the natives soon became aggressive and Ooligbuck took Richardson on his back and waded out to the *Dolphin* to get him clear of the trouble. The Eskimos then attempted to drag the boat ashore and loot its contents, but were fended off by the seamen. The mood changed when, as the boats continued on their way, they were joined by the Eskimo men in their kayaks and the women in their larger boats – oomiaks. Trading was carried out with the men as the women made gestures that Richardson noted 'could scarcely be misconstrued'. More Eskimo groups joined in the sea-borne pursuit and proved to be both agile and cunning in their attempts to steal from the boats. One Eskimo offered to guide the boats through a channel only to be the cause of it running aground, another leapt from his kayak, raced across the hulls of three others, and jumped into the *Dolphin*. At another stage, Kendall was so inundated with natives trying to get into the *Union* that he shouted across to Richardson for permission to open fire. Richardson approved, but only 'if necessary'. In the event, the raising of muskets caused the natives to flee, probably from experience with Indians armed with guns. Then the reason behind the Eskimo's bold attempts to get into the boats became clear. Only native women use the large oomiaks to row themselves across the water – and one of the natives had asked Ooligbuck if 'all the white women had beards'.

The day's hectic activities were followed by a miserable night. In an attempt to keep clear of the natives, the boats were rowed out to a small island, but were prevented from landing by shoals. As rain fell, the party raised sails and canvas to protect them as they tried to sleep, but it was to no avail and they were forced to huddle down in wet clothes. Before long a gale blew up and brought along waves that threatened to swamp the boats. Richardson decided to head for the lee of the island and found himself pushed over a sandy bar into the comparative safety of a small inlet (Refuge Cove). A tent was pitched on the shore for some of the men whilst others remained under cover on the boats. Just as they had reached a small degree of comfort, the *Union* – with Kendall and one man on-board – broke free from her mooring and was driven towards the breaking surf of a lee shore. The two men struggled to keep her clear as the *Dolphin* was launched to her rescue. At last, with the boats once more secured, the men returned to the tent where, as they strove to find sleep, the wind tore the tent pegs out of the ground and the tent collapsed. When he came ashore after the *Union* was recovered, Kendall slipped and fell. His knife – slung around his neck – penetrated his chest and was only stopped from reaching his heart by striking a rib.

The early hours of the following morning were spent on the flat shores of the island drying their clothing and stores and trying to obtain an hour's sleep. The strong wind continued until the evening, eventually dying away and allowing the party to set sail at nine o'clock. By the middle of the night the wind had turned to the north and driving ice flows forced the party to land. Ooligbuck shot a caribou and a welcome change of diet was enjoyed before divine service – it being a Sunday. The next day, Richardson issued all his men with a glass of grog – after their struggles through the delta marshes, they had, at last, reached the sea.

After a brief visit by Eskimos, who seemed better disposed towards the party than those they had left behind, the boats sailed along the low sandy shore with Richardson bestowing names upon the important features. Points were named after his friends Captains Toker and Warren, the Duke of Clarence's surgeon, Copeland Hutchison, was honoured with a bay, and Captain Charles Phillips (the inventor of the double-capstan) had his name bestowed upon an island. Kendall was allowed to name an island where they spent most of one night after a friend, Mr Atkinson. Atkinson Island produced a surprise no one had expected. Close by a deserted native village, the party found a large building, 27ft square, constructed of logs and covered with soil. Strong ridgepoles supported the log roof and the outside was decorated with twenty-one whale skulls. No-one, not even Ooligbuck, had seen anything like it. Richardson considered it as 'evidence of no small progress towards civilisation.'

Four days of good progress – though held up by occasional fogs – brought the party to the north shore of Harrowby Bay. Twelve Eskimo tents were seen on the beach whose occupants, on being alerted to the newcomers, ran to the waters edge waving knives and demanding the boats left. Richardson, shouting that he wanted to barter, saved the situation. Soon the boats were surrounded by kayaks and oomiaks and bits of old iron hoop and beads were being swapped for bows, arrows and spears (Richardson had come to the conclusion that one way to reduce the threat from aggressive natives was to get them to trade their weapons).

Cape Bathurst was rounded later that day with a line of grounded ice indicating shallow waters close inshore. Many large ice floes drifted offshore, the waters between them frequently broken by breaching whales. A favourable wind sped the boats along a gradually rising shore and round a large bay Richardson named after Franklin. The limestone cliffs forming the most easterly point of the bay were given the name 'Cape Parry'. In Darnley Bay, to the east of Cape Parry, Richardson named an island after a fellow naval explorer, Commander Hugh Clapperton, who, as his name was being immortalised among the ice floes off North America, was trekking towards his death on the sweltering, fetid banks of the West African River Niger. At that point, Richardson and his party were almost directly north of Fort Franklin, 313 miles to the south. The most easterly point of Darnley Bay was named 'Cape Lyon' after Captain George Lyon of the *Griper*, whilst the range of hills that followed the shore line was named after the First Lord of the Admiralty, Lord Melville.

Strong winds delayed the party for two days at Cape Lyon before progress could be resumed through churning brash ice pushed inshore by the wind. Beyond Point de Witt Clinton (named in honour of the respected Governor of New York State) the loose ice became more of a threat and, from a high point, Richardson could see that the route ahead was little more than a complete sheet of ice broken only by a few open lanes out to sea. For a time, the boats were able to continue their voyage by pushing loose floes out of the way with poles but, before long, Richardson was forced to land and set up camp in the face of impassable ice. By the next morning, however, a gap had opened up between the ice and the shore and the party were able to press on.

For some days, Richardson had been aware that the northern horizon had been lined with what appeared to be land. At first he took the dark shapes to be nothing more than fog banks but, when Kendall climbed to high ground on Cape Bexley to ascertain the direction of the coastline ahead of them, he was able to confirm Richardson's sighting. There was, indeed, land to the north. Richardson named the discovery after a philosopher, Dr. Hyde Wollaston, and called the ice-strewn waterway between his position and Wollaston Land 'Dolphin and Union Strait' after his boats.

From Cape Bexley it was found that the coast trended more and more to the south. With the wind generally astern, the boats weaved their way through the ice floes with little difficulty, only being forced to stop when the *Dolphin* was damaged by being trapped between the ice and the shore.

On 7 of August 1826, the party rounded Cape Krusenstern and entered Coronation Gulf. They had now made contact up with the land already surveyed by Franklin and Richardson five years earlier. Cape Hearne was reached that evening and the mouth of the Coppermine the following day.

Beyond Bloody Falls it was found that the rapids were too shallow for the boats. There remained no choice but to abandon them and they were dragged clear of the water and the tents erected close-by. A Union Flag was hoisted over the site and all the remaining gifts for the natives were put in boxes and left in the tents. Only the excess gunpowder was thrown away so that 'no accident might occur' to the lucky Eskimos who first came across the spot. The stores, scientific specimens, and food were shared out among the party with each man receiving a gun, ammunition, and a blanket. The weight carried by each individual came to 72lb and Richardson soon found that the seamen 'being unaccustomed to carry loads, advanced slowly.' An attempt was made to tow the supplies upriver in the 'wallnut shell', but the fast-flowing river frequently swamped the frail craft and, eventually, Richardson

The Dolphin *pushing her way through the loose ice.*

had to order its abandonment. Three days after they had begun their march, the Coppermine curved away to the south and the party struck out in a south-westerly direction across the Barren Lands towards the Great Bear Lake.

Two days after leaving the river, as they were about to settle down for the night, Kendall was scanning the horizon with his telescope when three Indians came into his view. Moss was immediately thrown onto the fire to create more smoke and a white ensign was attached to a musket and waved vigorously. The strangers turned out to be from the Hare tribe (frequent visitors to Fort Franklin) and had been ordered by their chief, It-chinnah, to keep a lookout for the white men. Delighted with their meeting, they now offered to guide the party to the Dease River and to warn other Indians that the party was passing through their territory. Richardson – equally delighted – accepted their offer and every man searched his belongings for something to give the Indians as a gift.

Other Indians were met during the three days it took to reach the mouth of the Dease River. All gave freely of their food stocks – a welcome addition to the supplies of Richardson's party as, by the time they reached the place appointed for the meeting with the canoes from Fort Franklin, not only was there no-one in sight, but only two days rations remained. Some fish was obtained from the river and five men, including Ooligbuck, were sent to find food on the north shore of the lake. Richardson was becoming concerned. Before leaving Fort Franklin he had stressed repeatedly the urgency of the party being met when they reached the Great Bear Lake, and had underlined his demands by offering a gun to the leader of the canoe party. If no-one appeared by 28 August, six days away, he and his men would have to start to walk the 300 miles around the lake, a journey of close on three weeks.

The following evening, as they were turning in for the night, voices were heard and on investigation, a boat and several canoes came into view. They carried four voyageurs, four Chipewyan hunters, and ten Dog-rib Indians – the latter accompanied by their families, making a total of about thirty people. It appeared that Dease had sent the party off in plenty of time, but bad weather had caused them delays. A further two days were lost in gathering together the hunting party that had been sent out, and it was not until the 28th – the day Richardson had feared they might have to start walking to Fort Franklin – that the canoes pushed off and set out over the lake.

The fort was finally reached four days later to a warm welcome from Dease. Richardson and his men had travelled 1,980 miles over land and water and had been away for seventy-one days. They had completed exactly what they had been ordered to do, they had discovered an unknown land, and had come back without the loss, or serious injury, of a single man. All that remained was to wait to see if their leader, John Franklin, had been equally successful. The wait, however, was not easy, for if Franklin failed to return to the fort, he could have reached the *Blossom* and be on his way to Canton, he could be preparing to winter on the northern shores – or he could be dead.

Having, with some difficulty, made his way through the mud-flats at the mouth of the MacKenzie River, Franklin and his party had arrived at a small bay that opened out to the sea. To the east lay a long, low, shore on which could be seen a large number of Eskimo tents. In accordance with his instructions, Franklin determined to meet the natives and prepared gifts to be presented to them. He strictly reminded his men that they were not to trade with the Eskimos and to leave all dealings to the officers. They were to have their muskets ready for use, but on no account were they to open fire unless ordered to do so by Back or himself.

With the Union Flag flying astern of the *Lion* and the White Ensign in a similar position on the *Reliance,* the two boats were rowed towards the tents. They grounded about a mile off the shore and had to be poled back into deeper water as the natives were hailed. Almost immediately, scores of kayaks and oomiaks took to the water and headed towards the boats. By the time the first of the natives arrived, almost a hundred of the Eskimo craft were in the water between them and the shore. On their approach, Augustus shouted across to explain that the visitors were friends and were hoping to find a passage for large ships which would come and bring much trade. At this a great roar went up from the crowd on the water and the first kayaks closed with the boats. Soon Franklin and Back were issuing small gifts and receiving bows, knives, and facial ornaments in return. Before long, there were almost 300 of the natives trying to get involved with the trading and Franklin, concerned at the numbers, attempted to get out to sea only to find that the boats were, once again, aground.

As the boat's crews tried to use their oars to get themselves afloat one of the kayaks was overturned. The *Lion's* seamen dragged the unfortunate Eskimo on-board and Augustus put his coat around the shoulders of the shivering man. The

The Eskimos looting Franklin's boat.

native promptly began to lift the canvas covering the stores and, on being dissuaded from further investigation, shouted to the other Eskimos to announce what he had seen. This promptly caused the boats to be pressed on all sides by natives suddenly eager to grab what they could as the seamen desperately tried to keep them out – even the ensigns and the masts had to be taken down to protect them from being removed. Eventually, Franklin was able to persuade a number of Eskimo chiefs to enter the boats in an effort to keep the others at bay. At first, this action succeeded and gave the crews a chance to get the boats afloat, but the natives had used the time to prepare a new strategy. Leaving their kayaks they jumped in the water and began to drag the boats towards the shore, at the same time smiling and making gestures of friendship. Three of the native men jumped into the *Lion* and pinioned Franklin to his seat whilst continuing to smile.

As the boats were hauled up on the beach, the *Reliance* was surrounded by knife-wielding Eskimos who grabbed what they could and handed the stolen items to their womenfolk standing behind. The voyageur, Vivier, had his knife snatched only to see it being used to cut the buttons from his coat. Another group surrounded Back and, using the threat of knives, demanded the gilt buttons from his jacket. Suddenly, a young chief went to Back's aid by sitting on the officer's knee and ordering the others away. As this was happening, Franklin left the *Lion* with Augustus, and ran along the beach towards the *Reliance*. He had not gone far when he heard Duncan, the coxswain, calling him back. The mob had now turned its attention to Franklin's own boat. The crew was busily fending off the natives with the butts of their muskets and Duncan had tied the box containing the astronomical instruments to his leg in response to repeated attempts to steal it. After fending off the attacks of three natives who were trying to steal his pistol, Franklin saw the marine, Wilson, raising his musket at an Eskimo. Unaware that the marine had been stabbed (albeit saved by the thickness of his coat), Franklin shouted at him to hold his fire and went to his

Back's men raising their muskets to frighten off the attacking Eskimos.

assistance, throwing natives over the boat's bow. The young chief who had been of help to Back then clambered into the *Lion* but could not stop more natives entering the boat by the stern. Just as the crew prepared to meet the new attack, the natives suddenly leapt out of the boat and Franklin and his men watched in astonishment as the Eskimos ran up the beach and hid behind driftwood and the beached kayaks.

The reason behind this precipitate flight became clear when they looked across to the *Reliance*. As the natives concentrated their attack on the *Lion*, Back had managed to get his boat afloat and was, by now, some yards offshore. Sensing that the situation was getting out of hand he had ordered his men to raise their muskets and aim in the general direction of the Eskimos. Probably aware of what the muskets were capable of from experience with Indians, the Eskimos had fled. The *Lion* was immediately pushed off the beach and joined the *Reliance*. As they rowed clear of the shore, the natives returned to their kayaks, but were warned off by Augustus who impressed upon them that anyone coming in range would be shot.

A quick muster of the boats' contents revealed that the Eskimos had managed to steal all the copper cooking vessels, a set of jib-sails, a tent, a bundle of blankets and shoes, and one of the men's bags. Many of the sails had been damaged as the natives had tried to cut free the metal fittings. Franklin was deeply impressed by the way his men had behaved in not opening fire despite severe provocation. He had been convinced that – outnumbered as they were – the entire party would have been massacred if one of his men had panicked and fired his musket. The site of the attack was given the name 'Pillage Point'.

Contact was again made with the Eskimos as the boats remained offshore and Augustus returned to the beach to remonstrate with his fellow natives over their behaviour. After protracted negotiations, the tent, a cooking pot, and some shoes were returned.

The boats were rowed six miles up the bay's western shore before Franklin allowed a camp to be set up to give his men a chance to rest after an exhausting day. A watch was set and it was not until late morning that the expedition was ready to get under way. The final touches were being made to the repair of the sails when Back spotted a vast flotilla of kayaks appearing out of the mist. Franklin promptly ordered everyone into the boats. By the time they were out into deep water the leading kayaks were within hailing distance. Out in front was a kayak whose occupant held up one of the copper kettles that had been stolen the day before. He shouted across that he wished to return the stolen item and that one of the oomiaks to his rear carried the remainder of the white men's property. But Franklin would have nothing to do with any further risk of conflict and replied that any natives approaching would be fired upon. This threat had no effect until he fired a shot just ahead of the leading kayak. At this, all the native boats veered round and paddled off in the direction they had just come.

Having shaken off the native threat, a favourable wind allowed the party to set their sails and follow the coast as it trended west by north-west. Ice drifted well offshore leaving open waters to the high mud-banks that skirted the coast. At eleven o'clock that evening, a low island appeared just off the shore and Franklin decided to stop for a few hours to rest his men and to prepare the boats for a sea-journey. Eager to press on, and with the wind remaining in the right quarter, the party set off at three o'clock the following morning. At first all went as well as the previous day but, before long, ice was seen lining the shore. After achieving twelve miles the boats were brought to a halt. The ice out at sea and along the shore had merged to form a glittering barrier right across their path. Franklin was forced to retreat until the shore ice allowed him to take the boats to a beach where he set up camp, consoling himself with the thought that his supplies were enough to allow him a few days detention.

The tents were erected on the muddy shore beneath giant stranded ice floes. To the south and west of their position, mountains rose beyond plains laced with small

Making contact with a group of Eskimos.

Another mass threat from the Eskimos.

lakes and rivers. Franklin named the range directly to the south after Richardson, and those to the west in honour of a Professor Buckland. Just as the party turned in for a welcome sleep the alarm went up from the men on duty as guards. Three Eskimos had stumbled on the camp and appeared to be on the verge of loosing arrows at the white men. Augustus shouted at them to lower their weapons. They did so and, after cautious negotiations, simple trading was soon in progress. The natives asked if they could bring other members of their tribe to see the newcomers and Augustus agreed to go with them to their tents. Before they left, Franklin had Augustus explained to the Eskimos that they were not to come closer than a series of marks he had set up 150 yards from his tents.

Five hours later, Augustus returned with twenty men and two women. They had left their weapons behind and showed none of the aggression that had been experienced at Pillage Point. Once exchanges of goods had been made to everyone's satisfaction, the natives told Franklin that the ice could be expected to move from the shore once the wind came from the right direction, thus leaving open a lane of water along which the boats could travel. They warned, however, that further barriers of ice could be expected as the passage to the west progressed. The following day, the Eskimos returned with their wives and children, and a group of forty-eight engaged with the seamen in an amicable trade of seal-skin boots for beads, fish-hooks, and metal tools as Back sketched their portraits.

Three days after their arrival, a westerly wind began to break up the ice and force it from the shore. The boats were launched but, after a mile and a half, they were forced back onshore. Once again, a solid sheet of ice barred their path. A night of rain was followed by a southerly wind which, to their delight, pushed the ice out to sea, but they were not able to advance much beyond Point Sabine. As they established a camp on the western shore of the low headland they saw the ice closing up the route they had just taken – with only a short delay their boats would have been crushed.

This was to be the pattern of their progress over the following days. Seizing every opportunity as the wind and rain helped to break up the ice, the boats were urged forward through narrow lanes that always threatened to close up, or were poled through loose ice floes that ground against each other with a menacing roar. More Eskimos were met, but all proved to be friendly and provided the party with food in the shape of caribou meat or dried fish. Herschel Island was passed and slow progress made through ever-increasing fog – a new hazard that added to the dangers from the ice. The party suffered a long delay just beyond the western edge of the Buckland Chain and Franklin chose to climb the most westerly of the mountains, Mount Conybear, with Duncan and one other man. At the top they built a cairn of rocks and placed beneath it a note describing the purpose of the expedition. To their disappointment, the view revealed the sea to be a solid mass of ice.

After three days of torment by clouds of mosquitoes they were, once again, able to push forward, but only in short journeys. On 27 July, the party came across a wide river that flowed from the newly named 'British Chain' of mountains. The river was named after the Duke of Clarence, the lord high admiral, as it was likely to be the last river before Russian territory was reached. At the naming ceremony, a tin box containing a silver medal was buried, the Union Flag hoisted, and three cheers given – 'the only salute we could afford'.

Point Demarcation (where the party drew level with the border between the British and the Russian territories) was reached four days later. Beyond the point, the wind pulled round and they were able to hoist their sails before running aground on a reef in thick fog. After a delay of three days on 'Icy Reef', the boats were dragged over the shallows of Beaufort Bay to a stretch of open water. This exhausting work was rewarded by an uninterrupted voyage of twenty-eight miles to Point Griffin (named after the family of his late wife's closest friend, Jane Griffin).

A new range of mountains that rose to the south were named the 'Romanzoff Range' (in honour of a recently deceased Russian chancellor) as an easterly wind drove the boats and accompanying ice floes around Point Manning. To the west of the point, the wind died away and the men were pulling at the oars when a native encampment was seen on the shore. On closing with the beach it appeared, at first, that the site was deserted. No movement, apart from sledge dogs, was seen until a naked woman suddenly emerged from one of the tents. Her shouts of alarm roused the camp and within moments, the beach was alive with naked people shouting and waving knives. Calling across from the *Lion*, Augustus managed to calm the tumult down, but Franklin decided against landing. With over fifty natives in the camp, he had not enough gifts to satisfy all their undoubted demands. Four kayaks, however,

Foggy Island.

were launched from the beach and their occupants rewarded with small gifts to demonstrate goodwill.

Camden Bay was crossed with little difficulty despite the occasional grounding and the brief visit of more natives. A landing was made on Point Brownlow before the boats were rowed through loose ice to Flaxman Island. Once again, the ice was locked onto the shore and no open passage remained for the boats to get further west. The island proved to be a dismal place to have their progress halted. About four miles long and no more than 50ft in height, the place had no water and little driftwood for use as fuel. Overnight, the water in the kettles froze as a gale failed in its promise of removing the barrier. But, two days after their arrival, a lane of water opened up and, with sails crammed on, the boats raced ahead until the *Lion* ran aground on 'Lion and Reliance Reef'. Hauled free by her crew, the boat had sustained enough damage to require her to be beached and repairs to be carried out. A site on the low coast was found at an old Eskimo camp, but the crews of both boats had to wade ashore with much of the stores in order to get the vessels over the shallow water. A brief exploration revealed that they were not on the mainland, but on an island separated from it by a narrow stretch of water. Fog prevented any further progress once the repairs had been completed and the following morning saw the ice closing in with the shore. To pass the time, astronomical observation were made during moments of clear weather and Augustus went hunting, returning with a welcome caribou.

On the fourth day, an attempt was made to reach an island that could be seen about three miles off, but the return of the fog forced them to row back to 'Foggy Island' (as Franklin had named their dreary refuge). Shortly after their arrival, another gap in the fog prompted a further attempt to head westward but, once again, incoming fog forced their return. The effort required to drag the boats through the mud of the shallow waters exhausted the party and resulted in several men suffering from swollen legs. Franklin found himself forced to compare his journey to the east of the Coppermine River five years earlier. At that time, fog had been a rarity and the ice had stopped his progress on just three occasions. He also regretted not having designed boats that had been decked in. This would have provided shelter for both his stores and his men.

On Sunday 13 August (their sixth day on Foggy Island) Franklin held a church service before the party retreated to their damp tents to 'amuse themselves'. The fog was so thick that it prevented even the shortest of walks or the taking of observations. The retreat beneath canvas was also caused by the lack of driftwood available at the site. What little fuel was available had to be saved for cooking the meals. Ice was beginning to form on the island's pools of water.

On the early morning of the 16th, the sun rose to a morning clear of fog. No time was wasted in getting the boats loaded and pushed out into deeper water. Spirits rose as it looked, at last, as if they were to escape from the 'detested island'. The island they had failed to reach six days earlier turned out to be a low headland that provided its own share of risk as its shoaling waters were encountered. Franklin named it 'Point Anxiety'. Eight miles further west, Point Chandos was rounded to reveal the entrance to Yarborough Inlet. Whilst crossing the inlet's mouth, the fog began to return and a freshening wind stirred the shallow waters causing the boats to steer away from the land to avoid being driven ashore. Soon they found themselves surrounded by drifting ice floes and were forced to try and find a place to land. An attempt at Point Heald, and another on the western tip of Prudhoe Bay, failed when rolling surf threatened to overturn the boats in the shoaling waters. With the situation becoming desperate, Franklin decided to head out to sea once again in the hope that the boats could be secured alongside a large floe. They had not gone far when their keels grounded on a gravel reef that barely showed above the water's surface. Seizing the opportunity, the boats were dragged onto the shingle and the tents erected to provide shelter from the icy wind. A temporary lifting of the fog revealed that the reef was no more than five hundred yards in circumference, had no fresh water, and enough stunted Arctic willows to provide fuel for just one fire.

As the party huddled beneath damp blankets in an effort to keep warm, Franklin began to apply his mind to their situation. For some days the flight of birds to the south and the freezing of open waters had announced that winter was on its way. Before long, the last of the caribou would follow the birds and snow would blanket the land. As testified by their swollen legs, his men had suffered greatly in the constant hauling of the boats through the cold waters. He knew he could depend upon them to stretch themselves to the limit, but had no desire to inflict more suffering upon them – 'though no one who knows the resolute disposition of British sailors can be surprised at their more than readiness to proceed, I felt that it was my business to judge of their capacity of so doing, and not allow myself to be seduced by their ardour, however honourable to them, and cheering to me.' Finally, his instructions from the Admiralty ordered him to return on a date between 15 and 20 August if it was clear to him that he would be unable to reach Kotzebue Sound (over 700 miles away) that season. In the fading evening light, Franklin assembled his men and told them that they had reached their furthest point. As soon as the weather abated, they would begin the journey back to Fort Franklin. The news was received with 'the good feeling that had marked their conduct throughout the voyage.'

The next day the fog was swept away by a violent gale that prevented the boats from being launched. Franklin was, however, permitted to see what would have lain ahead had he pressed on. The coastline arced away into a bay that terminated in a low headland about eight miles away. Beyond that, a similar headland could be made out. The first of these features Franklin named after 'my excellent companion Lieutenant Back', the other after 'my friend Captain Beechey'.

On Friday 18 August 1826, 'Return Reef' was quitted beneath double-reefed sails. Two hundred and seventy miles to the west, Beechey was bidding farewell to the *Blossom's* barge as Elson took her towards Point Barrow. Five days later, Elson would turn back 160 miles from Return Reef. Had Franklin been able to emulate his best sailing distance, twenty-eight miles, for every one of those days, he would still have missed the *Blossom's* barge by twenty miles. In all probability, however, any attempt to press further to the west would have been delayed by fog and ice, and a meeting with Elson missed by a far wider margin.

A gale drove the *Lion* and the *Reliance* to Foggy Island where a pile of drift timber was erected on the highest part of the island's northern shore. Beneath it Franklin had buried a record of their voyage, a halfpenny coin, and a silver medal. He also had enclosed a letter addressed to the Russian fur traders in the hope that it might find its way to them via the natives. The pile was draped in metal implements to attract the Eskimos and a red pennant was flown from its top.

The continuing gale delayed departure from the island for two days, but this was followed by good progress to Flaxman Island. Boulder Island was reached after nineteen hours of hard rowing and a brief rest was enjoyed before another exhausting haul brought them to Barter Island. In crossing Beaufort Bay it became necessary to steer out into the pack of drifting ice in order to avoid the bay's shallow waters. Constantly under threat from the wind-driven ice, the boats reached Demarcation Point where a family of Eskimos was so overjoyed to see them that one of the men hastened to put on his best clothing and insert his favourite mouth ornaments. More natives were met on Herschel Island and, at Point King, Eskimo women sewed seal-skin soles onto the party's moccasin shoes – an invaluable improvement to their footwear with the likelihood of having to tow the boats from the shore in the near future. It was, however, the natives that the party found just to the west of the MacKenzie that were to prove the greatest help.

On the morning of 29 August, after Franklin and his men had been driven ashore by a gale, a large group of natives visited the expedition camp. Following the usual exchange of goods, the Eskimos left at mid-afternoon. Not long after they had departed, two young natives were seen returning across the rocks in great haste and in a state of much excitement. They brought the news that a large party of Indians was approaching the camp with the intention of killing all the white men. News of Franklin's visit had reached the Indian's ears, and they were determined that no new trade would be allowed to interfere with the arrangements they already had with the Eskimos. The threatened attack had been intended to take place along the coast off Herschel Island but, when they found no trace of the white men, they had moved to the mouth of the MacKenzie where they could find sustenance whilst waiting. The information was vital to the expedition's safety but – as was learned subsequently – the young messengers had not brought the news out of respect for the white men, their chief concern lay with their fellow Eskimo, Augustus. Nevertheless, they warned Franklin that he should leave with all speed and try to get on the MacKenzie before the Indians as the would-be attackers had brought no canoes with them. They also suggested that, if the white men were to set up a camp, they should make it on an island well away from the shore as the Indians were armed with muskets.

Armed with this news, Franklin determined to leave immediately, but was held up by the absence of Spink who had wandered off in an attempt to find caribou. An anxious time was spent waiting for the missing seaman before he returned and the boats could be pulled clear of the shore and out of immediate danger. Franklin aimed straight for Pillage Point and, after having to drag the boats for two hours through shallow water, the point was rounded. A wind, bringing with it several showers of snow, then helped their progress up the river. Four days later, Point Separation was reached and a copper cooking pot located. They had left the pot for the natives but, having been robbed of all but one of their other pots by the Eskimos at Pillage Point, they were delighted to find it remaining where it had been deposited. A letter and a bag of pemmican were left in case Richardson and his party were ascending the river behind them.

Fort Good Hope came into sight in the late afternoon of 7 September. There they learned that, not for the first time, rumours had been spread that both Franklin's and Richardson's parties had been killed. In response, Franklin had the fort's manager send two Indians down the river to see if any information regarding Richardson could be obtained.

His fears were put at an end thirteen days later when the boats reached the lakeshore beneath Fort Franklin. Richardson himself was not at the fort – he had taken a canoe to the Great Slave Lake to study the geology of the district – but Kendall and Dease provided a cheery welcome.

Franklin and his party had been away from the fort for almost exactly three months. They had journeyed over 2,000 miles and contended with hostile natives, ice, fog, and gales. Six hundred and ten miles of the North American coastline had been revealed to European eyes for the first time. Not a man had been lost, nor serious injuries sustained. Franklin noted that his men had 'met every obstacle with an ardent desire to surmount it, and cheerfully exerted themselves to the utmost of their power'.

The arrival at Fort Franklin had been marred by the failure of the Indian hunters to bring in enough food to see them through the approaching winter. During his absence, a derisory three caribou had been shot and, for some time, the fort had been existing solely on fish taken from the lake. Franklin immediately sent Kendall to Fort Norman for supplies he had previously ordered to be delivered there. On his return, Kendall brought – in addition to a modest amount of food – warm clothing and letters. Among the latter was an official notice informing of the promotion of George Back to the rank of commander.

By mid-October, the snow was firmly set in and, a month later, the lake had frozen over. The remainder of the stores at Fort Norman was collected by canoe. The food, in particular, proved to be vital to the occupants of Fort Franklin as the number of Indians bringing in food dwindled away when it was learned that the fort no longer held goods that could be exchanged for furs. Once again, fish proved to be the mainstay of the diet though, unfortunately, several men were affected by stomach problems as a result. A programme of entertainments was introduced on the same lines as the previous winter, and Franklin and Kendall concentrated on the summer's charts, maps, and observations.

The highlight of Christmas 1826, was a performance of cut-out figures that – behind an illuminated screen – enacted a play written by Back. So successful was the opening night that the play had to be repeated on three subsequent occasions. A dance to Wilson's bagpipes on New Year's Eve brought the festive season to an end. On the fourth day of 1827, the temperature fell to a level low enough for Kendall to use a bullet-mould to make a pistol-ball out of mercury.

By the middle of February, the first of the caribou returned to the region and seven were brought down, introducing a welcome change in the Fort's diet. Another reason that Franklin was pleased to see the return of the animals was that he could leave the fort under the command of Back and begin his journey to the south (Back and the remaining men would follow with the spring thaw). Using dogs and sledges, he set off with five of his men and two Indians, the latter pulling sledges loaded with pemmican. Less than two days after his start, the Indians disappeared, taking the food with them, and Franklin was forced to carry on with much reduced rations. A week was spent at Fort Simpson as Franklin sorted out the administration required to settle his accounts with the Hudson's Bay Co. before he moved on, first to Fort Resolution, then to Fort Chipewyan.

A frustrating six weeks was spent at the fort on the Athabasca Lake waiting for the Hudson's Bay Co. brigade of boats to be prepared for their journey along the Athabascan and Saskatchewan rivers. At last, on 31 May, Franklin set off and arrived at Cumberland House eighteen days later. There he was re-united with Richardson.

It had been eleven months since they parted at Point Separation not knowing when, or if, they would meet again. The naturalist, Drummond, was also at Cumberland House. It had taken him four months to reach the Rocky Mountains via Fort Edmonton and he had spent the winter alone under a crude shelter made from tree branches. His summer was spent crossing the mountains northwards towards the headwaters of the Peace River in the company of an Indian hunter who brought along his family, and whose skills rarely extended beyond the capture of young porcupines. Drummond then turned southwards and headed off in the direction of the Columbia River but, on receipt of a letter from Franklin, started his return journey to Carlton House. There, after a journey in which he suffered grievously from snow-blindness and starvation, he met Richardson. With at least two months remaining before Back and the rest of the party would arrive at Carlton House, Drummond chose to stay behind in order to carry out more work in the region.

Franklin and Richardson continued their canoe voyage down the Saskatchewan River until it met Lake Winnipeg. At Norway House they said farewell to their faithful companion Augustus. His skills, whether in hunting or in negotiations with his fellow Eskimos, had been of immense value to the exhibition. Shedding a tear at the separation, the brave Augustus pleaded, on behalf of himself and Ooligbuck, to be allowed to accompany any future expedition led by Franklin, Back, or Richardson. No such future could be offered with any degree of confidence, but Franklin took firm steps to ensure that the payment owing to the two Eskimos was forwarded to the Hudson's Bay Co.

Travelling via Lake Champlain, New York was reached in August and, just as on the outward passage, the party was treated with generous hospitality and assistance. The packet-ship was boarded on 1 September and, after twenty-five days at sea, Franklin stepped ashore at Liverpool. It had been just over two and a half years since he had left England. Three days later, 'accompanied by Dr. Richardson' he 'had the honour of laying the charts and drawings before his Royal Highness the Lord High Admiral'. Franklin could take pride in an enterprise that had added over 1,200 miles of previously uncharted coasts to the map of North America. He had missed connecting with Beechey by a bare 160 miles under circumstances that were beyond his control – and all without the loss of a single life.

It was not long before Franklin was proposing that a new expedition should be mounted. He urged that a ship should be sent to seek a north-west passage from the west. Once Richardson's Cape Bathurst had been passed, a wintering place would be found and the vessel supplied by an overland expedition supported by the Hudson's Bay Co. During the following summer a passage through Dolphin and Union Strait would bring the ship within range of Parry's Hecla and Fury Strait. If that route proved to be blocked, there was always the possibility of finding a way through to one of Parry's other routes to the north and east. However, whatever happened, Franklin noted in the conclusion to his account of the expedition that

Arctic discovery has been fostered principally by Great Britain; and it is a subject of just pride that it has been prosecuted by her from motives as disinterested as they are enlightened; not from any prospect of immediate benefit to herself, but from a steady view to the acquirement of useful knowledge, and the extension of the bounds of science...And it is sincerely to be hoped that Great Britain will not relax in her efforts until the question of a north-west passage has been satisfactorily set at rest, or at least until those portions of the northern shores of America, which are yet unknown, be laid down in our maps.

But the world was moving on. In a letter to a friend written less than two months after his return, Franklin observed 'The brilliant battle of Navarino (27 October, 1827) will certainly for a time lead the Naval attention to other pursuits than those connected with science – and if war should unfortunately break out I should prefer trying my fortunes in the more active line of service.'

The chance for glory in a new war did not arise. Instead Franklin was to be rewarded for his enterprise by the presentation of the Paris Geographical Society's gold medal and – in common with Parry – Oxford University awarded him an honorary degree of Doctor of Civil Law. He was also, much to his disappointment, made a Knight Commander of the Guelphic Order. Franklin had been keen to be appointed a Companion of the Bath (CB) 'as being a more Professional distinction than Knighthood'. The problem was that the CB was awarded for leadership in battle and, although Franklin had seen plenty of action, he had been serving at too junior a rank to qualify. Moreover, Earl Bathurst had 'expressly' told him that the earl personally wished that CBs could be awarded to officers on the grounds of scientific research – but nothing came of it.

Before the announcement of his knighthood, Franklin achieved one further distinction. In November 1828, he married Jane Griffin – the best friend of his late wife. He had taken Jane with him to St Petersburg with the intention of marrying her there 'However on our arrival at that place we found so few conveniences for a new married party, that we both considered it better to defer our union until it could be cemented in England'.

With no vacancy available at one of the major naval hospitals, Richardson returned to his appointment as surgeon to the Chatham division of marines. His subsequent lectures to the Geological Society provided a valuable appendix to Franklin's account of the expedition.

Commander Back's return to England from Fort Franklin had been marred by the death of two men, one from disease, the other by drowning. He and Kendall had arrived in October, some six weeks after Franklin. Kendall learned that he had been promoted lieutenant with his commission back-dated to April that year. Neither officer however, was given employment and both were put on half-pay.

The navy never employed Kendall again. He died in 1845 having achieved the position of superintendent of the Peninsular and Oriental Steam-Packet Co.

CHAPTER TEN

'GO AND SEE!'

On his return from Spitsbergen in 1818, Franklin had proposed to John Barrow that it might be possible to reach the North Pole by crossing the frozen Arctic Sea. The idea was supported by the writings of others who had seen the vast sheet of ice barring their own attempts to reach northwards. Phipps, who had come across the barrier in 1773, had written that his way had been blocked by 'one continued plain of smooth unbroken ice, bounded only by the horizon.' More recently, the whaler-scientist, William Scoresby Junior, had reported that he 'once saw a field (of ice) that was so free from snow, a coach might have been driven many leagues over it in a direct line without obstruction or danger.'

Barrow sent a copy of Franklin's idea to Parry — already feeling uncomfortable in the 'sedentary occupation' of hydrographer. Parry grasped the proposal with both hands and wrote to the First Lord of the Admiralty, Lord Melville, recommending that the idea be followed up using 'sledge-boats over the ice, or through any spaces of open water that might occur'. To Franklin — at that time at Fort Franklin preparing for his expedition down the MacKenzie River — he wrote that 'the true reply to all doubts is, go and see!' For a time there was no reply from the Admiralty so, on Barrow's advice, Parry re-submitted the proposal, this time supported by a scientific programme to be carried out during the expedition. This, in turn, gained the backing of the Royal Society (of which Parry was a fellow) and the society's distinguished president, Sir Humphrey Davey. In July 1826, approval was granted and Parry was given his old ship, *Hecla,* for the undertaking.

For his officers, Parry was able to choose from a wide range of experienced polar seamen. James Ross was selected to be the *Hecla*'s first lieutenant and given the job of preparing the ship for the task ahead. Lieutenants Henry Foster and Francis Crozier were appointed as was Midshipman Edward Bird. John Halse was appointed as purser (his fifth expedition under Parry's leadership). The expedition naturalist was Charles Beverly who had served under both John Ross and Parry as assistant surgeon, but had lost his place on the navy list after refusing an appointment. It was hoped that his time in the *Hecla* would lead to his re-instatement. The only newcomer to the ice was the assistant surgeon, Robert McCormick.

The 'sledge-boats' Parry intended to take across the ice to the North Pole were solidly built of fir and oak. Twenty feet long and seven in the beam they were intended to be manned by two officers, ten seamen, and two marines. Secured alongside the keel of each boat were steel-shod sledge runners for use when crossing the ice. In addition, two large wheels were fixed to the fore-end of the boats and a smaller wheel aft, the stern wheel being attached to a steering arm. A single, 19-ft, mast could carry a sail that also served as an awning. It was intended that Norwegian reindeer would do the boat hauling. Should, however, the animals prove to be unfitted for the job, the boats would have to be pulled by the officers and men, a load – when full – of 268lb per individual. Parry was to take one of the boats over the ice with Beverly as his second-in-command. The other was to be in the charge of Ross with Bird as his second.

In March 1827, Parry's father-in-law, Sir John Stanley, gave a dinner for the entire ship's company after his daughter (Isabella) had hoisted her husband's pendant to the mast-top. She also gave Parry a silk white ensign to fly at the North Pole. She had stitched the flag herself and it had last flown over the church at their marriage. In addition, an announcement was made that an order-in-council had approved an award of £1,000 if the expedition could reach 83 degrees north.

The *Hecla* left Deptford on 26 March and moved downriver to Sheerness. On the way a tragedy occurred off North Fleet. John Gordon, a seaman who had served under Parry on all his previous expeditions, was sent out to lay a kedge anchor from a boat. As the anchor was thrown from the boat, one of its flukes caught on the vessel's gunwale. The weight of the anchor, combined with a fast flowing stream, threatened to turn the boat over. Gordon raced from the boat's stern sheets and lifted the anchor clear just as the craft was about to be swamped. Unfortunately, his foot became caught in a bight of the anchor-rope and he was dragged over the side by the descending anchor. He was never seen again. Parry found he was unable to 'describe the sensation this melancholy catastrophe occasioned in the ship, for Gordon was respected and beloved by all.'

Captain William Parry.

But, tragedy or not, the expedition was on its way. Several days were spent at Hammerfest in northern Norway collecting eight reindeer and practising – with some hilarity – walking on skis. A week after their departure from the Norwegian port, the *Hecla* fell in with a fleet of whalers and stayed in company with them until the coast of Spitsbergen was reached on 12 May. Parry's plan was to be on his way northwards with the sledge-boats by 1 June but, first, he had to find a secure anchorage for the *Hecla*. Several suitable harbours were passed, but the ice prevented him from finding a secure haven. At Smeerenburg Harbour – on the north-west corner of West Spitsbergen – a southerly gale drove the ship hard against the pack ice and Parry was forced to seek refuge amongst the ice floes. This gave him protection from the rough sea but, inevitably, he soon found himself beset and unable to break free.

Although trapped, Parry found that the ice was drifting in a north-easterly direction, thus following the route he had intended to take. Whilst waiting for the ice to break up he had the sledge-boats lowered onto the ice and carried out trials in their use. At first, all did not go well. Both the wheels and the reindeer were found to be useless and an attempt by Foster and Crozier, using a large part of the ship's company to drag them over the rough ice, took fourteen hours to cover four miles. A subsequent attempt on level ice, however, proved much more promising and it was felt that, under the right circumstances, twenty miles a day could be achieved. The skis also proved to be ineffective as snowshoes and were adapted for use as personal sledges.

It was to be twenty-four days before the *Hecla* was freed from the ice and another ten days were spent in seeking a suitable harbour. At last, on 18 June after cutting through the ice for a quarter of a mile, a safe anchorage was found in Treurenburg Bay (Sorg Fjorden). Well behind his schedule, Parry lost little time in setting out with the sledge-boats (by now named *Enterprise* and *Endeavour*). Leaving the ship under the command of Foster, and accompanied by Crozier in the ship's cutter, Parry set sail northwards on 21 June.

A landing was made on Walden Island and a site chosen as a rendezvous for the return journey. Crozier was ordered to bring a boat from the *Hecla* to the spot in case a spare vessel was needed.

As Crozier bid farewell and returned to the ship, Parry set off through calm waters towards the ice. It took three days of paddling (oars were left behind to reduce the weight) before they were stopped by the vast sheet of ice that stretched to three horizons. It was 24 June and their position was 81 degrees, 12' 51". By noon the boats had become sledges and Parry began the ordered pattern that would control their daily lives for the remainder of the time on the ice.

He intended that travel should be done only at night. As the sun never set at that time of year there would be no difficulty in navigating, and there would be the advantage of firmer snow, less risk of snow-blindness, a warmer time of day to sleep, and higher temperatures to dry out wet clothing. Parry had provided himself with a twenty-four hour pocket chronometer to prevent the risk of confusion between night and daytime – and to ensure that a navigational mistake did not send him down an opposite meridian after reaching the pole.

When hauling the boats they wore racoon-skin caps and blue box-cloth (i.e. thick wool) hooded jackets and breeches – the latter having a square of white, waterproof, canvas sewn over the seat. Canvas gaiters were attached to the breeches by a buckle and strap. On their feet they wore low leather boots as worn by Laplanders. Fur clothing was used for sleeping beneath blankets and Parry insisted that the fur 'sleeping dresses' were always to be kept dry. To that end, the day clothing had to be put on when rising, even if they were still wet from the day before.

For food each man was allowed a daily ration of 9oz of pemmican, 10oz of biscuit, 1oz of cocoa powder, and 1 gill of rum. In addition there was a weekly allowance of 3oz of tobacco. Water for the cocoa was heated in a boiler that used seven wicks and took over an hour to boil three and a half gallons (one pint per man). The 'day' started with prayers followed by a breakfast of cocoa and biscuits. The boats were then stowed and hauled for five hours before an hour-long lunch break was taken. Then, depending on conditions, a further four to six hours was spent dragging the boats before a halt was called. On completion of the day's pulling, the boats were hauled alongside each other and the sails used to cover them as an awning. Any repairs needed were carried out before supper and a watch set to guard against polar bears. Most men smoked their pipes and chatted, fighting 'all their battles again'. Parry, however, was a non-smoker and preferred to sniff at a bottle of eau de Cologne (known to the men as 'the captain's pipe'). Evening prayers were then said, fur clothing was donned, and sleep sought in cramped condition which forced them to 'stow rather closer than was agreeable.' In the 'morning' the sharp blast of a bugle-call announced that the cocoa was on the boil.

But the best planning can fail in the face of a challenge from the elements. Instead of the level sheet of ice Parry had been led to believe might be found north of Spitsbergen, all that could be seen ahead was a vast, quarry-like, jumble of 40ft hummocks and giant pressure-ridges. Open lanes of water were frequently encountered requiring the sledge-boats to be launched and then hauled out onto the next floe – an exhausting exercise. Areas of knee-deep, slushy snow proved to be particularly difficult to cross. The sledge-boats had to be emptied and both crews put to heaving on a single boat to drag it forward making several journeys to cover the same amount of ground. Pools of meltwater, that were too shallow to float the boats, had to be waded through, and thin ice was a constant threat. Even worse was the frequent rain which carved the surface of the ice into sharp 'penknives' that slashed at the men's soft leather boots. At times the men were reduced to crawling on all fours just to urge a boat over a few yards of broken, snow-covered ice. On top of everything there was little in their surroundings that could provide inspiration.

Hauling Parry's sledge-boats northwards.

After scanning the horizon through his telescope from the top of a tall hummock, Parry wrote

> Nothing could well exceed the dreariness which such a view presented. The eye wearied itself in vain to find any object but ice and sky to rest upon. From want of variety, the most trifling circumstances engaged a more than ordinary share of our attention – a passing gull, or a mass of ice of unusual form, became objects which our situation and circumstances magnified into ridiculous importance.

Parry's leadership kept the party pressing forward through day after day of appalling conditions. Always encouraging, always to be seen heaving with the best of them, he kept his men cheerful despite the inadequate food and the constantly challenging ice. But he – and the other officers – harboured a secret that was beginning to affect his own morale. Through his frequent observations and calculations it had become obvious that the poor conditions over which the sledge-boats were being hauled was not the worst of his problems. Far more serious was his discovery that the ice over which he was travelling was drifting continuously *to the south*.

Snow-blindness had begun to effect many of the men and Parry noted that his 'eyes were so painful with having strained them in looking out for the road, that I was unable any longer to see my way, and was therefore obliged, for a time, to give up the pioneering duty to Lieutenant Ross'. Oddly, despite seeing the Eskimo's 'spectacles' during his wintering in Hudson's Bay, Parry had not thought to introduce such items to the expedition. The following day, Ross himself suffered an accident that gave cause for much concern. Whilst helping to push the *Endeavour* over a scatter of hummocks, the boat heeled over and trapped him. At first the surgeon/naturalist, Beverley, feared that Ross's spine had been damaged but, on closer examination, the injury amounted to no more than painful bruising.

The seamen, although maintaining their good humour, began to comment that they 'were a long time in getting to this 83 degrees!' (and, of course, their share of the £1,000 prize). On 22 July an observation revealed that – on that day – they had hauled the sledge-boats ten or eleven miles, but had drifted southwards by six. Four days later they had managed to drag the boats over rough ice for a maximum of another twelve miles – only for Parry to discover that they had drifted so far southwards that they were three miles south of where they had started on the 22nd. It was time to call a halt.

After explaining the problem to the seamen, Parry decided on a day of rest before beginning the return journey. The day (27 July) proved to be warm and sunny so the men took the opportunity to wash and repair their clothing whilst the officers took observations. These revealed that they had reached 82 degrees 43' 32" north – less than twenty miles from the prize-earning 83 degrees. Parry calculated that, in five weeks, they had travelled 292 miles in total with 100 miles over water. However, the frequent requirement to journey over the same stretch of ice carrying stores and hauling the sledge-boats separately, increased the actual distance covered to about 580 miles – a figure not far removed from the distance between Spitsbergen and the pole. Despite five weeks of gruelling effort, on their day of rest, the party was no further than 172 miles from the *Hecla*. Ross took from his pocket a red leather bound copy of 'The Economy of Human Life' which his sister had given him before departure. In it he wrote 'Written on board the *Endeavour* in Latitude 82 3/4 N 27th July 1827 Jas. C. Ross'.

That evening, Parry hoisted his wife's silk ensign and toasted the health of the king. Ross then stepped forward with a toast to 'Mrs Parry', followed by the sergeant of marines raising his glass to 'Sir John Stanley', Parry's father-in-law. On the following day, with 'little satisfaction', the party turned southwards.

The sparse ration which had been provided began to take its toll as the party retraced its steps. A polar bear was sighted but, much to everybody's annoyance, managed to avoid the musket balls. Most of the men, noted Parry, had in 'anticipation, consigned a tolerable portion of his flesh to their cooking kettle, over a fire of his own blubber.' Ross rectified the situation a few days later by bringing down a bear. The animal had hardly sunk to the ice before a seamen was at its side with a knife ready to put part of it into a conveniently-boiling pot. Soon after they had gorged themselves, several of the men suffered severely from over-eating, yet blamed their condition on the quality of the meat. This result of over-indulgence prompted Parry to write – after another bear was seen and wounded – that 'luckily for us, it escaped.'

The camp at Parry's furthest north.

With a lighter load and the southward drift, the journey away from the pole took considerably less time than the haul to the north. On 11 August, fourteen days after they had turned, and forty-eight days since they had lifted their boats out of the sea, Parry and his party heard the sound of waves breaking against the ice. In less than an hour the boats were, once again, united with their natural element and heading towards the *Hecla*.

On Table Island they found supplies left by Crozier (although the bread had been eaten by polar bears) and a note informing Parry that his dog, Fido, was fit and well. A tiny islet, just to the north of Table Island, and at that time the most northerly known land in the world, was named after James Ross for 'no individual can have exerted himself more strenuously to rob it of this distinction'. On Walden Island, the spare boat left by Crozier was collected and, after several days battling against a southerly wind, the *Hecla* was reached in the late afternoon of 21 August. To the welcoming cheers of the ship's company they learned that, in their absence, the tough old ship had been driven ashore, re-floated, and then deliberately beached to protect her from wind-driven icebergs. But their return saw the vessel safely back upon the waters of Treurenberg Bay and ready for the voyage home. A delay of a few days was caused by a wait for Foster's return from his surveying expedition and the ship eventually raised anchor on 28 August.

A month after their departure, the expedition reached Orkney. Again, the southerly wind was the cause of a slow voyage and its continuation led to Parry taking up the offer of a passage to Inverness in the revenue cutter *Chichester*. On his arrival at the Admiralty to present his report to the lord high admiral (the Duke of Clarence) he was astonished to find himself followed into the waiting room by Franklin and John Richardson, newly returned from their MacKenzie River expedition. The meeting had taken place by chance and gave rise to great congratulation and celebration. Parry, however, would have been almost equally pleased with the fortnight's leave granted by the lord high admiral. Ross, on the other hand, now in command of the *Hecla* as it sailed down to the Thames, must have been less than excited to learn that the duke had decided that he would pay a call upon the ship and that, under no circumstances, was he to allow the vessel to be in anything less than 'good order and cleanliness'.

The *Hecla* arrived in the Thames on 6 October 1827, and the lord high admiral paid his promised visit eleven days later. The ship was paid off on 1 November and Parry hauled down his pendant for the last time. He was never to have command at sea again nor to mount any further polar exploration. He had, nevertheless, scored his name deeply into polar history. His furthest north remained unsurpassed for almost fifty years, and his standing amongst his contemporaries may be judged from the fact that, before his death, the then most southerly known point on the globe was named Parry Mountains at the same time as the most northerly point – Mount Parry, north of Smith Sound – was also named in his honour.

Parry returned to his role as hydrographer to the navy on decommissioning the *Hecla*. He made his mark on the world of surveying and charts by producing the first ever sales catalogue of Admiralty charts and organising the production of the department's 'Sailing Directions'. In 1829, he accepted both a knighthood and the post of commissioner for the Australian Agricultural Co. He returned to England in 1834 and spent a year as assistant poor-law commissioner in Norfolk before returning to the navy as controller of the steam machinery and packet department. After ten years Parry was appointed captain-superintendent of Haslar Royal Naval Hospital where he remained until 1852 when he was promoted to rear admiral. A year later he was appointed as lieutenant-governor of Greenwich Hospital. In late 1854 he suffered a breakdown in his health and went to the Rhineland resort of Ems in search of a recovery, but found only death. Rear Admiral Sir William Edward Parry – 'the beau ideal of an Arctic officer' – died in Germany on 8 July 1855. His body was returned to England and buried in the grounds of Greenwich Hospital. His grandson, Rear Admiral John Parry, was appointed hydrographer in 1914 and served in that post throughout the First World War.

The *Hecla*, at that time the most experienced polar surveying vessel in the world, was sold out of the Royal Navy's service in April 1831.

CHAPTER ELEVEN

'TODAY WAS AS YESTERDAY, AND SO WAS TODAY, SO WILL BE TOMORROW'

At the beginning of the 1819 grouse shooting season, Captain John Ross returned to Scotland with his wife. He had been in the Royal Navy for thirty-three years and was now, for the first time, on half-pay with practically no prospect of future employment with the Admiralty. He took to the study of phrenology and recommended that the navy should instruct its officers in reading the bumps on the heads of their ships' companies in order that the men might be employed to the best advantage of the service. Needless to say, their lordships failed to see the advantage of this and ignored Ross's advice. A more practical study was made of the newly developing science of maritime steam propulsion. Ross voyaged on as many steam vessels as he could and even conducted experiments in a tank at his home in order to increase his understanding of steam engines. In an anonymous letter to *Blackwood's Magazine* in April 1827, he accurately predicted the Royal Navy's reluctance to take advantage of the new form of propulsion. This was followed by the publication of '*A Treatise on Navigation by Steam; comprising a History of the Steam Engine, and an Essay towards a System of the Naval Tactics Peculiar to Steam Navigation, as Applicable both to Commerce and Maritime Warfare.*' In his pamphlet Ross pointed out the obvious advantages of a system of propelling a vessel that depended upon neither wind nor human effort. He suggested regulations for the qualifications of engineers and stokers, and earned the support of both by recommending a double ration of beer whilst they operated the engines. Despite the work being published in three editions, the First Lord of the Admiralty, Lord Melville, commenting on a proposal to employ steam-packets in the Mediterranean wrote 'Their Lordships feel it their bounden duty to discourage to the utmost of their ability the employment of steam vessels, as they consider the introduction of Steam is calculated to strike a fatal blow at the supremacy of the Empire.' Melville's reasoning was perfectly sound. Britain had absolute mastery of the seas whilst her sailing men-of-war remained unchallenged, but to support the introduction of a system that threatened that mastery *and* could be made easily available to less fortunate nations, was clearly foolhardy. Ross, however, determined upon a plan that would, he hoped, demonstrate the utility of the steam-engine. What could be better than taking a steam vessel into the Arctic ice, and navigate it through the north-west passage?

His first approach was to the Admiralty but, with his old enemy, John Barrow, still firmly in office, their lordships turned the idea down. He then tried an old friend and dry gin distiller, Felix Booth, a man who had frequently revealed himself to be public spirited and generous, but Booth refused him on the grounds that he did not wish to be seen to be in pursuit of the £20,000 prize that was still available through an Act of Parliament. Other hoped-for benefactors – including the Duke of Wellington – were tried but none were able to help. Then, at last, support came from Booth, by now the sheriff of London. The Board of Longitude had been abolished by Parliament, and along with it went the £20,000 prize – Booth could no longer be accused of attempting to profit from the proposed expedition.

With his finances now secure, Ross searched for a suitable vessel for the expedition. He found her at Liverpool; an eighty-five-ton, oak-built paddle-steamer named *Victory*. She had served as a mail packet between the port and the Isle of Man and had proved capable of towing a 600-ton ship at three miles an hour against the wind and tide. Ross purchased the *Victory* for £2,500 and set about preparing her for service in the Arctic. He began by replacing her paddlewheels with a new design that allowed the paddles to be lifted clear of the water within a minute. This innovation would be of great importance if the paddles were threatened by ice. Also, with paddles raised, the ship's sailing qualities would be greatly improved when running under canvas. Ross then turned his mind to the ship's engines. The 30hp engine that had proved adequate for the vessel's previous owners was to be powered by a newly designed high-pressure boiler patented by the firm of Braithwaite and Ericsson.

Next, Ross informed the Admiralty of his plans. This, in turn led to news of the proposed expedition reaching a wide public and Ross found himself inundated with volunteers. At one stage he was able to state with complete accuracy that he could have manned the ship entirely with Royal Naval captains. Even the immensely experienced and well-respected whaling captain William Scoresby Junior applied for a berth, but Ross had already decided on the team that would accompany him northwards. For his second-in-command (and expedition naturalist) he had chosen his nephew, Commander James Ross. The third officer was William Thom, an experienced seaman who had served as purser on Ross's voyage in the *Isabella*. In order to avoid the ignominy of a naval officer being referred to as the ship's 'master', Thom was appointed to that post whilst John and James Ross took the respective titles of first and second 'directors of the expedition'. Three mates were appointed; Thomas Blanky, who had served with Lyon in the *Griper*; Thomas Abernathy, an

Captain John Ross.   Victory *leaving the Thames.*

ex-*Fury* seaman; and George Taylor, who had been serving as the master of the *Victory* when Ross purchased her. Six seamen were taken on and joined a carpenter and his mate, a chief and second engineer, three stokers, an armourer, a cook and a steward. This ship's complement was completed by the appointment of Dr George McDiarmid who had experienced northern waters in a whaling ship.

The engine and boiler were tested over two days in early May, the test being superintended by the Admiralty engineer from Portsmouth Dockyard. The results proved to be less than spectacular. At first the engines failed to hold the ship against a very modest tidal stream and an attempt to warp her forward resulted in the ship's rigging becoming entangled with another vessel's bowsprit. The following day the dockyard engineer was standing close to a safety-valve when it lifted drenching him in scalding steam. Having obtained first aid from James Ross, the man returned to his task only to see the paddle-wheels revolving at an un-inspiring seventeen revolutions per minute.

Problems with the engine and boiler did not stop a steady stream of distinguished visitors from making their way to the *Victory* at her Thames-side berth. In addition to the Duke of Orleans (the future king of France) and the marquis of Sligo, the ship was visited by Sir Thomas Byam Martin, the Controller of the Navy; the hydrographer, Captain Francis Beaufort; Captain Sir John and Lady Jane Franklin; and Captain William Parry, who regarded the expedition as having 'a better chance of succeeding than any of us' but – in referring to the ship's machinery – considered that there was 'rather too much that was new and untried'.

The Admiralty had supplied Ross with a sixteen-ton decked tender to which he gave the name *Krusenstern* in honour of the Russian explorer. He also hired a whaler – the *John* – as a supply ship intended to accompany the *Victory* as far as the entrance to Prince Regent's Inlet. To encourage her crew, and to assist in covering the costs of the expedition, Ross had promised that, once the stores had been transferred, the *John* could immediately return to its whaling role. He arranged to meet her at Loch Ryan – within sight of his house.

Painted all over (including masts and yards) in bright red, the *Victory* set sail at six o'clock in the morning on 23 May to rendezvous with the *John*. From the very beginning the ship's machinery proved to be troublesome. After proving of little help to the sails in a modest breeze, Ross had the paddle wheels raised, but the engines were kept going to help pump the bilges clear of water finding its way in through a serious leak. Before long, a piston rod required a temporary repair and a connecting key on the main shaft broke. The boiler leaked constantly and, despite applying the recommended temporary repair of packing the leak with animal dung and potatoes, the flow of water became so serious that it eventually put out the boiler fire. Delayed by stormy weather, the *Victory* reached the Isle of Man by 4 June where new shaft keys were manufactured (no spares had been held on-board). Three days later, and well on their way to Loch Ryan, the senior stoker, William Hardy, emerged from the engine room with his left arm horribly mangled and almost severed above the elbow. He had fallen against the machinery yet had managed to extricate himself and make his own way to the upper deck. With the surgeon, McDiarmid, waiting at Loch Ryan, Ross had no option but to use the surgeon's instruments to amputate Hardy's arm himself. The gruesome task completed, the injured man had to be got ashore as quickly as possible and Ross headed for Port Logan. At this point, just when speed was of the essence, the boiler joints parted and a gearwheel was stripped of all its teeth. Harbour was eventually reached the following day and Hardy was put ashore cursing to the skies that he would 'now not be able to go on the expedition'.

The wretched ship's machinery and the loss of an experienced man were soon to be seen as just part of Ross's problems. On reaching Loch Ryan, the crew of the *John* were found to be in a state of mutiny. They were convinced that the delay caused by the slow voyage of the *Victory* meant that the whaling season would almost be over by the time they parted off the entrance to Prince Regent's Inlet. Two attempts by Ross to recover the situation failed and he was mortified to see the crew of his store-ship engaging in drunken brawls within view of his own house. Eventually, the *John*'s involvement with the expedition was abandoned and the stores transferred to the *Victory* and the *Krusenstern*.

It was probably with a degree of relief that the *Victory,* with the *Krusenstern* in tow, finally left the waters of Loch Ryan on the evening of 13 June 1829. The following day a gale snapped the foremast. Undeterred, and with the mast given a temporary repair, Ross pressed on and rounded Cape Farewell on 1 July. Three weeks later they arrived at the Danish community of Holsteinsborg where, in addition to a warm welcome, they found the wreck of the whaler *Rockwood* stranded in the harbour. Ross, who had known the *Rockwood* when she had served with the Royal Navy

A contemporary cartoonist's view of John Ross's expedition. Not only has the North Pole been reached, but Ross has somehow learned of the death of King George III and the crowning of William IV.

as HMS *Rattler*, was delighted to find that her mizzen-mast was undamaged and purchased it to replace his damaged foremast.

As the seamen traded old clothes for Eskimo boots and gloves, both the Rosses tested their navigational and other scientific instruments ashore, and James Ross joined the surgeon in collecting plants. On 26 July, after attending church, Ross and his expedition sailed out of the harbour and tacked northwards to disappear amongst drifting ice floes.

Almost two years later, thirty-seven-year-old Commander George Back, placed on half-pay since his return with Franklin, was touring Italy and improving his already highly skilled talent for painting, when he heard a report that Ross and his party had perished. Believing this to be unlikely, and that Ross would have made his way to Fury Beach where he and his men could have survived on the stores piled up on the shore, Back rushed home and offered his services to lead an expedition in search of the missing Ross. A proposal of a similar nature had already been put forward by John Richardson, but it had been turned down on the grounds that Ross's expedition had not been sponsored by the government. Back's arrival, however, coincided with an attempt to raise funds by George Ross – brother of John and father of James. Before long a 'Committee for promoting the Arctic Expedition by Land' was put together under the patronage of the Duke of Sussex and the chairmanship of Vice-Admiral Sir George Cockburn. George Ross acted as secretary. The government offered £2,000 if a further £3,000 could be raised by subscription. Cockburn appealed to the public

> Shall we allow it be said of us by the rest of the world (as it assuredly will be, if we do not timely prevent it,) that we cared not for them? That we thought of their sufferings with apathy, and were indifferent to the terrors that awaited them, when it was our duty to succour them, and a trifling general subscription would enable us to do so? Let us not then become the scorn of surrounding nations, by omitting such a duty.

The plea worked and the money was raised. Back was ordered to make his way to the Great Slave Lake via New York, Montreal, and the well-established fur-trade route. He was then 'to strike off to the north-eastward, or in such other direction as you may ascertain to be most expedient, in order to gain the Thlew-ee-choh-desseth, or Great Fish River, which is believed either to issue from Slave Lake, or to rise in its vicinity, and thence to flow with a navigable course to the northward, till it reaches the sea.'

Little was known of the Great Fish River beyond a few sketchy Indian reports, and it was not known if the mouth of the river was to be found at the Polar Sea or on Hudson's Bay. It was assumed, however, to flow through the treeless barren lands. Once the river's source had been found, Back was to leave some of his party behind to build a winter base whilst he descended the river to its mouth. There he was to build a landmark with a message for Ross that he would be returning the following spring. If, on his return, nothing was heard from Ross, Back was to make his way to Fury Beach. If this failed to find Ross, Back was ordered to carry out a survey of the coast between the mouth of the Great Fish River and Point Turnagain.

To accompany him, Back would take three soldiers – Royal Artillery gunners, two of whom were Woolwich trained carpenters who would be responsible for the expedition boats – and another fifteen men who were to be obtained from Hudson's Bay Co. volunteers. As an additional 'officer' and expedition naturalist, Back agreed to take the newly-qualified Dr Richard King. The twenty-three-year-old King was the son of an employee of the Ordnance Office in the Tower of London and an ex-pupil of St Paul's School. After a seven-year apprenticeship with the Society of Apothecaries he qualified as a surgeon at Guy's Hospital, shortly afterwards becoming a member of the Royal College of Surgeons.

The party left Liverpool in the packet *Hibernia* on 17 February 1833, arriving in New York to a warm welcome from its citizens. Back (ever concerned about the funding at his disposal) was delighted when the steamboat company, in whose vessel he travelled from New York to Albany, refused all payment for their passage or for the carrying of their stores. The large canoes used to travel across lakes Huron and Superior were exchanged for smaller 'north' canoes at Fort William and King was ordered to take charge of the stores whilst Back went on ahead to make sure that no unseen difficulties slowed down their progress. The raising of men proved to be more difficult than expected and Back complained in a letter to a friend that he was 'in the midst of bustle and annoyance – hiring and persuading men to go.' He was, however, able to report in the same letter that King had proved to be 'very amiable, and will make a good voyageur.'

Fort Resolution on the Great Slave Lake was reached on 8 August. Four days later Back set off eastwards across the lake with an addition to his party in the person of Alexander McLeod, a Hudson's Bay Co. chief trader who had been promised promotion if he gave his services to the expedition. Back's plan was to take three men and an Indian guide to search for the source of the Great Fish River. Once it was found, the small party would descend it whilst McLeod took charge of the building of 'Fort Reliance' at the eastern end of the lake, and whilst King made his way to the fort with the remainder of the supplies.

By heading just east of north and crossing three lakes by light canoe, Back discovered the headwaters of the Great Fish River with little difficulty. An attempt was made to descend the river, but a series of rapids proved impassable for their light craft. Consequently, Back returned to Fort Reliance, reaching his winter base in early September. McLeod had done a good job in the short time Back had been away and the fort boasted separate accommodation for Back, King, and McLeod (who had been joined by his family), 'houses' for the men, a large 'hall' for the Indian guides, and an observatory. The winter, however, proved to be difficult with game so scarce that much of the expedition's supplies of pemmican had to be used to see them through a winter so cold that Back claimed the temperatures were lower than he had experienced on his two expeditions with Franklin. Back, nevertheless, ensured that the fort was run in an orderly fashion. He wrote

> My day is spent chiefly thus – before breakfast I read a portion of scripture, and afterwards attend to my observations, study, draw, (I have plenty of pencil sketches,) work up my survey, take notes on Aurora, etc. At the same time I have my eye on whatever duty is going on, have an evening school twice a week, and read the service in French and English every Sunday.

Not everything went as smoothly as hoped:

> My guitar is cracked, and jars abominably.

The arrival of late spring brought more than just the chance to prepare for the forthcoming descent of the Great Fish River. It also brought a messenger racing across the ice of the lake. On 30 April, Back read a letter dispatched six months earlier from Admiral Sir Charles Ogle who had taken over as chairman of the Land Expedition Committee from Cockburn. From its contents, Back learned to his astonishment and delight that Ross and his party had arrived safely back in England.

Just before midday on 26 August – four and a half years after Ross had disappeared into the Arctic – his old ship, the *Isabella*, was under full sail off the southern shore of Lancaster Sound when the wind dropped. As the sails hung empty and the crew idly scanned the sea around them, one of them spotted three small boats heading their way. A boat was launched from the *Isabella* in response and, as it came up alongside the leading boat, a voice was heard shouting a request for the name of the ship. The mate shouted back 'The *Isabella* of Hull, once commanded by Captain Ross.' In reply, the stranger stated that he was, indeed, that same Captain Ross – only to have the mate assure him that he could not be, as Captain Ross had been dead for two years. But Captain Ross it was.

On leaving Holsteinsborg, Ross had found that the feared 'middle ice' did not exist that year and he was able to make passage directly for Lancaster Sound – the scene of his declared 'Croker's Mountains' and the cause of his subsequent humiliation at the hand of John Barrow. The Sound was entered on 7 August and, five days later, the bow of the *Victory* was pointing southwards down Prince Regent's Inlet. An anchorage was found five miles south of Fury Beach on the same day as the duchess of Clarence's birthday and consequently named Adelaide Harbour in her honour. Both the Rosses,

Thom, and the surgeon were taken by boat beneath the towering limestone cliffs until James Ross – who had been serving as a lieutenant in the *Fury* when she grounded – recognised a landmark leading to the site. On arrival they found that polar bears had wrecked the tents but the contents; sugar, bread, cocoa, tinned meat, vegetables, wines, and spirits all remained in perfect condition. A neat pile of sails also appeared to be undamaged as were several barrels of gunpowder, but of the ship itself, not a trace remained. Ross burned off the gunpowder for fear that, if it fell into the hands of the Eskimos, it was liable to cause the natives injury or even loss of life. The *Victory* was then packed as tightly as possible with enough stores to extend Ross's victualling supplies by almost three years. Ten tons of the *Fury*'s coal was picked up from the beach and some of the sails taken to be used as tents and awnings.

The anchor was weighed on 14 August and, two days later, a landing was made at 'Possession Point' where formal possession of the land was made in the name of the king. The bay in which the landing was made was named 'Brentford Bay' and the name 'Felix Boothia' (Boothia Peninsula) was given to the whole of the land in honour of the expedition's main sponsor. From a nearby high point, Ross noted what appeared to be 'the entrance to a great inlet' but decided not to investigate the possibility further.

So far, the expedition had found little trouble from ice but, three days after leaving Brentford Bay, the *Victory* found herself beset and unable to break free. The ice, however, was, in the beginning, drifting south and, when the direction of drift changed to the north, Ross moored the ship alongside a grounded ice floe. The following day the ice opened up and Ross resorted to his, by now, utterly despised engine and paddles to take him on a slow cruise to an anchorage Ross named 'Port Logan'. Heavy weather held them in the harbour for a few days before they could make their way still further south to another anchorage Ross named 'Elizabeth Harbour' after Booth's sister. On 25 September, a small island was sighted and named 'Andrew Ross Island' for John Ross's son. Two islands to the east were named 'Hecla and Fury Island' as they were on the same latitude as Parry's strait, and a further island was named Isabella Louisa in honour of Parry's wife.

With the approach of winter it was important that a secure anchorage should be obtained. Just such a site was found at a point on the coast south of Elizabeth Harbour. 'Felix Harbour' was about 150 miles south of Parry's furthest point and was a sheltered anchorage in a wide bay Ross named 'Lord Mayor Bay' – both names being further gratitude to the expedition's sponsor. The two ships were cut into the ice and stationed with their bows to the north. The topmasts were taken down, the boats were landed, and the upper deck roofed by an enclosed canvas awning. Around the ships' sides a wall of snow was built for added insulation and an observatory was built ashore.

On his arrival at Felix Harbour, Ross took action on a decision he may have made some time before. The engine and boiler that had given so much trouble and had provided very little advantage had to go. He gave orders that the machinery was to be removed and placed ashore – from that moment on, the *Victory* was to be solely a sailing ship. The extra room gained by the equipment's removal was turned over to the men as extra accommodation space.

The crew was formed into five watches (i.e. four hours on watch with sixteen hours off) and a working day from six o'clock in the morning to nine o'clock in the evening was introduced. Dinner was served at noon and compulsory exercise had to be taken by walking around the upper deck in the late afternoon. Between six o'clock and nine o'clock in the evening, a voluntary school taught reading, writing, mathematics and navigation. On Sundays, the ship and men were inspected and, after prayers and a sermon, religious tracts donated by a Mrs Enderby were made available. An evening Sunday school at which psalms were sung and the scriptures read completed the day of rest. Ross was convinced that such a rigid attention to religious duties brought about 'mutual kindness, with a regularity and tranquillity of behaviour which are not very general on board of a ship.'

On 9 January 1830, the duty lookout at the observatory announced that a group of about thirty Eskimos was approaching. Armed with guns, both the Rosses, McDaimid, and a few men went out to meet the visitors. When the natives were seen to be carrying only knives, Ross ordered the guns to be ostentatiously cast aside. The Eskimos responded by throwing away their weapons and, before long, a friendly rapport had been established between the two communities. Gifts of iron hoop were handed over and arrangements were made for the officers to visit the native village the following day. This proved to consist of eighteen igloos housing near a hundred people – the women, in particular, delighted with gifts of beads and needles. Eight of the native leaders paid a return visit to the *Victory* and the growing friendship underlined by the gift of a wooden leg to an Eskimo who had lost a limb in an encounter with a polar bear. The natives responded by sketching a map of the region on which was recognised Repulse Bay and Akkoolee. It also showed a large gulf between Akkoolee and Felix Harbour and an exciting narrowing of Boothia Felix to the south that might just have been a waterway to the west.

James Maslin, the armourer, who had been suffering from tuberculosis since before his departure from Britain, died on 20 January and was buried ashore.

During March, James Ross spent time learning the art of sledging with dogs from the natives and, on 5 April, set off westwards with the mate, Thomas Blanky, and two natives with ten day's rations. They soon found the dogs preferred to attempt to eat the sledges (which were made of frozen Arctic char – a fish similar to salmon) than to pull them. After three days, they arrived at a frozen sea which the natives explained was clear of ice during the summer. To the south, the Eskimos further informed them, there was only land and, if the ships were to reach the sea on which they gazed, they would have to return northwards as there was no passage to the south.

They also indicated the existence of a large island to the west. Returning by the route over which they had set out, one of the Eskimos suffered from snow-blindness and had to be carried on a sledge as the two naval men walked alongside.

Despite the assurances that there was no west-leading waterway to the south, James Ross and Blanky set off on 21 April with seven days rations to see for themselves. They were back the following day having discovered little more than a melt-water stream. The natives had been right all along – there was no water passage to the west across the narrow neck of Felix Boothia.

It was now time to have a look to the north. James Ross was particularly keen to have a closer look at the ice-blocked 'great inlet' which his uncle had noted on their way south. With him, Ross took the mate Abernathy and two Eskimo guides. They reached a point about forty miles from the ship before they had to turn back due to both time and the ice conditions. On the return journey Ross impressed the natives by shooting a musk ox and picking off a brace of ptarmigan in flight. He, in turn, was impressed by the Eskimo's ability to slice off the raw meat and devour it in great mouthfuls.

In mid-May, James Ross set off once again, this time returning to the west. As his journey was expected to take longer than his previous expeditions, his uncle arranged to lead out sledges of his own in order to leave depots of supplies for the return journey. Taking Abernathy and three other men with him, Ross travelled by

Victory *in Felix Harbour.*

Ross's first contact with the Boothia Felix Eskimos. The weapons have been left on the ground as the two groups meet.

night to reach the frozen sea. After a probe to the south which revealed a chain of lakes extending north-eastwards across the peninsular, he returned to a point where he could strike out westwards across the ice (James Ross Strait). Fifteen miles of sledging brought the party to the northern tip of an island. Ross took possession of the land using a silk flag that had been donated to the expedition by the ladies of the Matty family. He consequently named the island in their honour before continuing westwards where he fell in with the low shores of a coast trending to the north-west. The shore was followed for about eighty miles until it turned sharply south-west around a low cape that Ross named 'Cape Felix'. By now convinced that the coast was part of the North America continent and would eventually link up with the shores travelled by Franklin, Ross named the ground on which he was walking 'King William Land'. He pressed on for a further thirty miles until he reached a point where he was in danger of reducing his supplies (already reduced to half-rations) beyond that need to get him back to the first return depot being established by his uncle. Leaving the three men to set up camp, Ross and Abernathy pressed on for a further hour until, on climbing a slight rise, they saw before them a large bay interrupted to the south by an elevated promontory. This was to be the furthest extent of his expedition and he and Abernathy built a small pillar of rocks to mark the event, naming the spot 'Victory Point'. He named the bay after his friend George Back, the promontory was honoured with the name 'Cape Jane Franklin' whilst the lady's husband was equally honoured by having the farthest edge of the bay as it curved south and west named 'Franklin Point' – an eminently suitable name with Cape Turnagain being no more than 220 miles to the south-west.

Ross returned to the west coast of Felix Boothia by passing to the south of Matty Island. As he did so he searched the horizon to the south and south-east 'but a thin haze covered the land which prevented me from tracing it very distinctly to the south-eastward.' Ross was assuming that, to his south, the eastern shores of King William Land linked up with the coast of Felix Boothia and that he was crossing a large bay, an idea supported by the Eskimos. Despite finding that natives had eaten the contents of his return depots (which the natives replaced with fish) Ross reached the *Victory* safely after being absent from the ship for twenty-three days.

With the season well into June, the time had come to prepare the ships to leave Felix Harbour and to head north to examine closely the coast down which they had come the previous year. But the ice proved agonisingly slow in clearing and no open water could be seen out to the east. When, in early August, the ice did begin to move, constant northern winds drove the floating ice into the bay. The little *Krusenstern* was able to break out but, after a month waiting for the conditions to improve, Ross ordered the *Victory* to be unloaded and had her warped northwards for four miles. It was a most difficult and dangerous task that saw the vessel frequently grounding and being placed at risk from drifting ice. By the end of September, it was clear that no amount of effort was going to extricate them from their situation. Ross mustered his men and told them that they must expect to spend another winter on the coast of Felix Boothia.

All of October was spent in cutting the ships into the shelter of the newly named 'Sheriff's Harbour'. John Ross noted that he blamed his nephew for their predicament. He had suggested an earlier attempt to move slowly up the coast, but James Ross had assured him that the ice would clear and enable an easy departure.

By the middle of November the vessels were secured for the winter. The routine of the previous year was re-introduced, but the Eskimos failed to put in an appearance. In general, the health of the men remained good. Ross, nevertheless, was keen that they should try to get used to 'Greenland food' for he firmly believed that the consumption of large amounts of oil and fat – such as was normal among the natives – would be the 'true secret of life in these frozen countries.' There is little evidence that his seamen shared his belief.

Once again spring arrived late, and it was not until April that James Ross could set off on a further sledge journey to the north in search of the supposed waterway across the peninsular. Plunging temperatures and storms cut the journey short and, on their return, the mate, James Taylor, suffered serious frostbite to one of his feet. Speed was now of the essence, but their rate of travel was severely reduced by a six-mile wide barrier of ice ridges that took twelve hours to cross with Taylor strapped to the sledge. Ross then decided to press on alone to get help and covered the remaining twenty miles in nine hours. When rescued, Taylor had to have part of his foot amputated.

Victory finally stopped by the ice.

Both the Rosses set off on a sledge journey in mid-May. John Ross went to have a look at the lakes James had seen stretching across the peninsular the previous June. One of the lakes he named 'Krusenstern', another was named after Admiral Saumarez – a friend who, unbeknown to Ross, would soon be serving on the committee raising funds for the expedition's rescue.

James Ross, in the meantime, headed westwards once again. Having achieved the western sea, Ross turned north and followed the coast towards his target – the north magnetic pole. The spot – 70 degrees 5' 17" north; 96 degrees 46' 45" west – was reached at eight o'clock in the morning on 1 June 1831. A giant cairn was built on the spot and a message buried beneath it. The moment was completed when Ross unfurled the Union Flag and took possession of the magnetic north pole in the name of Great Britain and the king (who, unknown to Ross, was now William IV). A return journey of twelve days brought them back to the ship 'excepting petty grievances, all in good health.'

There was little else to do but to wait for the break-up of the ice and their escape from the anchorage. August was almost finished before the ice began to drift out of the bay. Four miles was achieved before, in avoiding an iceberg, the ship grounded and the rudder was broken. The following day, a further ten or eleven miles was achieved before the ice forced them into an anchorage (Victory Harbour, later 'Victoria Harbour'). For a month they waited expectantly for a break in the ice that would allow them further progress but, by the beginning of October, they had given up hope and the ships were prepared for a third winter in the Arctic. The tedium was beginning to tell, and Ross noted 'To-day was as yesterday, and as was to-day, so would be to-morrow.' Christmas was celebrated with a round of beef that had been part of the *Fury*'s stores for eight years even before it found its way onto Fury Beach.

The new year, 1832, had hardly opened before one of the seamen, James Dixon, died of dropsy and another, Andrew Buck, began having fits and went blind. The mate, Taylor, was crippled, one of John Ross's old wounds began to open up, and the effects of scurvy began to be seen. With limited provisions available, and with the threat of the expedition falling apart around him, Ross came to the conclusion that their only hope lay in abandoning the ships and striking out northwards in the hope of meeting up with the whaling fleet.

Ross planned to get his men to Fury Beach and use the boats left there to get up to Barrow Strait but, just in case the boats turned out to be unusable, he arranged for two of the *Victory*'s boats to be placed on sledges and, under his command, twelve men dragged them eighteen miles north of Victory Harbour. When exhaustion brought on the need for rest, a trench was dug in the snow, canvas was laid across and covered with snow, and the men crouched beneath, huddled together for warmth. On the return of the boat party, both Rosses set out with ten men and 2,000lb of provisions in the same direction. When the boats were reached, both they and the stores were relayed forward another twelve miles (Ross calculated that they had needed to travel 329 miles to get the boats and stores thirty miles from the ship).

The *Victory* and the *Krusenstern* were formally abandoned on 29 May. The ensign was nailed to the mast, a toast was drunk, and Ross said goodbye to 'an old friend'. He now planned to haul the two ship's boats as far as Elizabeth Harbour. From there he intended that the party would press on with half the rations to a point where a small party could be sent on to Fury Beach. The difficult terrain, however, severely tested the men to such a degree that – with sixteen miles still to go – the mate, Blanky, approached Ross with the request that the boats and spare provisions could be abandoned and the party be allowed to head straight for Fury Beach. Ross let his temper get the better of him and Blanky was reprimanded 'for the extreme impropriety of his conduct' and the men were told to proceed 'in a manner not easily misunderstood, and by an argument too peremptory to be disputed'. Clearly, Ross was determined not to lose his grip on the situation.

Elizabeth Harbour was reached six days later and, on the following morning, the entire party set off with three sledges loaded with stores and provisions for three weeks. On the 12th, with Fury Beach 150 miles to the north, James Ross, Abernathy and a seaman, John Park, headed off with a light sledge as an advanced party. The three men crossed the ice of Brentford Bay in a light mist which prevented Ross from investigating the possible 'great inlet' his uncle had noted on the way south. Arriving at Fury Beach, Ross found that three of the *Fury*'s boats had survived, a

Ross ordering the ensign to be nailed to the mast before abandoning the Victory.

welcome discovery as it now meant that the boats they had hauled as far as Elizabeth Harbour could be abandoned. He returned to join his uncle and inform him of the situation and learned that John Ross had made a cursory investigation of the 'great inlet' and had come to the conclusion that the only eastern outlets were a number of rivers 'there was no opening, or passage to the western sea at this place'.

The last of the party reached Fury Beach on 1 July and Ross immediately set about building secure accommodation. Using timber and the *Fury's* sails a large tent-like structure – 31ft by 16ft and 7ft high – was built within twenty-four hours of their arrival and named 'Somerset House' in recognition of Parry's name for the land – North Somerset. The carpenters then turned their attention to the boats and prepared them for the voyage northwards. A month to the day after their arrival, the ice cleared from the shore and the entire party, with three boats under the command of the two Rosses and Thom, set sail with provisions for six weeks. By that evening, they found themselves beneath the precipitous cliffs where the *Fury* had been wrecked eight years earlier – and similarly under threat from the advancing ice. In great haste the boats were hauled up the rocky beach and Ross found himself trapped for six days before a gap in the ice allowed him to proceed a mere two miles further before being forced ashore once again. With the ice to the north stretching unbroken to the horizon it was clear they were to be held at that spot for some time so Ross sent Thom back with one boat to bring up more supplies from Fury Beach.

It was to be almost three weeks after their stranding before a westerly wind forced the ice from the shore, opening a wide lane of water allowing progress to the north. Four days later they had reached a point eight miles south of Cape Clarence and Ross made an attempt to cross the forty-mile wide mouth of Prince Regent's inlet to reach Cape York. Frustrated by the ice, he had to settle for the Leopold Islands just off Cape Clarence. From a high point he could see Barrow Strait, Lancaster Sound, and Prince Regent's inlet. But to his, and his party's, deep disappointment, all he could see was 'one vast solid and unbroken mass of ice'.

It did not take long to come to the conclusion that there was no other option available but to return to Fury Beach. Due to the ice conditions, the boats could be used for only part of the journey. At Batty Bay, after being forced to cut their way through the ice, they hauled the boats out of the water and built sledges from the staves of the bread casks. Supplementing their rations with a few foxes and ptarmigans, they took six days to cover the thirty-two miles to Fury Beach, their progress being slowed down by the crippled mate, Taylor, who had to be carried for most of the way on a sledge.

On their arrival, Somerset House was covered in blocks of snow to prepare it for the approaching winter – the party's fourth in the Arctic. Thanks to the still abundant stores remaining stacked on the beach there was no shortage of food. Only meat and alcohol proved to be in short supply and Christmas was celebrated with roasted Arctic fox washed down with water.

The forty-eight-year-old senior carpenter, Chimham Thomas, died of scurvy in February. Two other men showed symptoms of the disease and John Ross's old wounds were giving him some trouble (he was now aged fifty-five). The situation was not help by the sheer lack of any activity, and Ross noted that those with 'the enviable talent of sleeping at all times, whether anxious or not, fared best.'

Towards the end of April, 1833, under the direction of James Ross, the fittest of the men relayed supplies across the sea ice to Batty Bay. The boats – which had remained in good condition – were caulked and prepared once again for the journey north. For the second time, Somerset House was abandoned and the party, carrying and dragging its sick, reached the boats on 12 July only to find that the ice remained as solid as ever. It was to be a frustrating further four weeks before an open lane appeared leading to the north. In the early hours of the morning all those who could, turned out to hack a passage through the ice to reach the open water. Within four hours they were under sail and, just thirty- six hours later, they were at the same point where they had been forced to return the previous year. On 17 August, first by pulling on the oars, then under sail, Prince Regent's Inlet was crossed and a landing on a beach west of Cape York. In the twenty hours since they had set out that morning, they had travelled over seventy miles. A number of gales impeded their further progress but, mainly by the use of their oars, they passed Admiralty Inlet and reached the shores just west of Navy Board Inlet late on the 25th. At four o'clock in the morning the following day, the lookout, a seaman named David Wood, shouted that he could see a sail. Using his telescope James Ross confirmed the sighting and the boats were launched amidst a cloud of signal smoke produced by burning wet gunpowder. The party pulled hard towards the ship only to see it disappear before a strengthening breeze. Two hours later another ship appeared in view but, it too, looked as if it was about to leave. But, to their utter relief, the wind fell and Ross and his party saw a boat being lowered and pulled towards them. It was the *Isabella* – Ross had been saved by his old ship after four and a half years in the Arctic.

Wearing seal-skin trousers beneath his faded naval uniform coat, Ross arrived at the Humber port of Kingston Upon Hull on 18 October to a hero's welcome. Flags flew from all the port's vessels, bells rang out, and the mayor, aldermen, wardens and brethren of Trinity House, along with members of the local Philosophical Society, all queued to shake his hand. A public dinner was provided at the Vittoria Hotel in his honour at which he was granted the freedom of the city (a precedence soon to be followed by London, Liverpool, Bristol and Wicklow). The following day he, in company with James Ross, reported to the Admiralty and was honoured the next morning by an audience with the king. William IV – known, amongst other things, as 'Sailor Bill' from his long service in the Royal Navy – was delighted to accept the

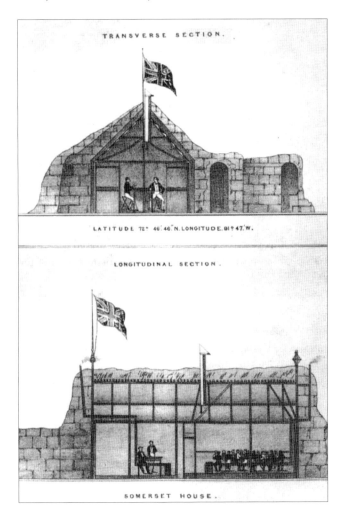

Ross's 'Somerset House' on Fury Beach.

Union Flag that had been flown at the north magnetic pole and granted permission for his name to be applied to the land claimed by James Ross.

Before long, John Ross's knighthood was announced along with his gazetting as a Companion of the Order of the Bath (the restrictions denying Franklin the order having been relaxed). His arms were to carry the top portion of the globe with the motto *Arctaeos Numine Fines* ('The Limits of the North') beneath a crest bearing a Union Flag which bore the date '1 June 1831' flying above a dip-circle whose needle pointed vertically downwards. Honours and awards also poured in from Prussia, Sweden, France, Russia, Belgium and Denmark. At Leicester Square a great panorama was painted for exhibition to the public, 4,000 letters of congratulation were received, and the poetess, Sibella Elizabeth Hatfield, celebrated his return with verses such as:

All, all, but that most noble boast,
So well by manly daring earn'd;
All but the thoughts of Ross, long lost,
And *ROSS TO ENGLAND SAFE RETURNED!*

Despite, however, the blaze of tributes, Ross's head was not entirely turned and he was soon persuading the Admiralty to give his men full-pay for the whole four and a half year they were away instead of the mere fifteen months wages they had been contracted to receive. He then embarked on a bitter pamphlet war against the suppliers of the machinery which he had abandoned on the shores of Boothia Felix.

James Ross was appointed to Nelson's old flagship, HMS *Victory,* in order to complete the service time required for his promotion to captain. William Thom was appointed as purser to HMS *Canopus*, an eighty-gun third rate that had been captured by Nelson at the Battle of the Nile – by a strange twist of fate her name in the French navy had been *Franklin* (albeit after the American scientist-diplomat, Benjamin). McDairmid, the expedition's doctor, was awarded the rank of assistant surgeon. The remaining men were all taken into the Royal Navy with those having previous service being promoted.

In the meantime, Back was still at Fort Reliance, on the eastern shore of the Great Slave Lake. When news reached him of Ross's escape, Back was able to concentrate on the second part of his instructions. He was to descend the Great Fish River and, from its mouth, survey the coast as far as Franklin's Point Turnagain. Back was immediately faced with a problem. He knew that canoes were probably the best means of travel on the river, if for no better reason than that they were easily carried around possible stretches of rapids, but his own experience told him that such canoes – particularly in the hands of unskilled artillerymen and voyageurs – placed his party at much greater risk when on the far rougher waters of the Polar Sea. Accordingly, he chose to have his carpenters prepare one of the two strongly built boats he had brought with him. Weighing a ton and a half and with a length of 30ft, the single boat could easily accommodate the two officers, two Metis translator-guides, three Hudson's Bay Co. men, and three Royal Artillery gunners. Unfortunately, between them, the eleven men could not lift the boat.

Back and his party set off down the river on 4 July 1834. His progress was repeatedly hampered by rapids (eighty-three in total) which the boat had to be forced through. Numerous broad lakes were encountered, all requiring a search for the river's outlet. At one stage, it seemed that the boat was condemned to defeat them when they came across a series of rapids so violent that they could have caused serious damage to the craft. By extraordinary good fortune, there appeared on the scene, a tribe of Indians who cheerfully gathered around and hauled the boat past

Ross rescued by the Isabella.

the hazard. After twenty-five days and a voyage of 230 miles through 'an iron-ribbed country without a single tree on the whole line of its banks' Back found himself tasting salt-water as the river emerged into a wide inlet (Chantry Inlet).

Hampered by ice, Back worked his way along the flat, western shore of the inlet as a series of headlands loomed up to the east backed by a range of hills. At what appeared to be the most northerly of these headlands (Cape Hay), the coast trended towards the east. In order to confirm this, Back climbed a small hill he had named 'Mount Barrow'. To the north-west, Back saw a stretch of open water with land on the far side that continued across his northern front. To the east lay a wide expanse of water. The only barrier between the two stretches of water was 500 yards of solid ice which Back could clearly see would prevent his passage to the west. He came to the conclusion that the open water to the north-west was, in all probability, a strait between the land on which he stood, and the land to the north which, (from the copy of Ross's chart that he had been sent along with his new orders) seemed clearly to be part of King William Land. To the east he seemed to be looking at a strong possibility of a waterway linking with the bottom of Prince Regent's Sound, thus making Boothia Felix an island. And what about King William Land? Despite James Ross's opinion (supported by the Eskimos) that he had been crossing a bay when he sledged between King William Land and Boothia Felix, it was now clear that there was a considerable body of water to the south. This did not exclude the possibility that there was a narrow isthmus linking the two which was beyond Back's field of vision. However, he was in no position to confirm any of the possibilities that lay open to his investigation. His fuel and food was beginning to run dangerously low and there was no chance of getting his heavy boat across the ice barrier that prevented his reaching the open waters to the west.

It was at this stage that matters took a serious turn. From Mount Barrow, Back had seen land far to the north-north-east and reckoned it to be an island. King, however, felt that the land was part of a mainland. For a third opinion, Back sent his three artillerymen to have a look. What happened to this party was only reported on their return, and then only in sketchy detail. Whilst away from Back and King the three men fell in with a party of Eskimos and an altercation took place ending with three of the natives dead. None of this was mentioned to the officers. Two of the men agreed with King that that the land to the north-west was part of a coast – thus increasing the likelihood that the eastern open water was a wide bay. King was eager to examine the situation more closely, but Back was conscious of the fact that he was, by now, very low on supplies, and that a marked depression had descended on some of his men on their return from Mount Barrow. It also seemed strange to him that, whilst Eskimos were seen, they remained far off, thus thwarting any hopes he may have had of gaining their aid in getting the boat across the ice barrier. With his orders telling him to begin his return journey between 12 and 20 August, he mustered his men for the voyage up the Great Fish River on the 15th. They did not leave until King had built a cairn containing a cache of supplies on Montreal Island. He intended to return and conduct a wider search of the area.

On his return to England in August 1835, Back's report meant different things to different people. Sir John Barrow – newly knighted, still at the Admiralty, and smarting over the fact that he had been forced to write a congratulatory letter to Ross on his return, gleefully announced that Ross's declaration that Felix Boothia was a peninsular was 'humbug'. Ross himself, used Back's information to snipe at his nephew by stating that James Ross's idea that there was a bay south of Matty Island, linking the coast of Felix Boothia with King William Land, was 'incorrect'. If so, there was a strong possibility that King William Land was, in fact, King William *Island*. James Ross argued that he had only used a dotted line to delineate the southern shore of the supposed bay on his chart, and he now believed that the west coast of King William Land was probably connected to the western coast of Chantry Inlet (despite such an isthmus not having been seen by Back), thus including the inlet in the bay the Eskimos had told him about.

On his return, some weeks after Back, King revealed his lack of experience in dealing with people by criticising Back for being too friendly with his men, for delegating too many of the expeditionary tasks to King himself, and for leaving the area too quickly. Even worse, for someone with ambitions to return to the river, he even took pains to criticise the Hudson's Bay Co. Needless to say, when King tried to raise support and funds for his own proposed expedition, the response caused him to retreat to a medical practice in London.

In the meantime, Back had been promoted to captain by a special order-in-council (an honour previously only awarded to the future King William IV) as a reward for his endeavours, and the Great Fish River was re-named the 'Back River'.

In December 1835, James Ross, who had received his promotion to captain a year earlier, was working on a magnetic survey of the British Isles with Edward Sabine when he was asked by Parry if he would take a ship into Baffin Bay to supply eleven whaling vessels trapped in Davies Straits. Also on-board the whalers were men from ships that had been 'nipped' (crushed) by the ice. Among the ships that had been lost was the *Isabella*.

Ross immediately accepted and, authorised by the Admiralty, went to Hull and selected for his first command the thirty-seven-year-old, 280-ton *Cove*. She was straightaway commissioned as HMS *Cove*, manned by volunteers, and prepared for her voyage by her new master – Captain Humphreys who, as captain of the *Isabella*, had rescued John Ross and his party in August, 1833. As his first lieutenant, Ross selected Francis Crozier with whom he had served in Parry's *Hecla*. The newly promoted Lieutenant Erasmus Ommanney was also appointed. Henry Mapleton entered as second master, and the quartermaster's position went to James Sefton who had served with Parry on three Arctic voyages. Among the volunteers unable to go was Captain George Back.

Ross's instructions were to make his way to the edge of the ice where he could expect to pick up any men forced to abandon their ships, and then to proceed to the Danish settlements to see if any survivors had made their way there. In the meantime, HMS *Terror* and HMS *Erebus* – two bomb vessels – were being fitted out and strengthened at Chatham and Portsmouth respectively. The *Terror* had already been commissioned under the command of Commander Edward Belcher. These two ships would join Ross in March. However, even as Ross sailed from Hull he was receiving reports of several of the trapped ships being freed and arriving at their home ports. By the time he arrived at Stromness, the Admiralty informed him that it was now unlikely that both of the supporting ships would be sent out to join him.

The *Cove* sailed on 11 January 1836, and forced her way through severe gales for the next two weeks. Then, on the 28th, whilst fighting the worst seas she had encountered since leaving port, she was hit on the starboard bow by a huge wave that wrenched away her bowsprit and split the stem open. Most of the ship's company, including the master (who had lashed himself to the rigging), thought that the ship had been forced so far over that she would never recover. Ross, however, 'cooly' gave orders and brought the ship about. His calm action made him 'perfectly idolized' by everyone on-board. Unfortunately, the ship was so badly damaged that he was forced to return to Stromness to carry out repairs. Whilst this was being put under way more of the previously trapped ships arrived at the port. Soon it became clear that all that remained was one ship missing and another still locked in the ice.

Ross was able to sail on 24 February and, after another rough passage, arrived at the ice in early April. Five weeks were spent scouring the ice edge before he learned from a passing whaler that the missing ship had returned safely – only the Hull-based *William Torr*, last seen trapped in the ice, was left to be found. After 100 days at sea, the coast of Baffin Island was seen and Ross crossed the Davis Strait to Holsteinborg where he expected to find the *Erebus* and *Terror*, or at least one of them. Neither ships were in harbour so he sailed north to the Whalefish Islands where he learned from a whaling captain that it had been decided not to send either of the supporting ships. From another whaler, he received new Admiralty orders confirming the cancelled sailings and telling him to return home once he had considered he had done all that he could to find the lost ship. A final cruise to the north (where he came across a fleet of fifty whaling ships held up by the ice) and a final sweep along the ice edge completed the search, The *Cove* returned to Hull on 31 August. Some years later it was learned that the *William Torr* had been nipped as Ross sailed from Hull. Twenty-two of her crew had died whilst being cared for by Eskimos, and the captain had taken the remaining men over the ice to where he believed a whaling ship would be found. None were ever seen again.

Whilst the voyage had achieved little, Ross had proved to be a resolute captain and skilled seaman. His work had also established a good working relationship between the Royal Navy and the whaling fleet. He was offered a knighthood for his efforts but turned it down, later explaining that he did not want to run the risk of being confused with his uncle, Captain Sir John Ross. Crozier was promoted to commander.

With the return of Back from the Great Fish River, the Royal Geographical Society in concert with the hydrographer to the navy, Captain Beaufort, urged the government to launch another expedition to try and finally settle the problem of the insularity, or otherwise, of Boothia Felix and King William Land. The Admiralty was not averse to the idea and, when it became clear that the *Terror* was not to be required in support of James Ross's Baffin Bay rescue mission, Back was offered command with the instructions to enter Hudson's Bay, make his way to either Wager River or Repulse Bay and, taking boats with him, cross the Melville Peninsular to the shores of the Gulf of Boothia. From there one party was to explore the coasts of the gulf whilst a second party was to head westwards to the mouth of the Back River using the seaway if Boothia Felix was, in fact, an island, or by crossing the land if it proved to be a peninsular. From the Back River they were to continue to Point Turnagain and then on to 'cross the strait which is supposed to separate America from the islands to the north, tracing the shore to the furthest point of James Ross's discovery (i.e. Victory Point)'.

Back's first lieutenant was William Smyth who had made a name for himself by crossing the Andes and canoeing down the Amazon. The other lieutenants were Owen Stanley, the son of the bishop of Norwich and whose cousin, Isabella, had married Parry (Stanley had also served under Franklin), and Archibald McMurdo who had earned his early promotion by rescuing the crew of a whaler from the clutches of New Zealand Maoris. Among the mates were Robert McLure and Graham Gore. The master was James Saunders.

Supplies for eighteen months were crammed into the ship. Messrs Donkin and Gamble provided tinned meat, pigs and sheep were housed on the forecastle, and almost 6,000lb of pemmican were stored below decks ready for use with the expeditions. Long fur-lined pea-jackets made of thick, closely woven, boxcloth were supplied to go over trousers of the same material. Fur caps, bear-skin blankets, woollen clothing, leather boots, and thick socks provided extra protection against the coming cold. A newly designed heating system consisting of a furnace, pump, and pipes had been installed to keep the inside of the ship warm and dry.

Back sailed in the newly strengthened *Terror* in June 1836, and passed through Hudson's Straits on 1 August. The ice was met the following day but a passage leading to the north remained open. Taking this route enabled the *Terror* to arrive safely off the northern shore of Southampton Island and within two days sailing of their destination, Repulse Bay. Easterly winds, however, brought the ice and, before long, the ship was surrounded and trapped. Helpless in the ice, the *Terror*, drifted westwards beneath the imposing cliffs of Cape Comfort. On 20 September, a storm sent huge masses of ice against the ship's sides causing several of the ship's fastenings to spring from their housings and the rudder to be badly damaged. A week later they were within ninety miles of Repulse Bay when the ice closed firmly around the ship and lifted her stern 7½ft out of the water. The pressure caused the main beams to crack, and Back had the ship's boats prepared for lowering. Suddenly a loud crackling noise was heard and the ice fell away from the ship, revealing an imprint of her sides pressed into its dazzling whiteness. Back had any remaining ice hacked away and the now useless rudder unshipped. The *Terror* had suffered serious damage and the officers began to sleep with their cabin doors open for ease of escape.

At the beginning of October, open water was seen along the shore. The entire ship's company rushed out onto the ice to try and cut a channel to reach it, but so thick was the ice that all the effort was in vain. In consultation with his officers, Back decided that their best chance lay in preparing the ship for a winter locked into the ice. He gave order for a dock to be cut into the surrounding ice floe but, just as the saws were being prepared, the floe split and a driving wind forced the shattered ice against the ship. A large floe reared up at the ship's bow and, in falling, not only lifted the stern again, but cracked the stem post and sprung the bowsprit. In this position, with her stern raised, the ice froze the *Terror* again into its rigid grip. If the ice floe was to crack again, they would be at the mercy of the driving ramparts of ice; if they remained locked in, there was not only the risk of the ship being slowly squeezed by enormous pressure, but they would be forced to drift at the whim of the ice – and the northern shore of Southampton Island was little more than a few miles distant. No ship would survive being forced onto that rocky coast. There was little that Back could do – so he ordered that a theatre should be organised to take his men's minds off their plight. He found enough to occupy himself by trying to raise the temperature inside the ship after the heating system broke down. Not only was the temperature in the mess decks and cabins constantly below freezing point, but condensation was so bad that all clothing and bedding was perpetually sodden. Eventually, heaters from the ship's boats were brought on-board; an adaptation which successfully raised the temperature, but caused the ship to fill with suffocating smoke. After considerable experimentation a canvas tube was installed to the outside which allowed the smoke to clear and the conditions inside the ship to attain a modest degree of comfort. In thus manner 'we drifted to and fro off the high land of Cape Comfort; at times carried so close to the rocks as to excite alarm for the safety of the ship.'

Christmas was marred by the first signs of scurvy. Within days the disease had claimed its first victim. Graham Walker, a seaman, died in early January. A hole was cut in the ice for the sea to receive his body, but the funeral became a grisly affair when, after the corpse was lowered into the water, it refused to sink. A cannonball had to be hastily brought from the ship and used as a weight before the body reluctantly disappeared.

The close proximity of the shore allowed several minor expeditions to be made and Lieutenant Stanley carried out a survey of the previously uncharted coastline. None of the visits ashore produced the slightest evidence of any form of life, human or animal. From the heights nothing could be seen but ice, wisps of 'frost-smoke', and the masts of the *Terror* rising out of her icy prison.

On 18 February 1837, the ice began to split apart and 30ft-high ridges began to bear down upon the ship 'which complained much'. The shocks of the ice striking her caused the decks to split and deck-beams to lift from their bases. Lashings parted, bolts began to withdraw, and boxes of stores – used to support the decks – collapsed. So severe were the blows to the ship that men were frequently knocked off their feet. A month later the elements tried again. The sternpost was smashed and the stern plunged as the bows were lifted out of the water and deposited on an ice floe. Water poured in through the stern-frame as the ship listed to starboard, and the ship's company spent the night in full expectation of having to abandon the ship in temperatures that froze both brandy and mercury. Yet again, however, the ice froze around them and, with the *Terror* twisted and strained, the eastward drift continued. By May, Southampton Island was cleared and Cape Wolstenholme, the south-west corner of Hudson's Strait, was in sight at the end of June.

Top: *The ship's company of HMS* Terror *attempting to cut a channel to open water.*

Above left: *Captain George Back.*

Above right: *The* Terror *in the grip of the ice.*

Two more deaths occurred from scurvy and the officers tried to grow shoots from dried peas to feed to the sick. The pemmican that had been intended for the exploring parties was now being issued to the ship's company. Robert McLure joined others in eating a case of pemmican that had gone bad and stank foully but, never having eaten pemmican before 'we ate it, thinking it was the proper taste.' A better source of food appeared in the shape of large flocks of duck which flew overhead and fell easily to the ship's marksmen.

The approach of July brought higher temperatures and lanes of open water began to appear snaking through the surface of the ice. None, however, were within reach of the ship. Then, on the morning of the 11th, with a loud crack the floe on which the *Terror* was trapped split along the length of the ship and drifted away from the larboard (port) side. Back immediately hoisted sails but the ice refused to release its grip on the starboard side. Orders were given for men to go over that side to see if they could free her with saws and axes. When this proved to be ineffective, ice-anchors were taken out and an attempt was made to warp the ship free. As this was being done, the ice near the starboard bow cracked and parted. A great cheer went up from both officers and men as the ship rolled to larboard, a cheer that died on their lips as, instead of a return roll to starboard, the ship continued its increasing list to larboard. Soon it became impossible to stand on the sloping deck and water began to pour in through the damaged hull. Back rushed to the starboard side and looked over. He was horrified by what he saw. The break-up of the ice had not only freed the ship, it had also liberated a great mass of ice that was fast beneath the waterline of the *Terror's* starboard side. This ice was now rising to the surface, slowed down only by the buoyancy of the *Terror* – a buoyancy which was gradually disappearing as water flooded into the ship. Three parties were immediately organised, one prepared the ship's boats in case the vessel had to be abandoned, another manned the pumps, whilst a third clambered over the starboard side and attacked the threatening ice with saws, axes and ice-chisels, working 'with the characteristic indifference to peril which has been so often admired in British seamen.' For twenty-four hours they laboured until, seeing that some men were about to collapse with exhaustion, Back called a halt to all but the party manning the pumps. Everyone, officers and men, lay about the upper deck of the ship, most in a deep sleep until they were startled awake by the sound of crashing ice. The frozen mass that held onto their starboard side had begun to break up. The ship shook as the ice 'four fathoms thick' smashed against its side. But none of that mattered as the *Terror*, gradually freed of its clinging enemy, hauled itself upright onto an even keel. Now the cheers were permitted to ring their full course.

With a jury-rigged rudder and the ship's carpenter hard at work trying to make the vessel seaworthy, the *Terror* made its way through Hudson's Strait and reached the open Atlantic on 6 August. The first part of their passage provided for a smooth

The ice breaking up around the Terror.

The mass of ice rising to the surface and threatening the Terror *with destruction.*

voyage but subsequent gales put a dreadful strain on the badly damaged ship and Back was forced into the extraordinary position of having to pass a chain-cable around the ship's hull to hold it together. By the time they arrived off the north Irish coast, the *Terror* was little more than a waterlogged hulk and Back decided to make for the small port of Lough Swilly. Attempts by using blue lights and gunfire failed to attract the attention of a pilot so Back decided to take the ship into harbour himself despite the risk of grounding in unfamiliar waters. Just before midnight, the *Terror* limped quietly into the sleeping harbour and the ship's anchor was dropped for the first time in fifteen months. Within days, the battered ship had to be run ashore to prevent her from sinking at her anchorage. Upon examination it was found that her forefoot had disappeared completely and twenty foot of the keel, along with 10ft of the stern post, had been driven 3ft to one side leaving a huge hole through which water had continued to pour. Back wrote to the secretary of the Royal Geographical Society telling him that 'The ship is broken and strained in every part.'

The failure of the expedition, even to arrive at the start of its intended route across the base of Boothia Felix, was soon lost in universal admiration for Back's achievement in bringing his men home safely. William Smyth was immediately promoted to commander and appointed to warmer climes. Owen Stanley was given his own command as a lieutenant before being promoted to commander in 1839. As captain of HMS *Rattlesnake* in 1846 he surveyed much of the coast of Northern Australia and New Guinea and had the Owen Stanley range of mountains named in his honour – the highest peak being named Mount Owen Stanley. The mates, McLure and Gore, both received their lieutenant's commission.

Back, already with the rank of captain, could not be further promoted (flag rank was earned by seniority on the captain's list). He was, however, showered with prizes. The Royal Geographical Society presented him with its gold founder's medal and the silver patron's medal. The Geographical Society of Paris presented him with its gold medal. He was knighted in 1839, elected a fellow of the Royal Society, given an honorary degree by Oxford University and became vice-president of the Royal Geographical Society. He married a widow in 1846 and was promoted to flag rank eleven years later. George Back never went to sea again, being 'very much shaken' by his experiences off the northern coast of Southampton Island. He died in 1878.

The *Terror*, battered almost to the point of sinking, had demonstrated that the bomb-vessel, when strengthened for polar seas, could take an enormous amount of punishment. She was returned to Chatham Dockyard where she was repaired and brought back to a seaworthy condition. The Admiralty was soon to have further use for her.

CHAPTER TWELVE

'REGIONS FAR BEYOND WHAT WAS EVER DREAMED'

Forty-five years after Cook had sailed into Antarctic waters, the vast fields of ice were once again penetrated, this time by the Russian explorer Bellingshausen. The continent was circumnavigated and, in all probability, the mainland was sighted but Bellingshausen never made such a claim. The same year (1819) that Bellingshausen began his voyage, a British sealing captain, William Smith reported that he had discovered land to the south of Cape Horn. On his next voyage he was accompanied by a Royal Navy master, Edward Bransfield, who took possession of the land (South Shetlands) before pressing further to the south where more land was discovered. Smith and Bransfield had discovered the Antarctic Mainland. They had found the north-west corner of a peninsular and Bransfield landed and claimed the territory on behalf of the king giving it the name 'Trinity Land' (after Trinity House). In turn, the waterway between the South Shetlands and the tip of the peninsular was named 'Bransfield Strait'.

Later that year, the American sealer, Nathaniel Palmer, stood on the volcanic rim of the most southerly of the South Shetlands, Deception Island, and saw, across the southern end of Bransfield Strait, distant mountains even further to the south of the peninsular.

Between 1822 and 1824 another Royal Navy master, James Weddell, explored the eastern seaboard of Trinity Land and reached 74 degrees, 15' south. He gave the name of the ice-strewn waters through which he sailed 'Sea of George VI' (Weddell Sea). Six years later, the former midshipman and acting master, James Biscoe, circumnavigated the Antarctic and discovered Enderby Land (named after the owners of his vessels). On reaching the west coast of the Antarctic Peninsular he discovered Adelaide Island and Graham Land.

All these achievements did not add up to a great deal in explaining the overall nature of the land around the South Pole. It was still not known whether or not there existed a great landmass, or if Antarctica was a mass of islands. Only a national enterprise could start to reveal some of the mystery. Unfortunately – as far as the British were concerned – such national enterprise was about to be shown by both the French and the Americans.

Both the French and the British were heavily involved in researching the earth's magnetism. In pursuit of knowledge that could be gained from the far south, the French sent out two ships in 1837 under the command of Jules-Sebastien-Cesar Dumont d'Urville, an experienced commander and explorer amongst whose claims to fame was in the discovery of the limb-deficient statue – Venus de Milo. Two years later, whilst hove-to in an Antarctic fog, d'Urville was astonished to see a vessel of the United States Navy pass within hailing distance yet fail to acknowledge his signals. The American ship later proved to be one of a small squadron under the command of Lieutenant Charles Wilkes USN that had been sent out by the United States government as the 'US South Seas Surveying and Exploring Expedition'.

In Britain, the British Association for the Advancement of Science had, on several occasions during the 1830's, put forward proposals to the government suggesting that an expedition should be sent to the Antarctic to test the current theories on magnetism and to try and locate the south magnetic pole. In 1838, a proposal led by the famous astronomer, Sir John Herschel, found government favour and, with the support of the Royal Society, the plans were put into operation.

The two bomb vessels *Erebus* and *Terror* were both already adapted for polar waters and available for service. To command the expedition there could be little doubt about the selection of Captain James Ross. Not only was he vastly experienced in polar sailing, but was well known to have great skill in magnetic observations. Ross was to have the *Erebus* and he arranged for his second-in-command and captain of the *Terror* to be Commander Francis Crozier. The first lieutenant in *Erebus* was Edward Bird, veteran of three Parry voyages and second-in-command of Ross's boat during the attempt on the North Pole. The *Terror*'s first lieutenant was Archibald McMurdo who came with valuable experience in that ship under Back. Another of the *Terror*'s lieutenants was Joseph Kay, a nephew of Sir John Franklin.

Robert McCormick was appointed as surgeon and naturalist of the *Erebus*. Something of a prickly character, McCormick had served in the *Hecla* on Parry's 1827 expedition and later sailed in HMS *Beagle* with Charles Darwin being carried as the ship's naturalist. The two failed to reach any rapport and Darwin came to consider McCormick 'an ass'. Finally, with no-one to challenge his diagnosis, McCormick had himself invalided home. Appointed to the West Indies, he once again had himself invalided home to spend the next four years on half-pay. He passed the time by walking the length and breadth of England studying natural history before applying to join Ross in the *Cove,* but was turned down as the post had already been filled.

McCormick's assistant in the *Erebus* was twenty-one-year-old Joseph Dalton Hooker, the son of Sir William Hooker, professor of botany. His role, in addition to his medical appointment, was – not surprisingly – as expedition botanist. As *Erebus*'s gunner, Ross took Thomas Abernethy, his experienced (and hard drinking) sledging companion who had accompanied him to Victory Point and to the north magnetic pole.

Above left: *James Weddell.*

Above right: *Weddell in the Antarctic, 1822.*

Right: *Captain James Ross.*

Whilst Ross finished the work he was doing on magnetic surveying, Crozier was left to prepare the ships. Once he had finished loading the vessels with coals, warm clothing, 6,000lb of canned meat, 6,000lb of canned soup, 15,000lb of canned vegetables, 5,000lb of canned gravy, wine and spirits, each ship was as 'full as an egg'. Crozier, however, was somewhat disgruntled at having to pay for many of the expedition's instruments out of his own pocket ('sad day this'). Ross was having difficulty with the parents of a young lady, Ann Coulman, whose father fended off his advances with a brusque letter 'Sir, your age compared with my daughter's, your profession and the very uncertain and hazardous views you have before you, all forbid our giving any countenance to the connection.' Ross was seventeen years older than Anne.

The ships sailed without ceremony from Margate roads on the evening of 30 September 1839. After a slow voyage, calling at numerous islands to take magnetic surveys, the *Terror* arrived at Hobart Town, Van Dieman's Land (Tasmania) on 14 August 1840, and (the ships having been separated during the voyage) the *Erebus* appeared the following day. They were met by that most kindred of spirits, the lieutenant governor, Captain Sir John Franklin. On his return from his journey down the MacKenzie River, Franklin had married Miss Jane Griffin who, like his first wife, was a woman of very independent mind. A best friend of Eleanor, Franklin believed 'that there exists between us the closest congeniality of mind, thought, and feeling.'

Between 1830 and 1833 he had been in command of HMS *Rainbow*, seeing service in the Mediterranean where he was awarded the Golden Cross of the Greek Order of the Redeemer for his work off the Greek coast during that country's war with Turkey. In 1836, Franklin was appointed as lieutenant governor of Van Dieman's Land and found working with civilian government officials markedly different from working with his fellow naval officers. He was, therefore, delighted with the arrival of Ross and ensured that the ships were given the best possible welcome at the start of their stay.

Ross, Crozier, and Kay all stayed at Government House during their time in Van Dieman's Land. An observatory was set up at a site named 'Rossbank' and a series of magnetic observations carried out. To ensure that there was more to the visit than just the pursuit of scientific data, a constant series of dinners, balls and parties were arranged. A return dinner was held on-board the *Erebus,* and a ball was arranged by the expedition officers at the Custom House. Crozier found himself strongly attracted to Sophia Cracroft, Franklin's niece and lifelong companion of Lady Franklin. Unfortunately, however, Miss Cracroft had eyes only for Ross – and Ross was too pre-occupied with Anne Coulman to begin any extra romantic diversion.

Whilst at Hobart, Ross learned of the outcome of the French and American expeditions. Dumont d'Urville had discovered 150 miles of land between longitudes 142 degrees east and 136 degrees east. He had named it 'Adelie Land' (Terre Adelie) after his wife. This had been followed by a 60-mile westward cruise past giant ice-cliffs until he had been forced to turn northwards when sickness broke out amongst his men. Wilkes wrote to Ross telling him that he had made considerable discoveries between 165 degrees east and 96 degrees east. Ross was deeply annoyed by the information. He had assumed that, as both expeditions would have known before their sailings that he intended to strike out for the magnetic pole, they would have searched for land in another part of the Antarctic. They had not, however, penetrated any further south than 67 degrees of latitude and that, combined with the knowledge that the whaling captain, John Balleny, had seen land (Sabrina Land) in the vicinity of 120 degrees east, persuaded him to 'select a much more easterly meridian (170 degrees), on which to endeavour to penetrate to the southward, and if possible reach the magnetic pole'.

Dumont d'Urville returned to France in November 1840, and was awarded the Paris Geographical Society's gold medal. He died eighteen months later, along with his wife and only surviving son, in a train crash at Versailles. Wilkes arrived back in the United States in 1842 and found himself facing a court martial on several charges of illegally punishing some of his men. In 1861, he almost precipitated war with Great Britain by boarding the British mail-steamer *Trent* and removing two confederate commissioners accredited to France. As a rear-admiral he was court-martialled for disobedience and retired from the service. He died in 1877. Wilkes' expedition was the only major maritime expedition ever sent out under United States government sponsorship during the age of sail.

Erebus and *Terror* sailed from Hobart on 12 November 1840, and called at the Auckland Isles and Campbell Island on their way south. Observatories were set up and plant and wildlife specimens collected from both. Christmas Day was spent riding out a gale. Two days later the first iceberg was seen, its huge size, sheer sides and flat top being markedly different from the splintered and jagged ones Ross knew well from his northern travels. On New Year's Day 1841, the Antarctic Circle was crossed and the pack ice reached. Warm clothing was issued to the ship's companies as Ross skirted the edge of the pack studying it from the masthead. A north-westerly wind arriving on the 5th gave Ross the opportunity he had been waiting for and the *Erebus* followed by *Terror* turned their bows and charged the pack ice. After an hour or so's 'thumping', the ships broke through into much looser ice which enabled them to make progress without any great difficulty. Within three days they were in clear water with 'not a particle of ice to be seen.'

In the early morning of the 11th, a spectacular shoreline revealed itself to the ships. A range of mountains ('Admiralty Range') swept to the north-west, their snow-capped peaks rising to ten 10,000ft above the sea. The following morning Ross and Crozier, accompanied by men from their ships landed on an island and, to toasts in sherry and rum, took possession of the land in the name of Great Britain and its young queen. The solemn occasion was spoilt for McCormick by the masses of penguins which combined to produce a particularly pungent smell – 'The perfume arising from this colony was certainly not of an Arabian sweetness.' A further range of mountains that equalled the Admiralty Range in grandeur followed the coastline to the south and was given the names of eminent scientists from the Royal Society and the British Association. The land fronted by the mountains was named 'Victoria Land'. Continuing south, Ross came across a large island to which he gave the name 'Coulman Island' with its most southerly point being named 'Cape Anne' – another arrow in his quiver with which to persuade Anne Coulman's parents to reconsider his pursuit of their daughter.

Weddell's furthest point south at 74 degrees 15' south was passed on the 23rd before ice fixed to the mountain-lined shore ('Prince Albert Mountains') forced the ships out to the east. Four days later, Franklin Island was discovered and named, followed the next day by Beaufort Island. Continuing to head southwards under full sail in a slight breeze, Ross and his men were suddenly exposed to a sight that caused them great astonishment. Fine on the starboard bow, land that had been named simply as 'High Land' (Ross Island), proved to hold a most spectacular surprise. The western of two large mountains could be seen to be 'emitting flame and smoke in splendid profusion'. It was, in fact, an active volcano, its smaller companion now extinct. Hooker wrote

> This was a sight so surpassing everything that can be imagined and so heightened by the consciousness that we have penetrated, under the guidance of our commander, into regions far beyond what was ever dreamed practicable, that it really caused a feeling of awe to steal over us…

Ross named the volcanoes 'Mount Erebus' and its consort 'Mount Terror'.

From the easternmost point of the island (Cape Crozier) another, equally astonishing, sight awaited them. A huge wall of ice that towered above the masts of the ships extended east to the far horizon. Well over 100ft in height and flat along the top, the frozen barrier revealed no inlet or strait, suggesting a passage further south. Ross sailed for over 300 miles along the front of the barrier, reaching on the way his highest latitude – 78 and a quarter degree south. The voyage along the spectacular ice cliffs carried its own danger. If a northerly wind had arrived in any force, Ross would have found himself off a frozen lee shore with the grave risk of his ships being thrown against the ice. Even this risk was ignored on 8 February when Ross came across a large bay in the ice wall. With the sails hanging from the yards in the windless silence the ships' companies of the two vessels looked around in awestruck wander at the glittering blue and white walls that almost surrounded them. At one point, the ice cliffs reduced in height, allowing a view from the masthead which revealed an 'immense plain of frosted silver'. They could not, however, afford to tarry as the threat of a northerly wind was ever present. A further attempt to go eastwards was thwarted by pack ice and, on the 11th, Ross turned his bows to the west. Five days later he was north of Mount Erebus and the island's most northern point, 'Cape Bird'. To the west of this cape he found, what appeared to be, a large bay which he named after Lieutenant McMurdo (McMurdo Sound).

Ross had planned to winter in the Antarctic and, as pancake ice – the first sign of surface freezing – was beginning to form on the water, it was clear that a base would soon have to be found. They were only 160 miles from the magnetic pole but, as he moved further north along the coasts of Prince Albert and Victoria Lands, nowhere offered itself as a landing place. Eventually, as it was too late for any of the shore ice to break away and offer the hope of a suitable landing site, Ross and Crozier agreed to return to Van Dieman's Land after having had a look at the discoveries of Balleny and Wilkes.

With Cape North – the northernmost part of Victoria Land – rounded, the Balleny Islands were found without much difficulty but, as the ships were approaching the land charted by Wilkes, a severe storm blew up and a dark night was spent in fear of

Erebus *and* Terror *discover an Antarctic volcano – Mount Erebus.*

Ross at the ice barrier.

being grounded on a lee shore. But, with the return of daylight, and with the rigging of both ships crowded with men on the lookout, no sign of land could be seen. Ross searched the area from every point of the compass, at one stage sailing directly 'along the mountain range'. It soon became clear that Wilkes had, at best, been charting a mirage, at worst, a cloud formation. Ross put Wilkes' error down to 'the very cursory manner of his proceedings' and his 'unpractised eye in Icy Regions'. Later examination of Wilkes' charts suggested that the problem was probably one of hydrographic surveying and that the land Wilkes had seen was further to the south than his charts indicated. The name 'Wilkes Land' was given to the area in 1939.

Having, to his own satisfaction, settled the question of Wilkes' 'discovery', Ross turned to the north-west and, the following morning, found himself surrounded by pack ice. Pushing the ships through with some difficulty, Ross then found himself at the mercy of the Antarctic swell. The ships were pushed helplessly towards a line of eighty-four massive icebergs surrounded by hundreds of smaller bergs. So dangerous, and seemingly hopeless, was their situation that Ross turned to prayer in preparation for 'the awful destruction that threatened in one short hour to close the world and all its hopes and joys and sorrows upon us forever.' His prayers, however, were answered at the last moment and an increasing breeze drove him clear of the danger.

After a call at Kerguelen Island, Ross and his ships arrived at Hobart Town on 7 April after an absence of five months – sixty-three days of which had been spent below the Antarctic Circle. There they found the hospitality as warm as ever to help them pass the three months it took to refit the ships. In return, the officers held a grand ball on the forty-seventh anniversary of Howe's victory over the French at the battle of 'The Glorious First of June'. The *Erebus* and *Terror* were lashed together and an awning placed over both vessels. The *Erebus* served as the ballroom and the *Terror* as the dining room. Three hundred and fifty guests were invited and danced to the band of the 51st Regiment until dawn. Hooker considered the event to be 'without doubt the most splendid thing ever given. The expense however was enormous.'

Refreshed and eager for another probe amongst the ice, the ships left Hobart on 7 July leaving Lieutenant Kay behind in charge of the Rossbank Observatory. Sydney, the New Zealand Bay of Islands, and Chatham Islands were visited to carry out magnetic observations before Ross turned south along the 146 degree west meridian towards the ice. The first floes were reached on 18 December and the Antarctic Circle was crossed on New Year's Day 1842. With the ships unable to reach southwards due to a southerly breeze, much of the following week was given over to dancing and games on the ice.

On 19 January, still deep in the pack, the wind swung round to the north and brought with it a deep rolling swell that had the ships pitching and rolling in 'an ocean of rolling fragments of ice, as hard as floating rocks of granite'. Before long, the rudders of both ships had been smashed. At one stage, the ships found themselves on tops of neighbouring waves, only to plunge simultaneously into the succeeding trough and losing sight of all but the topmasts of the other ship. The storm subsided after two days, but it was not until the 24th that the rudders could be replaced.

The southern edge of the ice was reached on 1 February. It had taken them five days to cross through the pack the previous year, on this attempt it had taken forty-seven. With open water ahead, Ross was able to push southwards despite occasional southerly winds which sent up a spray coating the ships' bowsprits in ice. Whilst this ice was being chipped off the bows of the *Terror*, a fish was found frozen fast to the ship. It must have been thrown up with the spray and held by the ice. The surgeon of the *Terror*, Dr Robertson, decided to sketch the fish, but had only just begun when one of the ship's cats leaped on it and bore it away as an unexpected meal.

Above: *A ball on the ice – New Year's Day, 1842.*

Left: Erebus *and* Terror *at the mercy of the Antarctic waters.*

In the pack ice.

Return to the ice barrier.

The Great Ice Barrier was met on the 23rd some ten miles further east than had been achieved the previous year. It was also six miles further to the south enabling Ross to record his highest southern latitude at 78 degrees 9' 30" south. He then turned eastwards to follow the ice wall's course and found that it soon trended towards the north-east. He was not to get far. On the following day the pack was found to press up against the barrier, its leading edge trending away to the north-west. The long delay in getting through the pack ice on the way south had meant that, by now, the season was well advance. Already the surface of the sea was freezing into pancake ice and Ross knew that the time had come to leave the Antarctic.

After a week's run along the edge of the pack, its most westerly limit was reached. Once it was turned, the ships were able to steer north-east then east towards Cape Horn. In the darkness of midnight on 12 March, as the ships were running abreast of each other, a number of small icebergs were seen ahead. Ross immediately took measures to haul clear but, just as these were being carried out, a large iceberg was seen on the *Terror's* port bow and she took avoiding action by turning to starboard. At just about the same instant, the same iceberg was seen from the *Erebus* and her bows were turned to port. The collision that ensued was violent in the extreme. The starboard bow of the *Erebus* struck the port bow of her consort and the seas forced the two ships to grind past each other as high waves drove them up and down. Anchors, booms, boats, and catheads, were all carried away or wrecked as the two ships' rigging meshed, tore and strained in a fury of tangled ropes and splintered spars. Fortunately, the sea wrenched the ships apart leaving *Erebus* suffering the worst damage with her foretopmast and bowsprit gone. But, even worse was threatened by the sheer walls of the leeward icebergs, towering high above the mast tops. Crozier, taking charge 'as if he was steering into any harbour', headed for a vertical dark streak that had been seen in the wall of ice against which they were being forced. Hoping against hope that the darkness indicated a space between two icebergs rather than merely a break in the surface of the sheer ice cliff, the *Terror* charged forward to find, much to their relief that a gap – no wider than twice the beam of the vessel – allowed them through to the shelter of the iceberg's lee. Once they were out of danger, blue lights were lit and all eyes turned to their wake for sight of the *Erebus*.

Ross was facing a fearful situation. The *Erebus* was out of control and being driven hard towards the iceberg. Standing quietly on the quarterdeck with his arms folded, he calmly gave orders that the mainsail should be loosed. His only hope was to 'resort to the hazardous expedient of the sternboard'. He meant to use the wind and sails to drive the ship backwards. With extraordinary coolness, the seamen ran up the rigging and battled with the elements to free the encumbered mainsail as the ship rolled heavily and spray from the sea striking the iceberg drenched the upper deck. At last the ship gathered sternway and, with her stern awash and her yardarms scraping the lofty sides of the iceberg, the *Erebus* clawed herself clear of the danger

– only to find that she was now bearing down upon another mountain of ice. By skilled seamanship, the ship's head was turned and Ross was able to head for the same gap that Crozier had used in his escape.

Despite the continuation of the storm that had nearly sent them to the bottom, a jury bowsprit was rigged on the *Erebus* and, within three days, both ships were in a condition that allowed them to continue their voyage to the east. Cape Horn was rounded in the first days of April and the Falkland Islands reached on the 5th – their first sight of land for 136 days.

Although Ross ensured that his magnetic duties were carried out on the islands, his main task was the repair and refit of his ships. This meant hauling the *Erebus* up onto the beach and emptying both vessels. The carpenters set to with a will and, by the end of July the ships were, once again, ready for sea. Those of the ship's company not on duty were given leave in appreciation of their hard work and were found later by Hooker lying insensible through the effects of too much rum. Another cause for celebration was the fact that a recent copy of the 'Navy List' revealed that Crozier had been promoted to captain and Bird had been made commander.

Seamen from the Terror *breaking up ice for the ship's water.*

The collision between the Erebus *and the* Terror.

Erebus *and* Terror *escape the icebergs.*

A short visit to Cape Horn to carry out a magnetic survey was completed before the ships finally sailed from the Falklands without 'the smallest regret' on 17 December. Lieutenant McMurdo, suffering from an internal complaint, was left behind to be invalided home on the next ship taking passage.

Ross's plan for his third voyage into Antarctic waters was based on his belief that the ice would be driven from the eastern shore of the Antarctic peninsular leaving a wide lane of open water. Through this, he believed, he would be able to strike deep to the south. The pack ice was found on Boxing Day and land two days later. For the next five weeks Ross found himself in a cul-de-sac formed by fixed ice to the south and land to his west and north (Erebus and Terror Gulf). Formal possession of the land was taken on a small island (Cockburn Island) and a large snowless mountain to the south was named Mount Haddington in honour of the First Lord of the Admiralty. At the south-west corner of the 'gulf' (actually the route south was sealed off by ice-linked islands), both ships found themselves in difficulty as the pack ice was forced against the land and many hours of warping were needed to haul themselves clear. A final attempt to make his way south through the ice failed when the pack began to drift northwards. Ross now decided to follow the edge of the pack as it trended north and east. After crossing the track of Weddell's return from open water (and finding only ice) Ross found the pack suddenly taking a more southerly trend leading to open water. A week later the pack was once again encountered, but all efforts to penetrate further to the south were resisted. As they retreated from each attempt to breach the floes Ross saw the ominous sign of the surface water freezing between the broken ice. Unbeknown to him, he was only forty-five miles from undiscovered land (Queen Maud Land), but the time had come to leave the frozen wastes of Antarctica.

Their course was shaped for the Cape of Good Hope and Simon's Bay was reached on 4 April. A minor refit allowed the ships to leave by the end of the month and, after an uneventful voyage, they anchored off Folkestone on 4 September. Ross reported immediately to the Admiralty, the ships continuing on to Woolwich where they were paid off on the 23rd – almost four and a half years after they had been commissioned.

The homecoming proved not to be the heroic welcome that had been hoped for. The excitement caused by reports of the earlier discoveries had waned and nothing spectacular arose from the attempt to follow in the wake of Weddell. The land that had been discovered was far too remote and did not hold an eagerly awaited possibility to match that of a north-west passage. The magnetic surveys, although carried out with the greatest diligence, had little about them to catch the public imagination – and took another twenty-five years before the final results were published.

Franklin had written about Ross's officers that 'there was scarcely one above the ordinary run of the service', and Hooker was later to write that Ross 'would not take a

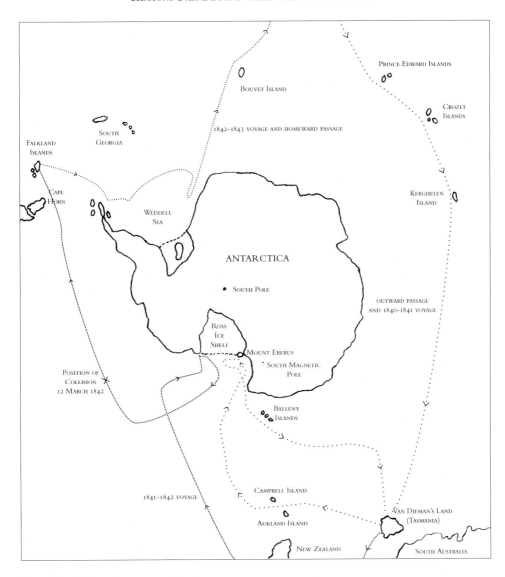

James Ross's Antarctic voyage 1840-1843

single officer of acknowledged position in the Service' and that not one of the officers was to rise 'above mediocrity'. These seem harsh judgements when there can be no doubt that the seamen amongst them were of a very high calibre. It may be, however, that like another Antarctic explorer in the following century, Ross only picked those who would represent no challenge to his leadership and who looked unquestioningly upon his record of achievements. As it was, several of the officers went on to complete careers that took them beyond 'the ordinary run of the service'.

Apart from those who had still a part to play in polar exploration, Archibald McMurdo died as a rear admiral on the retired list, Joseph Kay remained at Hobart and was, eventually, made a fellow of the Royal Society. Two others reached the rank of captain and a further two that of commander. Another became paymaster-in-chief at Greenwich Hospital and one achieved the post of clerk of the court of the Falkland Islands, working under the governor – who had served as a mate in the *Terror*. Joseph Hooker himself went on to a knighthood and to succeed his father in the post of director of the Royal Botanical Gardens at Kew. He survived to reach the age of ninety-four and was able to personally advise the great Antarctic expeditions at the start of the twentieth century.

Despite the cool reception he had received from the general public, Ross had achieved much during his voyage. This was recognised by the award of a knighthood, an honorary degree from Oxford, medals from learned societies, and the hand in marriage of Anne Coulman – but only on the promise that he would never again undertake a long polar expedition.

EPILOGUE

From the sixteenth to the nineteenth century, from Tudor to Hanoverian, from sailing barques to steamships, the Royal Navy sent its men to reach out for polar horizons. These men were to face danger with resolution, tedium with equanimity, and death itself with matchless courage. Men who were trained for war, yet found themselves against an enemy whose resources sprang from the elements themselves. Cold that froze their very breath, ice that destroyed their ships, and vast, empty, regions with nothing to sustain life. Despite the challenge, they had walked, sailed, paddled, and hauled sledges to the limits of their technology and, as the middle of the nineteenth century approached, their footprints stood at the highest latitudes both north and south. But it was not enough. There still remained a tantalising unknown in the route of the north-west passage, and the poles themselves still lay open for those with a will to reach them. Even worse, other nations were discovering the lure of the polar regions and threatened to take the icy laurels that Britain had strived so hard to win. This could not, must not, happen.

As candles burned in the Admiralty offices, men looked at the charts before them. To allow others to take the prize would be an intolerable disgrace. No flag of another country should be allowed to be first through the gates opened by British initiative and enterprise. What had gone before must be seen as steps leading directly to the pinnacle – an icy pinnacle to be adorned with the flag of Great Britain.

The men at the charts looked even more closely.

BIBLIOGRAPHY

Back, G. (1837) 'Letter to the Secretary of the Royal Geographical Society, September 11th, 1837' *Naval Chronicle* Vol VI, pp. 683–86

Beechey, F. W. (1831) *Narrative of a Voyage to the Pacific and Beering's Strait to co-operate with the Polar Expeditions, Performed in His Majesty's Ship* Blossom, *under the command of Captain F.W.BEECHEY R.N., F.R.S., F.R.A.S., and F.R.G.S., in the Years 1825-6-7-8* London: Colburn and Bentley

Carter, R. R. (1998) *Searching for the Franklin Expedition. The Arctic Journal of Robert Randolph Carter* Annapolis, Maryland: Naval Institute Press

Coleman, E. C. (2000) *Captain Vancouver, North-West Navigator.* Whitby: Caedmon

Colledge, J. J. (1969) Ships *of the Royal Navy: An Historical Index in two volumes* Newton Abbot: David & Charles

Cyriax, R. J. (1977) *Sir John Franklin's Last Expedition* Plaistow & Sutton Coldfield: Arctic Press.

Dodge, E. S. (1973) *The Polar Rosses. John Ross and James Clark Ross and their Explorations* Montreal: McGill University Press

Fluhmann, M. A. (1976) *Biography of Captain Francis Crozier RN, FRS, FRAS* Published by the Department of Information, Government of the Northwest Territories

Franklin, J. (1910) *Narrative of a Journey to the Shores of the Polar Seas in the Years 1819, 20, 21 and 22* Everyman

Franklin, J. (1971) *Narrative of a Second Expedition to the Shores of The Polar Seas in the Years 1825, 1826, and 1827 By John Franklin, Captain R.N. F.R.S. and Commander of the Expedition* Rutland, Vermont: The Charles E. Tuttle Company, Inc

Houston, C. Stuart (ed) (1974) *To the Arctic by Canoe 1819-1821: The Journal and Paintings of Robert Hood, Midshipman with Franklin* Montreal: McGill–Queen's University Press, Arctic Institute of North America

Houston, C. Stuart (ed) (1994) *Arctic Artist: The Journal and Paintings of George Back, Midshipman With Franklin, 1819-1822* Montreal: McGill–Queen's University Press

Jones, A. G. E. (1976) 'Commander D.C. Clavering's Voyage to East Greenland, 1823' *Muskox* Vol 9

Jones, A. G. E. (1992) *Polar Portraits* Whitby: Caedmon

Jones, A. G. E. (1978) 'Rear Admiral William Edward Parry: A Different View' *Muskox* Vol 21

King, H. G. R. (1969) *The Antarctic* London: Blandford Press

Lamb, G. F. Franklin (1956) *Happy Voyager, Being the Life and Death of Sir John Franklin* Ernest Benn Limited

Lehane, B. (1981) *The Northwest Passage* Amsterdam: Time-Life Books

Lloyd, C. (1970) *Mr Barrow of the Admiralty, A Life of Sir John Barrow 1764-1848* London Collins

Markham, A. H. (1891) *Life of Sir John Franklin* London: George Phillip & Son

Morris, R. (1996) 200 Years of Admiralty Charts and Surveys *Mariner's Mirror* Vol 82, No.4

Neatby L. H. (1970) The search for Franklin. Published by Edmonton, Canade: M. G. Hurtig Ltd

Ommanney, E. *The Unpublished Rough Journal of Captain Erasmus Ommanney RN* Archives, Glen Bow Museum, Calgary, Canada.

Parry, A. (1963) Parry *of the Arctic, The Life Story of Admiral Sir Edward Parry 1790-1855* London: Chatto & Windus

Parry, E. (1863) *Memoirs of Rear Admiral Sir W. Edward Parry* Eighth edition London: Longman, Green, Longman, Roberts & Green

Peard, G. (1973) *To the Pacific with Beechey: The Journal of Lieutenant George Peard of HMS Blossom 1825-1828* Cambridge: Cambridge University Press for the Hakluyt Society

Poulsom N. W. & Myres, J. A. L. (2000) *British Polar Exploration and Research: An Historic And Medallic Record with Biographies, 1818-1999* Savannah Publications

Richardson, R. *Narrative of Sir John Richardson to the Admiralty Secretary* Admiralty Library Collection.

Richardson, R. (1984) *Arctic Ordeal: The Journal of John Richardson, Surgeon-Naturalist with Franklin 1820-1822* Montreal: McGill-Queen's University Press

Richards, L. R. (1985) *Dr John Rae* Whitby: Caedmon

Ross, Sir J. *Narrative of Sir James Ross to the Admiralty Secretary* Admiralty Library Collection.

Ross, M. J. (1994) *Polar Pioneers, John Ross and James Clark Ross.* Montreal: McGill-Queen's University Press

Ross, M. J. (1982) *Ross and the Antarctic* Whitby: Caedmon

Wallace, H. N. (1980) The *Navy, The Company, and Richard King* Montreal: McGill-Queen's University Press

Other Sources

Arctic Voyages: Being an Account of Discoveries in the North Polar Sea in the Years 1818, 1819, & 1820. With an Account of the Esquimaux People Compiled from the most Authentic sources. Printed by Richard D. Webb, Dublin, 1831.

A Calendar of Letters and Documents in the Collection of the Arctic Institute of North Amercia, University of Calgary. Calgary, October 1980

The Dictionary of National Biography

The Geographical Magazine June 1875

The Life and Correspondence of Jane, Lady Franklin Lincolnshire Archives

The Nautical Magazine Vol I, Number 10, 1832

The Nautical Magazine Vol II, Number 21, 1833

The Nautical Magazine Vol III, Number 34, 1834

The Nautical Magazine June 1850

The Nautical Magazine November 1851

The Nautical Magazine January 1852

The Weekly Visitor, No. LXVIII, Vol II, February, 1834.

INDEX